Sacred Ecology
Third Edition

Sacred Ecology examines bodies of knowledge held by indigenous and other rural peoples around the world, and asks how we can learn from this knowledge and ways of knowing. Berkes explores the importance of local and indigenous knowledge as a complement to scientific ecology, and its cultural and political significance for indigenous groups themselves. This third edition further develops the point that traditional knowledge as process, rather than as content, is what we should be examining. It has been updated with about 150 new references, and includes an extensive list of web resources through which instructors can access additional material and further illustrate many of the topics and themes in the book.

Fikret Berkes is Distinguished Professor and Canada Research Chair at the Natural Resources Institute, University of Manitoba, Canada. His studies on community-based resource management have led to explorations of local and indigenous knowledge. He has authored some 250 scholarly publications and nine books, including *Linking Social and Ecological Systems* (Cambridge University Press, 1998) and *Navigating Social-Ecological Systems* (Cambridge, 2003).

Sacred Ecology

Third Edition

Fikret Berkes

NEW YORK AND LONDON

Third edition published 2012
by Routledge
711 Third Avenue, New York, NY 10017

Simultaneously published in the UK
by Routledge
2 Park Square, Milton Park, Abingdon, Oxon OX14 4RN

Routledge is an imprint of the Taylor & Francis Group, an informa business

First edition published by Taylor & Francis 1999
Second edition published by Routledge 2008

Library of Congress Cataloging in Publication Data
Berkes, Fikret.
    Sacred ecology / Fikret Berkes. -- 3rd ed.
        p. cm.
    1. Environmental sciences--Philosophy.   2. Traditional ecological
    knowledge.   3. Indigenous peoples.   4. Human ecology.   I. Title.
GE40.B45 2012
179'.1--dc23   2011040040

ISBN13: 978–0–415–51731–7 (hbk)
ISBN13: 978–0–415–51732–4 (pbk)
ISBN13: 978–0–203–12384–3 (ebk)

Typeset in Times New Roman by RefineCatch Limited, Bungay, Suffolk, UK.

SFI Certified Sourcing
www.sfiprogram.org
SFI-00453

Printed and bound in the United States of America
by Edwards Brothers, Inc.

Contents

Illustrations

Figures

Tables

Boxes

Photos

Preface to the First Edition

When I started to write this book, I had to remind myself of the oft-repeated conventional wisdom that the amount of knowledge in the world has been doubling every decade in recent times. Aside from the questions of just who measured the amount of knowledge and how, the obviously rapid pace of the growth of information all around us is sobering to anyone interested in traditional ecological knowledge. Has ancient knowledge perhaps become irrelevant, or has it simply been swamped by modern knowledge and reduced merely to a footnote? Just what can the study of traditional knowledge contribute to the contemporary world? This volume tries to answer these questions somewhat along the lines of the quotation attributed to the British philosopher Bertrand Russell: "One of the troubles of our age is that habits of thought cannot change as quickly as techniques, with the result that as skill increases, wisdom fades."

The interest in indigenous systems is not merely academic. The lessons of traditional knowledge, especially of the ecological kind, have practical significance for the rest of the world. There is a growing line of thought, as this volume documents, that we are moving in the new millennium toward different ways of seeing, perceiving, and doing, with a broader knowledge base than that allowed by modernist Western science. For many of us, the science of ecology has a historic role to play in this process. As Theodore Roszak observed in his 1972 book, *Where the Wasteland Ends*, "ecology already hovers on the threshold of heresy." Some three decades ago, ecology held a great deal of promise to step across this threshold, and "in so doing, revolutionize the sciences as a whole. . . . The question remains open: which will ecology be, the last of the old sciences or the first of the new?" (Roszak 1972: 404).

It may be an exaggeration to say that the science of ecology as a whole has such a momentous choice to make. No doubt much of ecology will continue as conventional science, and at least for the foreseeable future, such ecology will have a role to play in the advancement of knowledge. The fact of the matter is, an overwhelmingly large part of ecology tries to adhere to the tenets of conventional science. It tends to be quantitative, reductionistic, and not at all sacred or spiritual, seemingly bent on dashing Roszak's hopes, as Evernden (1993) later noted. But for me the more interesting kinds of ecology are the unconventional ones—if not quite "heretical," certainly at the edge of scientific respectability! Thomas Kuhn's (1970) *The Structure of Scientific Revolutions* argues that new scientific paradigms arise at the peripheries of mainstream science. New ways of looking at phenomena come about as the conventional paradigm proves less and less capable of explaining observations. A case in point is the replacement of Newton's mechanistic model of the universe by Einstein's relativity principle. Does traditional ecological knowledge represent some such paradigm change (in a small way) in the field of ecology? Only time will tell.

Before entering the world of traditional ecological knowledge, let me explain how I came to develop an interest in it. I first became involved in the human ecology of an indigenous group, the Cree Indians, in 1971, but I did not start my field studies in James Bay in subarctic Canada until 1974. At the time, I had just finished my Ph.D. work as a marine scientist and applied ecologist, and I had spent much of my graduate student years practicing being a "good scientist," always skeptical and always questioning the evidence. I also believed that all phenomena could be studied by the use of the scientific method. This latter belief was shaken somewhat in 1972 when I first started to teach at McGill University in Montreal. The course was about environmental studies and social change, taught by a team led by John Southin and Wade Chambers, themselves unconventional thinkers. I was exposed to a great many new ideas, and for the first time, to philosophy of science. Now this was a new field for me; science students (and scientists) almost never read philosophy of science! One book, perhaps the earliest one that forced me to take a broader view of knowledge, was R. G. H. Siu's *The Tao of Science*.

By 1974, I was in James Bay fishing with the Cree. I had turned down an excellent opportunity to do a postdoctoral fellowship with a leading marine ecologist, to work instead with my anthropologist colleague, Harvey Feit, a move considered quite suicidal professionally by many of my scientist friends. My early studies of human ecology, fisheries, and environmental assessment in James Bay actually went very well. I had a little innovative twist in my study plan. Instead of setting my own nets and sampling my own fish as scientists normally do, I was accompanying Cree fishers to go to *their own* fishing areas and collecting the usual biological data from their catch, as well as collecting data on the Cree fishery itself. The reason for the unusual study design was only in part deliberate as a study of *human* ecology; in part it was dictated by the limitations of my budget.

I was comfortable with the collection of "objective" and quantitative data, and the Cree fishers and their families were quite content that I was not the kind of researcher who was always asking questions. We did a lot of fishing; the fishery was not a commercial one but subsistence, carried out only for household and community needs. One year I calculated that with my puny research grant, I had outfished (outsampled) the government research team, which had a quartermillion-dollar budget to conduct fisheries assessment in the same waters. But it was really the Cree who were doing the fishing. I was only the guest and inept helper, as they effortlessly set nets and pulled in the fish, zipping up and down the most complicated coastline you could ever imagine, where the configuration changed at each phase of the tide. I was beginning to develop a healthy respect for their knowledge and capabilities.

Twice I thought I would wrap up the James Bay project, once in 1978 and again in 1982, but somehow I ended up going back. I was finding that the more research I did in James Bay, the more interesting research questions presented themselves. Many were questions I had not asked at the start of my research, such as, "With no government regulation, how come the Cree did not overfish, and how come the resources did not suffer from the tragedy of the commons?" The answer was that the Cree had community-based resource management, and the analysis of common property resources became my main line of research (e.g. Berkes 1989a). There were other questions as well, some of which I did not get to until quite recently. Traditional knowledge is one of them. I had made considerable progress in describing and analyzing traditional, community-based resource management of the Cree. But this analysis had been based on *my* academic interpretation of the system, what some anthropologists would call the *etic* view. (Chapter 7 gives a detailed account of that work.) I had not given much thought to the *emic* view or how the Cree themselves saw their systems, nor did I think the unique Cree worldview of nature, as documented by an earlier generation of anthropologists, was particularly relevant in James Bay of the 1980s. I was soon proven wrong.

It started with a comment by one of my Cree associates. He said: "Now that you have been doing work here (on and off) for ten years, you must have learned something of our hunting and fishing. How about doing something useful for the community, writing down for us some of our rules and practices to help educate the younger generation?" We had an unwritten agreement about the conditions of my research in the community: I would come back and be accountable (they did not approve of researchers who disappeared with the data after a year or two), and I would help put the information to the use of the community as needed. Now my associate was taking me up on it. A promise is a promise, although I should admit, I initially regarded the task as free consultancy, or worse, as a secretarial/editorial job, but in any case the request was consistent with the Cree practice of reciprocity and therefore impossible to refuse without losing face.

My fears about the drudgery of the job were quickly dispelled when I started meeting with the self-selected task force organized by my associate, George Lameboy, and by the head of the Chisasibi Cree Trappers Association, Robbie Matthew. It was a group of brilliant, humorous, and wise people. I found myself as the invited scribe in a latter-day "Black Elk Speaks" (Brown 1953), with an internal check and consensus mechanism thrown in, because I had not one elder but a whole group with me! We proceeded Cree-style, slowly and deliberately, with many digressions and much good humor. They set the agenda; I made the notes, and edited and brought them to the next meeting. Then they went over each line, translated back to Cree for the benefit of the members who did not speak English, and they made sure, as only meticulous hunters can, that I eventually got everything right. This process continued though five meetings in 1984, and at the end of the year I presented the group with the final report. It was later turned by the Cree into a small book, *Cree Trappers Speak* (Bearskin *et al.* 1989). Chapter 5 of the present volume borrows heavily from the report, and Chapter 6 gives a flavor of the Cree-style discourse that led to it.

The slow pace of the proceedings meant that I could keep up with the notes and did not have to use a tape recorder, which many of the older Cree dislike as a symbol of white man's technology. It also meant that I had time to absorb the discussion and seek clarification every now and then. Here was a group of elders and experts, speaking without the prompting of a meddlesome researcher, about their views of life, spirituality, rituals in the bush, uncomfortable relations with missionaries (Berkes 1986b), the cycling of animal populations, the proper ways to hunt caribou and geese, and on and on. In my ten years, I had never asked questions about these things, and some of these matters I did not think they would talk about at all.

Out of the discussion emerged a worldview different from the mainstream Euro-Canadian one, a worldview in which nature pulsated with life, compelling in its spiritual ecology. In one of the stories Cree elders told, a famous and influential missionary of the James Bay coast of the 1930s was quoted as repeatedly telling the Cree, "there are no spirits in the bush." The Cree elder sighed and added, "No matter how much he repeated that, we all knew that the land was sacred and full of spirits." Here we were, in 1984, on the sacred land where the animals determined the success of the hunt. Violate rules of respect and reciprocity, you came back from the hunt empty-handed. Many of the Cree believed that; some of the younger hunters were skeptical but not willing to take a chance either (although many others violated the rules nevertheless).

Somewhat to my surprise, I found myself comfortable with the Cree view of nature, even though, by virtue of my Western education and scientific training, I was heavily inclined to resist it. My generation had grown up with the marvels of the space age and the glorification of science and technology. Later, the environmental movement of the 1960s and the 1970s had provided a devastating critique of the misapplications of science and technology, but we were short on prescriptions, especially of the nonscientific kind. The standard view of ecosystems on which I had been brought up was rather machine-like. The influential ecologist, Eugene Odum (1971), for example, characterized ecological cycles as giant wheels powered by the energy of the sun. In this mechanical ecology, there was little room for the discussion of ecological ethics and even less of the sacred.

There were other views of ecology, but they were not a part of the discussion among ecologists. As Paul Shepard once observed, although ecology is a science, its greater and overriding wisdom is universal. That wisdom can be approached mathematically, experimentally, or it can be danced or told as myth. It is in Australian aboriginal people's "dreamtime" and in Gary Snyder's poetry. I discovered Aldo Leopold's (1949) "land ethics" only in the 1970s. Among the exceptions to conventional ecology was the work of Ian McHarg. He was writing about nature and environment, not as an ecologist but as a landscape architect and planner, inspiring dissatisfied ecologists such as myself to widen our radius of intellectual search. The chapter "On Values" in his *Design with Nature* (1969) talked about Iroquois bear rituals preceding a hunt. The hunter talks to the bear and assures the bear that the killing is motivated by need; at the same time, the ritual reminds him of his ethical obligations. McHarg observed, "Now if you would wish to develop an attitude to prey that would ensure stability in a hunting society, then such views are the guarantee." The science of ecology did not discuss such views, but Siu, Leopold, McHarg, and later Bateson (1972) mentally prepared me to be receptive to a traditional ecology that did.

A large number of people (academics, resource managers, and practitioners) contributed to the development of this volume by sharing their ideas and insights and by sending material. I am grateful to them all. They include Arun Agrawal, Upali and Mala Amarasinghe, Mac Chapin, Johan Colding, Iain Davidson-Hunt, Jocelyn Davies, Roy Dudgeon, Nick Flanders, Carl Folke, Milton Freeman, Madhav Gadgil, Anne Gunn, Chris Hannibal Paci, Jeff Hutchings, Bob Johannes, Stephen Kellert, Gary Kofinas, Allice Legat, Robin Mahon, Henrik Moller, Barbara Neis, Garry Peterson, Dick Preston, Kent Redford, Yves Renard, Mere Roberts, Allan Smith, Frank Tough, Ron Trosper, Nancy Turner, Marty Weinstein, and Elspeth Young. I would like to pay a special tribute to Mike Warren (Iowa State University) who passed on prematurely in 1997; his enthusiasm and generous friendship will be sorely missed.

A large number of people shared their traditional and local knowledge with me, in Quebec, Ontario, Manitoba, Northwest Territories, British Columbia, Newfoundland, and Labrador (all in Canada), the Caribbean area, Turkey, India, Bangladesh, and Sri Lanka. I cannot possibly name them all and do justice, but I am nevertheless much indebted to them. In regard to the three chapters on the James Bay Cree, the key people who influenced me include George and James Bobbish, William and Margaret Cromarty, George Lameboy, Robbie Matthew, John Turner, and their families.

For chapter reviews I am thankful to Frank Tough, Yves Renard, Allan Smith, Kent Redford, and my wife, Dr. Mina Kislalioglu Berkes. My son, Jem Berkes, assisted a great deal with the technical production. Prabir Mitra drew the figures. The assistance of the Taylor & Francis team, especially that of Alison Howson, Catherine Kovacs, and Elizabeth Cohen was greatly appreciated.

Preface to the Second Edition

When *Sacred Ecology* first came out in 1999, I received a number of invitations to speak. One was from the Anishinabek/Ontario Fisheries Resource Centre in North Bay, Ontario. The Centre is an independent body that provides a forum for information sharing and participation in fisheries management in the Anishinabek area on the Canadian side of the upper Great Lakes. They were proposing to organize a meeting for me with the Ojibwa resource managers of the area. Red flag: Ojibwa are famously guarded and sensitive over issues of traditional knowledge. The celebrated artist Norval Morrisseau, founder of the woodland school or medicine painting, had been censured heavily by his own people two decades earlier for painting Ojibwa legends. What would they do to me—a non-native—for daring to write and talk about traditional knowledge?

I showed up in North Bay with a great deal of trepidation. It was a cool winter day on the icy shores of Lake Nipissing off Georgian Bay/Lake Huron. There were 35 or so Ojibwa tribal resource managers at the meeting, most of them in their thirties and Western educated. They were all quite familiar with the contents of the book and had copies of it in hand. They did not attack me at all. In fact, they were so appreciative and so receptive. The one thing they wanted to discuss, over and above all else was, how does one talk to elders? How does one learn from them? Now almost a decade later, I think they meant, how do you access elders' ways of knowing. That is, as Katja Neves-Graça would put it, "knowledge, the process" was what they were interested in; not "knowledge, the thing known."

This second edition of *Sacred Ecology* has a greater emphasis on knowledge as process. There are two new chapters and one of them (Chapter 8) is about climate change, based on an Inuit-initiated project that started just after the first edition came out, a project that has had considerable policy impact since the release of its video in 2000. The chapter shows how the Inuit people made sense of climate change. Indigenous people do not of course have prior or "traditional" knowledge of climate change. What they have is sensitivity to critical signals from the environment that something out of the normal is happening.

The other new chapter (Chapter 9) is about how indigenous knowledge deals with the complexity of the world around us. The chapter mainly uses examples of environmental change in the North to build a theory of how indigenous ways of knowing can help observe and monitor complex systems. Along with new material in Chapter 10 about the evolution of knowledge, and in Chapter 11 about how traditional knowledge gets modified in response to local economic needs and global opportunities, I think we have a stronger, better rounded book, both in theory and in practice. All the chapters have been modified in major ways and updated with recent references.

The second edition of *Sacred Ecology*, as with the first edition, contains a great deal of material with which I am familiar first-hand. It is based on the work undertaken by colleagues and graduate students affiliated with the University of Manitoba's Centre for Community-based Resource Management that started in 2002 when I received the Canada Research Chair in Community-based Resource Management. I thank the Canada Research Chairs program (www.chairs.gc.ca) for allowing me to concentrate on research and graduate education. Also important for the contents of the book, I have had the benefit of a network of other colleagues and partner groups, including many indigenous groups and other rural communities.

In putting together the revised book, I relied on a large number of people. In addition to continuing collaboration with many colleagues and former students listed in the original preface, I thank the following for their help and insights: Derek Armitage, Grazia Borrini-Feyerabend, Nancy Doubleday, Emdad Haque, Eugene Hunn, Igor Krupnik, Frank Lake, Louis Lebel, Micheline Manseau, Charles Menzies, Katja Neves-Graça, Douglas Nakashima, Theresa Nichols, Per Olsson, Jules Pretty, P. S. Ramakrishnan, Marie Roué, Colin Scott, Kaleekal Thomson, and David Turnbull.

It gives me pleasure to thank a growing number of our graduate students whose research has contributed to the field. Many of them have produced works that are cited in this volume: Tikaram Adhikari, Eleanor Bonny, Damian Fernandes, Colin Gallagher, Sandra Grant, Carlos Idrobo, Anne Kendrick, Serge LaRochelle, Kenton Lobe, Maria M'Lot, Alejandra Orozco Quintero, Brenda Parlee, Claude Peloquin, Dyanna Riedlinger Jolly, and Cristiana Seixas. Carlos also assisted with the redrawing of figures. I thank our secretary, Jacqueline

Rittberg, for technical assistance, Routledge editors, Siân Findlay, Stephen Rutter and David McBride, their staff, and Susan Leaper and the Florence Production team for making the book possible.

I wish to pay special tribute to two pioneers of indigenous knowledge/traditional ecological knowledge who passed away recently, Bob Johannes and Darrell Posey. Bob's *Words of the Lagoon* (1981) was a major inspiration for my own traditional fisheries knowledge work. For its detail of documentation, I don't think it has been surpassed. Darrell Posey did his signature work with the Kayapo of Brazil. He used to say, yes, he is an American, but a Brazilian too, and really a citizen of the world. In my mind, he embodied the paradoxical nature of indigenous knowledge: it is intensely local, but at the same time, it is universal.

Preface to the Third Edition

This edition of *Sacred Ecology* has been updated with about 150 new references and that is only a fraction of the literature that has emerged since 2008. As David Turnbull observed in the 2009 special issue of *Futures*, the future of indigenous knowledge lies in the creation of a knowledge space, and the explosion of the literature in recent years indicates that this seems to be happening. Major contributions in the area of biodiversity conservation, with various volumes cited here, and the creation of "modern" indigenous knowledge in such areas as local environmental monitoring indicate the continuing relevance of local and traditional knowledge.

This new edition further develops the point that traditional knowledge as process, rather than as content, is what we should be examining. Also important is the issue of a knowledge dialogue. Scholars have wasted in my view too much time and effort on a science vs. traditional knowledge debate; we should reframe it instead as a science *and* traditional knowledge dialogue and partnership. The issue of a power differential between science and traditional knowledge will never be completely resolved. But in recent years, as documented in *Sacred Ecology*, we have made great progress in the co-production of knowledge for problem-solving in critical issues such as climate change. Here we are not referring to somehow synthesizing science and traditional knowledge, but rather the generation of new knowledge through the synergy of combining what is already known to science and to local and traditional knowledge.

The major change in this third edition is the addition of web links in a section at the end of the book. This electronic supplement provides links to web pages to enrich the material in the book, extra case studies, and web-based open-access publications. Through these links, readers and instructors who use this book for teaching can access additional material and can follow up many of the topics and themes in the book. I have taken some care to include sites with practical applications of local and traditional knowledge, and have added teaching tips and study questions organized by chapter.

I am fortunate to have many supportive colleagues. In addition to those mentioned in the earlier editions, I am grateful to a number of scholars: Alpina Begossi, Sébastien Boillat, David Bray, Josh Cinner, Inger Marie Gaup Eira, Michael Ferguson, Bruce Forbes, Natalia Hanazaki, Eugene Hunn, Erjen Khamaganova, Gita Laidler, Mimi Lam, Raul Lejano, Gabriela Lichtenstein, Flora Lu, Ole Henrik Magga, Andrei F. Marin, Svein Mathiesen, Leticia Merino, Gonazlo Oviedo, Helen Ross, Jan Salick, Sylvie Shaw, and Renato Silvano.

My students are my best teachers. For their work and for sharing their insights, I thank Catie Burlando, Nathan Deutsch, Arthur Hoole, John-Erik Kocho-Schellenberg, Andres Marin, Andrew Miller, Eva Patton, Ryan Pengelly, Julia Premauer, Lance Robinson, Shailesh Shukla, Kate Turner, and Melanie Zurba, in addition to those mentioned in earlier editions.

I have augmented the illustrations in this new edition with photographs; I am grateful to Upali Amarasinghe, Yilmaz Ari, Catie Burlando, Carl Folke, Frank Lake, and James Robson for permitting me to use their photos. I thank Ron Jones for his expert work in researching websites, and Nancy Turner and Robin Kimmerer for additional suggestions. It was a pleasure working with Routledge editors Stephen Rutter, Leah Babb-Rosenfeld, and Gail Newton, and the Routledge production team.

CHAPTER 1

Context of Traditional Ecological Knowledge

Most of us have lost that sense of unity of biosphere and humanity which would bind and reassure us all with an affirmation of beauty. Most of us do not today believe that whatever the ups and downs of detail within our limited experience, the larger whole is primarily beautiful.

Gregory Bateson, *Mind and Nature*

Ecological awareness will arise only when we combine our rational knowledge with an intuition for the nonlinear nature of our environment. Such intuitive wisdom is characteristic of traditional, nonliterate cultures, especially of American Indian cultures, in which life was organized around a highly refined awareness of the environment.

Fritjof Capra, *The Turning Point*

We live in a world densely populated by humans in close communication with one another over the surface of the earth. More and more, the world looks like a single society, a "global village." But in fact, human society consists of a great many groups, as different from one another as the city dwellers of New York, rice farmers of India, and aboriginal hunters of northern Canada. People of our global village differ not only in their daily occupations and material wealth, but also in the ways in which they view the world around them. This multitude of perceptions is directly related to cultural diversity around the world, a diversity that is rapidly shrinking. Surrounded by the built landscape, it has become difficult for many people to relate to the environment. This alienation from nature has contributed to the environmental problems of the contemporary world. But at the same time, it has triggered a search for new ways of relating to nature.

The science of ecology, or at least one school of ecology that takes a broader holistic view, provides a new vision of the earth as a system of interconnected relationships. Emerging out of the discourse of ecology is a view of human society as part of a web of life within the ecosystem. Researchers are discovering, in the words of Berry (1988), "a universe that is dynamically alive: a whole system, fluid and interconnected. . . . Science is discovering a new version of the 'enchanted' world that was part of the natural mind for most of human history." This view is a radical departure from the static, mechanical, disembodied view of the world formulated by Descartes, Newton, and other thinkers of the Age of Enlightenment, and which has dominated our thinking.

The land ethics of Aldo Leopold (1949), deep ecology (Naess 1989), Gaia (Lovelock 1979), a sense of place, bioregionalism, topophilia or love of land (Tuan 1974), and biophilia or love of living things (Kellert and Wilson 1993; Kellert 1997) are some of the ways in which people concerned with environmental ethics have searched for the personal and spiritual element of ecology that has been missing in scientific ecology. Yet others have explored Eastern religions and Native American worldviews for insights (Callicott 1994; Bruun and Kalland 1995; Grim 2001). These efforts are very much a part of the broader context of the interest in traditional ecological knowledge, since it represents experience acquired over thousands of years of direct human contact with the environment.

The term *traditional ecological knowledge* came into widespread use only in the 1980s, but the practice of traditional ecological knowledge is as old as ancient hunter-gatherer cultures. Although this book is about traditional *ecological* knowledge and deals with environment and resources, the study of other types of traditional knowledge is valued in a number of fields. In fact, in comparison to some of these fields, the study of indigenous knowledge in ecology is relatively recent.

The earliest systematic studies of traditional ecological knowledge were carried out by anthropologists. As part of this endeavor, ecological knowledge was studied by ethnoecology, an approach that focuses on the conceptions of ecological relationships held by a people or a culture (Toledo 1992, 2001; Nazarea 1999; Hunn 2008; Johnson and Hunn 2010). Ethnoecology is a subset of ethnoscience (folk science), defined by Hardesty (1977: 291) as "the study of systems of knowledge developed by a given culture to classify the objects, activities, and events of its universe." As the definition indicates, much of the early research in ethnoscience was concerned with folk taxonomies. Pioneering work by Conklin (1957) documented, for example, that traditional peoples such as the Hanunoo of the Philippines often possessed exceptionally detailed knowledge of local plants and animals and their natural history, recognizing in one case some 1,600 plant species.

Various kinds of indigenous environmental knowledge have come to be accepted and used by scientific experts in a number of areas. For example, there has been growing recognition of the capabilities of traditional agriculturalists (Warren *et al.* 1995; Anderson 2005), pharmacologists (Schultes 1989), water engineers (Groenfelt 1991; Tiki *et al.* 2011), and architects (Fathy 1986). Increased appreciation of ethnoscience, ancient and contemporary, paved the way for the acceptability of the validity of traditional knowledge in a variety of fields. In the area of ecology, various works showed that indigenous groups and other traditional peoples in diverse geographical areas, from the Arctic to the Amazon, had their own understandings of ecological relationships and systems of managing resources. The feasibility of applying traditional ecological knowledge to contemporary resource management problems in various parts of the world was gradually recognized in the international arena, as reflected in the following quotation from *Our Common Future*, the report of the World Commission on Environment and Development:

> Tribal and indigenous peoples' . . . lifestyles can offer modern societies many lessons in the management of resources in complex forest, mountain and dryland ecosystems.
>
> (WCED 1987: 12)

> These communities are the repositories of vast accumulations of traditional knowledge and experience that link humanity with its ancient origins. Their disappearance is a loss for the larger society, which could learn a great deal from their traditional skills in sustainably managing very complex ecological systems.
>
> (WCED 1987: 114–15)

Defining Traditional Ecological Knowledge

There is no universally accepted definition of traditional ecological knowledge. The term is, by necessity, ambiguous since the terms *traditional* and *ecological knowledge* are themselves ambiguous. In the dictionary sense, *traditional* usually refers to cultural continuity transmitted in the form of social attitudes, beliefs, principles, and conventions of behavior and practice derived from historical experience. It is cumulative and open to change (Nakashima 1998; Ellen *et al.* 2000). Hunn (1993a: 13) explains: "New ideas and techniques may be incorporated into a given tradition, but only if they fit into the complex fabric of existing traditional practices and understandings. Thus traditions are enduring adaptations to specific places. . . . Traditions are the products of generations of intelligent reflection tested in the rigorous laboratory of survival. That they have endured is proof to their power."

For some, *tradition* and *change* are contradictory concepts, and it is difficult to define just how much and what kind of change would affect the labeling of a practice as "traditional." Worse, as Lewis (1993a) points out, the traditional "may be dismissed or denigrated because the custodians of such knowledge are no longer considered 'traditional' by outsiders, particularly those in positions of power and authority." This is one of the reasons why some scholars avoid using the term *traditional* and instead favor the term *indigenous*, thus avoiding the debate over tradition, as Warren explains:

> In 1980, David Brokensha, Oswald Werner and I were struggling to find a term that could replace "traditional" in the designation "traditional knowledge." In our view, "traditional" denoted the 19th-century atti-tudes of simple, savage and static. We wanted a term that represented the dynamic contributions of any community to problem-solving, based on their own perceptions and conceptions, and the ways that they identified, categorized and classified phenomena important to them. At the same time Robert Chambers and his group at Sussex were struggling with the same issue. Independent of each other, we both came up with the term "indigenous."
>
> (Warren 1995: 13)

For many others *traditional* does not mean an inflexible adherence to the past; it simply means time-tested and wise. In particular, for many groups of indigenous people the word *tradition* carries many positive meanings. For example, when the Inuit participants in a 1995 conference were asked to describe traditional knowledge, there was consensus on the following meanings: practical common sense; teachings and experience passed through generations; knowing the country; being rooted in spiritual health; a way of life; an authority system of rules for resource use; respect; obligation to share; wisdom in using knowledge; using heart and head together (Emery 1997: 3).

Notable among these descriptors is traditional ecological knowledge as a way of life (Witt and Hookimaw-Witt 2003) and an abundance of references to ways of knowing (Simpson 2001) and doing things, knowledge as process—as opposed to knowledge as content. Indigenous scholars Battiste and Henderson (2000: 46) write, "what is traditional about traditional ecological knowledge is not its antiquity, but the way it is acquired and used." When the young Anishinaabe resource managers of the Great Lakes area were reacting to the first edition of *Sacred Ecology* (see Preface to the Second Edition), the word *traditional* was not a concern and neither was the content of the book. What they were really interested in discussing was how to talk to elders, the processes by which this traditional knowledge is acquired and transmitted.

The term *ecological knowledge* poses definitional problems of its own. If ecology is defined narrowly as a branch of biology concerned with interrelationships in the biophysical environment, in the domain of Western science, then *traditional ecological knowledge* is an oxymoron. If, on the other hand, *ecological knowledge* is defined broadly to refer to the knowledge, however acquired, of relationships of living beings with one another and with their environment, then the term becomes tenable. It is what Lévi-Strauss (1962) has called the *science du concret*, the native knowledge of the natural milieu firmly rooted in the reality of an accumulation of concrete, personal experiences, as opposed to book-learning.

In this context, *ecological knowledge* is not the term of preference for many traditional or indigenous peoples themselves. For Australian indigenous people, knowledge comes from *country*; knowledge is a situated process tied to a specific place (Weir 2009; Lauer and Aswani 2009; Muir *et al.* 2010). In the Canadian North, aboriginal peoples often refer to their "knowledge of the land" rather than to ecological knowledge. *Land* to them, however, is more than the physical landscape; it includes the living environment. For example, the Dogrib Dene (Athapascan) term *ndè* is usually translated as "land." But its meaning (like *country* in Australia) is closer to "ecosystem," except that *ndè* is based on the idea that everything in the environment has life and spirit (Legat *et al.* 1995). Interestingly, in the history of the science of ecology, *land* was also often used as a synonym for *ecosystem*, as in the "land ethic" of Leopold (1949).

In this book, *ecological knowledge* is used in this sense of knowledge of the land. It is a fairly broad consideration of ecology, but not broad enough to encompass all aspects of knowledge. Indigenous knowledge cannot be reduced simply to its ecological aspects (McGregor 2004), but a book has to have a focus and this is the focus of this book.

To arrive at a definition of *traditional ecological knowledge*, it is necessary to sift through the various meanings and elements of the concept through the development of the fields of ethnoscience and human ecology (see Chapter 3). The study of traditional ecological knowledge begins with the study of species identifications and classification (ethnobiology) and proceeds to considerations of peoples' understandings of ecological processes and their relationships with the environment (human ecology). Implied in the concept is a component of local and empirical *knowledge* of species and other environmental phenomena. There is also a component of *practice* in the way people carry out their agriculture, hunting and fishing, and other livelihood activities. Further, there is a component of *belief* in peoples' perceptions of their role within ecosystems and how they interact with natural processes.

Boxes 1.1 and 1.2 illustrate the idea that purely ecological aspects of tradition cannot be divorced from the social and spiritual. Stories and legends are part of culture and indigenous knowledge because they signify meaning. Such meaning and values are rooted in the land and closely related to a "sense of place." Writing about the tribal area of Shimshal in northern Pakistan, Butz (1996: 52) notes that indigenous "ecological knowledge and activities [are] symbolically and instrumentally embedded in the places and life worlds out of which they developed and which they help constitute." Writing about another tribal group, the Penan of Sarawak, eastern Malaysia, Brosius (2001: 148) adds, "The landscape is more than simply a reservoir of detailed ecological knowledge. . . . It is also a repository for the memory of past events, and thus a vast mnemonic representation of social relationships and of society."

Box 1.1 The Tradition of Coyote Stories

"Traditions include ideas of religion, patterns of artistic expression, and familial relationships, for example, in addition to knowledge of economically valuable resources. However, close examination will reveal that it is not possible to divorce the ecological aspects of a tradition from the religious, the aesthetic, or the social. For example, among native American people of the Columbia Plateau of northwestern North America, moral precepts are inculcated by means of a body of 'Coyote stories,' " explains Hunn. An elder from the Columbia Plateau tribes may know more than sixty such stories, each one constituting a full evening's performance. "To appreciate the meaning these stories convey requires an intimate knowledge of the local natural environment, local animals and plants being the main characters and local places the stage on which they act out the human drama. Children learn the moral precepts that will guide them in their social and ecological relationships by listening to their elders tell these stories. Thus religion, art and ecology are one. Traditions are thus ecological in the sense that they represent a complex and integrated system of practices and beliefs."

Source: Hunn 1993a: 14.

Box 1.2 A Cree Legend of Flood and Origin of the Earth

According to archaeological evidence, the Cree have been living in the James Bay area for thousands of years. According to native beliefs and legends, the Cree have lived on this land "from the beginning," since time immemorial. They lived through major floods that destroyed the rest of the earth.

After the flood, according to the legend, the Cree trickster-hero, Wesakachak, found himself floating helplessly along with otter, beaver, and muskrat. The Creator gave Wesakachak the power, not to create, but to remake the world if only Wesakachak could bring up some earth from underneath the flood waters. Wesakachak turned to his companions for help. First, he called on the otter to dive down and bring up a piece of the earth. But the otter failed. Wesakachak then asked the beaver to do the same, but the beaver was also unsuccessful. Finally, Wesakachak, in desperation, turned to the muskrat. Small as he was, the muskrat had a strong heart and he tried very hard. Twice he dove and twice he failed. On the third attempt, he dove so deep that he almost drowned. But when he came up, against his breast in his forepaws, he held a piece of the old earth . . .

Source: Traditional. There are many versions of this popular legend. I collected this version from Moose Factory, Ontario. In some Mushkego (West Main) Cree legends, Wesakachak is the first human or the creator of all things. He is a teacher but also a fool who finally puts a barrier between all the earth's creatures so that they can no longer talk to one another. The older Chisasibi Cree hunters still refer to the ancient "time when humans and animals talked to one another."

Putting together the most salient attributes of traditional ecological knowledge, one may arrive at a working definition of traditional ecological knowledge as *a cumulative body of knowledge, practice, and belief, evolving by adaptive processes and handed down through generations by cultural transmission, about the relationship of living beings (including humans) with one another and with their environment*. This definition, evolving from our earlier work (Berkes 1993; Gadgil *et al.* 1993; Berkes, Folke, and Gadgil 1995a), is the operational definition used in this volume. Traditional ecological knowledge is a way of knowing; it is dynamic, building on experience and adapting to changes. It is an attribute of societies with historical continuity in resource use on a particular land. By and large, these are non-industrial or less technologically oriented societies, many of them indigenous or tribal, but not exclusively so. Some non-indigenous groups, such as inshore cod fishers of Newfoundland (Neis 1992, 2005; Murray *et al.* 2008), some ranchers of northwest Colorado (Knapp and Fernandez-Gimenez 2008, 2009), and users of Swiss Alpine commons (Netting 1981) no doubt also hold traditional ecological knowledge, in the sense of multi-generational, culturally transmitted knowledge and ways of doing things.

Traditional ecological knowledge as used here refers to ways of knowing (knowing, the process), as well as to information (knowledge as the thing known). The distinction between the two is important for analytical reasons and for understanding traditional ecological knowledge properly (Box 1.3). The type of empirical knowledge readily accepted cross-culturally (e.g. species names, life cycles, habitats) could be more aptly described as information (Spak 2005).

The various problems with the term *traditional ecological knowledge* have sent scholars to look for other terms. For example, some in the Canadian Arctic prefer to use the term *Inuit Qaujimajatuqangit*, abbreviated as IQ (Arnakak 2002; Wenzel 2004). The term covers all aspects of Inuit values and way of life, and may be too broad to use in place of traditional ecological knowledge (Wenzel 2004). Pretty (2007) prefers the term *ecological literacy* that gets around several issues. Others use *experiential knowledge* (Fazey *et al.* 2006). *Local knowledge* is the term of choice of some scholars "because it is the least problematical" (Ruddle 1994a: 161). But Raffles (2002) questions if *local knowledge* adequately captures the fact that indigenous knowledge is relational or situated knowledge. There are other shortcomings: the term *local knowledge* conveys neither the *ecological* aspect of the concept, nor a sense of the temporal dimension and cumulative cultural transmission.

Box 1.3 Some Aboriginal Definitions of Traditional Ecological Knowledge

"Aboriginal people define TEK as much more than just a body of knowledge. While this is a part of it, TEK also encompasses such aspects as spiritual experience and relationships with the land. It is also noted that TEK is a 'way of life'; rather than being just the knowledge of *how* to live, it is the actual *living* of that life. One way of looking at the differences between Aboriginal and non-Aboriginal views of TEK is to state that Aboriginal views of TEK are 'verb-based'—that is, action-oriented. TEK is not limited, in the Aboriginal view, to a 'body of knowledge'. It is expressed as a 'way of life'; it is conceived as being something that you *do*."

Source: McGregor 2004: 78.

Likewise, the term *indigenous knowledge* has its own critics. First, it implies a kind of knowledge that is restricted to indigenous people. Second, it implies that there is a category of knowledge that can be clearly labeled as indigenous. Ellen and Harris (2000) point out that the epistemic origins of much knowledge are obscure, constraining the perceived divide between kinds of knowledge. Is indigenous knowledge clearly separable from other kinds? Bjorkan and Qvenild (2010) argue that all knowledge, including indigenous knowledge, is situated and hybrid. Analyzing the knowledge of rubber production among Asian smallholders, Dove (2002) shows that their agroecological knowledge could hardly be less indigenous in nature. The rubber tree itself is not indigenous to the region (it came from the Amazon). The historical construction of rubber knowledge in Asia shows that it is a kind of hybrid knowledge that involved many partners. It developed iteratively through multiple steps and local innovations.

In this volume, *local knowledge* is used when referring to recent knowledge, as in the nontraditional knowledge of some Caribbean region peoples discussed in Chapter 10. The term *indigenous knowledge* is defined as the local knowledge held by indigenous peoples or local knowledge unique to a given culture or society, following Warren *et al.* (1995). It is used as the broader category within which *traditional ecological knowledge* fits. There is a good reason to proceed this way.

Much of the indigenous knowledge literature is not about *ecological* relationships but about many other fields of ethnoscience including agriculture (Warren *et al.* 1995; Armitage 2003), ethnobotany (Schultes and Reis 1995; Cunningham 2001; Laird 2002), ethnozoology (Clement 1995; Sillitoe 2002; Anderson and Tzuc 2005), ethnopharmacology (Marles *et al.* 2000), irrigation systems (Mabry 1996), soil and water conservation (Reij *et al.* 1996; Tiki *et al.* 2011), soils or ethnopedology (Pawluk *et al.* 1992), ethnoveterinary medicine (Mathias-Mundy and McCorkle 1995; SRISTI 2011), human food and healing (Pieroni and Price 2006), weaving (M'Closkey 2002), basketry (Athayde *et al.* 2009), ethnoastronomy (Ceci 1978), ethnoclimatology (Orlove *et al.* 2000, 2002) and others.

There is even a literature on indigenous knowledge and classification of snow (Pruitt 1984; Magga 2006) and freshwater ice (Basso 1972). The sea ice literature is very substantial (Nelson 1969; Freeman 1984; Riewe 1991; Oozeva *et al.* 2004; Krupnik *et al.* 2010). Some of these areas of ethnoscience (e.g. soil and water conservation) are directly related to ecological knowledge, but others (e.g. ethnoastronomy) are less so. The terms *traditional ecological knowledge* and *indigenous knowledge* have often been used interchangeably. But in this volume, the use of *traditional ecological knowledge* is limited to more explicitly land-related knowledge and is considered a subset of the broader category of indigenous knowledge.

Traditional Ecological Knowledge as Science

There are both similarities and differences between traditional science and Western science. Bronowski considers the practice of science (including magic) as a fundamental characteristic of human societies: "to me the most interesting thing about man is that he is an animal who practices art and science and, in every known society, practices both together" (Bronowski 1978: 9). Both Western and indigenous science may be considered, along with art, the result of the same general intellectual process of creating order out of disorder.

More controversial is the question of the existence of curiosity-driven inquiry among traditional peoples. Opinions differ, but there is a great deal of evidence that traditional people do possess scientific curiosity, and that traditional knowledge does not merely encompass matters of immediate practical interest. In his classic study, *The Savage Mind*, Lévi-Strauss (1962) argues this point on the grounds that ancient societies could not have acquired such technological skills as those involved in the making of watertight pots without a curiosity-driven scientific attitude and a desire for knowledge for its own sake. As Lévi-Strauss (1962: 3) states it, "the universe is an object of thought at least as much as it is a means of satisfying needs."

Lévi-Strauss's work is groundbreaking in part because he avoids Western society's long-standing prejudice against non-Western cultures, especially those of "primitive" societies. He prefers to call the latter " 'prior' rather than 'primitive' "; "it was no less scientific and its results no less genuine. They were secured ten thousand years earlier and still remain at the basis of our own civilization" (Lévi-Strauss 1962: 16). The worlds of the shaman and the scientist are two parallel modes of acquiring knowledge about the universe, "two distinct though equally positive sciences: one which flowered in the Neolithic period, whose theory of the sensible order provided the basis of the arts of civilization (agriculture, animal husbandry, pottery, weaving . . .)." However, the two kinds of sciences are fundamentally distinct in that "the physical world is approached from opposite ends in the two cases: one is supremely concrete, the other supremely abstract" (Lévi-Strauss 1962: 269).

Banuri and Apffel Marglin (1993) also consider traditional ecological knowledge to differ from Western scientific ecological knowledge in a number of substantive ways. They use a systems-of-knowledge analysis, of which the philosophical and anthropological background goes back to Weber and Nietzsche, to contrast indigenous and Western scientific knowledge. According to this analysis, indigenous knowledge systems are characterized by embeddedness of knowledge in the local cultural milieu; boundedness of local knowledge in space and time; the importance of community; lack of separation between nature and culture, and between subject and object; commitment or attachment to the local environment as a unique and irreplaceable place; and a noninstrumental approach to nature. These features contrast, respectively, with Western scientific knowledge systems, which are characterized by disembeddedness; universalism; individualism; nature:culture and subject:object dichotomy; mobility; and an instrumental attitude (nature as commodity) toward nature.

One important point of difference is that many systems of indigenous knowledge include spiritual or religious dimensions (beliefs) that do not make sense to science or fall outside the realm of science. For example, some Dene (Athapascan) peoples of the North American subarctic consider that not only plants and animals but also rivers, mountains, and glaciers are alive. Working in the area of St. Elias Mountains, a glacier field that straddles Alaska, Yukon, and British Columbia, Cruikshank (2001, 2005) found that Tlingit and Tagish storytellers considered glaciers to be sentient and responsive, and attributed human-like characteristics to them. Stories told about periodic surges of glaciers (a geophysical fact) but also about glacier responses to human folly, such as cooking with grease on the glacier or making disrespectful remarks.

Animists everywhere in the world impute life and spirit to parts of the environment that Western science considers inert. Ingold (2006) points out that *life* should perhaps not be restricted to be an attribute of things (e.g. whether it contains DNA or not). Life can also be "immanent in the very process of that world's continual generation or coming-into-being" (Ingold 2006: 10). One can argue, as Ingold does, that extending the definition of life to consider the continuous birth of the world, may serve the purpose of "recovering the sense of astonishment banished from official science" (Ingold 2006: 9). It can also help restore the "sacred" into ecology, to inject some life-force into the machine-like scientific conceptualizations of ecosystems that was once fashionable.

Traditional knowledge systems tend to have a large moral and ethical context; there is no separation between nature and culture. In many traditional cultures nature is imbued with sacredness, as in Paul Shepard (1973) and Gregory Bateson's (Bateson and Bateson 1987) sense of *sacred*. This is " 'sacred ecology' in the most expansive, rather than in the scientifically restrictive, sense of the word 'ecology' " (Knudtson and Suzuki 1992: 15). It is also the "sacred," as proposed in Gregory Bateson's *Angels Fear*, as a venue for addressing the complexity of human-environment relations from a non-reductionist perspective (Katja Neves-Graça, personal communication).

As told by Catherine Bateson, Gregory "had become aware gradually that the unity of nature . . . might only be comprehensible through the kind of metaphors familiar from religion . . . an integrative dimension of experience that he called the sacred" (Bateson and Bateson 1987: 2). He did not think "religion" captured what he had in mind; "he searched for an understanding of the related but more general term, 'the sacred', moving gingerly and cautiously into holy ground, 'where angels fear to tread'" (Bateson and Bateson 1987: 8). The present book continues this line of thinking, and further explores sacred ecology as a way to approach the unity of human and environment (Chapter 12).

Some of these distinctions between traditional science and Western science are fundamentally important. However, the distinction between the two kinds of knowledge should not be exaggerated. As seen earlier in the case of rubber agro-ecology in Asia (Dove 2002) the two kinds of knowledge are nearly impossible to delimit. The distinction is often "a difference of degree (quantitative) rather than of type (qualitative)," as Giarelli (1996) puts it. Various authors have offered many other (sometimes simplistic) distinctions, including the alleged *inability* of traditional systems to use controlled experiments, to collect *synchronic* (simultaneously observed) data, and to use quantitative measures.

These generalizations simply do not hold up to evidence. Examples are available in fact to show that traditional knowledge experts are capable of carrying out controlled experiments (Chapter 7, the Cree fisher's experiment on species selectivity of gill nets). Some traditional management systems are based on *synchronic* data collected over large areas, rather than merely *diachronic* data, or a long time-series of local information. Examples include the Dene system of monitoring caribou movements over a broad front across the subarctic region of central Canada (Chapter 6) and regional observations of environmental change (Chapters 8 and 9).

As well, examples are available to show that quantitative thinking in some cases can be part of traditional systems of management. The case in point is Barnston's nineteenth-century estimate of goose populations, which must surely be one of the earliest published uses of traditional knowledge for resource management. Barnston (1861) was one of the first biologists/naturalists to attempt an estimate of wild goose populations in North America. Based on a field survey that indicated that the Cree Indians of James Bay killed some 74,000 geese per year, and an elders' rule of thumb that "for every goose killed, 20 must leave the Bay," Barnston came up with a total goose population figure of 1,200,000 for the region. This is an entirely plausible figure and well within modern population counts, which give a range of one to two million geese that use James Bay as a flyway, including two species, Canada goose (*Branta canadensis*) and the lesser snow goose (*Anser caerulescens*).

Differences: Philosophical or Political?

The relationship between Western science and traditional science is complex. Considering that there are a number of different traditions of Western science, and a range of indigenous knowledge systems, caution is necessary in generalizing about differences. Agrawal (1995a) argues that finding clear demarcations between indigenous and Western knowledge is futile, given the failure of philosophers of science to find satisfactory verification criteria to distinguish science from non-science. Further, Agrawal (1995b) points out that "it is difficult to adhere to a view of indigenous and Western forms of knowledge being untouched by each other." He examined supposed differences between indigenous and Western knowledge with respect to substantive, methodological, and contextual matters and found less than a clear-cut separation.

According to some scholars, the philosophical differences between the two kinds of science are not sharply defined; rather, it is our reductionist analysis that tends to exaggerate the differences (Cordell 1995). Others think that the exclusion of non-science is "because these ways of knowing often employ non-standardized methods which are not 'transparent' in the same way as science and therefore easily dismissed" (Marlor 2010: 513). Some of these issues are explored further in Chapter 12 from a political ecology point of view in which indigenous knowledge is treated as a challenge to the dominant positivist-reductionist paradigm in Western science. Suffice to point out that the sources of conflict between practitioners of Western science and traditional science often have to do with power relationships between Western experts and aboriginal experts, who have different political agendas and who relate in different ways to the resource in question. Keith and Simon (1987: 219) emphasize the issues of authority and legitimacy: "It is important to understand that conflicts between northern peoples and those seeking to implement conservation strategies are not merely philosophical." Such conflicts can also occur with non-indigenous groups, for example, subsistence hunters in the greater Yellowstone National Park area. Robbins (2006: 185) writes: "Often dismissed as 'barstool biology', the ecological knowledges of local hunters in the northern Yellowstone ecosystem are rooted in environmental experience and situated politics."

Local and traditional knowledge, as situated knowledge (Nazarea 1999; Raffles 2002; Knudsen 2008), embodies claims to authority over land and resources, especially in the face of counter-claims from outsiders. Hence when noted Walmajjari artist Jimmy Pike learned that the designation of his country (land) in northwestern Australia as "Vacant Crown Land" means that it belongs to the Queen, he is reported to have declared, "The Queen never bin fuggin walk around here! Bring her here and I will ask her: All right, show me all the waterholes!" (Davies 1999: 61). In the native Australian worldview, knowing the waterholes, the songs that go with the trails, and the names of places is what establishes legitimacy of claim. In a story of the Gurindji people, as retold by Mulligan

(2003), a settler moves his homestead and the place name that goes with it. This provides proof enough to the Gurindji that the "whitefella" interloper had no serious connection with the land that he claimed.

Just as there is tension over control of land and resources, there is tension over authority and legitimacy of knowledge. Johannes (1989: 5), a biological scientist himself, observes that "the attitudes of many biological scientists and natural resource managers to traditional knowledge have frequently been dismissive." But these attitudes may have more to do with the question of the authority of knowledge than the quality of the knowledge. Consider, for example, the contrasting views of two tropical forest ecologists, Janzen and Gómez-Pompa. According to Janzen (1986), only biologists have the competence to decide how the tropical landscape should be conserved. As "representatives of the natural world," biologists are "in charge of the future of tropical ecology" and have the expertise to "determine whether tropical agrospace is to be populated" by humans or whether it should also contain "some islands of the greater nature"—that is, a landscape without humans. By contrast, Gómez-Pompa and Kaus (1992a) point out that "the concept of wilderness as untouched land is mostly an urban perception" and has little to do with the reality of tropical forests in which the current composition of mature vegetation is the legacy of human use over millennia:

> The first step is to recognize that conservation traditions exist in other cultural practices and beliefs that are separate from Western traditional conservation. . . . The view of the white ashes of forest trees that have been felled and burned for an agricultural plot may appear to an urbanite outsider to be a desecration of the wilderness, but a farmer may see it as an essential stage of renewal.
>
> (Gómez-Pompa and Kaus 1992a)

As Lewis (1989) comments, "It is difficult for people from 'advanced' cultures to accept the idea that people from 'primitive' cultures might know something scientifically significant, or even know more about a subject within the fields of natural science, in this case fire ecology, than do scientists." These observations are echoed in the critique of Feyerabend (1987) of the intolerance of many scientists toward knowledge and insights that originate outside institutionalized Western science. Scientists tend to dismiss understandings that do not fit their own; this includes understandings of other scientists using different paradigms. Interestingly, indigenous knowledge holders can also behave that way themselves (see Box 1.4).

Box 1.4 Skepticism Works Both Ways

It is well known that many scientists are skeptical of indigenous knowledge. But skepticism can work both ways. For their part, many traditional knowledge holders are skeptical of book learning, and tend to dismiss scientists who do not have extensive first-hand knowledge of a specific area. I remember the story told by a caribou biologist about his first visit to Baker Lake in Canada's Nunavut Territory. He made the mistake of introducing himself as an expert on caribou. The local hunters were incredulous. "You mean," they said, "you know about all caribou, including our caribou here too?" It was clear from their response that what the biologist knew about the caribou, which is universal knowledge according to the positivist tradition, carried not one bit of weight in Baker Lake.

The biologist's knowledge was not considered legitimate unless it was specific to the area, obtained largely first-hand, and in apprenticeship with a local knowledge-holder. The Baker Lake Inuit had no trouble with Western science, as long as it fit *their* understanding of the caribou, and if it was obtained at least in part through the kind of learning process that *they* considered legitimate, that is, through first-hand observations and guided by the teachings of elders. In this regard, their attitude hardly differed from that of Western scientists when confronted by "other" experts. The Baker Lake Inuit expected the knowledge of these other experts to live up to *their* standards of legitimate knowledge and pass *their* tests of verification.

Feyerabend's (1987) analysis provides one explanation for the contemptuous attitude of some scientists toward traditional ecological knowledge. Many scientists would probably lean toward another explanation: it is the duty of the scientist to remain skeptical, especially when confronted with an area such as traditional knowledge, which does not easily lend itself to scientific verification (Davis and Ruddle 2010). Hence the issue is complex, even if one agrees with Feyerabend and Lévi-Strauss, among others, that Western scientific methodology is merely one way, and not the only way, to acquire knowledge (Nakashima 1998; Ingold 2000; Atleo 2004; Geniusz 2009; Kassam 2009).

This is not to say that tradition is necessarily virtuous. Obviously, many traditional practices and belief systems are not, or were not, adaptive (Diamond 2005). For example, Taoist sages in the third century recommended ingesting cinnabar, a toxic ore of mercury, for a long life. Some Chinese traditional medicine still prescribes potions of bear gallbladder, ground-up tiger bone, and rhino horn. A conservation ethic may be lacking among some traditional groups with detailed environmental knowledge (Redford and Stearman 1993; Callicott 1994). For example, New Guinea natives possess remarkably detailed knowledge of plants and animals, but their practices nevertheless have a heavy impact on the native biota (Diamond 1993). Exaggerated claims of indigenous wisdom of the "noble savage" have hurt the study of traditional ecological knowledge (for more on this, see Chapter 11). As well, misapplications of indigenous knowledge have caused problems. With regard to overeager and ill-conceived attempts to replicate Mexico's traditional *chinampa* agriculture, Chapin (1988: 17) writes, "we become blinded by the beauty of the conceptual model [*chinampa*] and lose our bearings, mistaking it for reality itself. We end up seducing ourselves."

With the increasing acceptance of traditional ecological knowledge in recent years, a new kind of political problem has emerged. Many national and international programs incorporate indigenous values and knowledge; in some cases, there is a legal obligation to do so. This has resulted in the creation of a "traditional ecological knowledge industry," often using rapid rural appraisal kinds of techniques (Grenier 1998) to generate material to be used as mandated. There are two problems with this approach. First, the material so generated is often out of cultural context (Nadasdy 1999). Second, traditional ecological knowledge often becomes co-opted into non-indigenous frameworks that may be fundamentally different from indigenous ways of thinking (White 2006). In reference to northern territories in Canada where the use of traditional ecological knowledge is legally required, Simpson explains:

> Governments often require their bureaucrats to include TEK in policy and legislation without proper consultation with Aboriginal peoples, in unrealistic timeframes, and without appropriate financial support. Governments also regularly require TEK to be written down or documented before it is considered useful. Documented TEK is then integrated into processes and frameworks that remain strongly rooted in Western science, and much of the transformative potential of indigenous knowledge is assimilated in the process.
>
> (Simpson 2005: 1650)

To explore these issues further, we need to consider the kinds and context of traditional ecological knowledge. As traditional ecological knowledge is not merely a body of knowledge (McGregor 2004), we need a framework to distinguish between empirical kinds of indigenous knowledge and ways of life; between information and ways of knowing.

Knowledge–Practice–Belief: A Framework for Analysis

Many authors have noted that traditional knowledge may be considered at several levels of analysis, consistent with the description of traditional ecological knowledge as a *knowledge–practice–belief complex*. According to Lewis (1993a), traditional ecological knowledge begins with local knowledge at the level of taxonomic systems and then proceeds to the understanding of processes or functional relationships. Kalland (1994) identifies three levels, starting with empirical or practical knowledge. The second level is "paradigmatic knowledge," or the interpretation of empirical observations to put them in a context, and the third is "institutional knowledge," or knowledge embedded in social institutions, the rules and norms of society. Orlove and Brush (1996), following Nabhan (1985), make a distinction among three levels, different from Kalland's: indigenous environmental knowledge; management practices based on this knowledge; and religious beliefs about and ritual uses of plants and animals. Stevenson's (1996) "interrelated components" of traditional ecological knowledge are different again: specific environmental knowledge; knowledge of ecosystem relationships; and a code of ethics governing appropriate human–environmental relationships.

There appears to be a consensus that there are multiple layers or levels of indigenous knowledge, even though there is no agreement about the delineation of these layers (Usher 2000; White 2006). In the present volume, traditional knowledge is considered at four interrelated levels (Figure 1.1).

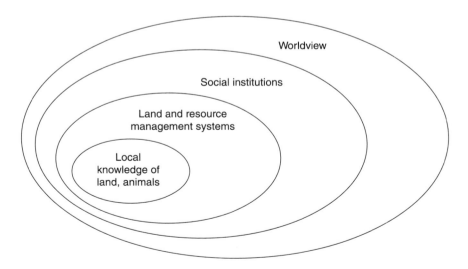

Figure 1.1 Levels of analysis in traditional knowledge and management systems.

First, there is the local and empirical knowledge of animals, plants, soils, and landscape. This level of knowledge includes information on species identification and taxonomy, life histories, distributions, and behavior. Based on empirical observations, all such information has obvious survival value, and is readily accepted cross-culturally. This is the "documented TEK" that is often incorporated into government reports and may at times be out of cultural context (Simpson 2005).

At the second level of analysis, there is a resource management system, one that uses local environmental knowledge *and also includes* an appropriate set of practices, tools, and techniques. Those ecological practices require an understanding of ecological processes, such as the functional relationships among key species and an understanding of forest succession. This second level of analysis is comparable to the second level of Orlove and Brush (1996).

Third, a traditional system of management requires appropriate social institutions, sets of rules-in-use, norms and codes of social relationships. For a group of interdependent hunters, fishers, or agriculturists to function effectively, there has to be a social organization for coordination, cooperation, and rule-making (Berkes 1989a). Social institutions may include *institutions of knowledge* that frame the processes of social memory, creativity, and learning (Davidson-Hunt and Berkes 2003).

Finally, a fourth level of analysis is the *worldview*, which shapes environmental perception and gives meaning to observations of the environment. It is comparable to Kalland's (1994) "paradigmatic knowledge." As Whitehead (1929) argued, knowledge has components of *observational order* and *conceptual order*. The first of these orders is constituted by our direct perceptions and observations. The second is constituted by our ways of conceiving the universe. The concepts supplied by our conceptual order, the worldview, invariably provide the interpretation of our observations of the world around us. The fourth level includes religion, ethics, and more generally, belief systems (Grim 2001; Taylor 2005, 2009; Jenkins 2010), and rounds out the knowledge–practice–belief complex that describes traditional knowledge.

Figure 1.1 shows the four levels of analysis as concentric ellipses, with the management system encompassing local and empirical knowledge, the institutional level enveloping the management system, and all three levels embedded within a worldview or belief system. However, it must be emphasized that the four levels are not always distinct. In particular, the management system and the social institution that governs it are often so closely coupled that the distinction between them may seem artificial (Berkes and Folke 1998). One might argue that the management system and the institution are one and the same. It must also be pointed out that there are feedbacks among the levels, and the linkages are in dynamic relationships. Local knowledge may grow; both management systems and institutions may adapt, change, and fall apart and may be renewed. Worldviews shape observations and social institutions but may themselves be affected by changes occurring at the other levels, such as the collapse of management systems, as illustrated in Chapter 6.

Objectives and Overview of the Volume

A major issue of our times is how humans can develop a more acceptable relationship with the environment that supports them. Growing interest in traditional ecological knowledge since the 1980s is perhaps indicative of two things: the need for ecological insights from indigenous practices of resource use, and the need to develop a new ecological ethic in part by learning from the wisdom of traditional knowledge holders. However, it is becoming clear that "resource management" as a concept is too Western-centric. Many indigenous languages do not even have words for "resource" or "management." Traditional knowledge provides lessons not in resource management but in dealing with human–environment relations. The objective of this volume is to explore these ideas toward a "sacred ecology" that addresses human–environment relationships in a holistic and humanistic way.

The book examines a diversity of traditional knowledge systems and discusses the usefulness of traditional ecological knowledge in terms of providing an understanding (not merely information) that is complementary to scientific ecology. At the same time, the book explores a diversity of relationships that different groups have developed with their environment. Here the approach is evolutionary, with emphasis on the dynamics of relationships between societies and their resources, in exploring how environmental practices develop over time. There is no clear separation of empirical and theoretical material in the organization of the volume, except that the early chapters cover concepts; the middle chapters contain empirical material; and the final chapters contain the bulk of theory and conclusions.

In more detail, Chapter 2 reviews the literature and builds on the concepts and definitions introduced in this chapter. It discusses the emergence of the field of traditional ecological knowledge and its significance, both for indigenous cultures and more broadly for humankind. The intellectual roots of the discipline in ethnobiology and human ecology and the expansion of the meaning and range of traditional knowledge are the subjects of Chapter 3.

The next cluster of chapters contains substantive material on how traditional ecological knowledge and management systems work. Chapter 4 provides an international context for the practice of traditional knowledge, followed by three chapters on one indigenous society living in the eastern subarctic of North

America. Of these, Chapter 5 deals with the distinctive Cree Indian worldview of nature and animals and quotes Cree hunters extensively to provide insights into a culture "from the inside." Chapter 6 is about the *actual* behavior of hunters, and it tells the story of how the Cree learned to deal with the experience of declining caribou, based on historical evidence and contemporary observations of cultural evolution in action. Chapter 7 provides a detailed analysis of the Cree system of fishing and its interpretation from the point of view of resource management science. The examples and illustrations in the core of the book, Chapters 5 to 7, are from northern Canada, based on some 30 years of work. They involve the Cree, the Anishinaabe (Ojibwa), the Dene, the Inuit and the Inuvialuit (the Inuit of the western Canadian Arctic), with comparative material from other places and societies.

Chapters 8, 9 and 10 deal with a number of issues regarding the nature and use of traditional ecological knowledge, making indigenous knowledge applicable to contemporary problems. Chapter 8 is about climate change as observed by an Arctic community, using their own ways of observing and interpreting change. It shows how the use of different knowledge systems can broaden the scope of information available and contribute to the understanding of change. Chapter 9 continues on the theme of local and indigenous observations of the environment, and provides an interpretation of indigenous holism and complex systems. Using examples from a traditional society (Inuit hunters of Hudson Bay) and a nontraditional one (fishers of Grenada, West Indies), the chapter shows how people develop rules of thumb and build mental models of their environment in an approach that resembles fuzzy logic. Chapter 10 is about the development of traditional knowledge. The main examples come from a nontraditional society, the islands of the West Indies, which provide a laboratory-like setting for the study of local knowledge and practice, and the evolution of management institutions.

The last two chapters are both reflexive and forward-looking. Chapter 11 examines critical perspectives of traditional ecological knowledge, its limitations, and the debate over indigenous conservation, and explores some possible ways in which conservation ethics develop and indigenous knowledge itself evolves. Chapter 12 starts with the political ecology of traditional knowledge, examines traditional knowledge as a challenge to the positivist–reductionist paradigm in Western science, and concludes with a discussion of the potential of traditional ecological knowledge to inject a measure of ethics into the science of ecology and resource management, thereby restoring the "unity of mind and nature" (Bateson 1979).

CHAPTER 2

Emergence of the Field

Ethnobiology was for many years an esoteric subject. Work by Conklin and others showing the potential for the application of traditional biology to agricultural development was done more than half a century ago. Why is it then that traditional ecological knowledge is receiving so much attention lately?

Traditional ecological knowledge transcended academic circles and spilled into the popular media in the 1990s. One sure sign of its popularity was the cover story in *Time* magazine devoted to "Lost tribes, lost knowledge" (Linden 1991). There has been an increasing number of international symposia and workshops, and a rapidly expanding list of books and other publications on the subject. But this in itself cannot be the sole explanation of increasing attention to traditional ecological knowledge. Scholarly discovery of new findings is not a one-way transfer of information from an objective nature to receptive minds. The process is reciprocal and interactive: minds must be sufficiently receptive to receive the information in the first place, in turn stimulating new research and understanding, and these in turn stimulating greater receptivity.

There are probably several factors involved in the increased attention accorded to traditional ecological knowledge: the presence of a dedicated core group of scholars producing not only academic material but also feeding information into international policy circles; parallel developments in other interdisciplinary, policy-relevant fields such as environmental ethics, commons, and environmental history; public dissatisfaction with the outcomes of modernist analysis in fields such as resource conservation and management; and the emergence of indigenous scholarship to claim and use indigenous knowledge in education, culture, and politics. Perhaps it is the case that the accumulation of a "critical mass" of knowledge in the subject area happened to coincide with a search by the public, policy makers, scholars, and professionals for *alternatives* to a materialist tradition in ecology and environmental science.

The chapter starts with a review of the emergence of traditional ecological knowledge in the international scene since the 1980s, and the evolution of the literature. It deals with the complementary relationship of indigenous knowledge with three interdisciplinary fields: environmental ethics, commons (common property or common pool resources), and environmental history. It then proceeds to explore the cultural significance of traditional ecological knowledge for indigenous peoples themselves, and how the subject has necessarily become politically volatile in recent years. Indigenous people have begun to assert control over their knowledge as intellectual property, sometimes related to cultural revitalization movements. The chapter explores the reasons why it is important for indigenous peoples to control the research conducted on their knowledge, and a number of ways in which their voices have been heard. Indigenous control of indigenous knowledge has to be balanced against the possibilities for its practical use for humankind in a number of areas: biological and ecological insights, resource management, protected areas, biodiversity conservation, environmental monitoring, international development, disaster management, and environmental ethics.

Evolution and Differentiation of the Literature

Following the classical work in ethnoscience (see Chapter 3), a number of international organizations developed an interest in indigenous knowledge. Active from 1984 to 1989, the Traditional Ecological Knowledge Working Group of the International Conservation Union (IUCN) was founded on the idea that traditional ecological knowledge for natural resource conservation and management had been undervalued. The IUCN had already been receptive to the idea (McNeely and Pitt 1985), and the group published a newsletter and stimulated further interest through workshops and publications (Johannes 1989; Freeman and Carbyn 1988; Williams and Baines 1993). Since about 1993, IUCN's Inter-Commission Task Force on Indigenous Peoples has assembled materials to assist governments, development agencies, and other groups to work more effectively with indigenous peoples toward sustainability (Posey and Dutfield 1997). Since the early 2000s, IUCN has been specifically interested in indigenous and community-conserved areas (ICCAs) (Borrini-Feyerabend *et al.* 2004a; Brown and Kothari 2011; Martin *et al.* 2011).

Several international initiatives were undertaken through the United Nations system. One was UNESCO's program in traditional management systems in coastal marine areas (Johannes *et al.* 1983; Ruddle and Johannes 1985, 1990). A second was UNESCO's Man and the Biosphere (MAB) Program, part of which resulted in scientific investigations of traditional systems (e.g. Ramakrishnan 1992). A third was the work undertaken by the United Nations Research Institute for Social Development (UNRISD), which included an examination of the role of indigenous knowledge in the context of participatory management, for example, in protected areas (Pimbert and Pretty 1995). A global network of indigenous knowledge resource centers emerged in the 1990s, focusing mostly on agriculture and sustainable development. It was coordinated by the Centre for International Research and Advisory Networks (CIRAN/Nuffic), The Hague, Netherlands. CIRAN/Nuffic also produced a newsletter, *Indigenous Knowledge and Development Monitor*, building on *CIKARD News*, published earlier by the Center for Indigenous Knowledge for Agriculture and Rural Development at Iowa State University, USA. These activities resulted in the formation of a global indigenous knowledge network of some 30 centers in the late 1990s.

The outcome of all these activities is reflected in the rapid increase in scholarly and practical outputs, the proliferation of the kinds of traditional knowledge, the audiences for traditional knowledge, and the kinds of media used for recording and transmitting traditional knowledge. Table 2.1 summarizes a selection of areas of local and traditional knowledge that have been recorded in the literature. The list is not meant to be comprehensive and the categories are no doubt overlapping.

These kinds of knowledge include ethnobotany that historically started with the documentation of empirical knowledge of species, and later moved into the study of ecological relationships (ethnoecology) and resource use systems. It includes the kinds of knowledge that deal with resource use systems, institutions, and worldviews—the analytical levels of traditional knowledge (Figure 1.1). But the categories in Table 2.1 often cut across the four analytical levels. As well, the table includes bodies of literature (education, politics, and epistemology) that are about traditional knowledge but fall outside the analytical levels in Figure 1.1. Some of the areas of knowledge in Table 2.1 can be expanded and subdivided further. For example, "land use and occupancy" as a category hides the fact that there are distinct bodies of practice within it (Chapin *et al.* 2005). Table 2.2 captures some of these different approaches and methodologies within the broader area of land use and occupancy.

The range of kinds of traditional knowledge in Table 2.1 was not developed only by academics for scholarly purposes. For indigenous people, traditional knowledge is lived knowledge (e.g. Ingold 2000; McGregor 2004) but,

Table 2.1 A selection of areas of indigenous knowledge research as reflected in the literature

Kind of knowledge	Nature and potential uses	References
Ethnobotany and indigenous classification	Plants used as food and medicine; plants in language, ceremonies, and narratives. May be used in support of programs for promoting traditional knowledge	Balée 1994; Cunningham 2001; Turner 2004; Alexiades 2009
Resource use knowledge and practice	The diversity of land and resource use practices, such as use of fire, succession management, selective harvesting. May be used for input into resource management; cultural preservation	Pandey 1998; Deur and Turner 2005; Anderson 2005
Social institutions for resource use and stewardship	The role and development of institutions (local rules and norms) that mediate the use of knowledge, govern environmental practices and the way people make a living. May be used for capacity building	Berkes and Folke 1998; Boyd 1999; Trosper 2009
Land use and occupancy	Harvest areas, camps, travel routes, based on integrated map biographies of knowledge holders. Used in support of land claims and to fight development projects	Tobias 2000, 2010; Chapin and Threlkeld 2001
Landscape and biophysical knowledge and terminology	Local and indigenous terminology of landforms and species assemblages; specialized terminology such as for sea ice. May be used for local education, park planning, baseline for climate change monitoring	Oozeva et al. 2004; M'Lot and Manseau 2003
Resource harvesting and subsistence economy	Current or historical harvesting locations and use of key species in the subsistence economy. May be used for local history and culture; input into conservation and co-management	Hart and Amos 2004; Hunn 1999
Oral history	Lived experience and elders' stories, including events earlier than living memory. May be used for local history, oral tradition and cultural documentation	Cruikshank 1998, 2005
Indigenous ideology and worldview	Ways of seeing the environment, relations between human and non-human persons. May be used in education; documenting culture and philosophy	Hunn and Selam 1990; Posey 1999; Preston 2002
Traditional knowledge education	Elders' teachings; indigenous principles for living on the land; cultural practice and environmental relations. May be used in youth education	Bearskin et al. 1989; Cajete 2000; Atleo 2004; Brown and Brown 2009
Decolonizing knowledge	Indigenous knowledge in the context of colonial relations; reclaiming knowledge; intellectual property rights. May be used for raising political awareness	Smith 1999; Battiste and Henderson 2000; Rose 2004
Epistemology and knowledge systems	What constitutes knowledge; role of local and traditional knowledge in pluralistic approaches. May be used in co-management, environmental assessment	Turnbull 2000, 2009; Reid et al. 2006

Table 2.2 Different approaches and methodologies employed in land use and occupancy studies

Methodology	Description
Map biographies	Researchers record the lifetime extent of land use (resource harvesting, habitation, travel routes, and sometimes place names, stories and legends associated with places, and sacred sites) of individual traditional people. Individual maps are then combined to provide the land use map of a community (Freeman 1976, 2011; Riewe 1992; Tobias 2000, 2010).
Resource use area mapping	The spatial extent and the quantitative importance of resource use (wildlife, fisheries and other resources) can be determined with a questionnaire-based study. This can be scaled to show the quantitative values of various kinds of resources harvested over a specific period of time (Berkes *et al.* 1995).
Oral history, sketch maps and GIS	Oral history and local information on sketch maps, with use of geographic information systems (GIS) technology, produce information to help with resource planning and to identify management alternatives (Sirait *et al.* 1994; Ontario Ministry of Natural Resources 1994; Alcorn *et al.* 2003; Hoole and Berkes 2010).
Territorialization	Community mapping or participatory mapping uses spatial information technologies to map and document indigenous tenure systems, termed "territorialization" in Southeast Asia (Peluso 1995; Vandergeest and Peluso 1995; Rocheleau 1995; Fox 2002).
Ethnocartography	Information from land use questionnaires can be summarized into cartographic records by geographic zone and by community, showing all the resources and land features that are of importance to local groups (González *et al.* 1995; Chapin and Threlkeld 2001).

nevertheless, documented traditional knowledge also has its uses: enhancing political voice; documenting land and resource claims; fighting development projects; educating local youth; preserving indigenous cultures or revitalizing them; recording history from local perspectives; educating decision-makers and policy makers; communicating with outside scientists and governments; and creating materials for resource management, co-management, or environmental assessment (Bonny and Berkes 2008). Traditional knowledge outputs have become tools for political, educational, and cross-cultural communication purposes. It is not uncommon for a single output to be communicated to several audiences, with multiple uses in mind (Butler 2004; Lewis 2004; Stephenson and Moller 2009).

The diversity and range of traditional environmental knowledge and its audiences has expanded over the years. When the first indigenous knowledge outputs were produced in the 1970s, only a few target audiences were identified, such as negotiators and policy makers in indigenous land claim processes (Freeman 1976, 2011). It was not clear to whom and for what uses the recorded knowledge would be useful. Since that time, a number of key purposes have emerged, ranging from youth education to ecological restoration (Kimmerer 2002; Anderson and Barbour 2003). Traditional knowledge outputs have taken on their own social lives, and in some cases have been put to uses other than those for which they were originally intended. Accompanying this trend, there has been an increasingly greater presence of indigenous researchers, building capacity, developing ownership, and ensuring that knowledge is organized and presented in a culturally appropriate manner (Menzies 2006; Moller et al. 2009; Miller et al. 2010).

Incentives for indigenous and other rural communities to develop such outputs come from a desire to strengthen cultural norms and practices, as well as to apply traditional ways of knowing to new challenges (M'Lot and Manseau 2003). In the case of land and resource claims negotiations, for example, land-use maps allowed indigenous knowledge to come to bear on political arenas where it had previously not been considered (Fox 2002; Alcorn et al. 2003; Chapin et al. 2005; Freeman 2011). The early maps proved the extent of indigenous knowledge and use of the land, and made that knowledge available for decisions about new political boundaries. Beyond documenting information for outside uses, indigenous and other rural communities are increasingly finding motivation to record their knowledge for local purposes (Oozeva et al. 2004). Rapid social change that has taken place over the last century has, in many cases, ruptured local practices, and the social relations and the language necessary for oral traditions to thrive. This has created a need to record knowledge for reasons of cultural preservation and continuity (Nabhan 2000a; Turner and Turner 2008; Pilgrim and Pretty 2010).

The audiences for whom such products are developed represent a broad mix of both traditional and new actors. Recording traditional knowledge is a means of making it accessible to outside audiences accustomed to written tradition and book-learning. However, the same publications are also being used to support indigenous and other rural groups that are taking on the new challenge of caring for the land through local organizations and co-management bodies (King 2004; Spak 2005). The education of youth, often a local priority, is being supplemented by book, video, and computer-based learning. Each generation re-discovers its cultural knowledge and must combine what is remembered from the past with what is experienced in the present. It is this change between generations that drives the evolution of traditional knowledge and practice (Ingold 2000). In the rapid global environmental change experienced in the twenty-first century, indigenous and other rural communities face the challenge, perhaps more than before, of integrating the wisdom of past generations with the reality of the present (Kimmerer and Lake 2001; Kwan 2005).

Along with the expansion of our understanding of the diversity and range of traditional environmental knowledge and its audience, there has been an expansion of the diversity and range of media types to communicate this knowledge. Traditional knowledge is no longer limited to the realm of books, reports and academic papers. In addition to the print media and atlases, we have several powerful media types suitable for local use and control, as well as outside dissemination: DVD/video (IISD 2000); audio tapes, CD-ROMs (Fox 2003); and websites (WFMC 2011). These new media options allow us to mix and match to find the best fit between kinds of knowledge, the intended audience, and the media type used to transmit knowledge (Bonny and Berkes 2008). A major implication for researchers is the increasing feasibility of reaching indigenous and other rural audiences, using multiple ways of communicating findings and allowing for multiple uses of research results. Knowledge exchange is not one-way; it is reflexive, iterative, and adaptive.

Growth of Ecosystem-based Knowledge

One of the contributions of indigenous knowledge has been an improved understanding of different kinds of ecosystems. Table 2.3 provides a survey of examples, by ecosystem and resource type, from major works dealing with traditional knowledge and resource management systems. Some of these examples are examined in more detail in Chapter 4 and elsewhere. In addition to those sources cited in the table, there are a number of other major works on indigenous knowledge concerned with tropical forests (Balée 1994; Redford and Mansour 1996; Alexiades 2009), grassland or savanna ecosystems (Leach and Mearns 1996; Fairhead and

Table 2.3 Examples of traditional knowledge and resource management systems from selected ecosystems and resource types

System	Description
Tropical forests	The Mareng of New Guinea practice shifting cultivation (Rappaport 1984). Similar systems are found in many parts of the world (De Schlippe 1956; Spencer 1966; Redford and Padoch 1992). Ecological succession is used to produce a sequence of food crops and other useful products (Alcorn 1984; Posey and Balée 1989).
Grasslands	Many traditional herding peoples of the African Sahel have elaborate grazing systems that involve rotation and alternation of areas used by the herds (Niamir 1990). Many herders move their animals to wet season pastures at the edge of the Sahara, mimicking the seasonal migration of wild ungulates (Niamir-Fuller 1990).
Mountains	Terracing as a soil and water conservation method seems to have been independently discovered by mountain cultures of the Mediterranean, South Asia, Philippines, and South America. Communal pasture use (Netting 1981) and migratory herding systems (Galaty and Johnson 1990) are found in many mountainous regions worldwide.
Tropical fisheries	Customary restrictions (taboos) by species, seasons, and area help prevent overfishing in many parts of Oceania (Klee 1980). Such reef and lagoon tenure systems are found throughout the Asia-Pacific region (Ruddle and Johannes 1990; Freeman *et al.* 1991).
Irrigation water	Traditional irrigation systems include the *zanjera* of the Philippines, a derivative of the *huerta* irrigation system used in Spain that dates back to ancient Arabic rule in Iberia (Maass and Anderson 1986), and the subaks of Bali, Indonesia, devised by temple priests (Lansing 1991).

Leach 1996), coastal resources and fisheries (Freeman *et al.* 1991; Haggan *et al.* 2006; Lutz and Neis 2008; Trosper 2009), northern ecosystems (Freeman and Carbyn 1988; Kassam 2009; Crate and Nuttall 2009; Krupnik *et al.* 2010), and water resources and the water environments (Mabry 1996; Reij *et al.* 1996; Shaw and Francis 2008). Others deal with conservation (Morauta *et al.* 1982; McNeely and Pitt 1985; Schaaf and Lee 2006; Painemilla *et al.* 2010; Verschuuren *et al.* 2010), development (Brokensha *et al.* 1980; Warren 1991a; Warren *et al.* 1995; Sillitoe 2006; Heckler 2009; Subramanian and Pisupati 2010), ethnobiology (Alcorn 1984; Berlin 1992; Nazarea 1999; Cunningham 2001; Johnson and Hunn 2010), intellectual property rights (Posey and Dutfield 1996), biocultural diversity (Maffi 2001; Kassam 2009; Maffi and Woodley 2010), and indigenous environmental ethics (Knudtson and Suzuki 1992; Anderson 1996; Grim 2001; Taylor

2005). Guides for indigenous knowledge researchers are also available (Grenier 1998; Geniusz 2009; Kovach 2009; Tobias 2010).

This critical mass of literature may be appreciated more fully when considered alongside other interdisciplinary areas sympathetic to traditional ecological knowledge. This chapter examines three such areas.

The first of these fields is environmental ethics (Callicott 1989; Engel and Engel 1990; Callicott 1994), which developed a discussion around the subject of indigenous cultures, especially those of American Indian peoples, as a possible source of inspiration for a new environmental ethic (Callicott 1982; Hughes 1983). However, exaggerated claims of American Indians as "the original ecologists" invited refutations and caused scholars to become skeptical of source materials and interpretation. A case in point is the speech of Chief Seattle, which was a hoax knowingly perpetrated by some (see Chapter 11 for the story). Scholarly skepticism gave way to the acceptance of a new subfield but only after many comparative studies were carried out.

Many of these studies documented the existence of a generalized reverence for life, a "community-of-beings" worldview, representing the wisdom of many cultures in many parts of the world (White 1967; Worster 1988; Gadgil and Berkes 1991; Callicott 1994, 2008; Snodgrass and Tiedje 2008). Yet nature reverence is certainly not a universal traditional ethic (Diamond 1993; Callicott 1994). Another stream of the literature emphasized religion, or religious ethics, as a prescription for encoding conservation (Dudley *et al.* 2008; Dominguez *et al.* 2010; Bhagwat *et al.* 2011) and wise management in general (Rappaport 1979; Taylor 2005). For example, Anderson (1996: 166) argues that "all traditional societies that have succeeded in managing resources well over time, have done it in part through religious or ritual representation of resource management. The key point is not religion *per se*, but the use of emotionally powerful cultural symbols to sell particular moral codes and management systems."

A second related field is commons and the investigation of the role of traditional communal property institutions in the management of common–pool (common property) resources. A large literature base has developed in this area since the 1980s, documenting that some traditional social organization and common-property systems were capable of avoiding the dilemma of the "tragedy of the commons" and leading to sustainable resource use (McCay and Acheson 1987; Berkes 1989a; Bromley 1992; Ostrom *et al.* 2002). Traditional knowledge was initially of secondary, perhaps even marginal, interest in the commons literature that focused on institutions and property rights relations. There was a need, however, to document commons institutions and resource systems that had persisted over historical time, that is, those that were sustainable. Two schools of thought developed on historically rooted commons institutions.

One school of thought chose its examples from Western societies. For example, the book by Ostrom (1990) relies on examples such as the *huerta* irrigation system in Spain (Maass and Anderson 1986) and the Swiss Alpine commons (Netting 1981), both of which have historical roots that extend well beyond five hundred years. A second school of thought concentrated on traditional knowledge and management systems, not as mere "traditions" frozen in time as anthropological curiosities, but as *adaptive responses* that have evolved over time (Berkes 1989b; Dei 1992; Berkes and Folke 2002; Agrawal 2005). Recognizing traditional knowledge as the source of ecological adaptations, some studies explicitly and deliberately sought for examples of non-Western resource management systems for their insights (Colding and Folke 1997, 2001; Turner 2005; Trosper 2009). The rationale was that indigenous groups may offer practices and adaptations that may expand the range of the rather limited set of Western resource management prescriptions, with its roots in the mechanistic, linear Newtonian science. Thus, the search for alternatives for resource management came to include traditional management systems and their commons institutions (Berkes and Folke 1998; Berkes *et al.* 2000; Trosper 2009; Johnsen 2009).

A third related field is environmental history that started to develop a dynamic view of ecological change, with a fresh look at the root causes of environmental problems (Cronon 1983; Turner *et al.* 1990). Discussion centered on such themes as how, after the great transformation generated by the industrial revolution, ecological relations became more destructive as they became more distant, providing a larger context for the appreciation of traditional knowledge and worldview (Worster 1988). Environmental historians developed interests not only in interpreting ancient landscapes but also in making ecological sense of the ancient peoples and their resource use practices that *resulted* in these landscapes (Gadgil and Guha 1992; Redman 1999). For example, landscape ecology bears traces of past land use in terms of species compositions and soil profiles, long after that land use ceased (Berkes and Davidson-Hunt 2006). The history of land use, in turn, has the imprint of ecological and economic changes. Cronon's (1983) study of the colonization of New England states and European–Indian relationships traced the history of two competing economies. One of them, the Indian economy, took what we would today call an ecosystem approach and treated the environment as a portfolio of resources and services that supported livelihoods. The other economy, that of the colonists, turned the environment into commodities, exploited sequentially one resource after another following market demands, and caused depletion and environmental degradation in the process.

Similar inquiries in environmental history from diverse geographic and cultural areas, as far apart as California (Blackburn and Anderson 1993; Anderson 2005) and India, revealed ecologically sensible traditional practices being displaced by the push for commodity production. For example, throughout much of India, forest resource use followed a sequence of exploitation from the more valuable (such as teak) to the less valuable species, and from the more accessible to the less accessible areas (Gadgil and Guha 1992). Under colonial rule, there was a general change from the production of a wide variety of goods for local needs to the production of a few commodities for export (Gadgil and Thapar 1990).

In summary, the development of interest in traditional ecological knowledge is related to major changes in perspectives among scholars, policy makers, and the public. Dissatisfaction with a science that places an artificial divide between mind and nature (Bateson 1972), as discussed in Chapter 1, and a reaction to the materialist tradition in ecology, economics, and resource management (Norgaard 1994; Norton 2005; Jenkins 2010) are part of the driving forces. Interest in traditional ecological knowledge can be interpreted as a search for alternatives in human–environment relationships and in resource stewardship (Berkes and Folke 1998; Posey 1999; Ramakrishnan *et al.* 2006).

Cultural and Political Significance for Indigenous Peoples

In searching for alternative solutions for global issues, there is always the risk of abstracting traditional knowledge from its cultural and historical context (Nadasdy 1999; Natcher *et al.* 2005; Simpson 2005). Ecological knowledge held by a group is only one aspect of their overall culture. However, in contrast to Western science, there is little or no separation between such knowledge and other spheres of culture. Knowledge of the biophysical environment is embedded in the social environment. Many researchers in the past have tried to document traditional ecological knowledge for the sake of cultural preservation. It has been persuasively argued, though, that traditional ecological knowledge can only be conserved *in situ*: much of indigenous knowledge makes no sense when abstracted from the culture of which it is a part (Agrawal 1995a, 1995b). The questions of the cultural and political significance of traditional ecological knowledge involve a series of linked issues, including worldviews, cultural survival, ownership of knowledge or intellectual property rights, empowerment, local control of land and resources, cultural revitalization, and self-determination.

Traditional ecological knowledge may best be seen as an integrated package that includes the local knowledge and classification systems of the groups in question; their environmental practices and management systems; their social institutions that provide the rules for management systems such as tribal territories; and their worldviews that constitute the ideological or ethical basis of these systems. Among many North American aboriginal groups, hunting is not merely the mechanical use of the local knowledge of animals and the environment to obtain food, it is a religious activity (Preston 1975, 2002; Tanner 1979). Speck (1935: 72) said it well many decades ago: "To the Montagnais-Naskapi . . . the animals of the forest, the tundra, and the waters of the interior and the coast exist in a specific relation. They have become the objects of engrossing magico-religious activity, for to them hunting is a holy occupation."

Even for contemporary hunters in northern Manitoba, long acculturated and converted to Christianity, hunting continues as a spiritual activity in which "you got to keep it holy" (Brightman 1993: 1). The use of traditional ecological knowledge to make a livelihood sustains the distinctive cultural ideology of the group, as well as the very important social relationships within the group. It helps maintain social identity and provides a source of values. Social relations of cooperation, sharing, gift-giving, gender-role maintenance, and all-important reciprocity (with both humans and animals) are part of what Fienup-Riordan (1990) calls "the broader question of the relation of ideology to adaptation." Knowledge, values, and identity are transferred to succeeding generations through the annual, cyclical repetition of livelihood activities based on traditional ecological knowledge and practice (Hunn and Selam 1990; Freeman 1993a; Ellen *et al.* 2000; Rose 2005).

Just as the hunt carries symbolic meaning for hunting groups of North American aboriginal peoples, the shifting cultivation (*milpa*) cycle carries symbolic meaning for the indigenous people of northcentral Mexico (Alcorn 1984). For the aboriginal people of Australia, ancestors have provided songs, dances, narratives, ceremonies, sacred objects, and paintings in order to maintain the bond between land, people, and totemic beings (Wilkins 1993; Mulligan 2003). Constant engagement with land/country leads to knowledge building or learning, whereby knowledge emerges from the long-term relationship between people and place (Davidson-Hunt and Berkes 2003, 2010). Events are ordered by connections, often related to the seasonal timing of life cycle events or phenology (Lantz and Turner 2003; Muir *et al.* 2010). For example, the Gitga'at people of British Colombia, Canada, collect edible seaweed. Women harvesters watch the growth of stinging nettle plants in the camp to tell when the seaweed is ready, without wasting time to go out to the seaweed grounds (Turner and Clifton 2009). In Australia, indigenous people know that when March flies are biting, crocodiles are laying eggs. It is not necessary to keep going to the waterhole to see if the crocodiles are laying eggs; it is enough to be bitten by the March fly (Rose 2004, 2005). Country tells you what is going on; many indigenous cultures have developed ways to read the narrative of the land. "The landscape painting is the country itself," as phrased by traditional elder Wenten Rubuntja (see Box 2.1). The spiritual domain of dreaming can, however, also serve a conservation role, as in the case of red kangaroo taboo sites in Central Australia (Newsome 1980).

Box 2.1 "One Flesh–One Spirit–One Country–One Dreaming": The Australian Aboriginal Conception of the Environment

Wilkins explains that the Dreamtime is the unifying thread binding social relations, land, and totemism among the Australian Aborigines. *Dreamtime* is the Aboriginal concept that refers to the spiritual domain or dimension in which ancestral totemic beings arose from beneath the uninhabited and unshaped land and, through their actions and movements and their very existence, created, and continue the creation of the physical, spiritual, cultural, and social world that now exists and that must be perpetuated through continuing all the practices handed down from the ancestors during this time. Because the land is a living record of Dreamtime events, Aborigines perceive their environment in a very different way from Anglo-Australians. For example, in discussing Aboriginal art, Sutton goes so far as to claim that for Aboriginal Australians "there is no geography without meaning or without history. . . . The land is already a narrative—an artifact of intellect—before people represent it."

One should question, Wilkins points out, whether Australian Aborigines themselves would articulate these matters in the same way as anthropologists have, and, he says, it is very clear that they do. Wenten Rubuntja, a respected elder within the Mparntwe Arrernte community and a well-known artist, makes the following pertinent observations:

> These rocks we've got to worship. The rainmakers, the caterpillars, or the kangaroos, emus, we got to pray for it. In this country, and every other country, we were looking at worship, before the settlers came here. When the settlers came here they started cutting trees. We shouldn't be cutting trees. We shouldn't be getting rocks, making holes in the country. . . . Country was pretty and country was *tywerrenge* (something associated with sacred ceremonies; it can also refer to land itself). We don't forget about *tywerrenge*. We still keep going, singing, and ceremonies all the time, singing all the time and painting all the time, shield and dancing. What belongs to this country, belongs to the Aboriginal culture, we never lost, keep going ahead. . . . The landscape

> painting is the country itself, with *tywerrenge* himself.
> *Tywerrenge* and songs come out of the body of the country.
> See all this one, this little waterhole. We're not like white-
> fella who can take a photograph and say what pretty country
> it is; we've got the song to sing for that country.
>
> *Source*: Wilkins 1993: 73.

It is clear enough from the above considerations that the broader social and cultural aspect of traditional knowledge is a very serious matter for many indigenous peoples. Partially for this reason, dealing with traditional ecological knowledge has become politically volatile: knowledge is an intensely political matter. "Although studies on indigenous peoples, societies and communities continue to be carried out, researchers no longer have *carte blanche* to work independently from the people themselves. Nor can they treat the data that they collect as if it was a value-free product which can be extracted and used at will" (Inuit Circumpolar Conference 1992). These considerations have had a major international impact on the way indigenous knowledge research has been carried out (Mauro and Hardison 2000; see also Chapter 8).

Indigenous peoples are beginning to assert control over their knowledge systems for at least two reasons. First, especially in the area of medicinal plants, some indigenous groups have seen how their knowledge and biological resources have been turned by others into profit-making commodities that can be bought and sold. Thus, they have started to ask the question of who benefits from the recording of the knowledge, investigating how they themselves can control and market their knowledge and products (Posey and Dutfield 1996; Brush and Stabinsky 1996).

Second, indigenous knowledge has become a symbol for many groups, representing the regaining of control over their cultural information. Reclaiming their indigenous knowledge has become a major strategy in many parts of the world for revitalization movements, defined as "a deliberate, organized, conscious effort by members of a society to construct a more satisfying culture" (Wallace 1956: 265). For example, in Canada, the Berger Commission Inquiry, which helped articulate aboriginal views and lent credibility to local knowledge and management traditions of northern indigenous peoples, contributed to the development of a revitalization movement (Zachariah 1984). Some of the major aboriginal cultural groups in Alaska and northern Canada, including the Inuit, Dene, and Cree, have been carrying out their own traditional knowledge studies as part of an effort to strengthen their culture and assert their land rights (Dene Cultural Institute 1993; Gwich'in Elders 2001; Hart and Amos 2004; Oozeva *et al.* 2004).

Box 2.2 provides an example of using traditional knowledge, in this case, of biodiversity for cultural education and revitalization (Nabhan 2000a). There are similar efforts in other parts of the world as well (Ross and Pickering 2002; Edwards and Henrich 2006). Chapter 12 deals with some of the experiences in using traditional knowledge to prepare land and resource claims by aboriginal groups. Such revitalization is not merely a cultural exercise; it is about empowerment and political control.

A case in point comes from Hawaii, where the native revitalization movement has allegedly "re-invented traditional culture" to suit its political needs (Keesing 1989). According to this view, authentic, pre-contact Hawaiian culture is largely irretrievable, having been demolished by colonialism. The new cultural identity being created is "invented" through the use of symbols and values, but the resulting version of Hawaiian culture does not correspond to any specific time period (Linnekin 1983). These views have been challenged by some scholars: "As there are no longer any real Hawaiians, culture specialists are the only possible custodians of their former way of life," retorts Friedman (1992), and he proceeds

---

Box 2.2 Culture and Biodiversity Education in the Sonoran Desert

"Many Native American elders in the Sonoran Desert are aware that their children have diminished exposure to both common and rare species and to the oral traditional knowledge about them . . . As a solution to this problem, I am working with 16 Seri Indian 'para-ecologist' trainees who learn from both their elders and from visiting conservation biologists how to provide better protection not only for cultural resources but for natural resources such as endangered species as well. This course can be a model for other indigenous communities, for it honors both Western scientific and traditional ecological knowledge about biodiversity. . . . Indigenous peoples must be included in the conservation and management of the world's remaining biological riches. Otherwise, biodiversity conservation will be relegated to being a concern of an elite few, and indigenous communities will become further disenfranchised from their rich traditions of interactions with native plants and animals."

Source: Nabhan 2000a: 40–1.

to point out that the values in question are in the "lived experience" of contemporary rural Hawaii.

Questions of Ownership and Intellectual Property Rights

As pointed out by Posey and Dutfield (1997: 75), indigenous knowledge is treated by most legal systems as part of the "public domain"; it can be used by any person or corporation as soon as it leaves the community. When researchers publish the results of their work, they may place sensitive indigenous knowledge in the public domain, unwittingly passing it to corporations who can use it for financial gain without any obligation to return benefits to the community (Posey and Dutfield 1996, 1997).

Until recent years, the study of traditional knowledge was carried out by Western scientists and social scientists, mostly ethnobiologists and human ecologists (see Chapter 3). It is only relatively recently that indigenous peoples have begun to assert their control over their traditional knowledge. It is related to the significance of the information, as well as to a growing sense among these groups that research by outsiders has not served them well over the years (Smith 1999; Battiste and Henderson 2000). The argument is similar to the one articulated by Edward Said (1994) who pointed out that Western values have continued to permeate historical and ethnographic works on non-Western peoples, raising fundamental questions about how we can actually engage with and comprehend other societies and traditions. One way is to listen to indigenous peoples themselves as they intervene and challenge the academic discourse about themselves; but there are at least three other ways.

The use of traditional knowledge projects, community-initiated and carried out by aboriginal groups themselves, is perhaps the most common way in which indigenous voices are being heard. The book by Johnson (1992) is an attempt to capture the experience of a number of community-based and community-sponsored traditional knowledge studies. Early examples of such studies include the Darién indigenous lands project in Panama (González et al. 1995); the James Bay Cree trappers' traditional knowledge project in Quebec (Bearskin et al. 1989); the Mushkegowuk Cree land and resource use project in Ontario (Berkes et al. 1994, 1995b); the Marovo Project in the Solomon Islands (Baines and Hviding 1993; Hviding 2003), and the Forests for the Future project in Gitxaala, British Colombia, Canada (Menzies 2004). These projects are examples of the contribution of indigenous knowledge to political empowerment, and one such study, the Inuit Observations of Climate Change project, is the major topic of Chapter 8.

A second way that indigenous voices are heard involves the development of indigenous scholarship to provide a direct voice, for example Arnakak (2002),

Atleo (2004), Barreiro (1992), Brascoupe (1992), Brown and Brown (2009), Collier and Vegh (1998), Cordova (1997), Geniusz (2009), Holmes (1996), Kimmerer (2000), Lewis (2004), D. McGregor *et al.* 2010, Magga (2006), Menzies (2006), Oozeva *et al.* (2004), Ravuvu (1987), Roberts *et al.* (1995), Taiepa *et al.* (1997), Wavey (1993), Witt and Hookimaw-Witt (2003) and others. Community-based cultural documentation projects, such as those from Alaska and northern Canada, provide particularly strong examples of social action combined with indigenous scholarship (Cruikshank 1995).

A third way involves the recording of indigenous knowledge, with the holders of such knowledge as co-authors, together with the Western observations or interpretations. Such works include Anderson and Tzuc (2005), Beaucage *et al.* (1997), Davidson-Hunt *et al.* (2005), Gearheard *et al.* (2006), Hunn and Selam (1990), Kendrick *et al.* (2005), Kofinas *et al.* (2002), Krupnik *et al.* (2002, 2010), McDonald *et al.* (1997), Majnep and Bulmer (1977), Manseau (1998), M'Lot and Manseau (2003), Moller *et al.* (2009), Nichols *et al.* (2004), Parlee *et al.* (2005a, 2005b, 2006), Sable *et al.* (2006), Turner and Clifton (2009), and Turner *et al.* (2000).

Holmes (1996) provides a powerful voice regarding the significance of indigenous peoples researching their own knowledge and communicating it in a culturally appropriate format. She deals with traditional knowledge as "lived knowledge" based on an "ancestry of experience" of the elders *and the researcher*, and she uses stories as an elder does in her teachings, creating relationships and establishing personal meaning. The concept of ancestry of experience is a significant notion especially for a native Hawaiian because of the importance of genealogy in defining who and what a person is.

Holmes's approach to indigenous knowledge is fundamentally different from the research methodologies of most academics. As outsiders, they tend not to deal with indigenous knowledge as lived knowledge, they lack an ancestry of experience, and they often do not establish meaning by creating relationships. Instead, the researcher often "unpacks" the received knowledge, processing and "reformatting" it in accordance with her or his own cosmology, says Holmes, appropriating knowledge, if not appropriating voice. But such research leaves Western scholars unable "to understand indigenous values or cosmologies, except as 'myth' or 'data'" (Holmes 1996: 380). Indigenous knowledge further suffers because of the way it is communicated by the researcher and because the reader/receiver is often ill-equipped to understand it. Holmes (1996: 383) reflects: "when people hear or read voices of Native Peoples, they can't always attach those voices to particular *practices*. These voices most often arrive through text, not experience, and therefore without everyday referents." If indigenous knowledge is lived knowledge, the reader, lacking the ancestry of experience, will for example "read" Black Elk (Neihardt 1932; Brown 1953) but not hear him.

Holmes's challenge to the study of indigenous knowledge touches on fundamental paradoxes. If only indigenous peoples are truly competent to research indigenous knowledge, then most research would cease. This will solve the problem of knowledge and voice appropriation, but it would also eliminate the bridges being built between Western and non-Western knowledge and among aboriginal groups themselves. Similarly, for most readers written texts necessarily lack everyday referents, that is, lived experience that validates the lived knowledge. But if this means they are devoid of meaning, then all writings on indigenous knowledge are essentially irrelevant or futile.

Perhaps more constructively, one can define three guiding principles as inspired by Holmes's critique. First, the study of indigenous knowledge always needs to be participatory; it cannot be done without the collaboration of indigenous peoples as equals (Holmes 1996; Davidson-Hunt and O'Flaherty 2007). Second, it helps to remember that written accounts of indigenous knowledge will always be incomplete, unless the reader has lived that knowledge and can supply her or his own referents. *The written page will never be an adequate format for the teaching of indigenous knowledge.* It can only be taught properly on the land. Third, not only the researcher but also the reader of indigenous knowledge has to be prepared to question her or his own values, to be reflexive, and to be prepared to "unpack" one's own values before unpacking those of the indigenous culture in question. As such, cross-cultural sensitivity is at the heart of all research and understanding of traditional knowledge.

Practical Significance as Common Heritage of Humankind

The need for indigenous groups to control their knowledge has to be balanced against the need to share their insights as part of the common heritage of humankind. There are tangible and practical reasons why traditional ecological knowledge is so important for the rest of the world as well, apart from the ethical imperative of conserving cultural diversity. Many of the following points, of course, directly concern people at the local as well as the global levels.

The following list is adapted from various sources (IUCN 1986; Healy 1993; Berkes 1993). The seven areas identified here are not meant to be exclusive categories; they meld into each other. They deal with aspects of ecology and resource use only and exclude other areas of indigenous knowledge, such as pharmacological or medical applications. Traditional ecological knowledge is critical for biological information and ecological insights; resource management; conservation of protected areas; biodiversity conservation; environmental monitoring and assessment; development; dealing with disasters and modern crises; and environmental ethics. We look at each of these areas in detail below.

Traditional Knowledge for Biological Information and Ecological Insights

New scientific knowledge can be derived from perceptive investigations of traditional knowledge, for example, with respect to species identifications and crop varieties, natural history, behavior, life cycles, and species interrelationships (Nabhan 2000b; Laird 2002; Nazarea 2006). Traditional knowledge provides insights on ecosystem dynamics (Alcorn 1989), leading to important applications, for example in ecological restoration (Anderson and Barbour 2003). Classic examples of biological and ecological insights from traditional knowledge include the "three sisters" agriculture, as it is called by the Iroquois, a sustainable agricultural system of corn, beans, and squash widely practiced from the United States to Chile (Barreiro 1992), and traditional marine lagoon fish polyculture systems (Johannes *et al.* 1983).

Robert Johannes, an expert on tropical reef fish ecology, provides a telling example of the level of detail available from indigenous knowledge. When Johannes was working with fishers in the tiny archipelago of Palau in the Pacific in the mid-1970s, he obtained from local fishers the months and periods as well as the precise locations of spawning aggregations of some 55 species of fish that followed the moon as a cue for spawning. This local knowledge amounted to more than twice as many species of fish exhibiting lunar spawning periodicity as had been described by scientists in the *entire world* at that time (Johannes 1981). Tropical fisheries of the world provide ample opportunities to learn from traditional knowledge, simply because there are too many species and not enough biological science. Brazilian researchers, for example, have been making systematic use of local fisher knowledge to fill data gaps (Silvano and Begossi 2010; Begossi *et al.* 2011).

Other examples of traditional ecological insights come from the Canadian North, where local knowledge often far exceeds that of Western scientists who have a seasonally limited research period. It is common among northern field researchers to draw upon the knowledge of their local assistants. Systematic recording and acknowledging of such knowledge goes back to the work of Freeman (1970), who supplemented his own observations and scientific information with local knowledge from the Inuit of Belcher Islands to summarize the biology of 56 species of Hudson Bay birds. In addition to biological information on life cycles and distributions, scientists have also noted Inuit ecological knowledge of predation, competition, and mutualistic interactions among Arctic species. Examples include the Inuit knowledge of the interactions of narwhal (*Monodon monoceros*) and killer whales (*Orcinus orca*), and of eider ducks and great black-backed gulls (Freeman 1993b). Until the 1940s, the world of science did not even know that there was a major population of eider ducks (*Somateria mollissima sedentaria*) that lived year-round in Hudson Bay. Nakashima (1993) pointed out that as late as the 1960s, the standard book on the birds of Labrador stated that "the only authority for the wintering of this eider on the open waters of Hudson Bay" were the Inuit, a situation grudgingly described by the book as "acceptable for the present." The very considerable Inuit knowledge on the eider was finally recorded by Nakashima in what is probably the only Ph.D. thesis in traditional knowledge that concentrates on a single species (Nakashima 1991).

Traditional Knowledge for Resource Management

The current interest in indigenous peoples as resource managers goes back to the early 1980s (Klee 1980; Williams and Hunn 1982), even though strictly speaking "management" is not an indigenous concept. The idea of an environment that is actually controllable by humans is a uniquely modernist concept. Indigenous people talk about "caring for the country" (Weir 2009), "taking care of the land," or "keeping the land" (O'Flaherty *et al.* 2008; Miller and Davidson-Hunt 2010). But "management" that treats animals, and nature in general, as passive is alien to most if not all indigenous cultures (Schmidt and Dowsley 2010).

Much of the controversy about the resource management capability of traditional peoples stems from the fact that these societies have been impacted by social and economic changes that have resulted in loss of knowledge and altered practices. For example, the incorporation of practices favoring individual decision-making (as opposed to traditional cooperative hunting) among Kotzebue Sound Inupiat in Alaska has coincided with sharp declines in the numbers of beluga whales (Morseth 1997). As Polunin (1984) puts it, traditional management systems are often overtaken by events. Johannes (1978) wrote about the "demise" of traditional management in Oceania, but reversed his position 22 years later when he saw that many of the practices were re-emerging (Johannes 2002a).

Indeed, many resource use practices consistent with sustainability do remain and can be used for resource management (Manseau *et al.* 2005a). For example, Duffield *et al.* (1998) demonstrated the feasibility of using local knowledge to construct indicators to monitor the sustainability of mountain environments. Another practical application of local knowledge comes from Newfoundland. According to Hutchings (1998: 1) "the collapse of Newfoundland's northern cod fishery may have been predicted by changes in fishing practices and fishing effort by Newfoundland inshore and offshore fishers." Neis *et al.* (1996) concluded that information from fishers, combined with scientific data can:

1   contribute to knowledge of cod behavior, ecology, and stock structure;
2   help understand trends in catchability;

3   inform future research;

4   increase awareness of stock abundance inshore; and

5   increase awareness of interactions among different fisheries (e.g. juvenile cod by-catch in the capelin fishery).

The complementarity of local knowledge and scientific knowledge is an increasingly important theme in resource management (Berkes 2009a). For example, there is an emerging consensus in Oceania that, given the scarcity of scientific knowledge and research resources, alternative coastal fishery models are needed. These models involve the use of local knowledge to substitute for, or complement, scientific knowledge (Hunt 1997; Johannes 1998). The use of traditional ecological knowledge in an experimental way to learn from management interventions, with subsequent policy changes, makes it a potential tool for Adaptive Management (Berkes *et al.* 2000). The similarities between Adaptive Management (a branch of applied ecology) and traditional management are explored in Chapters 4, 6, 7, and 11. Both indigenous knowledge and Adaptive Management focus on feedbacks and the maintenance of ecological resilience (Alcorn 1989; Holling *et al.* 1995; Trosper 2009). These observations compelled us to ask: How can resource management be improved by supplementing scientific data with local and traditional knowledge? How can information from resource users themselves broaden the base of knowledge necessary for decision-making for sustainable resource use (Berkes and Folke 1998)? The present volume is in part a follow-up to these questions.

Traditional Knowledge for Conservation of Protected Areas

Conservation programs often need to encompass a broader view of the role of local people of the area, their knowledge and interests, and their social and economic needs. The World Conservation Union (IUCN) has been looking into conservation with people at least since the early 1980s (McNeely and Pitt 1985), and protected area management has increasingly become a social science (McNeely 1996). Protected areas may be set up to allow resident communities to continue their traditional lifestyles, with the benefits of conservation accruing to them as well as to the rest of the world. Partnerships between conservation and local peoples are feasible, especially where the local religion and values are consistent with conservation (Bhagwat *et al.* 2011).

The traditional basis of conservation is substantial (Borgerhoff Mulder and Coppolillo 2005). However, indigenous conservation, where it exists, is not based on the same ethic as Western conservation and uses social (rather than legal) enforcement, such as taboo systems. For example, Colding and Folke (1997) and Colding (1998) analyzed available data on species-specific taboos, and found that about one-third of the identified taboos prohibited the use of a species listed as threatened. Area-specific taboos or sacred areas are found in many regions of the world (Ramakrishnan *et al.* 1998), even at sea (McClanahan *et al.* 1997). Some of these traditional sacred areas, for example the indigenous-controlled Alto Fragua-Indiwasi National Park in Colombia, are being re-established formally as community-conserved areas, following a recommendation to the 2003 World Parks Congress (Borrini-Feyerabend *et al.* 2004b: 93, 116). Many new national parks around the world are established at the site of former traditional sacred areas, for example, the Kaz Mountain National Park in Turkey. Kaz Mountain (Mount Ida), near the site of ancient Troy, supports a healthy forest which includes 32 endemic plant species (found nowhere else in the world). The area has been home to Turkoman and Yoruk people since the 1400s whose culture includes pre-Islamic elements from their Central Asian ancestral homeland. Plant-gatherers and wood-workers, their sacred sites dot the landscape in the National Park area. But the Park technically excludes the uses that helped maintain the values that made the Park what it is in the first place (Ari *et al.* 2005).

Especially where the local community jointly manages such protected areas, the use of traditional knowledge for conservation is likely to be very effective

Photo 2.1 A sacred tree (the "Bride's Pine") at the Kaz Mountain (Mount Ida) National Park in Turkey. The local culture includes pre-Islamic elements such as sacred sites.

Photo: Yilmaz Ari.

(Berkes *et al.* 1995; Gadgil *et al.* 2000; Borrini-Feyerabend *et al.* 2004b). However, a survey of the conservation literature showed that only about 0.4 percent of detailed conservation evaluations have used local and indigenous knowledge over a 25-year period (Brook and McLachlan 2008). Hence there has been a growing interest in co-management, a partnership between government agencies, local communities, and others, in the sharing of authority and responsibility of management, also called collaborative management or joint management (Borrini-Feyerabend 1996; Ross *et al.* 2009). However, the dark side of co-management is the potential for the co-optation of indigenous knowledge and coercing people to work within Western-style governance that is foreign to their thinking (Stevenson 2006; White 2006; Ross *et al.* 2010).

Creating stakes in conservation facilitates the use of traditional ecological knowledge for conservation, provided of course that authorities are willing to use local insights in the true spirit of collaboration. For example, in the Keoladeo National Park in India, the local population argued for years that the grazing of water buffalo in the park was consistent with conservation objectives and should be allowed. After many years of strife between park authorities and local people, a long-term study by the Bombay Natural History Society finally corroborated the local view, showing that the grazing of water buffalo helped counter the tendency of the wetland to turn into grassland. The ban on grazing had adversely affected the wetland and the park, which was famous for its bird life, and the solution was to return to water buffalo grazing once again (Kothari 1996; Pimbert and Gujja 1997).

There is a growing number of such applications (Hunn *et al.* 2003; Eamer 2006; Xu *et al.* 2005; Lejano and Ingram 2007), but in various regions such as Latin America, the presence of indigenous peoples in protected areas is a matter of considerable controversy. There are debates on the questions of whether indigenous peoples' agendas are consistent with scientific biodiversity conservation objectives, and whether any level of human use compromises biodiversity (see Chapter 11).

The international protected area system increasingly recognizes sustainable use areas and the role of local people in conserving lands and waters. Of particular interest are areas traditionally conserved by the local people for various reasons, the sacred natural sites (Verschuuren *et al.* 2010), including sacred groves. Sacred forests and sacred groves are found on all continents, and have a huge conservation potential (Ramakrishnan *et al.* 1998). There are over 100,000 sites in India alone (Ormsby and Bhagwat 2010). These are mostly small sites but nevertheless hold a large reservoir of biodiversity useful for rural livelihoods (Gadgil *et al.* 2000). African sacred groves are also receiving a great deal of conservation attention (Juhé-Beaulaton 2008; Nyamweru and Kimaru 2008; Sheridan and

Nyamweru 2008; Sheridan 2009). The incorporation of these indigenous and community-conserved areas (ICCAs) into the national and global networks of protected areas is the subject of much debate (Borrini-Feyerabend *et al.* 2004a; Kothari 2006; Berkes 2009b; Robson and Berkes 2010).

Traditional Knowledge and Stewardship of Biodiversity

Much of biodiversity conservation is motivated to preserve protected areas, but there is a growing recognition of human involvement in social–ecological systems and the importance of conservation outside protected areas (Bhagwat *et al.* 2008; Bird *et al.* 2008; Berkes *et al.* 2009; Pilgrim and Pretty 2010). Some traditional knowledge and resource management systems are of special interest because they seem to allow less intensive use and greater biological diversity. Many of the areas of the world that contain high levels of biodiversity are also the areas in which indigenous peoples are found (Posey and Dutfield 1997; Maffi 2005). This relationship is probably not accidental, but the mechanism of the relationship is not clear. For some scholars, there is a close and perhaps causal relationship between biodiversity and cultural diversity, as measured by language diversity (Maffi 2001; Maffi and Woodley 2010).

For others, the explanation may lie in the use of indigenous practices such as succession management, rotational use, and the creation of patchiness by the use of fire and other kinds of disturbance (Berkes *et al.* 2000; Berkes and Davidson-Hunt 2006; Miller and Davidson-Hunt 2010; S. McGregor *et al.* 2010). The two views are not contradictory. In the first, the emphasis is on language (as a proxy of culturally diverse practices), whereas in the second, the emphasis is on the elaboration of the diversity of traditional ecological knowledge and practice (Anderson 2005; Turner and Berkes 2006; Pretty *et al.* 2009; Verschuuren *et al.* 2010).

Many indigenous practices tend to conserve biodiversity, as traditional groups rely on a portfolio of resources for their livelihoods. A study carried out in Oaxaca, arguably the most biologically and culturally diverse state of Mexico, is informative in this regard. In Oaxaca's northern highlands, low intensity forest use and rotational (*milpa*) agriculture have led to pronounced spatial heterogeneity in forest structure and composition, and created a high-biodiversity forest–agriculture mosaic. However, in recent decades, fewer people are farming, less land is cultivated, and fewer crop varieties are grown. With agricultural abandonment, the forest cover has increased, but contrary to the usual assumptions, local biodiversity has *declined* because of the decline of forest–agriculture mosaic. It appears that the land-use practices of these Zapotec and Chinantec indigenous communities enhance biodiversity, and that people are agents of landscape renewal processes that allow for both cultural and biological diversity to flourish (Robson and Berkes 2011).

Photo 2.2 Forest–agriculture mosaic in the cultural landscape of Santiago Comaltepec village, northern highlands of Oaxaca, Mexico. Note the denser tree cover near hilltops.

Photo: James Robson.

A mixed livelihoods strategy, rather than one concentrating on a few species for cash income and exports, is consistent with biodiversity conservation, as also noted in studies of early colonization of the United States (Cronon 1983), and in the colonization and "modernization" of areas previously controlled by indigenous groups (Oldfield and Alcorn 1991). But many traditional and rural peoples of the world cannot be considered conservationists if conservation requires proof of intent (Smith and Wishnie 2000). However, many indigenous groups, including those that have suffered loss of control of resources, do still retain elements of resource use practices that are consistent with the protection of biodiversity (Berkes *et al.* 1995). For example, Poffenberger *et al.* (1996) mapped tribal areas in India and areas of remaining forest cover. With the exception of semi-arid lands (where there is no forest anyway), the authors found a close correlation between the two.

The book *Global Biodiversity Assessment* includes examples of traditional practices that conserve biodiversity, and recognizes that "where indigenous peoples have depended on local environments for the provision of resources over long periods of time, they have often developed a stake in conserving biodiversity" (Heywood 1995: 1017). It provides examples from a variety of ecosystem types of multi-species, multiple-use resource systems that protect and enhance local biodiversity at the level of varieties, species, and landscapes. As sketched in Figure 2.1, patchy use of the landscape creates a mosaic whereby different patches are at different stages of succession. This creates landscape level diversity, supporting a larger number of species than would otherwise exist (Berkes and Folke 2002; for more on this, see Chapter 4).

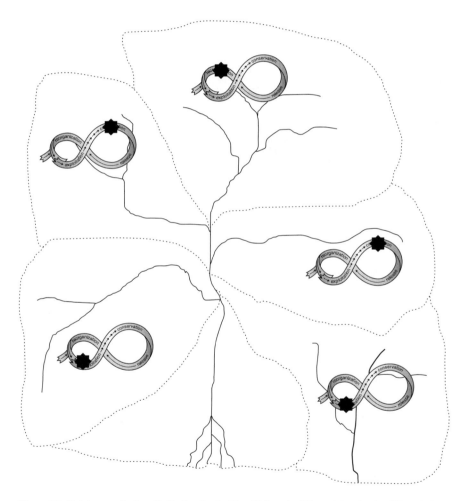

Figure 2.1 Patchy use of a hypothetical watershed in which each of the patches is at a different stage of successional development, with different complements of species. "Figure eights" denoting adaptive renewal cycles from Gunderson and Holling (2002).

Source: Adapted from Berkes and Folke (2002).

Traditional Knowledge for Environmental Monitoring and Assessment

People who are dependent on local resources for their livelihood are often able to assess the health of the environment and the integrity of the ecosystems better than any evaluator from the outside. As Chief Robert Wavey (1993) of northern Manitoba puts it, "people retain a record of what the land and resources have provided for generations, and the Aboriginal people are the first to see the changes." Their time-tested, in-depth local knowledge can be useful in monitoring local ecosystems. Such knowledge and locally constructed mental models of a healthy land or ecosystem (see Chapter 9) can provide key information for the monitoring of environmental change (Kofinas *et al.* 2002; Eamer 2006).

Environmental monitoring by the use of indigenous knowledge (Castello *et al.* 2009) and by use of local knowledge and observations (Anadón *et al.* 2009; Sullivan *et al.* 2009; Goffredo *et al.* 2010) has been successfully used in many cases. Local and indigenous knowledge may be used in environmental assessments (Ericksen and Woodley 2005), and in evaluating the environmental impacts of proposed developments. For example, Heaslip (2008) shows how indigenous knowledge can be used to monitor salmon aquaculture waste. As well, knowledge of the local social system is essential to any social impact assessment (Sadler and Boothroyd 1994). Given that many development projects push through before there is time for the proper completion of scientific studies, the use of local knowledge becomes even more important (Berkes and Henley 1997).

However, some of this information, such as the details of land use, are considered proprietary knowledge. The last thing an aboriginal group wants to do is advertise to the rest of the world its prime hunting and fishing locations! Reflecting on the Manitoba experience, Wavey (1993) argues that indigenous control of traditional land-use information is fundamental to maintaining the proprietary nature of such information and the way in which it is put to use in environmental assessment. In any case, there is no reason to think that an indigenous group will want to participate in the assessment of a project they consider to be damaging, if they have reason to believe that their participation will not result in any fundamental changes to the project. For example, the Cree refused to participate in the assessment of the James Bay II (Great Whale) hydroelectric development project in the early 1990s as a way of registering their opposition and withholding consent.

Even if they are willing to participate, the limited experience in this area shows that indigenous people may well have very different ideas about what constitutes a proper environmental assessment (Sadler and Boothroyd 1994; Stevenson 1996). A major study carried out by the indigenous peoples of the

Hudson Bay bioregion, and involving 27 Inuit and Cree communities around the Bay, focused on the cumulative impacts of a number of development projects (McDonald *et al.* 1997), impacts that government departments were having difficulty dealing with because of jurisdictional barriers and political sensitivities. The role of local-level knowledge was explored in some detail in the Millennium Ecosystem Assessment as well. Local-level inputs and traditional ecological knowledge were found to be essential in understanding and integrating regional and global change (Gadgil *et al.* 2000; Capistrano *et al.* 2005; Reid *et al.* 2006).

Traditional Knowledge for Development

The use of traditional knowledge may benefit development by providing more realistic evaluations of local needs, environmental constraints, and natural resource production systems. Involvement of the local people in the planning process improves the chance of success of development (Warren 1991b; Warren *et al.* 1995; Sillitoe 2006). The use of traditional knowledge in development has a relatively short history (Brokensha *et al.* 1980; Chambers 1983). Initially, "tradition" was seen by economists and development planners as an impediment, an unwillingness to break with the past to embrace scientifically developed agricultural and other improvements. However, as some of the unforeseen consequences of agricultural modernization (such as loss of crop biodiversity) became clear, interest in traditional knowledge was renewed. For example, Richards (1985) regarded indigenous knowledge as a neglected and marginalized resource that had a legitimate place in development programs. Putting indigenous knowledge to work, Richards argued, could result in a "peoples' science," a decentralized, participatory research and development system that would support rather than displace local initiative. Such populist science could then generate an indigenous agricultural revolution (Richards 1985).

A significant finding was that many rural groups were reluctant to abandon traditional practices because these practices were, in retrospect, more sustainable ecologically, economically, and socially. A case in point is the adoption of monocultures of high-yield crop varieties. They produce well in good years but may completely fail in bad. This is a risk that small farmers are reluctant to take. Such findings have been interpreted in terms of risk-aversion. Many traditional practices are adaptive precisely because they reduce the risk of failing to secure a livelihood. Poor people tend to be risk-averse, especially when the margin of safety is small (Chambers 1983). Yet, in areas such as the southern highlands of Bolivia, many local varieties of potato have been displaced by high-yielding but risky varieties in the name of "development" (Walsh 2010). People-oriented development, to Walsh (2010), turns the deficit argument ("the poor are lacking . . .") on its head, and endorses and supports sophisticated but threatened livelihood strategies of the poor.

There is increasing interest in indigenous knowledge and stewardship of medicinal plants (Begossi *et al.* 2002; Cetinkaya 2006; Pesek *et al.* 2010; Shukla and Sinclair 2009; Kassam *et al.* 2010; Byg *et al.* 2010), non-timber forest products (Begossi *et al.* 2000; Ruiz-Pérez *et al.* 2004; Belcher *et al.* 2005), and agro-biodiversity (Adoukonou-Sagbadja *et al.* 2006; Peroni *et al.* 2008; Brown and Kothari 2011). Cultural memory and its role in maintaining practices that conserve these species and varieties (Nazarea 1998), and gender roles in maintaining crop biodiversity (Nazarea 2006; Camou-Guerrero *et al.* 2008) are equally important. Traditional knowledge has come to be used as a major tool among practitioners who hold that development must be woven around people and not the other way around. It has been of more interest to those involved in social development and community development (Warren *et al.* 1995; Ishigawa 2006) and well-being (Subramanian and Prisupati 2010), rather than purely economic development.

The use of traditional knowledge has great potential also in designing strategies for culturally sustainable development (Preston *et al.* 1995). The work of Butz (1996) identifying symbolic values of herding yaks at Pamir pastures provides an example of sustainability planning that takes into account local world views. Yak herding not only carries instrumental values, such as milk and meat production, but also symbolic (or non-instrumental) values, such as those pertaining to self-identity, spiritual renewal, a role in local myth and history, ritual significance, and a sense of place.

Traditional Knowledge to Deal with Disasters and Modern Crises

In the 2004 tsunami in Asia, some communities were reportedly saved through their ability to identify early warning signs. Such abilities are not universal among traditional coastal societies; if they exist, they exist only among a few specialized island-living and fishing groups. For example, following the 2004 tsunami, we investigated the tsunami prediction capabilities of a number of coastal communities in India and Bangladesh and came up empty. We could not find any communities that could distinguish between a tsunami and a storm surge (when a storm, cyclone or hurricane piles up water onshore). Apparently, large tsunamis do not occur frequently enough to leave a strong social memory.

The case of hurricanes is different. There does seem to be a strong social memory of large hurricanes in at least some of the islands in the Pacific. When the anthropologist Raymond Firth returned to Tikopia (now part of the Solomon Islands) in the 1930s, he found an island devastated by a hurricane, which had destroyed houses and gardens and caused an acute food shortage. Hurricanes of such magnitude, he was told, occurred on the average once every 20 years or so.

Firth viewed the disaster as a test of Tikopia's social system to withstand disturbance. He found that the people had a portfolio of responses to the disaster. The
chiefs directed repairs, took measures to reduce theft, directed labor to planting
rather than to fishing, and sent workers abroad for wage work. Household-level
responses included changing diet, reducing hospitality, restricting kinship obligations, reducing ceremonies, and using unripe crops. Resource management strategies included shorter fallows, restriction of collecting rights, and stronger
enforcement of land boundaries (Berkes and Folke 2002).

The social memory of large hurricanes (once in a generation) can be contrasted
with that of large tsunamis (once in about a century). Most disturbance events
seem to be within the range of social memory. For example, when scientific information proved unavailable, Robertson and McGee (2003) used local knowledge
and social memory to assess the frequency of flood events in a wetland project in
Australia. Also in Australia, Schlacher et al. (2010) used local knowledge of
noxious algal blooms to devise a management plan for tourist beaches. Some
indigenous and traditional groups have not only local knowledge of past events but
also remarkable predictive abilities for natural disasters and weather phenomena.
One of the most remarkable cases is Andean ethnoclimatology documented by
Orlove and colleagues (2000, 2002).

For many centuries, indigenous potato farmers of the Peruvian and Bolivian
Andes have gathered in midwinter to observe the Pleiades. If this star cluster
appears big and bright, this is understood to predict abundant rains and large
harvests the following summer. If the cluster appears small and dim, people anticipate poor rains. These predictions are considered strong enough to dictate the
choice of crops. A superstition? Orlove et al. (2000, 2002) argue that Andean
ethnoclimatology actually works. "The apparent size and brightness of the Pleiades
varies with the amount of thin, high cloud at the top of the troposphere, which in
turn reflects the severity of El Niño conditions over the Pacific. Because rainfall in
this region is generally sparse in El Niño years, this simple method provides a
valuable forecast, one that is as good or better than any long-term prediction based
on computer modeling of the ocean and atmosphere" (Orlove et al. 2002: 428).

The ability to predict a good or a bad rainfall year has obvious survival value,
and several South American scholars have documented this indigenous forecasting ability from different places in the Andes, generally supporting the practice (Sébastien Boillat, personal communication) Better understanding of local
and indigenous knowledge, and the value of such knowledge, can help empower
communities to make their own decisions. This is the assumption behind the use
of local knowledge in disaster preparedness in mountain regions (Dekens 2007).
A book edited by Ellen (2007) gives many examples of local and indigenous
knowledge that may be relevant to food security and sustainability in the face of

crises and natural disasters, such as earthquakes, tsunamis, extreme weather events and pest outbreaks. Some of these "natural" disasters (e.g. extreme weather events) seem to be increasing in frequency and creating food security problems. The decline of local knowledge of famine and fallback foods is of concern in this regard (Turner and Turner 2008; Muller and Almedom 2008). However, prospects of co-production of knowledge by combining indigenous knowledge with appropriate science and technology have much promise (Ellen 2007). One additional aspect of the significance of indigenous knowledge and values is pursued in the next section.

Traditional Knowledge for Environmental Ethics

The concept of an external "environment" analytically separate from human society can be traced to post-Enlightenment thought in the West (Glacken 1967). It is the basis of the Cartesian dualism of mind versus matter, and hence humans versus environment (Bateson 1972: 337). "Man's dominion over nature," the official ideology of conventional Western science that aims to control the environment, has its philosophical background in Cartesian dualism. By contrast, traditional belief systems of many indigenous groups incorporate the idea that humans are part of the natural environment. As environmental ethicists discuss the re-establishment of this notion in modern society, it is worth recalling that the idea was once widespread throughout the world (Taylor 2005).

The wisdom of traditional knowledge is consistent with ecology and environmental ethics on the question of the control of nature. The relationship may be characterized in terms of a peaceful coexistence of humans-in-nature, or "flowing with nature," as in Taoist philosophy. Perhaps more to the point, some traditional ecology sees humans and nature in a symbiotic relationship, with mutual obligations (see Chapter 5). These mutual obligations may lead to "respect," which is a central idea in the relations of many Native American and other indigenous groups with nature (Callicott 1994; Trosper 1995).

The field of environmental ethics has received much inspiration from indigenous societies, but details are subject to much debate (e.g. Cordova 1997). At the level of the individual, Suzuki and McConnell (1997) argue for the need to rediscover and live the spiritual connection to nature. As well, there have been various attempts to incorporate ethical values from traditional systems into contemporary society. Indigenous ethics are relevant in a number of walks in life, including education (Cajete 2000) and development. For example, the Menominee of Wisconsin have a commercial forestry operation. They have been searching for economic policies consistent with native American values to guide their operations (Menominee Tribal Enterprises 2011; see Box 2.3). Chapter 11 further pursues the theme of using traditional knowledge and values for livelihoods.

Box 2.3 Designing Economic Policy Consistent with American Indian Values: The Menominee

"The Menominee employ principles of forest management that illustrate respect. They have given their forest manager the following management guidelines:

1   Produce trees with both quality and quantity.
2   Don't put all the eggs in one basket.
3   Remember that we are borrowing the forest from our grandchildren.

"The first two principles illustrate community and connectedness. Production of quality and quantity requires growing trees to large size for quality, which compromises quantity production. The large stock of older trees indicates that they are not high-graded, which cuts out all of the high-quality trees at once. All species are supported under the principle of keeping the eggs (forest productivity) in different baskets (species). The idea that the forest is borrowed from future generations, expresses the seventh-generation principle."

Source: Trosper 1995: 84.

CHAPTER 3

Intellectual Roots of Traditional Ecological Knowledge

Traditional ecological knowledge arose from two separate approaches: ethnoscience and human ecology. The first deals largely with folk taxonomies, ethnobotanical and ethnozoological classifications, of plants and animals. The second deals with indigenous understandings of natural processes, including the relationships of humans with animals, plants, and various environmental and sometimes supernatural factors. The two approaches have been joined by others emphasizing applications of traditional ecological knowledge to contemporary problems such as conservation, resource management, and sustainable development. The various approaches have intellectually distinct roots but are increasingly used together as traditional ecological knowledge matures as a discipline.

Thomas Huxley (as quoted in Gould 1980), once defined science as organized common sense. When I started my human ecology and fisheries studies in James Bay in the 1970s, I discovered that Cree fishers and I had a great deal in common in terms of interests and knowledge. I was amazed at the detail of their knowledge of seasonal cycles, distributions, and movements of fish; they were only mildly interested in my scientific bag of tricks, such as reading ages from fish scales. What was science to me regarding the ecology of James Bay fish was common sense to them. The fishers were pleasantly surprised that I could tell apart their species. They had noticed only the year before that the summer student field assistant working for the federal government had been mixing up two of their species. The problem was that the budding scientist did not have his biology right.

...erwise, there was no difference in the species identifications of the scientist and of the Cree fisher. One of the first things I did was to team up with a linguist to make sure I got the correct names and their acceptable variations in a standard orthography used by linguists (Berkes and MacKenzie 1978).

The study of traditional ecological knowledge, like the study of the Western science of ecology itself, begins with the identification and naming of species: ethnobiology. It proceeds to the study of ecological processes, or functional relationships, and people's perceptions of their own roles within environmental systems. This second area may be called ethnoecology, defined by Toledo (1992) to include four main streams: ethnobiology, agroecology, ethnoscience/anthropology, and environmental geography. More broadly, it may be called human ecology. It is practiced by a diverse group of scholars, dominated in numbers by anthropologists who are well-versed in ecology. Many of them consider themselves to be in the field of ecological anthropology or cultural ecology, which is considered a subfield of cultural anthropology (Netting 1986). Human ecology, however, is not a subfield of anthropology. It is also practiced by interdisciplinary scholars in other social sciences and by those ecologists willing to take a chance with the study of the ecology of the human species. Although Netting considers cultural ecology to be interdisciplinary, I prefer to use *human ecology* as a more inclusive term to account for the contributions of non-anthropologists as well as anthropologists.

Traditional ecological knowledge, as a field, is more than multidisciplinary; it is interdisciplinary (Jantsch 1972). Ethnobiology and human ecology fields are not clearly delineated but meld into one another, and many of the practitioners cross disciplinary boundaries. Thus the field of traditional ecological knowledge is integrative and involves synthesis and coordination by a higher-level concept, the definition of an interdisciplinary approach (Jantsch 1972). As traditional ecological knowledge develops into an increasingly distinctive field, one may expect that boundaries will become even more blurred in time.

The two intellectual roots of traditional ecological knowledge—ethnobiology and human ecology—are quite distinct with respect to the interests and backgrounds of the scholars who played a role in their development. They have, however, developed in a synergistic relationship with one another. As Cordell (1995) pointed out, there is a need to expose more of the intellectual roots of traditional ecological knowledge in ethnoscience and its relation to biology, especially biosystematics.

Ethnobiology and Biosystematics: A Good Fit

The story of ethnobiology is one of the triumphs of science as common sense. Ethnologists and linguists started the field as a study of folk classifications to gain insights into different cultures. But the classifications so obtained attracted the attention of biologists who saw ethnoscience as an opportunity to test whether species identifications were robust, that is, whether species as identified by scientific experts were the same as those identified by local experts in other cultures. The interest of biologists in turn helped infuse biological and ecological thought into the field of ethnoscience.

Before we get into the story of the common sense of species identifications, some background is needed on the development of ethnoscience as practiced by ethnologists and linguists. Ethnoscience has a relatively long history (Toledo 1992, 2001; Rist and Dahdouh-Guebas 2006). The earliest reference quoted by Lévi-Strauss (1962: 5) is Barrows's work from 1900 on Coahuila Indians of Southern California who made a living in an apparently barren desert environment by harvesting no less than 60 kinds of edible plants and 28 medicinal plants. Such early work contributed to the understanding of local knowledge and livelihoods of different cultures, but the development and systematization of ethnoscience is a much later event, beginning in the United States in the mid-1950s.

Ethnoscience emerged out of a need to describe cultures from the inside. It made use of the categories operative within those cultures themselves to gain access into their cognitive universes. It was based on the assumption that the existence of a word to name a concept is the most reliable indication that the concept exists in that culture. Thus, ethnoscience became involved at first with the description of systems of terminologies. Linguistic methodologies were used to provide more rigorous methods for gathering and analyzing data, and the field was sometimes referred to as "ethnographic semantics" (Sturtevant 1964; Colby 1966).

As practitioners became more specialized, they limited themselves to describing sets of terms covering specific areas such as kinship, anatomy, color, and fauna, and each of these areas became a field in itself. Ethnoscience soon turned almost exclusively into the study of systems of classification (Murray 1982). Comparative studies, which revealed the existence of universal principles in color nomenclatures, stimulated a similar search for principles of folk classification with regard to flora and fauna. In the 1980s, the *Journal of Ethnobiology* and a professional society devoted to the subject were founded in the United States. Many comparative studies were carried out, and an evolving sequence of classification systems of fauna and flora from around the world developed (Berlin 1992; Balée 1994). Other areas of ethnoscience concerned with environmental phenomena developed in parallel with ethnobiology and shared this focus on classification, for example, with regard to the ethnoscience of ice (Basso 1972), soils (Pawluk et al. 1992), and the prediction of seasonal cycles (Ceci 1978).

A long-standing debate in biosystematics is whether species are "real packages" or objectively recognizable units in nature, or "a fiction, a mental construct without objective existence" (Gould 1980: 206). Advances in ethnobiology provided an opportunity to put the question to the test. Here, finally, was "a way to obtain valuable information about whether species are mental abstractions embedded in cultural practice or packages in nature. We can study how different peoples, in complete independence, divide the organisms of their local areas into units. We can contrast Western classifications into Linnaean species with the 'folk taxonomies' of non-Western peoples" (Gould 1980: 207).

The idea of accepting the validity of folk science did not come easily to scientists. But some of the leading systematists of the day had first-hand experience with indigenous peoples and their local knowledge, and that helped the process of acceptance. Mayr (1963) wrote of his experiences with folk biology: "Forty years ago, I lived all alone with a tribe of Papuans in the mountains of New Guinea. These superb woodsmen had 136 names for the 137 species of birds I distinguished (confusing only two non-descript species of warblers)." Diamond (1966) published a more extensive study on the Fore people of New Guinea and found that they had names for all the species as identified by the scientific (Linnaean) classification system. Moreover, when Diamond brought Fore hunters into an area that had birds species they had never seen and asked them to give the closest Fore equivalent for each new bird, they placed 91 of 103 species into the "correct" Linnaean group!

Scientists are a skeptical lot, and soon the search was on for exceptions. An anthropologist, Berlin, and two botanists, Breedlove and Raven, published in 1966 their ethnobotany of the Tzeltal Indians of Chiapas, southern Mexico. Their explicit objective was to challenge Diamond's claim for the generality of extensive one-to-one correspondence between folk science and Western science. Their finding was that only 34 percent of the Tzeltal plant species matched the Linnaean list. The mismatches and the misclassifications, they thought, reflected cultural uses and practices. But a few years later after further study, Berlin's team reversed its opinion and affirmed the close correspondence of Tzeltal and Linnaean taxonomies. They had, in the earlier study, not fully understood the Tzeltal system of hierarchical ordering and had mixed names from several levels. Much to his credit, Berlin (1973) could now conclude that, "there is at present a growing body of evidence that suggests that the fundamental taxa recognized in folk systematics correspond fairly closely with scientifically known species."

Subsequently, Berlin *et al.* (1974) published a comprehensive book on Tzeltal plant taxonomy. Their complete catalogue of species contained 471 Tzeltal names. Of these, 281 or 60 percent were in one-to-one correspondence with Linnaean names. Of the remaining names, 173 (36 percent) were "underdifferentiated," that is, Tzeltal names referred to more than one Linnaean species. However, in more than two-thirds of these cases, there were subsidiary Tzeltal names to make distinctions within the primary groups, and all of these subsidiary names corresponded with Linnaean species. The remaining 17 names (4 percent) were "overdifferentiated." Seven Linnaean species had two Tzeltal names each. One Linnaean species, a gourd plant, had three Tzeltal names, one for plants with large, round fruits used for tortilla containers, one for plants with long-necked gourds for carrying liquid, and one for plants with small gourds not used for anything.

Other studies exist of comprehensive folk taxonomies. One of the most frequently cited studies in ethnobiology is a book, *Birds of My Kalam Country* (Majnep and Bulmer 1977), prepared cooperatively by an indigenous expert of the Kalam people of New Guinea and an anthropologist/natural historian. Of the entire Kalam catalog of 174 vertebrate (mammals, birds, reptiles, amphibians, and fish) names, more than 70 percent had one-to-one correspondence with Linnaean names. In most of the other cases, Majnep, the Kalam expert, lumped two or more Linnaean species under one Kalam name. In the other cases, Majnep made divisions within a Linnaean species on account of different uses or values. In some birds of paradise, for example, the sexes were named differently because only males carry the prized plumage. After accounting for understandable differences such as the one above, Bulmer, the Western expert, could find only four cases (2 percent) of inconsistency in the Kalam names by the rules of scientific nomenclature.

More on Linguistics and Methodology: How to Get the Information Right

The Tzeltal story shows, in addition to the tremendous scholarly integrity of Berlin, Breedlove, and Raven, some of the pitfalls in conducting ethnobiological research. Categories operative within a culture may not be so easy to figure out, and linguistic barriers may be very difficult to overcome. Hunn (1993b) provides a particularly telling case of ethnographic error leading to misidentification (see Box 3.1). Note that the error occurred in part because the indigenous language name was not recorded correctly in the first place, and in part because the indigenous informants used it in the English vernacular, no doubt for the benefit of a linguistically challenged researcher.

Hunn (1993b: 17) is very clear about the linguistic requirements of a novice ethnobiologist: "The researcher must first be able to ask this fundamental question in the native language: 'What is the name of X?' (while pointing to some individual organism). And he/she must be able to transcribe the answers accurately in that language. It is also necessary to know the difference between a name and other possible responses to that key question, e.g. 'I don't know', 'Yankee go home!', or 'The big, black, noisy bird that craps on your head.' "

Box 3.1 Identifying Species Correctly: The Puzzle of Camas

Hunn tells the story of "camas," a lily of northwestern North America with an edible bulb that was a staple food of local Indian groups. A local ethnographer published an account of the native food plants of one local group, a Salish-speaking group in the northern portion of the Columbia Plateau. He listed five species of "camas" as important in their diet, identifying "black camas" as *Camassia quamash* but also listing several species of "white camas" as *Camassia* species. These latter species were described as being harvested on extensive dry rocky flats south of the Columbia River. A generation of anthropologists searched for these camas digging grounds unsuccessfully.

Subsequent ethnobotanical research exposed the original ethnographic error: the term "camas" was borrowed originally from the Nez Perce Indian language (not a Salish language) by the explorers Lewis and Clark. The term was then appropriated by botanists for both the Latinate genus and species names. The term also entered the local English vernacular, but was generalized by English-speaking settlers to refer to most, if not all, Indian root foods. The Salish Indians described these plants to the ethnographer in the local English vernacular, in which "camas" has a much wider referential range than it had in the original Nez Perce (and related Sahaptin) language. "White camas" is not camas at all, in the Nez Perce or the botanical sense, but is used to refer to several species of "desert parsleys," members of the genus *Lomatium* of the parsley/celery/carrot family. There is no camas in this part of the Columbia Basin, but plenty of desert parsley. The two types of Indian foods are alike only in that the edible part of the plant is underground. They are found in quite different habitats, are harvested at different times, and are cooked and/or dried for storage in quite distinct ways. To confuse them is to miss a large part of the sophistication of local traditional ecological knowledge.

Source: Hunn 1993b: 17.

Learning a foreign language may not be easy for a researcher who may not have the time or resources for such an undertaking. This does not preclude the possibility of carrying out work in ethnobiology, but it makes care and caution in research even more important. Help may be obtained from bilingual members of the cultural group and from linguistic experts. Hunn (1993b) issues a series of precautions. Here is his list, as augmented from other sources:

(1) Indigenous classification systems are less comprehensive across taxonomic categories than the Western scientific system. In general, the gap between the two classification systems increases as the cultural and practical significance of a species decreases. Thus, one would anticipate that all the large mammal species will be named in a traditional system, but only a small fraction of the insects and other invertebrates may be recognized. For example, the Tzeltal language under-differentiates the numerous Linnaean species of bats and lumps them under a single name. Bats are, in fact, culturally significant (they are associated with evil forces in Mayan belief), but they are nocturnal and difficult to observe. Hunn (1993b: 19) argues that the use of lumped categories and residual categories "is in no way an indication of inability to distinguish species on a par with that of a Western scientific expert. Rather, it reflects a principle of mental economy" whereby attention is focused on the species that are important for livelihoods.

(2) Species of great importance to a culture may be overdifferentiated as compared to the Linnaean classification, as in the example of Tzeltal gourds. The Hanunoo of the Philippines have names for over 90 varieties of rice, and the Quechuan languages of the Peruvian Andes have several hundred named varieties of potatoes. In some cases, the indigenous system may have a series of names for a Linnaean species but no one general term. This is not surprising, Hunn reminds the reader, considering that the English language lacks a general term for the species *Bos taurus*, calling it "cattle," "cow," "bull," "bullock," "steer," "ox," "heifer," or "calf," depending on the sex and age of the animal and where it fits in the economy.

(3) Above the taxonomic level of species, the gap between indigenous classifica-tion systems and Western science tends to increase. Many biologists argue that only species are real units in nature, and the names at higher levels of taxonomy are to some extent arbitrary (Gould 1980: 210). Higher-level terms in folk systems will not, as a general rule, correspond closely to scientific systems. The Tzeltal, for example, have four named groups of plant species roughly corresponding to trees, vines, grasses, and broad-leafed herbaceous plants. This schema covers some three-quarters of their plant names but leaves the rest unaffiliated. The

Kalam of New Guinea divide their nonreptilian four-footed vertebrates into three groups: *kopyak* or rats, *kmn* for a mixed group of larger game mammals, and *as* for a diverse group of frogs and small rodents. The divisions reflect not biological similarities among the animals (which the Kalam acknowledge but dismiss as unimportant) but the gender division of livelihood activities. *As* are collected primarily by women and children, *kmn* are hunted primarily by men, and *kopyak*, associated with unclean environments, are not eaten at all.

(4) Basic names in indigenous classification systems may have two senses: a *core* reference, as Hunn calls it, to a particularly important or conspicuous species, and an *extended* reference to one or more similar species of lesser importance. Whether the term is being used to refer to the core species or to the extended group will depend on the context. In particular, binomial names may pose a problem. For example, the Tzeltal call all robins (Linnaean genus *Turdus*) *toht*. They distinguish up to five species by modifying the generic name, for example, *ch'ish toht* for the rufous-collared robin, *Turdus rufitorques*. Frequently, however, the core species of the folk genus will be referred to by the unmodified generic name. Whether the term is being used to refer to the genus or the species will depend on the context.

(5) Names of plants and animals in traditional systems have not been standardized. The terminology may vary by dialect, by village, and even by individual. Thus, the researcher has to cope with numerous cases of synonymy and homonymy, as Hunn calls them. For example, when I began the inventory of Cree fish names in the eastern James Bay area, my more experienced anthropologist colleague, Harvey Feit, warned me to watch out for acceptable equivalent terms in each community, as well as for differences among communities. Sure enough, we found both (see Table 3.1). To complicate matters, there also was an idiosyncratic system of "nicknames" for fish. Depending on his/her mood, a fisher might call northern pike (*Esox lucius*), "the prince of the waters" (a poetic translation) rather than refer to the species by the everyday Cree name of *chinusaw* (Berkes and MacKenzie 1978). Hunn mentions other complications that can further confuse a researcher. For example, some cultures in the Asia-Pacific region substitute alternative names or circumlocutions in referring to animals and plants, in order to avoid words that may call to mind the name of a recently deceased person.

(6) Different cultures have developed detailed classifications of those elements of the environment that are important to them. The researcher should be aware that ecologically or socially important ethnoscientific classifications are not limited to plants and animals. For example, northern indigenous peoples have a

Table 3.1 James Bay Cree Indian fish names in standard orthography used by Cree linguists

	Great Whale	Fort George	Wemindji	Eastmain	Rupert House	Waswanipi	Nemaska	Mistassini
arctic char	sùsàsù	sùsàsù	–	–	–	–	–	–
landlocked salmon	unàw	unàw	–	–	–	–	–	–
speckled trout	màsimàkus	màsimàkush	màsimàkush	màsimàkush	màsimàkush	màsimàkush	màsimekw	màsimekw masimekush
lake trout	kùkamàs kùkamàw	kùkamàsh kùkamàw	kùkamàsh kùkamàw	kùkamesh	kùkamesh	namekush	namekush	namekush
whitefish	atihkamàkw	atihkamàkw	atihkamàkw	atihkamekw	atihkamekw	atihkamekw	atihkamekw	atihkamekw
cisco	nùtimiwàsù	nùtimiwàsù	nùtimiwàsù	nùtimiweshish	nùtimiwesù	utùlipi uchùlipish	utùlipìsh	–
burbot	miy miyàhktù	miyàhkatù	miyàhkatù	miyàhkatù	miyàhkatù	miyàhkatù	miyàhkatù	miyàhkatù
white sucker	iyichàw	nimàpi	nimàpi	namepi	namepi	namepi	namepi	namepi
red sucker	nimàpi	mihkumàpi	mihkwàshàw mihkuchikàsh	mihkuchikàsh mihkwàshew	mihkuchikàsh mihkwàshew	mihkwàsew	mihkusew	mihkusew
sturgeon	–	nimàw	nimàw	namew	namew	namew	namew	namew
walleye	–	ukàw	ukàw	ukàw	ukàw	ukàsh	ukàsh	ukàsh ukàw
pike	chinusàw	chinushàw	chinushàw	chinushew	chinushew	chinushew	chinushew	chinusew

Great Whale = Poste-de-la-Baleine, Fort George = Chisasibi, Rupert House = Waskaganish
Note: Scientific names of the species and further details of Cree nomenclature in Berkes and MacKenzie (1978).

rich vocabulary of ice- and snow-related terms. Turkic peoples of Central Asia, traditional horsemen and women, have a detailed terminology of horse colors; modern Turkish carries these terms, even though contemporary urban Turks rarely see a horse. A lake is a lake in English. But in Bangladesh, which lies in the flood-plain of three great rivers, the Bangla language has several different terms to differentiate between different kinds of lakes, including *boar* (oxbow lake), *beel* and *haor* (two kinds of natural depressions in low-lying topography), and flood lands that become shallow, seasonal lakes during monsoon months (Ahmed *et al.* 1997).

(7) Traditional knowledge is often gendered (Turner and Turner 2008; Camou-Guerrero *et al.* 2008). Rocheleau (1991) writes, "half or more of indigenous ecological science has been obscured by the prevailing 'invisibility' of women, their work, their interests and especially their knowledge." Much of this knowledge is crucially important. Shiva (1988) points out that survival is the ultimate criterion for verification of poor rural women's knowledge. A steady stream of field research indicates the gendered nature of traditional work, such as agricultural specialization, and thus of traditional knowledge. This is reflected in some of the above examples, such as the Kalam division of animals. Even where there is no clear gender specialization in ethnoscientific knowledge, the researcher would do well to remember that differences in work and interests will likely translate into gender differences in depth of knowledge and the path of transmission. For example, among the Cree of James Bay, men and women share many items of traditional knowledge and bush skills. Nevertheless, most knowledge transmission follows gender lines. In one community, two-thirds of the instructors of young females in the transmission of bush skills were found to be women. This figure climbed to 80 percent in a smaller and more traditional community (Ohmagari and Berkes 1997).

(8) Caution should be exercised regarding culture-specific and referential meanings in ethnoscience. Hunn (1993b: 20) points out that the meanings of plant and animal names, such as those discussed above, are referential meanings, only one aspect of meaning of a term that may also include cultural meanings. For example, *dog* means *Canis familiaris*; but *dog* can also mean "man's best friend" in one culture, "sled-puller" in another, and "dinner" in a third. "Once the referential meaning has been established," says Hunn, "a whole world of other cultural meanings is accessible to the student of that system of traditional ecological knowledge."

(9) Finally, informants in a traditional ecological knowledge study need to be selected very carefully. Local and traditional knowledge is not distributed evenly in a community. There is usually a small number of locally recognized experts in

a given area of expertise, say, medicinal plants (Byg *et al.* 2010). Heterogeneity of knowledge, both within a community and among adjacent communities, is a reality (Ghimire *et al.* 2005). Davis and Wagner (2003) reviewed the published literature of local and traditional knowledge regarding how local experts were identified, and found that many studies did not meet even minimal methodological standards. In particular, many studies did not indicate how the interview sample was selected. Papers with exemplary methodology included Olsson and Folke (2001) which provided details of how expertise was identified and described the ways in which local knowledge informed institutions. Good research methodology does not necessarily rely on large sample size. For example, each of the classical traditional ecological knowledge studies by Majnep and Bulmer (1977), Johannes (1981), Hunn and Selam (1990), and Nakashima (1991) relied on *one* major informant (or co-author).

Although the present volume is not a book on methodology, it is probably fair to say that many of the better local and traditional knowledge studies rely on several methodologies and a triangulation of techniques, the use of several methods together. These methods may include participant observation (see Chapter 7), semi-directed interviews (Huntington 2000), focus groups (see Chapter 5), participatory mapping (Bryan 2011), participatory workshops (Kendrick and Manseau 2008; Knapp *et al.* 2011), network analysis (Crona and Bodin 2006; Evans 2010), and participatory rural appraisal (PRA) (Grenier 1998). Many researchers use variations of participatory action research (Fals-Borda 1987), and there is a trend to use culturally appropriate indigenous methodologies (Louis 2007; Wehi 2009; Geniusz 2009; Kovach 2009). Table 2.1 in the previous chapter provided a selection of areas of traditional knowledge research. Each of these areas has its own methodology and approaches. For example, land use and occupancy studies developed in different parts of the world use distinct approaches and methodologies. In Southeast Asia land use studies refer to "territorialization" (Peluso 1995; Vandergeest and Peluso 1995); in Central America, they refer to "ethnocartography" (Chapin and Threlkeld 2001).

Exaggeration and Ethnoscience: The Eskimo Snow Hoax?

One of the persistent problems in traditional knowledge research is the question of the reliability of information. Can indigenous knowledge be tested? Is it verifiable against scientific knowledge? Experienced researchers know that with some groups, *how* people say things may be more important than *what* they say. As Bielawski (1992) puts it, "Inuit knowledge resides less in what Inuit say than how they say it and what they do." The researcher must be familiar with the mode of communication of a particular group of people. For example, Felt (1994: 259) writes that Newfoundland fishers "communicate their understanding about their world through personal anecdotes and long stories and yarns about community members of yesteryear. Humor is frequently used, as are 'cuffers,' or exaggerated stories told in competition with other fishers." As an example, the author produces the cuffer about setting fish nets anchored to icebergs, an unlikely practice (because of safety concerns—icebergs tend to roll over), yet signaling the phenomenon that a retreating ice edge tends to be a good place to fish because of abundance of fish food (Berkes 1977).

The controversy over Eskimo (Inuit) snow terminology is a particularly interesting example about how exaggerated information may get perpetuated in the literature, in this case through no fault of the Inuit themselves. Geoffrey Pullum is a linguist who has written a book about fallacies that the general public commonly believes, despite the best efforts of experts to set the record straight. "In the study of language," he says, "one case surpasses all others in its degree of ubiquity: it is the notion that Eskimos have bucketloads of different words for snow" (Pullum 1991).

Borrowing from Martin (1986), Pullum traces the original source to the distinguished anthropologist Franz Boas, whose commentary about four distinct Eskimo root terms about snow was picked up in the 1940s by an "amateur" (that is, a nonlinguist, nonanthropologist) and embellished to produce seven or more categories. In the course of several successively more careless repetitions over several decades, as traced by Martin, the number of snow terms had been inflated to the order of one- to two-hundred!

Pullum (1991: 163) not only questions these numbers but also the evidence that the Eskimo terms are more differentiated than those in English. He points out that not only do some groups such as skiers use specialized terms such as powder and crust, but even among the general population there is a range of terms in common use: "the stuff in question is called *snow* when fluffy and white, *slush* when partially melted, *sleet* when falling in a half-melted state, and a *blizzard* when pelting down hard enough to make driving dangerous."

Pullum's points about scholarly sloppiness and the susceptibility of the public to cling to misinformation are well taken. However, some of his analysis shows a poor reading of ethnoscience: "When you come to think of it, Eskimos aren't really that likely to be interested in snow. Snow in the traditional Eskimo hunter's life must be a kind of constantly assumed background, like sand on the beach. And even beach bums have only one word for sand" (Pullum 1991: 166). And further: "The fact is that the myth of the multiple words for snow is based on almost nothing at all. It is a kind of accidentally developed hoax perpetrated by the anthropological linguistics community on itself" (Pullum 1991: 162).

These conclusions are of course not accurate. In a discourse of traditional ecological knowledge, it is important to point out that there is not only anthropological but also ecological evidence that bears on the question. Arctic ecologist Bill Pruitt has been using Inuktitut (Eskimo language) and other indigenous terminology for types of snow for decades (Pruitt 1960). He says, "Boreal ecologists deal with aspects of nature, particularly snow and ice phenomena, for which there are no precise English words. Consequently, our writings and speech are larded with Inuit, Athapascan, Lappish and Tungus words, not in any attempt to be erudite but to aid in the precision in our speech and thoughts" (Pruitt 1978: 6).

Table 3.2 provides a sampling of some of this specialized snow terminology and illustrates the importance of ecological considerations in the study of languages and ethnoscience. As for the question of the actual number of terms, the Saami educator and linguist, Ole Henrik Magga (2006: 34) writes that "there are 175–180 basic stems on snow and ice." Adding related terms and all the derivations, the total may "come up to something like 1,000 lexemes with connections to snow, ice, freezing and melting." It is clear that the Saami, as well as other northern peoples, are interested in snow, and the existence of a rich vocabulary is not a hoax at all. The case illustrates cross-cultural shortsightedness that one has to guard against. It also shows how wrong a narrow disciplinary perspective (in this case linguistics) can be, if the evidence from the broader interdisciplinary view is not consulted.

Table 3.2 Some specialized snow terminology

Term	Source	English equivalent
Aŋmaŋa	Inuit	Space formed between drift and obstruction causing it
Api	Inuit	Snow on the ground, forest
Čiegar	Saami	"Feeding trench" through undisturbed api
Čuok'ki	Saami	Layer of solid ice next to the soil
Fies'ki	Saami	"Yard crater" of thin, hard and dense snow caused by reindeer digging
Kaioglaq	Inuit	Large hard sculpturings resulting from erosion of kalutoganiq
Kalutoganiq	Inuit	Arrowhead-shaped drift on top of upsik; moves downwind
Pukak	Inuit	Fragile, columnar base layer of api
Qali	Inuit	Snow on trees
Qamaniq	Inuit	Bowl-shaped depression in api under coniferous tree
Sändjas	Saami	Fragile, columnar basal layer of api (= pukak)
Suov'dnji	Saami	"Feeding crater" excavated in the api
Upsik	Inuit	Wind-hardened tundra snow cover

Source: Adapted and condensed from Pruitt (1984). The Inuit terms are from the Kovakmiut; Saami = Lappish from northern Scandinavia.

Human Ecology and Territoriality

In Chapter 2, we touched upon the social and cultural significance of traditional ecological knowledge with regard to the sometimes sacred dimensions of indigenous knowledge, such as symbolic meanings and their importance for social relationships and values. Linguistics is one key to the understanding of social and ecological relationships in a culture. However, the study of functional relationships between people and the environment, and people's perceptions of how they fit within environmental systems, falls into the area of human ecology, and more specifically cultural ecology.

Cultural ecology is an ethnological approach that sees the modes of production of societies around the world as adaptations to their local environments. The field has its origin in the work of Steward (1936) on the social organization of hunter-gatherer groups. Steward argued against environmental determinism, which regarded specific cultural characteristics as arising from environmental causes. Using band societies as examples, he showed that social organization itself corresponded to a kind of ecological adaptation of a human group to its environment. He defined cultural ecology as the study of *adaptive processes* by which the nature of society and an unpredictable number of features of culture are affected by the basic adjustment through which humans utilize a given environment (Steward 1955).

Subsequent work showed that the study of processes of human adaptation to the environment was a productive line of inquiry in cultural anthropology, and that sound empirical data were available to document wide-ranging and systemic ecological relationships (Lee and Devore 1968; Netting 1986). Even though traditional ecological knowledge is generated locally, comparative analysis has shown the existence of similar ecological adaptations in comparable areas. In some cases, such as in shifting cultivation systems and the use of fire, traditional systems may show functional equivalents in quite different cultural and geographic settings (see Chapter 4). All of this makes the study of traditional ecological knowledge more than just locally significant. Because traditional systems often involve long-term adaptations to specific environments and resource management problems, they are of interest to resource managers everywhere (Turner *et al.* 2003; Turner and Berkes 2006). One example of such an adaptation is human territoriality and the use of resources on a territorial basis.

An early practitioner of cultural ecology was the American ethnologist Speck (1915), who saw the system of hunting territories used by the aboriginal people of Labrador as a method of resource conservation. His findings were later attacked on the basis that family-based hunting territories came into being *after* the fur trade and therefore could not have represented an aboriginal land tenure system

(Leacock 1954). The latter argument about the origin of the family territory system is probably correct, although the point is still debated (Bishop and Morantz 1986). From a resource management point of view, however, Speck's original point is valid. Community-based (but not family-based) territories were probably the primary practice for resource management at one time in North America. According to Sutton (1975), probably most native peoples in North America had systems of land tenure that involved rules for resource allocation within the group and for control of access to resources, and the prerogative to convey to others certain resource-use rights but not outright alienation. That is, the produce of the land was subject to rules and allocation decisions, but the land itself was never "for sale" (see Box 3.2). The point is, rights apply to specific resources but not to land because land belongs to the Creator (Trosper 1998, 2002).

Most indigenous land tenure systems in North America have disappeared; the James Bay area is one of the exceptions. Since the 1970s, much detailed work has been carried out to determine how these territorial land tenure systems work (Feit 1991). Forms of territorial systems found among the James Bay Cree, who live in the lands to the west of the Naskapi and Montagnais (Innu) of Labrador, are of the communal property type. Each community (in this case Chisasibi) holds a communal territory that is further subdivided into hunting territories of family groups (Berkes 1989b). A senior hunter leads each group and enforces the community's rules. Only members of the family or people invited by them are permitted to trap furs on this land, but it is generally understood that any community member can hunt or fish to feed his or her family. Within a territory, individual hunters lay claim to beaver lodges. Violations of general rules of hunting, fishing, and trapping are dealt with through customary law and enforced by social sanction.

Hunting rights limit the number of hunters who can operate in the family territories and in the communal territory as a whole. This way, high levels of productivity can be obtained with a limited hunting pressure. Where the human population is large and growing, the territory system can have the effect of limiting the number of active hunters and stabilizing the overall hunting pressure. We tested this hypothesis using an 18-year data set. Over this time period, the population of the eastern James Bay Cree nearly doubled and the percentage of participation rate in the traditional land-based economy declined, but the size of the population participating (i.e. the number of active hunters) in fact remained stable, as did the resource base (Berkes and Fast 1996).

Fishing, hunting, and gathering territories also exist in the Pacific Northwest. Their continued use has been well documented from northern British Columbia (Collier and Vegh 1998). The Nass River area near the British Columbia–Alaska border provides an example of the use of territorial systems in the management of Pacific salmon (Berkes 1985). The Nass River watershed is claimed as traditional

Box 3.2 Cree Humor: Land as "Real Estate"

Cree people use a great deal of humor in their daily interactions, as do many groups of North American aboriginal people. In the contemporary world, much of Cree humor deals with the absurd or inexplicable things that Euro-Canadians (*wapstagushio*, white man) do. Such as regarding the Creator's land as a commodity.

It was spring, just at the end of the goose hunting season. Ice was slowly clearing off James Bay, and a Cree companion and I went down the coast from Chisasibi to check some fish nets. As we took a tea break on a high piece of rock overlooking the Bay, we spotted two large canoes approaching. Several families were returning to the village of Chisasibi after a month or so in a goose hunting camp. The Cree are a gregarious people, never missing an opportunity to visit and to catch up on local gossip. So the canoes stopped at our tea-break camp, offering some smoked goose and not refusing some fresh boiled fish. They noticed me, of course; an outsider and a white man in the bush is always a curiosity. Shortly after, my companion was asked about my business in being there. His response, delivered in Cree, left the visitors helpless with laughter – several minutes of prolonged laughter – or so it seemed to me, as I sat feeling uncomfortable but also curious. What *did* he say that was considered so outrageously funny?

My companion explained later that he had merely said, "Oh, yes, this *wapstagushio*. He is here to look over some real estate." I must admit, I did not see the humor at that time. But the Cree had just concluded a land claims case and were negotiating a treaty with a government that was intent on redefining aboriginal rights and land claims to clear the way so that hydroelectric dams could be built. So imagine, hunters go to the peace and quiet of a month-long goose hunt, away from court cases and the threats of the mad industrialized world trying to grab their land. When they return at the end of the goose season, the first thing they run into is this *wapstagushio*, drinking tea and snacking on boiled whitefish, sitting on bare rock in the middle of nowhere. He is casting his greedy eyes about, appraising the real estate value of this piece of the Creator's land.

Source: Berkes field notes, Chisasibi, James Bay.

tribal territory by the Nishga. Within it, each Nishga community used one part of the watershed, within which specific salmon fishing sites were controlled by a chief on behalf of a *house*, a kinship-based social group. Thus, resource territories were organized hierarchically, from the watershed level down to specific fishing sites. In many parts of the Pacific Northwest, rules of sharing and reciprocity ensured that house chiefs took responsibility for allocating resources equitably within the house. Periodic *potlatches*, commonly held by many groups, were a mechanism for sharing the surplus of their fishing activities. Trosper (1998, 2009) suggests that potlatches may have served the function of solving the "tragedy of the commons" by creating a disincentive to accumulate individual wealth.

However, to view territoriality merely as a resource management mechanism is to miss half of the story. The potlatch is not only for resource sharing; it is culturally significant in its own right. Land is important for cultural reasons as well. For example, it is important for the education of the young and for knowledge transmission among the Cree (Ohmagari and Berkes 1997), among the Raramuri of Mexico (Wyndham 2010), and others. It is also important for the perpetuation of social values such as sharing and reciprocity, and the reproduction of culture, which is unconsciously known and embodied in action (Preston 1975, 2002). As Feit (1991: 227) explains, "Hunting territories are both systems of practice and culture, intertwined and closely linked to distinctive social forms and relations. . . . The replication of distinctive ideologies of land and social relations has been central to the ability of Algonquian peoples to maintain distinctive systems of land rights."

Much work in classical human ecology was concerned with territoriality and land tenure systems in a diversity of cultural groups and geographic areas. For example, no fewer than five of the 11 chapters in the book by Williams and Hunn (1982) deal with territories. Such territories were found in marine coastal as well as in terrestrial environments, for example in Oceania (Johannes 1978) and among the tribes of the Pacific Northwest. The Kwakiutl had named fishing banks (Boas 1934). Among non-aboriginal groups, Acheson (1975) reported territorial resource use among commercial lobster fishers in Maine. Such findings led various international resource management circles to suggest that land and marine tenure systems should be used as the basis of management. For example, Christy (1982) proposed that governments should consider recognizing local territorial use rights in fisheries (TURFS) toward improving resource management, and this approach has been the basis of some of the better coastal fisheries management systems in the world (Gelcich *et al.* 2010).

The basic ecological reasoning behind territoriality is simple. Ecologists consider territories as a mechanism by which population size can be matched to the limits of available resources. Territoriality is considered a behavioral self-regulatory mechanism found among many mammal and bird species, especially the predatory ones such as wolves. The presence or absence of territories and variations in resource control patterns have been explained by the use of economic and ecological models. These models, first developed in animal ecology, were applied to human groups by Dyson-Hudson and Smith (1978: 22), who defined territory as "an area occupied more or less exclusively by an individual or a group by means of repulsion through overt defense or some form of communication." The economic defensibility model predicted territorial behavior when the costs of exclusive use and defense were exceeded by the benefits gained. Dyson-Hudson and Smith (1978: 21) argued that the most important factors in determining the cost–benefit ratio were the predictability and abundance of a resource: "territoriality is expected to occur when critical resources are sufficiently abundant and predictable in space and time." If a resource was not critical for the well-being of a group, it was not worth defending. Similarly, if a resource was too rare or too abundant, there was no benefit to be gained from territoriality.

Richardson (1982), among others, applied the economic defensibility model to the data-rich Northwest coast from California to Alaska. He found that the model was generally useful in explaining patterns of resource control; the resources most frequently subject to access restrictions were those that were predictable and abundant, such as salmon. He also found, however, that the Dyson-Hudson and Smith model was inadequate to explain patchiness of resource use and of territories. As well, he suggested that some cases of territoriality may have purely cultural (as opposed to ecological and economic) explanations. In a similar vein, Chapman (1985) pointed out that marine tenure in parts of the South Pacific may be explained more simply in terms of local politics and power relations, rather than in terms of resource management. Yet others noted that traditional management may exist in the *absence* of territories, as in the case of Icelandic inshore fishers (Palsson 1982).

Since the 1980s, the emphasis on territories and economic models seems to have been replaced by a broader view of the social role of territoriality as part of culture, as argued for example by Feit (1991). As well, territoriality-based analysis has been largely replaced by one that emphasizes property rights and commons institutions. For many, territoriality is important, but it is only one aspect of a larger system of rights, obligations, and rules. As ecologists remind us, all species adapt to the resource limits of their environments. However, behavioral self-regulatory mechanisms among human groups are more complex than those found in other species. Many animal populations have territories; many human groups have commons institutions that are often systems of access rules, sharing rules, and appropriate resource use behavior (Berkes 1989b; Wilson *et al.* 1994; Cox *et al.* 2010).

Integration of Social Systems and Natural Systems: Importance of Worldviews

One of the major areas of study in human ecology of recent years is the integration of resource management and social systems. The book by Williams and Hunn (1982), dealing mainly with the indigenous groups of the Pacific Northwest and of Australia, is one of the earlier examples of the study of comparative cultural ecology and resource management. A large body of literature on traditional management systems in Oceania, compiled by interdisciplinary groups of marine ecologists, geographers, anthropologists, and others (Johannes 1978, 2002a; Klee 1980; Ruddle and Johannes 1990; Freeman *et al.* 1991), has revolutionized management thinking. Similarly, the tropical forest use of traditional cultures of the Amazon region has come under study by interdisciplinary teams, leading to a reconceptualization of tropical forest conservation (Posey and Balee 1989; Redford and Mansour 1996; Posey 1999; Holt 2005).

These studies have contributed to a search for alternative resource management systems. They have provided insights for more holistic, systems ecology-based approaches (Regier 1978), and for adaptive systems based on local knowledge and practice. The rediscovery of ecosystem-like concepts among traditional cultures in many parts of the world was an important stepping stone in the appreciation by ecologists of traditional holistic understandings of nature (see Table 3.3). Basically, two characteristics make these examples ecosystem-like concepts. First, the traditional unit of land or water in each of these cases is defined in terms of a geographical boundary (usually a watershed boundary). Second, the traditional concept considers everything within this environmental unit to be interlinked.

The territories of the Gitksan (Gitxsan) and Wet'sewet'en people of the Pacific Northwest provide an example. These territories are closely associated with a specific group of people. They are used for a variety of resource gathering activities and are controlled by chiefs on behalf of kinship groups. Chiefs describe their territorial boundaries as "from mountain top to mountain top" and orient themselves by two directional axes within this watershed framework: vertically up and down from valley bottom to mountain top, and horizontally, upstream and downstream (Tyler 1993). Detailed land use maps of the kinship-based house groups (*wilps*) of the Gitxsan show that there is a close correspondence between watershed areas and *wilps* or clusters of *wilps* (Collier and Vegh 1998). A close examination of these maps reveals that they are not merely territories but watershed-ecosystems-as-territories.

The examples in Table 3.3 provide only a sampling of a wide range of indigenous applications that resemble the ecosystem concept. However, the important

Table 3.3 Examples of traditional applications of the ecosystem view

System	Country/region	References
Watershed management of salmon rivers and associated hunting and gathering areas by tribal groups	Amerindians of the Pacific Northwest	Williams and Hunn (1982); Swezey and Heizer (1993)
Delta and lagoon management for fish culture (*tambak* in Java), and the integrated cultivation of rice and fish	South and Southeast Asia	Johannes *et al.* (1983)
Vanua (in Fiji), a named area of land and sea, seen as an integrated whole with its human occupants	Oceania, including Fiji, Solomon Islands, ancient Hawaii	Ruddle and Akimichi (1984); Baines (1989)
Family groups claiming individual watersheds (*iworu*) as their domain for hunting, fishing, gathering	The Ainu of northern Japan	Watanabe (1973); Ludwig (1994)
Integrated floodplain management (*dina*) in which resource areas are shared by social groups through reciprocal access arrangements	Mali, Africa	Moorehead (1989)

point to keep in mind is that there are many differences, as well as similarities, between these traditional and Western concepts of ecosystems. It would not be correct to label the examples in Table 3.3 simply as prescientific ecosystem concepts because they differ in context and conceptual underpinning. In Chapter 1, we considered the Dogrib Dene (Athapascan) notion of *ndè*, which could be translated as "ecosystem" except that *ndè* is based on the idea that everything in the environment has life and spirit (Legat *et al.* 1995). This makes it considerably different from mechanistic concepts of ecosystem.

This brings us to the consideration of these conceptual underpinnings, worldviews, or cosmologies. One of the classical studies of indigenous cosmologies was carried out by Reichel-Dolmatoff (1976) among the Tukano of the Colombian northwest Amazon, showing how the belief in the spirits of game animals restricted overhunting, and how shamanism functioned in the management of natural resources. Reichel-Dolmatoff drew attention to Tukano cosmology as representing a blueprint for ecological adaptation, positing worldviews as the organizing concept behind the cultural ecology of a group (Box 3.3). Tukano cosmology is not unique in the Americas. It has many features in common, for example, with Andean indigenous cosmologies (Valladolid and Apffel-Marglin 2001).

Box 3.3 Tukano Cosmology

According to Reichel-Dolmatoff, in Tukano culture, the individual person considers himself or herself as part of a complex network of interactions that include not only society but the entire universe. An essential interrelatedness of all things means that a person has to fulfill many functions that go far beyond his or her social roles, and that are extrasocietal extensions of a set of adaptive norms. These norms guide a person's relationships not only with other people but also with animals, plants, and other components of the environment. The rules the individual has to follow, says Reichel-Dolmatoff, "refer, above all, to cooperative behaviour aimed at the conservation of ecological balance as the ultimate desirable quality. Thus the relationship between man and his environment is being formulated not only on a cognitive level, but clearly it also constitutes an effective personal relationship in which individual animals and plants are treated with respect and caution."

The Tukano, argues Reichel-Dolmatoff, are aware that, to maintain resources, "a number of regulatory mechanisms have to be instituted and, what is more, have to be fully respected by all members of the society. These social controls of necessity possess marked adaptive implications and must be enforced primarily in those aspects of existence which, to a large degree, determine survival. I shall mention here: population growth, the exploitation of the physical environment, and aggression in interpersonal relations. It is quite clear to the Tukano that, in order to ensure individual and collective survival and well-being, adaptive rules have to be established to adjust the birth-rate, the harvest-rate, and to counterbalance all socially disruptive behaviour."

Reichel-Dolmatoff emphasizes the role of the shaman as a healer of illness, not so much at the individual level, but at the level of "supra-individual structures that have been disturbed by the person. To be effective, he has to apply his treatment to the disturbed part of the ecosystem. It might be said then that a Tukano shaman does not have individual patients; his task is to cure a social malfunctioning. The diseased organism of the patient is secondary in importance and will be treated eventually, both empirically and ritually, but what really counts is the re-establishment of the rules that will avoid over-hunting, the depletion of certain plant resources, and unchecked population increase. The shaman becomes thus a truly powerful force in the control and management of resources."

Source: Reichel-Dolmatoff 1976: 311, 312, 315.

One of the major lines of inquiry in the field of traditional ecological knowledge concerns cosmologies and worldviews. Are traditional worldviews relevant to present-day resource stewardship, and to the re-examination of our current attitudes toward the environment? Our view of the world and the universe and how we relate to them is the *source* of our values, our cosmology (Skolimowski 1981). Our observations of the world around us are invariably structured through the concepts supplied by our cosmology. Modern Westerners have a characteristic worldview regarding the place of humans in nature, one to which Bateson, Capra, and Berry allude, as cited in Chapter 1. Evernden (1993) argues that, in the dominant Western society of the post-Enlightenment period, humans are akin to aliens because they have a self-identity distinct from the world around them. The ecologist as a scientist "is forced to treat nature as essentially non-living, a machine to be dissected, interpreted and manipulated" (Evernden 1993: 20). In a similar vein, Skolimowski (1981) argues that our cosmology is based far too heavily on empiricism and scientism and is too mechanistic and analytic; it is insufficiently based on humanistic notions and morality toward nature.

Such generalizations are not universally true for all cultures. Even some Western traditions reject the view of a secularized and depersonalized nature. These include the alternative Christian views of nature, such as those of St. Francis (White 1967) and St. Benedict (Dubos 1972). There has been much discussion, as well, regarding Taoist, Zen Buddhist, and Sufi views on the environment (Pepper 1984; Callicott 1994, 2008; Selin 2003). Some of these views are consistent with pantheistic traditions of many indigenous peoples. Perhaps the explanation is that both the present-day indigenous groups and some of the spiritual traditions of Eastern and Western mainstream religions have been borrowing from the same wellspring of ancient wisdom of human–environment relationships. The question of worldviews is crucial to the analysis of traditional ecological knowledge. Chapter 5 provides one example of the unique worldviews of indigenous societies.

To summarize, ethnoscience and human ecology are at the intellectual roots of traditional ecological knowledge. The discipline started with the documentation of species lists of different cultures, and it elaborated a science of folk taxonomies of plants and animals and, later, of other environmental variables. It proceeded to the study of functional relationships of the elements of local knowledge so documented, including the study of human perceptions of ecological processes, and the process of human adaptation to the environment (Steward 1955). Some of the work of human ecologists in the 1970s and the 1980s emphasized territoriality (Malmberg 1980; Berkes 1986a). Although this work is important and has continued to date, others have approached traditional resource management systems using a framework that deals with commons rights and institutions. In this new emphasis, access rules are only one set of rules within a larger set of rights and obligations. Finally, context and worldviews are of key importance in human ecology. As Reichel-Dolmatoff (1976) pointed out, the researcher needs to study the worldview as the organizing concept behind the cultural ecology of a group, without which the logic of many traditional management systems would be difficult, if not impossible, to access. The next chapter proceeds to examine in more detail a selection of traditional ecological knowledge systems.

CHAPTER 4

Traditional Knowledge Systems in Practice

Throughout history, all human groups have depended on careful observations of the natural world. If they learned from these observations, they adapted successfully. If they did not, the consequences were probably deadly. Survival is the ultimate criterion for verification of traditional ecological knowledge, and adaptation is key. Thus, the practice of indigenous knowledge is, above all, the story of how social/cultural systems adapt to specific ecosystems. The accomplishments of traditional societies in such areas as agriculture are not easily deniable, as almost all major domesticated species of plants and animals predate Western science.

Traditional knowledge and resource management practice have the potential to contribute to the current understanding and use of a wide variety of ecosystems. Western civilization is largely based in north temperate regions of the world, and it is not surprising that most of Western resource management science has concentrated on temperate ecosystems. This has created some problems for resource management elsewhere. For example, many tropical marine ecologists have pointed out that fishery management designed for the characteristics of the North Atlantic does not at all work in tropical marine ecosystems. The same could be said about a number of other environments that we, as inhabitants of temperate ecosystems, consider "marginal." These include tropical forests, arid lands, mountains, and Arctic ecosystems. Hence *Our Common Future*, one of the first international documents to raise these issues, drew attention to the relevance of tribal and indigenous peoples' knowledge, with their long-term views and a contextual understanding of the local environment, for lessons in the management of resources in tropical forest, mountain, and arid land ecosystems (WCED 1987: 12; also quoted in Chapter 1).

However, the mere possession of knowledge does not guarantee that a given human group will live in harmony with its environment. There are many known cases of environmental mismanagement by traditional societies. We can, however, make an educated guess that, everything else being equal, societies with time-tested environmental practices *and* a capacity to learn from experience are more likely to be sustainable than those without. As we are dealing with a knowledge–practice–belief complex, one can further guess that the possession both of an appropriate social organization to put knowledge into resource management practice and of a worldview consistent with ecological prudence were also adaptive. Here *ecological prudence* is used in the sense of Slobodkin (1968), who observed that many predatory species generally act in a way that prevents the depletion of their food supplies. He found this to be so even with fairly simple organisms, as well as with mammals with their often elaborate systems of social regulation, such as territoriality.

Ecologically speaking, the human species may reasonably be characterized as a K-strategist, that is, a species adapted to maintain populations close to the ecological carrying capacity (Gadgil 1987). Thus, in human groups, one would expect to find social regulation of resource use, including territoriality and a range of other social mechanisms designed to prevent resource depletion, as discussed in Chapter 3. After all, basic principles of evolutionary ecology are applicable to the human species, too.

Several chapters coming up make reference to two concepts, Adaptive Management and social learning. Adaptive Management is an integrated method for natural resource management (Holling 1986; Lee 1993; Gunderson *et al.* 1995). It is *adaptive* because it acknowledges that environmental conditions will always change, thus requiring management institutions to respond to feedbacks by adjusting and evolving. Adaptive Management, like some traditional knowledge systems, takes a dynamic view of ecosystems, emphasizes processes (including resource use) that are part of ecological cycles of renewal, and stresses the importance of resilience, that is, the buffering ability of the system to absorb change without breaking down or going into another state of equilibrium. As well, Adaptive Management, like many traditional knowledge systems, assumes that nature cannot be controlled and yields predicted; uncertainty and unpredictability are characteristics of all ecosystems, including managed ones. In both cases, feedback learning is the way in which societies deal with uncertainty (Berkes *et al.* 2000). Often, this is not learning at the level of the individual, but *social learning* at the level of society or *institutional learning* at the level of institutions (Ostrom 1990; Gunderson and Holling 2002; Armitage *et al.* 2007).

The objective of this chapter is to describe the workings of a sample of indigenous knowledge and resource management systems in a variety of ecosystem settings. The emphasis is on the traditional system, as a linked social–ecological system (Berkes and Folke 1998; Berkes 2011), rather than on local and traditional knowledge itself. Two themes run through the chapter. The first is about evolutionary ecology and cultural evolution: traditional knowledge represents the summation of millennia of ecological adaptations of human groups to their diverse environments. The second theme concerns the compatibility of traditional wisdom with some current ecological approaches to resource management, specifically Adaptive Management. The chapter begins with examples of resource management from tropical forest ecosystems, and then moves to semi-arid lands, uses of fire, island ecosystems, and coastal lagoons and wetlands.

Tropical Forests: Not Amenable to Management?

Until the 1970s, our conventional view of tropical forests, as summarized by Lugo (1995), was that they were biological museums in which a vast inventory of biodiversity had accumulated in part due to the absence of ecological disturbance. Tropical ecosystems were thought to be both stable over time and "mature"; ecosystem complexity was believed to be related to stability, in turn a function of maturity. Tropical forests were thought to be fragile and not amenable to management because they were adapted to constant (or stable) conditions and ill-adapted to withstand the unpredictable effects of human activity and resource exploitation.

By the late 1970s, many ecologists had abandoned the idea that ecosystem complexity and stability were necessarily related. Moreover, the concept of stability was seen to be problematic because it was used to mean several different things. Holling (1973) proposed instead the concept of ecosystem *resilience* as the ability of a system to absorb change and still persist. The use of this concept has proved useful in many areas, and has been expanded to deal with integrated systems of humans and nature (Gunderson and Holling 2002; Berkes *et al.* 2003; Chapin *et al.* 2009). Lugo (1995) suggested that the key to managing the tropical rain forest is to focus on its resilience, rather than on its supposed fragility and unmanageability.

What is the evidence for the resilience of tropical ecosystems? At the theoretical level, ecologists are increasingly recognizing the importance of natural disturbances in maintaining tropical forest ecology (Denslow 1987). At the empirical level, there is an accumulation of evidence that forests once believed to be primary are in fact the products of human disturbance and management dating back perhaps millennia (Sanford *et al.* 1985; Gómez-Pompa and Kaus 1992a). These findings stimulated research on local traditional systems, not only in the Amazon but also in other tropical forest areas. A number of traditional systems used in the tropics illustrate how human use and disturbance can be made compatible with sustainability. Shifting cultivation or swidden systems are common in all tropical areas of the world—the Amazon, parts of Africa, South and Southeast Asia, and New Guinea (De Schlippe 1956; Spencer 1966; Redford and Padoch 1992; Brookfield and Padoch 1994; Ramakrishnan 2007). Swiddening involves the clearing, planting, harvesting, and fallowing of small areas over a multi-year cycle. Shifting cultivation, sometimes pejoratively called slash-and-burn, has received much attention as one of the major degradative processes in tropical forest areas when population pressures increase and rotation time is shortened. When that happens, land degradation may occur and biodiversity may be reduced as a result of repeated intervention in the regeneration process (Ramakrishnan *et al.* 2006).

However, many environmentalists have confused indigenous shifting cultivation that is properly carried out, with slash-and-burn as practiced by outsiders for short-term gains, inadvertently exaggerating the role of local people in tropical deforestation (Dove 1993). "Slash-and-burn agriculture accounts for only 30 percent of tropical deforestation in Latin America. . . . Slash-and-burn agriculture by colonists (under government incentives to clear the land) is different from the shifting agriculture practiced over millennia by the indigenous inhabitants" (Gómez-Pompa and Kaus 1992b). Likewise, Brookfield and Padoch (1994) state, "wholesale burning of the Amazon rainforest by settlers has helped stigmatize all burning, including that practiced sustainably by indigenous peoples."

Studies elsewhere also show that traditional shifting cultivation is not a part of the problem of tropical deforestation but rather part of the solution. Ramakrishnan (1992) describes multi-species systems of four to over 35 crop types, based on locally adapted native varieties, in the tribal areas of northeastern India. The indigenous system (locally termed *jhum*) requires sophisticated local ecological knowledge. The farmers optimize the use of soil nutrients by appropriate changes in the crop mixture depending on the length of the *jhum* cycle and the consequent high/low soil nutrient levels. On hill slopes, farmers combine r-strategist species (prolific cereals and legumes) with K-strategists with emphasis on vegetative growth, such as leafy vegetables. The aim is to maximize production from the site by mixing these two kinds of species with different reproductive strategies, in imitation of the early stages of plant succession in these forests (Ramakrishnan 1992).

Shifting agriculturalists studied by Ramakrishnan (1992) seem to have an intuitive understanding of the ecological requirements of two groups of plants that biologists call C-3 and C-4 species. The soil on steep hill slopes is highly hetero-geneous and the availability of nitrogen uncertain. The C-4 species with high nutrient-use efficiency could grow well in nutrient-poor microsites, whereas C-3 species with low nutrient-use efficiency are suited to nutrient-rich microsites: "Such a C-3/C-4 strategy helps in coexistence of species through mutual avoid-ance. The positioning of the C-3 and C-4 crop species under *jhum* in northeastern India imitates the local natural communities, with the more nutrient-use efficient species being located in the nutrient-poor upper parts of the slope and less effi-cient species situated at the base of the slope" (Ramakrishnan 1992: 381).

Some earlier work found that shifting cultivation conserves ecological processes but, in general, swiddens did not compare in complexity to the surrounding forest. However, when shifting cultivation was analyzed as an *agro-forestry system* and the use of trees was also taken into account, then the overall results of managing forest patches were conservative of biodiversity as well. Such are the findings of Alcorn (1984) with Huastec agroforestry in eastcentral Mexico, Posey (1985) with the Kayapo who create "forest islands" at the edge of the Amazon rain forest (the forest–savanna ecotone), and Irvine (1989) who found that the succession management of the Runa of the Ecuadoran Amazon actually enhanced forest biodiversity. The mechanism of biodiversity enhancement was shown in Figure 2.1 in Chapter 2.

In effect, many of these indigenous systems manage forest succession, as illustrated by the work of Denevan *et al.* (1984) with the Bora of Peru. The inves-tigators selected fields of different ages to examine vegetation changes in the staged process of abandonment and fallow. The Bora planted a wide variety of crops, the main staple being manioc (a starchy root crop) of which they recog-nized some 22 varieties. Peanuts, another major crop, were grown in second- or third-year fields. The three-year-old field contained at least 20 crop varieties, including fruit trees that were still young. The five-year-old field, with maturing fruit trees, looked more like an orchard than a field, with crops such as manioc almost phased out. The nine-year-old field consisted mainly of bushes and a 10- to 15-meter-tall secondary growth; coca was the most valuable crop. The oldest field studied, a 19-year-old fallow, contained some 22 useful tree species for edible fruit, medicines, construction wood, and other materials. Denevan *et al.* (1984) found that the most productive fallow stage was at 4 to 12 years. Before that, the fruit trees had limited production; after that, many of the useful species had been shaded out. Harvesting of some species continued, however, for 20 to 30 or more years.

Similar forest succession management systems are found in other parts of Latin America as well. Figure 4.1 shows a *hubche*, the traditional shifting cultiva-tion system of the Yucatec Maya in Mexico. Barrera-Bassols and Toledo (2005)

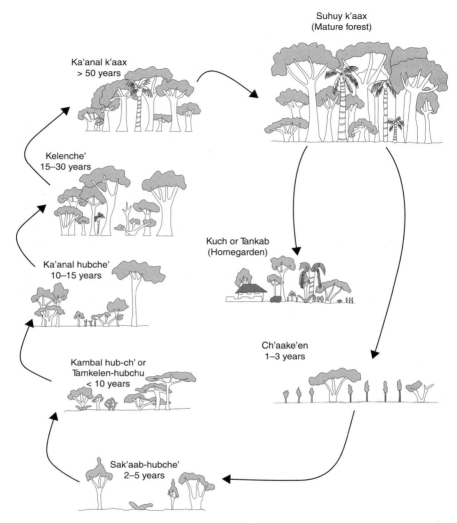

Figure 4.1 The Yucatec Maya of Mexico use ecological succession principles for the multiple-use of tropical forest resources.

Source: Adapted from Barrera-Bassols and Toledo (2005).

characterize *hubche* as a multiple-use system for tropical forests because of the different products and uses at different stages. The Yucatec Maya have a detailed repertory of terms for ecological succession processes. There are at least six terms that characterize each forest renewal stage. They identify soil–relief–vegetation relationships, and use numerous key-plant species as ecological indicators of productive practices and soil fertility (Barrera-Bassols and Toledo 2005).

One of the reasons why such good examples of shifting cultivation come from Latin America is that it is a region that is relatively less densely populated than, for example, South and Southeast Asia. In these more densely populated areas of the tropics one finds more intensive management systems—systems in which the fallow stage has been shortened or bypassed. For example, two of the most common traditional agroforestry systems in West Java, Indonesia, are *kebun-talun* (rotation between mixed garden and tree plantation) and *pekarangan* (home garden intercropping system) (Christianty *et al.* 1986). *Kebun-talun* is a system that increases overall productivity and serves multiple functions by sequentially combining agricultural crops with tree crops. The system consists of three stages, each serving a different function. The first stage is *kebun*, a planting of a mixture of annual crops, mainly for the market. After two years, *kebun* evolves into *kebun campuran*, a transition stage in which annuals are mixed with half-grown perennials. When the harvesting of annuals is completed, the field is usually abandoned for two or three years and becomes dominated by perennials (*talun* stage) before the cycle starts all over again (see Figure 4.2). However, even a short fallow has become difficult to maintain, as Java has turned, due to population increase, into one continuous urban concentration.

Even better adapted for higher population densities and found in various parts of the world is the home garden, a multi-species plantation around a house that may include food crops, medicinal plants, bushes, and fruit trees. They are found in various parts of Central and South America, for example, in Costa Rica. The Yucatec Maya home garden (*kuch*) may have 250 to 350 plant species (Barrera-Bassols and Toledo 2005). Home gardens may be found in many countries of the world, especially in South and Southeast Asia, Latin America and Africa (Eyzaguirre and Linares 2004). The Javanese version of home garden (*pekarangan*) consists of a mixture of annual and perennial crops grown on land surrounding a house. A *kebun-talun* may be converted to a home garden by building a house on it. Instead of clearing the trees to plant field crops as in *kebun-talun*, some of the home garden trees are usually kept as a permanent source of shade for the house and the garden. Field crops are planted continuously under the trees. There is no rotation but year-round harvest at irregular intervals. Plant species diversity is higher than in *kebun-talun* and may often be in the hundreds. As well, animals are always an integral part of the home garden. *Pekarangan* may look chaotic, but it makes full use of available space and diversity of resources (see Figure 4.3). Both of these above-mentioned systems retain some of the essential elements of the original tropical forest ecosystem, such as relatively high biodiversity. It is also possible in some instances to convert a tropical forest ecosystem into a completely different system of production, such as an irrigated rice system, but that is another story (see Chapter 11).

Figure 4.2 Successional stages of the *kebun-talun* system, West Java, Indonesia.
Source: Modified from Christianty *et al.* (1986).

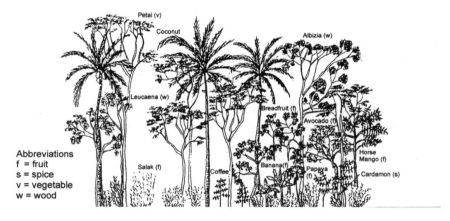

Figure 4.3 A representative home garden (*pekarangan*), West Java, Indonesia.
Source: Modified from Christianty *et al.* (1986).

Semi-arid Areas: Keeping the Land Productive

Much of the traditional ecological knowledge literature on arid and semi-arid lands concentrates on soil and water conservation techniques in agriculture (e.g. Bocco 1991; Pawluk *et al.* 1992; Reij *et al.* 1996; Tiki *et al.* 2011). An example is provided in Box 4.1. The material selected here instead considers how traditional management systems can directly alter the habitat and increase the productivity of the environment. This section describes one kind of active intervention: the establishment of forests at the edge of semi-arid lands. The next section describes another: the use of fire for habitat management in semi-arid (as well as other) environments.

**Box 4.1 Water Harvesting in Semi-arid Environments:
The Zuni**

"In many cases, soil and water conservation is the principle underlying indigenous farming methods. A common technique used by
traditional peoples from Mesoamerica to the Sahel includes the use of
weirs, dams, or terrace walls to slow runoff and foster the deposition
of upland sediments. In this way, eroded slopes are rehabilitated as
topsoil builds up behind structures. . . .

"Native Americans in the southwestern United States have
farmed successfully in a precarious arid and semiarid enviornment for
over a millennium. Some of the methods used by the Zuni include the
careful placement of fields on alluvial fans, complex manipulation of
runoff, and management of gully formation. It appears that harvesting
water and sediment from drainages has allowed the Zuni to favorably
influence soil moisture, nutrient status, and texture of soils within
their fields."

Source: Pawluk *et al.* 1992: 300.

Adaptations of herders (pastoralists) to their semi-arid environment have long
fascinated human ecologists (Behnke *et al.* 1993; Scoones 1999; Robinson and
Berkes 2010). A striking example of traditional ecological knowledge systems
helping forest growth in semi-arid lands comes from northwestern Kenya. For
over half a century, African pastoralists and their livestock have been blamed for
over-grazing and desertification. The assumption of negative pastoralist impact on
rangelands continues to shape resource management policy (Niamir-Fuller 1998).
It is true that cattle concentrations near villages and towns can pose sustainability
problems, especially if cattle owners remain in one spot. Traditionally, however,
African pastoral systems were characterized by large-scale movements and the
rotation of grazing areas. The large-scale movements of pastoralists and their
cattle mimicked the migrations of wild ungulates. Like wild herbivores, domestic
herds followed the annual cycle of rainfall and new grass growth, moving to
seasonally productive lands to take advantage of the new growth of high-protein
grasses, followed by a return migration after the food supply was exhausted.

Smaller-scale movements (micro-mobility) and the rotation of grazing lands
were also important for sustainability (Niamir 1990). Carrying capacity and
stocking rate calculations, both equilibrium-based concepts of primary importance to Western range managers, were of no meaning in the Sahel, where rainfall
varied unpredictably from year to year as well as from season to season. Instead,

traditional herders had rules that tracked ecological conditions of the range and controlled micro-mobility, resulting in the flexible and adaptive management of the actual stocking rate. These rules acted through four main variables: the length of grazing on a patch by a herd; the frequency with which the same patch is visited; rotation time (rest interval) between each visit; and the distance between grazed sites (Niamir-Fuller 1998). The formulation of simple rules-of-thumb based on key variables is typical of traditional knowledge systems for dealing with complexity, a theme that is developed further in Chapter 9.

The Ngisonyoka Turkana of Kenya are nomadic pastoralists, still engaged in a relatively traditional lifestyle at the time of the study by Reid and Ellis (1995). They kept their sheep, goats, and camels in circular enclosures, moving them with the seasons, about once a month on the average. The researchers had observed that seedlings of *Acacia tortilis*, the dominant tree species in the dry woodlands of the region, often appeared during the first rainy season after pastoralists abandoned their corrals. The entire area of the old corrals was often covered with dense circular patches of seedlings and young trees, corresponding to cycles of movement (Reid and Ellis 1995).

Acacia seedpods made up an important part of livestock diets. The goats and sheep digested many of the seeds they ate. Some, however, were not digested but were scarified. These germinated at higher rates than did non-ingested seeds. The researchers compared *Acacia* growth in abandoned corrals with that in control plots and found that seed density was 85 times higher in corrals than in controls. Corral soils were enriched with organic matter (ninefold higher carbon than controls), nitrogen (threefold), and phosphorus (sixfold), and they retained more moisture. Successful germination and survival of *Acacia* in non-corral sites were restricted to the occasional year with high rainfall, but *Acacia* in corral sites found a highly favorable microhabitat—the abandoned corral provided an environment in which seeds ready to germinate were deposited in nutrient- and moisture-rich patches of dung and soil.

The memory of Turkana herders for both location and time is excellent. Using "Turkana event calendars" previously developed by anthropologists, Reid and Ellis (1995) relied on local traditional knowledge to age *Acacia* stands, and they considered this technique more reliable than tree-ring counts. Using this approach, they were able to reconstruct the history of development of 14 *Acacia* forest patches in the area, ranging in age from 1 to 39 years.

"Contrary to conventional wisdom," Reid and Ellis (1995: 978) point out, "pastorals may be improving rangelands in South Turkana by enhancing recruitment reliability in this important tree species." The Turkana case is probably not an exception. Similar pastoralist–livestock–*Acacia* interactions may be found in South Ethiopia and South Kenya. A similar mechanism may explain the presence of

Acacia stands in nutrient-enriched patches in the middle of nutrient-poor savanna in South Africa near Iron Age Tswana settlements. "If so," Reid and Ellis (1995: 990) conclude, "this suggests that livestock may have affected tree recruitment in some African environments, not just for the past few decades, but for hundreds of years."

Traditional practices help create forest islands in some semi-arid areas of South America as well (Posey 1985). In the savanna landscape at the southern fringe of the Amazon, the Kayapo people plant small mounds of useful plants. They tend these mounds casually and add to them over time, planting and harvesting a succession of plants from annuals eventually to trees, in some ways similar to the management of swidden plots. A newly planted mound, *apete*, peaks in crop production in about three years; sweet potatoes continue for five years, yams and taro for six, and papaya and banana for longer. Old *apete* are not abandoned but continue to be managed for fruit and nut trees and other products. The resulting forest islands are difficult to identify as human-made (see Box 4.2).

Conclusions from the Kayapo case apply to savanna–tropical forest ecotone areas in other parts of the world. Fairhead and Leach (1996) argue that the mixed forest savanna is the outcome of forest expansion into the savanna, resulting from the deliberate management of the soil, trees, and fire by peasant farmers of West Africa. The farmers' oral history indicates that the increase in forest area is due to their management interventions; time-series aerial photo comparisons support farmers' oral history. As Posey's experience illustrates emphatically, such landscape changes are difficult to see and interpret, even for an observer prepared for the subtleties of traditional management systems. The next section describes another kind of intervention, the use of fire for habitat management, which is also difficult for a Western observer to understand at first glance.

Traditional Uses of Fire

Fire has been used by traditional peoples, not only by horticulturalists but also by hunter-gatherers, for habitat management in a variety of geographic areas (Turner 1994; Barsh 1997; Kimmerer and Lake 2001; Bird *et al.* 2005, 2008; Miller and Davidson-Hunt 2010; S. McGregor *et al.* 2010). Such use of fire, along with other kinds of habitat modification (Sayles and Mulrennan 2010; Bhagwat *et al.* 2011) have resulted in cultural landscapes. Many of these cultural landscapes were "invisible" to researchers. For a long time conventional wisdom held that hunter-gatherers did not modify their habitat, much less use fire to do it. There was a romanticized belief, as Lewis (1993b: 395) put it, "that 'primitive people' live, or at least once lived, in some undefined condition of 'harmony with nature,' engaged in environmentally benign ways of exploiting resources which either could not or would not have allowed people to alter 'what nature provides.' "

Box 4.2 The Kayapo of Brazil: Managers of the Forest Edge

The Kayapo Indians of central Brazil live in the watershed of the Xingu River, which is near the southern limit of the tropical forests of Amazonia and includes *terra firme* and gallery forests interspersed with areas of more or less open *cerrado* (similar to savanna). Their knowledge, management, and use of the floral and faunal resources of the forests in their territory are astonishingly subtle and complex. It is unlikely that the Kayapo are unique—they are simply, and by far, the best-studied of the many Indian groups of Amazonia.

> Like almost all the Indian groups in Amazonia, the Kayapo hunt, fish, and gather a great many species of the fauna and flora of the forests and practice shifting cultivation. They also concentrate native plants by growing them in resource islands, forest fields, forest openings, tuber gardens, agricultural plots, and old fields, and beside their trails through the forest. . . . Forest patches (apete) are created from open *cerrado* in areas prepared with crumbled termite and ant nests and mulch . . . .
>
> Perhaps the most surprising and significant of their many resource management techniques is the creation of the *apete* forest patches. Posey became aware that these isolated patches of forest were man-made only in the seventh year of his research among the Kayapo. As he pointed out, "Perhaps the most exciting aspect of these new data is the implication for reforestation. The Indian example not only provides new ideas about how to build forests from scratch, but also how to successfully manage what has been considered to be infertile *campo/cerrado*."

Source: Taylor 1988, in reference to Posey 1985.

In reality, there is extensive literature from Asia, Australia, Africa, and the Americas on the traditional uses of fire for preparation of garden patches, agroforestry systems, habitat management for semi-domesticated species (such as berries and root crops), and rangeland or grazing habitat management. Table 4.1 provides a sampling of such systems from the Americas. Care should be taken not to

Table 4.1 Examples of the use of fire for succession management in the Americas

Society/area	Description
Bora, Peru Amazon	Multi-stage, multi-crop tropical shifting cultivation system (Denevan *et al*. 1984)
Ralamuli, Northern Mexico	Kumerachi: oak-pine forest burning for patches of corn and beans (Davidson-Hunt in Berkes and Davidson-Hunt 2006)
California, United States	Chaparral burning to open up corridors and fire yards, renew vegetation for wildlife, prepare areas for planting (Lewis 1973)
Northern interior British Columbia, Canada	Burning of patches to maintain production of berries, mainly mountain huckleberry and lowbush blueberry (Johnson 1999)
Southern coastal British Columbia, Canada	Burning of garry oak savannah landscape to prepare habitat for root crops, mainly camas (Turner 1999)
Northern Alberta, Canada	Boreal forest burning to produce yards, corridors, mosaics, and habitat attractive for wildlife (Lewis and Ferguson 1988)
Alaska, United States	Gwich's in burning to clear underbrush, travel lanes; stimulate growth of new grass (Natcher *et al*. 2007)
Northwest Ontario, Canada	Anishinaabe boreal forest burning for berry production and small-scale cultivation (Davidson-Hunt 2003)

assume that fire was universally used. For example, Natcher *et al.* (2007) have shown that the Gwich'in used fire but their immediate neighbors to the west, the Koyukon, did not. All of the systems in Table 4.1 are based on succession management, similar, for example, to those in the India (Ramakrishnan 1992) and Mexico (Barrera-Bassols and Toledo 2005) cases in the earlier section on tropical forests and shifting cultivation.

Figure 4.4 shows the details of the last example given in Table 4.1. The Anishinaabe (Ojibwa) people of northwestern Ontario used to burn the boreal forest selectively for berry production and small-scale gardening, depending on soil conditions. The cycle starts with the forest (*nopoming*). A recently burned site could become a vegetable garden or a blueberry area. On sandy or rocky sites that cannot be used for gardening, a blueberry heath would develop three to five years after a burn. This blueberry patch could be renewed by burning it every two years or so, or the area would revert back to forest by succession. Logging disturbance provides a cycle similar to burning (lower panel of Figure 4.4). With the prohibition on burning since the 1950s, the Anishinaabe tend to rely on clearcut logging carried out by forestry companies, to provide the needed disturbance to start succession leading to berry production (Davidson-Hunt 2003; Berkes and Davidson-Hunt 2006).

Some of the best descriptions of fire management come from California. There have been many fragmentary anthropological references to the use of fire by

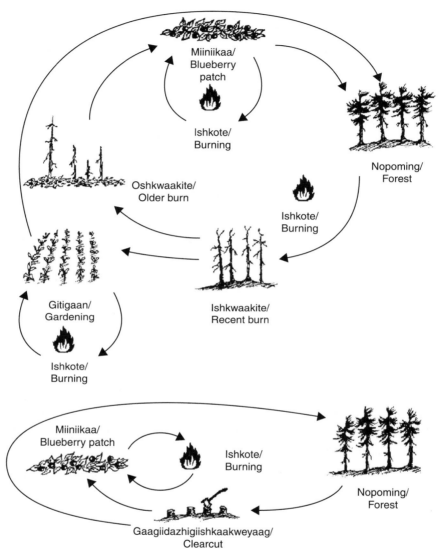

Figure 4.4 An Anishinaabe perception of forest succession following disturbance. The top cycle refers to fire as disturbance. The bottom cycle refers to forestry clearcuts as disturbance.

Source: Modified from Davidson-Hunt in Berkes and Davidson-Hunt (2006).

the aboriginal people of California, but the systematic study of the evidence did not start until the 1960s (Lewis 1973). Lewis was a young student when he first saw the effects of fire in a chaparral-dominated area and became receptive to the idea that fire may be used to make the environment more productive (see Box 4.3).

Box 4.3 Rediscovering the Wisdom of Chaparral Burning in California

Lewis writes that in 1960 he was involved "in the essentially futile effort of trying to stop a large, extremely intense brush fire in Sequoia Park, a fire which was only extinguished when it ran out of fuel along the crest of a mountain ridge. Ignited near the bottom of a canyon, ten thousand acres of dense chaparral erupted in what was described as a 'fire storm,' in an area which had not been burned for 70 or more years."

As a part of their efforts to contain the conflagration, a firebreak was cut from two directions across a drainage. Very near to where the fire lines were linked, Lewis and colleagues stumbled upon a long-abandoned Indian campsite that was probably used by the Western Mono in the trans-Sierran trade of obsidian and salt. All indications were that it had been regularly used over a long period of time; but in 1960, it was almost completely overgrown by dense brush and a large number of oaks, which were undoubtedly a source of acorns. The site was just a few yards from a ravine that, except for spring runoff, was apparently dry for most of the year.

Given the fact that the "natural growth" in the burn area consisted of an impenetrable thicket of chaparral, Lewis was puzzled: what made it a desirable campsite for the aboriginals? With instructions to get out as quickly as possible, he did not give much further thought to the question of the site's unlikely location, until a year later when he revisited the area to locate it for the park historian.

"Twelve months after what had been described in the newspapers as the 'total destruction' of brush and trees," Lewis writes, "a new and profuse growth of grasses, herbs, and sprouts of various chaparral species had emerged from the ashes. Most impressive was the number of deer observed browsing and grazing on the burn site. . . . At the same time—and during the same month as that of the previous summer—water was still running in the ravine, and the 'unlikely place' for a campsite offered views up and down the drainage. It was at this point that I began asking myself serious questions about why Indians would have set fires in chaparral stands—and, conversely, why we did not."

Source: Lewis 1993b: 390, 391.

Indeed, until the late 1880s, Kumeyaay bands of Southern California cultivated a kind of grain, since extinct, by harvesting, burning the stubble, and broadcasting seeds (Shipek 1993). Broadcast with the grain were seeds of leafy vegetables and other annuals; this produced an interplanted field not recognized by Europeans accustomed to plough-cleared monocultures. On steeper slopes, the Kumeyaay planted shrubs that produced food and medicine and broadcast seeds of annuals and perennials following controlled burns. Below-ground parts of chaparral survived the burning and resprouted. As the chaparral vegetation increased in size, the grains disappeared first, followed gradually by the other annuals and perennials. It was then considered time to reburn the slope (Shipek 1993).

Fire management was used for different purposes in different areas, but Lewis's cross-cultural comparative studies show that there are remarkable similarities as well. These similarities occur through functionally parallel strategies employed by hunter-gatherers to maintain "fire yards" and "fire corridors" in northwest California, western Washington, northwestern Alberta (Canada), Tasmania, New South Wales, western Australia, and Australia's Northern Territory (Lewis and Ferguson 1988). Thus, traditional knowledge lends support to fire ecologists and advocates of prescribed burning who emphasize the role of fire in the renewal cycle of ecosystems and who have successfully challenged the official dogma that all fires should be suppressed.

However, this is not to say that fire ecologists are necessarily comfortable with traditional practices. For example, in the Kakadu National Park, Australia's Northern Territory, where both sides agree that fire is a natural feature of ecosystems and a key to maintaining habitat diversity, great differences in opinion separate park managers from Aboriginal people. The managers want "controlled burns," planned in advance and based on the calendar and scientific criteria, and they believe that "fire is basically bad but *can be used* to good purpose," whereas the Aboriginal people's notions of the need to burn rest on many rules of thumb and a basic belief that "fire is good and *must be used*" (Lewis 1989).

Is there an element of wisdom in this belief in the good of burning? Careful studies by Australian researchers have shown that indigenous burning may lead to an increase in both plant and animal species richness (Bird *et al.* 2008). Indigenous burning in Australia's Western desert for small game hunting results in the formation of small-scale mosaics that maximize habitat diversity. In the absence of indigenous burning, these fine-grained mosaics dissolve, leading to a decrease in biodiversity at the local scale, and specifically to a loss of some of the small game species. As shown by satellite image analysis, these fire-mediated cultural landscapes contain a greater diversity of successional stages than landscapes under a natural (lightning) fire regime, similar to that shown earlier in Figure 2.1.

Lightning fires are hotter and burn larger patches; they result in a landscape that looks distinctly different in satellite images (Bird *et al.* 2008).

Island Ecosystems—Personal Ecosystems

It is said that island peoples see the limitations of their environment more readily than do those who live on continents. Thus, it is probably not a coincidence that the Asia-Pacific region is particularly rich in traditional knowledge and management systems, and many of these have been documented in detail, especially from Japan and parts of Oceania, that is, Melanesia, Micronesia, and Polynesia (Klee 1980; Johannes 1981; Ruddle and Akimichi 1984; Ruddle and Johannes 1985, 1990; Freeman *et al.* 1991).

The most widespread single marine conservation measure employed in Oceania was reef and lagoon tenure. The basic idea behind reef and lagoon tenure has to do with self-interest. The right to harvest the resources of a particular area was controlled by a social group, such as a family or clan (or a chief acting on behalf of the group), which thus regulated the exploitation of its own marine resources. As Johannes *et al.* (2000: 267) explained, "it was in the best interest of those who controlled a given area to harvest in moderation. By doing so they could maintain high sustained yields, all the benefits of which would accrue directly to them." A wide range of traditional regulations and restrictions applied to resource use. Some of these could be attributed to religious or superstitious beliefs (Johannes 1978) and some to power relationships in general (Chapman 1985) and regional differences in systems of political authority (Chapman 1987). But, by and large, reef and lagoon tenure rules operated as institutions for the management of inshore commons.

Some authors think that various cultural beliefs and rituals inadvertently served to conserve resources. For example, Polunin (1984: 267) argues that "exclusive areas became established not because people wished to conserve resources, but rather because they tended to exploit more and eventually came up against neighboring people doing the same sorts of things." Johannes (1978: 352), however, holds that many restrictions were clearly intended to conserve shellfish and fish: "almost every basic fisheries conservation measure devised in the West was in use in the tropical Pacific centuries ago." Table 4.2 lists some examples. Many of these locally devised regulations no longer exist, and reef and lagoon tenure systems themselves have been degraded through various episodes of colonization. However, they are being revitalized in some of the Pacific island nation states (Baines 1989; Ruddle 1994b; Johannes 2002a).

Environmental management in the Pacific goes beyond fisheries regulations. Chapter 3 pointed out that ancient conceptualizations of ecosystems exist in

Table 4.2 Traditional marine conservation measures of tropical Pacific islanders

Method or regulation	Examples
Closed fishing areas	Pukapuka; Marquesas; Truk; Tahiti; Satswal
Closed seasons	Hawaii; Tahiti; Palau; Tonga; Tokelaus
Allowing a portion of the catch to escape	Tonga; Micronesia; Hawaii; Enewetak
Holding excess catch in enclosures	Pukapuka; Tuamotus; Marshall Islands; Palau
Ban on taking small individuals	Pukapuka (crabs); Palau (giant clams)
Restricting some fisheries for emergency	Nauru; Palau; Gilbert Islands; Pukapuka
Restricting harvest of seabirds and/or eggs	Tobi; Pukapuka; Enewetak
Restricting number of fish traps	Woleai
Ban on taking nesting turtles and/or eggs	Tobi; New Hebrides; Gilbert Islands
Ban on disturbing turtle nesting habitat	Samoa

Source: Adapted and summarized from Johannes (1978).

several Amerindian, European, and Asian cultures, especially as watershed-based units (see Table 3.3). It appears that the richest set of examples was found in Oceania. Examples include the ancient Hawaiian *ahupua'a* (Lind 1938; Costa-Pierce 1987; Kaneshiro *et al.* 2005), wedge-shaped land units granted by the king to lesser chiefs, the *konohiki*. They encompassed entire valleys and stretched from the top of mountains to the coast and shallow waters. Figure 4.5 shows an idealized *ahupua'a*, with a forested mountain zone (functioning as a watershed conservation area protected by taboo), integrated farming zones in upland and coastal areas, a fringe of coconut palms along the coastline (storm and wind protection), and brackish water and seawater fish ponds (Costa-Pierce 1987). Such land use would be called integrated watershed planning in the contemporary terminology, and the land unit in question is clearly an ecosystem unit, with its biophysical boundaries. The Hawaiian *ahupua'a* disappeared with colonization, but made a comeback in the 1990s. Similar systems exist in other Pacific islands and some are considered functional.

The variations of the Hawaiian system may be found in the Yap *tabinau*, the Fijian *vanua*, and the Solomon Islands *puava* (Ruddle *et al.* 1992; Hviding 2006). In each, the term refers to an intimate association of a group of people with land, reef, and lagoon, and all that grows on or in them. This "integrated corporate estate" concept is effectively the "personal ecosystem" of the group in question: "*puava* is a defined, named area of land and, in most cases, sea. A *puava* in the widest sense includes all areas and resources associated with a *butubutu* (descent group) through ancestral rights, from the top of the mainland mountains to the open sea outside the barrier reef" (Hviding 1990: 23).

Photo 4.1 A Hawaiian *ahupua'a*, showing integrated farming in an upland zone, with terraces. Lava flows constitute the border of the *ahupua'a*. Forest cover in the upper reaches is commonly protected by taboo.

Photo: Carl Folke.

The Fijian *vanua* is conceptualized in similar terms (Ravuvu 1987; Ruddle 1994b). *Vanua* describes the totality of a Fijian community. Depending on the context, it may be used to refer either to a social group (*vanua* = tribe, descent group, lineage) or the territory it occupies (*vanua* = tribal estate), thereby expressing the inseparability of land and people in the Fijian ethos. Fijian spiritual affinity with land is illustrated in expressions such as *ne qau vanua* ("the land which supports me and to which I belong"), and *na vanua na tamatu* ("the people are the land") (Ravuvu 1987; Ruddle 1994b). Watershed-based descent groups are also found among the Maori, who are closely related to other Polynesian groups.

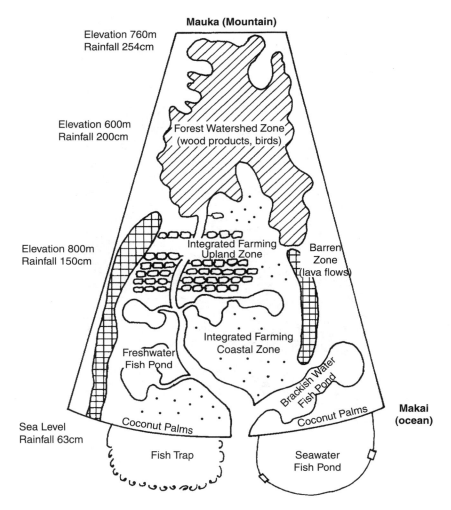

Figure 4.5 The *ahupua'a* system of ancient Hawaii.
Source: Modified from Costa-Pierce (1987).

One important and interesting feature of these ecosystem concepts, as pointed out by a number of researchers (e.g. Ruddle *et al.* 1992), is that land and sea space exist as a continuum, and that indigenous categories do not dichotomize resources into "ownable land" and "unownable sea" as Westerners do. Using the example of Roviana lagoon, New Georgia, in the Solomon Islands, Aswani (1997) challenges this view. He pointed out that the territorial unit (*pepeso*) is conceptually a single property domain that extends from the top of the mountains to the midpoint between South New Georgia and the next island. However, the people make a clear economic distinction between land and sea. Most significantly, Aswani (1997) argues, the sea cannot be claimed through its physical modification as can land. For example, the establishment of a small coconut plantation can be used as the pretext for privatizing land, but the sea remains an "untamed" domain in which communal tenure and access rules are strongly guarded by the chiefs. Examples such as these illustrate the difficulty in making geographical generalizations, and the difficulty in assessing the extent to which traditional systems are shaped by contemporary economic pressures.

Economic pressures influence not only the performance of traditional management systems but also the ethics of management. Johannes, who has extensive experience with traditional management systems in the Pacific, has been intrigued by the fact that some Pacific island peoples clearly possess a traditional conservation ethic, whereas other traditional peoples do not (Johannes and MacFarlane 1991; Johannes 1994). A group of people is said to possess a traditional conservation ethic if they have an "awareness that they can deplete or otherwise damage their natural resources, coupled with a commitment to reduce or eliminate the problem" (Johannes 1994: 85).

Among the people of the Torres Strait area between New Guinea and Australia, which has an abundance of marine resources, a traditional conservation ethic is lacking, according to Johannes and MacFarlane (1991). This contrasts with an often well-developed conservation ethic among people who live on the smaller Pacific islands such as Palau (Johannes 1981 and personal communication). Johannes has not attempted to provide a conclusive answer to this paradox, and some of his conclusions regarding the Torres Strait area have been contested (Kwan 2005). It seems possible that some of the differences may be related to the fact that people of small islands receive faster and clearer feedback on their resource exploitation strategies than do others, and these feedbacks increase their ability to learn and to revise not only their management systems but also their environmental ethics and worldviews. This point is revisited in Chapters 6 and 11 as part of the discussion of social learning and conservation.

Coastal Lagoons and Wetlands

One of the first international organizations to express interest in traditional management systems was UNESCO. In 1982, through its Division of Marine Sciences, UNESCO asked the International Association of Biological Oceanography to help organize a steering group to initiate work in this area. The group organized in 1983 at the UNESCO headquarters in Paris and quickly issued a report (Johannes *et al.* 1983) describing a range of traditional coastal management systems from around the world, pointing out the variations and similarities in the methods devised by peoples of very different areas and cultures. Their examples included:

- the *valli* (or *vallicoltura*) of the Venice region, Adriatic Sea, starting in the fifteenth to sixteenth centuries, designed so that young fish enter the pools with the tide but cannot get out; continued today as complex systems of dikes, gates and ponds;
- the *cherfia* of North Africa, installed at the mouth of lagoons, with openings equipped with concave basketwork that admits fish but prevents large fish from escaping, similar to the *lavoriero* of the Italian coast;
- the *acadja* of West Africa, which combines fishing with fish farming, and consists of immersing piles of branches in the shallow parts of the lagoon (serving to increase fish habitat);
- the Indonesian *tambak*, brackish water (mixed freshwater and seawater) fish ponds, dating back to the fifteenth century, usually installed in deltas and associated lagoons; and
- in freshwater areas, rice-fish (or rice-field) systems in their many variations, such as the Indonesian *minepadi* and *surjan* systems.

The above examples should be considered only a small sample of such systems. In fact, *cherfia* and *lavoriero* type of systems are also found in Greece and Turkey (Berkes 1992); *acadja*-like brush-pile fisheries are found in Bangladesh and Sri Lanka (Amarasinghe *et al.* 1997); and various kinds of rice-fish systems are found in India, Bangladesh, the Philippines, Vietnam, Laos, Cambodia, and China as well.

Some of these systems furnish excellent examples of the application of prescientific ecosystem views. One relevant example is from Indonesia, where traditional systems combined rice and fish culture, and nutrient-rich wastes from the rice-field fishery system often flowed downstream into brackish water aquaculture systems (*tambak*) and then into the coastal area enriching the coastal fishery (Costa-Pierce 1988). The *tambaks* themselves were polyculture ponds, often combining fish, vegetables, and tree crops (Figure 4.6).

Indonesia has many kinds of rice-fish and water management systems. Some of the more sophisticated kinds, such as the *subak* system in Bali for the management of irrigation water resources, were managed not locally but regionally. The *subak* was part of a water temple system, and the entire regional rice terrace irrigation was often managed as a system by resource manager-priests (Lansing 1987, 1991). The integration of rice-field fishery and *tambak* systems for combined production of rice, fish, and downstream products is an ecologically sophisticated application by any measure. These systems remained sustainable for several

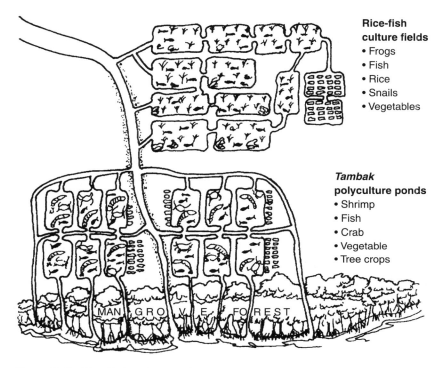

Rice-fish culture fields
- Frogs
- Fish
- Rice
- Snails
- Vegetables

Tambak polyculture ponds
- Shrimp
- Fish
- Crab
- Vegetable
- Tree crops

Figure 4.6 Traditional Indonesian coastal zone management.
Source: Modified from Costa-Pierce (1988).

centuries and combined livelihood activities with good conservation practice (note the integration of mangroves into the *tambak* in Figure 4.6). But they declined with population pressures and the wholesale conversion of coastal wetlands and lagoons into modern shrimp farms for international markets.

Coastal lagoons, especially in tropical areas, are very productive environments that support a multitude of often conflicting human activities. Not surprisingly, sophisticated local governance systems and allocation rules for lagoon resources have developed in a number of different geographical regions. Amarasinghe *et al.* (1997) describe one such contemporary lagoon management system from the Negombo estuary in western Sri Lanka. The case study illustrates the sophisticated level of governance that can be achieved by traditional systems and the key role of local institutions.

Of several kinds of fishing operations carried out in the Negombo lagoon, the one known as the *kattudel* or the stake-net fishery (which uses a bag-shaped net or trapnet) targeted high-value shrimp, *Metapaneus dobsoni*, as the shrimp migrated out to the sea. At the mouth of the lagoon, there were 22 named fishing sites at which 65 nets could be used at any one time. The sites were exclusive. The traditional fishing rights to the sites went back at least to the eighteenth century (and possibly to the fifteenth century) and were controlled by members of four Rural Fisheries Societies (RFS) based in the villages around the lagoon. Elaborate rules governed eligibility and membership in the RFS, the obligations of the fishers, the system by which the four RFS cooperatives shared the resource, and the allocation rules within each RFS. There were 306 members in the *kattudel* fishery out of some 3,000 fishers using the lagoon. The members took turns at the 22 fishing sites. A lottery system was used to allocate turns (one night of fishing at a time) for the members, and the turns rotated through the 22 sites to give each fisher a chance at the better sites (Amarasinghe *et al.* 1997).

An important feature of the *kattudel* fishery is that the rules of the fishery, most recently reorganized in 1958, have legal status under Sri Lanka's *Fisheries Ordinance* as "Negombo (Kattudel) Fishing Regulations." This is significant because only through legal enforcement can the strict limits on membership, and hence the limited-access nature of the fishery, be maintained. Closing access to a commons is important for its biological and economic sustainability (Amarasinghe *et al.* 1997). In fact, other examples of stake-net fisheries for shrimp in South Asian lagoons in which access control measures work poorly have sustainability problems (Lobe and Berkes 2004; Coulthard 2011).

The *kattudel* case shows that lagoon fisheries and associated traditional management systems can be sustainable over long periods, but this does not mean that such systems are stable throughout long periods. Rather, crises often punctuate relatively uneventful times. The real test of the management system in question is whether it can adapt (or be successfully redesigned) to respond to these crises. The *kattudel* fishery in the case study has been through turbulent times, most recently in the 1940s and the 1950s, and has evidently survived various conflicts and management crises. Some other systems in the South Asia region, for example a *kattudel*-type trap-net fishery near Madras, India, have not survived the intense conflicts brought about by caste group competition, apparently in this case because traditional resource use rights were not protected by government law (Mathew 1991), as they were in the case of the Sri Lankan *kattudel* fishery.

As recognized by the UNESCO working group (Johannes *et al.* 1983), traditional coastal and lagoon fisheries around the world provide a rich set of local adaptations from which modern management systems can learn. These systems are found not only in isolated parts of the world but also in industrialized areas. Examples include "fisheries brotherhood" systems that act to regulate resource use and manage resource conflicts, the guild-like *prud'homie* system of the French Mediterranean, and the *confreries* of Catalonia, Spain (Alegret 1995). It is true

Photo 4.2 Stake-net (*kattudel*) fishery for shrimp in the Negombo lagoon and estuary, Sri Lanka. A lottery system allocates turns for the use of the fishing spots.

Photo: Upali Amarasinghe.

that many of these systems have declined over the years. On the other hand, many new systems have in the meantime evolved in various parts of the world. Examples include the lobster territory system practiced among the commercial lobster fishers of Maine in the United States (Acheson 1975), and a system of managing net fishing sites, with remarkable parallels to the Sri Lankan *kattudel* fishery with its rotation of lottery-allocated fishing rights, that evolved in the 1980s in Alanya on the Turkish Mediterranean coast (Berkes 1992).

Conclusions

The theme of development–stability–crisis–adaptation appears over and over in many types of coastal and lagoon fisheries, and no doubt in other resource types as well. The findings in a variety of traditional resource management systems are in agreement with the central thesis of a book on Adaptive Management, *Barriers and Bridges to the Renewal of Ecosystems and Institutions* (Gunderson *et al.* 1995). *Barriers and Bridges* holds that resource crises are important for the renewal of management institutions (because the crisis forces social learning by the institution), just as dynamic processes, such as disturbances, are important for the renewal of ecosystems.

The use of fire that seems to be so widespread in traditional management systems is consistent with the Adaptive Management analysis. Small-scale disturbance, including the use of fire, helps ecosystem renewal. Thus, it is ecologically more sensible to let small, frequent fires burn to clear leaf litter ("fuel load") in forests before it accumulates, than to suppress all fires—which only sets the stage for fires of disastrous proportions when they finally do occur (Holling 1986). These ideas challenge conventional resource management science with its equilibrium-centered emphasis, and will be developed further in Chapter 9 in the context of complex systems.

There is another challenge posed by traditional management systems, supported by the dynamic view of ecosystem renewal in Adaptive Management, and it pertains to the role of resource use in maintaining healthy and productive tropical ecosystems. The lesson from shifting cultivation, *kebun-talun*, and *pekarangan* systems is that it is feasible to sustain a productive multi-functional landscape and a high degree of biodiversity by maintaining a variety of uses. Low-intensity productive uses are compatible with tropical forest ecosystems, and provide for ecosystem renewal and the maintenance of the resilience of the system. The tropical forest ecosystem can absorb the perturbation of long-fallow shifting cultivation, and in fact flourishes with it. Thus, if the objective is to conserve tropical forests, a strategy of focusing on resilience, through a knowledge of regeneration cycles and ecological processes such as plant succession, may be the key to tropical forest sustainability (Holling *et al.* 1995; Lugo 1995).

Seven principles that Alcorn (1990) derived from the indigenous agroforestry strategies of the Huastec and the Bora of tropical Mexico incorporate this kind of resilience thinking. These traditional strategies:

1   take advantage of native trees and native tree communities;
2   rely on native successional processes;
3   use natural environmental variation;
4   incorporate numerous crops and native species;
5   are flexible;
6   spread risks by retaining diversity; and
7   maintain reliable backup resources to meet needs should the regular livelihood sources fail.

Strategies such as these may be of value for creating better management practices in tropical forest ecosystems. In fact, practical applications of traditional knowledge in coffee agroforestry show that it is feasible to use ancient wisdom to create resilient modern cropping systems without destroying the essence of the tropical forest (Brookfield and Padoch 1994; Ramakrishnan 2007; Bhagwat *et al.* 2008; more in Chapter 11).

Thus, Adaptive Management focusing on resilience does not require that all uses of the tropical forest be eliminated. Nor does management require a precise capability to predict quantitative yields (such as food or timber), but only a qualitative capacity to devise systems that can absorb and accommodate future events. To do so necessitates greater attention to ecosystem processes rather than to ecosystem products (McNeely 1994; Chapin *et al.* 2009). The evidence from traditional knowledge systems is that such qualitative management capacity and attention to ecological processes were in fact developed by cultural evolution in many groups and ecosystems. The intuitive ecological sense of traditional knowledge, and the rules-of-thumb that are often used, are consistent with dynamic, multi-equilibrium, ecosystem-based analyses in contemporary ecology (Gadgil *et al.* 1993; Berkes *et al.* 2000; Gunderson and Holling 2002; Berkes and Kislalioglu Berkes 2009).

However, traditional knowledge and practice are often inconsistent with conventional resource management, and many Western-trained resource management professionals take a dim view of traditional systems. For example, Leach (1994), writing about Sierra Leone, West Africa, points out that many professional foresters see any conversion of the closed-canopy forest as degradation. Yet such conversion may be viewed positively by the local people, for whom the resulting bush-fallow vegetation provides a greater range of products than does the closed-canopy forest.

Similarly, in the case of herders and semi-arid lands, resource management professionals often blame pastoralists for overgrazing and desertification (Niamir-Fuller 1998). However, the Turkana example shows that pastoralists' activities can improve the vegetation cover. More generally, Leach and Mearns (1996) argue that pastoralists' herd management and land management strategies often make the most of productive opportunities in a dryland ecosystem—an ecosystem characterized by variability and non-equilibrium conditions. These conditions preclude the application of such conventional Western resource management tools as carrying capacity analysis and animal stocking densities (Behnke *et al.* 1993). Thus, traditional pastoralists "may have long been practicing resource management attuned to non-equilibrium ecological conditions," and hence any new and more appropriate resource management in savanna ecosystems would do well to build on the traditional knowledge, skills, and institutions of Africa's herders, rather than to replace them (Leach and Mearns 1996: 29; Robinson and Berkes 2010).

This chapter dealt largely with three kinds of ecosystems: tropical forests, arid lands, and coastal areas, and the traditional management of these linked social–ecological systems. The next four chapters deal with another type of ecosystem, the Arctic and the Subarctic. This concentration will allow us to deal with the full depth of the knowledge–practice–belief complex, from local knowledge, to management systems, to their social institutions, and to worldviews. Chapter 5 starts out by providing an *emic* account of the local worldview, that is, as seen by the local people themselves. Chapter 6 is the story of one major resource, the caribou, and the institutional learning and adaptation brought about by a crisis. Chapter 7 is a detailed human ecological analysis of one resource system, the Chisasibi Cree subsistence fishery in James Bay. It is an outsider's academic interpretation, an *etic* view. Chapter 8 explores indigenous ways of knowing by detailing how an Arctic community developed its own analysis of climate change unfolding in its area. Taken together, these chapters use different approaches to illustrate some of the principles and issues introduced here in Chapter 4.

CHAPTER 5

Cree Worldview "From the Inside"

Not all cultures in the world share the dominant Western view of a secularized, utilitarian, depersonalized nature. The existence of alternative views of the natural environment is important as part of the cultural heritage of humankind. This cultural diversity is akin to biodiversity as the raw material for evolutionarily adaptive responses (Gadgil 1987; Turner and Berkes 2006). Indigenous worldviews are diverse and different from the dominant Western worldview. This chapter provides a look into the worldview of one North American aboriginal group from the eastern Canadian boreal/subarctic.

According to the beliefs of the Cree of eastern James Bay, it is the animals, not people, who control the success of the hunt, a view that has parallels in many other indigenous groups such as the Inuit (Schmidt and Dowsley 2010). Hunters have certain obligations to fulfill toward the animals, maintaining a respectful relationship. A continued, proper use of resources is important for sustainability. Cree social values such as reciprocity apply to human–animal as well as to social relationships. These beliefs indicate a cosmology in which humans are part of a "community of beings" within the ecological system.

The Cree people of Chisasibi survived three centuries of fur trade as essentially hunter-gatherers. After settling into permanent communities in the 1960s and coming into close contact with the industrial society in the 1970s (due to the construction of the James Bay hydroelectric project), their lifestyle came to maintain an uneasy balance between being independent hunter-trapper-fishers and being rural North Americans at the margin of the dominant society. Although their philosophy of the natural environment has been changing rapidly, in pace with their integration into the dominant society, they still professed and practiced a distinctly different view of the world as of the 1980s.

The material presented in this chapter is based on focus group discussions with a volunteer, self-selected working group of senior hunters from the local Cree Trappers Association (CTA). The work was initiated by the Chisasibi CTA to provide educational material on Cree culture for youth, to record and strengthen traditional practice, and to educate the outside world in defense of Cree culture and subsistence economy. The report of the project was published by the Cree themselves (Bearskin *et al.* 1989); parts of it were published by the researcher as well (Berkes 1988b). The quotations are from the original report prepared for the Cree. Brackets are used to provide explanations for the reader.

The report was prepared through five sets of meetings and five drafts over a year-and-a-half (1984–5), and it was verified by members of the group through revisions at each step. Hunters' statements were written in standard English, as requested by them, and the text modified by them as necessary. The text of the chapter preserves the Cree narrative form and contains direct quotes. The researcher/compiler comes in merely to provide context, mostly at the beginning and the end of the chapter. The material is based on the then-current practice of mature hunters in Chisasibi; it is not an elders' account of past practice.

In the belief system or religious ideology of the Cree, the living environment is a community of beings that are supernatural as well as natural, as previously noted by other researchers working with Cree groups elsewhere (Preston 1975, 2002; Tanner 1979; Feit 1986; Scott 1989; Brightman 1993; Lemelin *et al.* 2010). These beings possess what Westerners might consider extranormal powers. They have spirits that are sentient; they are watchful and aware of people's behavior. This belief in animal spirits persists among the Chisasibi Cree despite the best efforts of missionaries to eradicate it (Berkes 1986b), and it shapes their worldview.

The chapter focuses on a selection of three Cree beliefs to illustrate their unique worldview:

1 it is the animals, not people, who control the success of the hunt;
2 hunters and fishers have obligations to show respect to the animals to ensure a productive hunt; and
3 a continued, proper use is necessary for maintaining production of animals.

The hunter's obligations toward animals are intertwined with social obligations, so that the environmental ethic of the Chisasibi Cree is an integral part of a comprehensive philosophy of life. The chapter includes some comparative material from the Anishinaabe, the Innu, the Koyukon and the Iroquois.

Animals Control the Hunt

In Western science and its applications to fish and wildlife management, it is assumed that humans can control animal populations. In Cree worldview, by contrast, "human management" of animals and environment is not possible. Rather, it is animals who control the success of the hunt. The Cree believe that animals know everything humans do; they are aware of hunters' activities. In the past all living things talked, communicated with humans. Many Cree legends carry this theme, and the idea is alive among contemporary hunters as well:

> I had a fish net out in a lake and at first I was getting quite a few fish in it. But there was an otter in the lake and he was eating the fish in the net. After a while, fish stopped coming into the net. They knew there was a predator there. So similarly game know about the presence of hunters as well. The Cree say, "All creatures are watching you. They know everything you are doing. Animals are aware of your activities." In the past, animals talked to people. In a sense, there is still communication between animals and hunters. You can predict where the black bear is likely to den. Even though the black bear zigzags before retreating into his den to hibernate, tries to shake you off his trail, you can still predict where he is likely to go to. When he approaches his den entrance, he makes tracks backwards, loses his tracks in the bush, and makes a long detour before coming into the den. The hunter tries to think what the bear is thinking. The hunter and the bear have parallel knowledge, and they share that knowledge. So in a sense they communicate.

The hunter always speaks as if the human is the passive partner in this relationship. If the animal decides to make himself available, the hunter is successful. The hunter has no power over the game; animals have the last say as to whether they will be caught. The hunter has to show respect to the animals because the hunter is dependent on game. The game is not there for the taking. There is no guarantee of a kill; the game must be pursued. Increase in the hunter's success, as he reaches his prime, goes hand in hand with the increase of his respect for the animals. Another way of putting this would be that he develops respect for game as he becomes a better hunter. The two factors are mutually related. The Cree notion of "success" or being a "good hunter" is not measured by the size of the hunter's kill; it is measured by the ability of the hunter to "get what he/she needs."

Young people are taught early on to show respect to the animals. If a hunter does not follow the expected practices of respect, it happens very easily that the disrespectful individual will kill nothing. For such a person, game would be scarce. Even if he sees game in the bush, the Cree believe, something happens, something prevents him from getting the game. This includes all animals, not just big game and fur animals, but also small game and fish. This is a fundamental belief shared by almost all hunters. A hunter never gets angry at game. If a hunter has no luck, he looks at himself to blame, not the animals. When the animals are not making themselves available, quite often they are only "returning the discourtesy," as the Cree see it. Sometimes a hunter may be unlucky for no apparent reason, but this is rare. In a community of hunters, it is an obligation of the more successful hunters to share their catch with the unlucky hunter. Sometimes a hunter is disrespectful to animals without intending to be.

> My brother was trapping otter. He had left his trap in the water a bit too long. Normally, one checks traps quite often. There was an otter in the trap, but it has been in the water too long. The fur was coming off. My brother was really worried: he had caused the fur to spoil, and knew that this was a crime against the animals. He said the otter would retaliate for this by not being caught. He thought it would take perhaps three years before the otter will decide to come back to his traps again.

Since hunting success ultimately depends on the willingness of animals to be caught, a hunter familiar with an area will often have the best success. Conversely, a stranger in an area will have poor hunting success for, as the Cree say, "The land is unfamiliar with him."

> I once invited a coaster [someone who has a hunting territory on the James Bay coast], a good hunter, to my trapline north of the Chisasibi [La Grande] River. He was a stranger there. Even though he was a good hunter and had done nothing wrong to the animals, he did not have much luck. There is a saying, "the land and game would feel unfamiliar or uneasy with you if you are a stranger there." Such a person may have poor luck at first, but later on game will get to know him.

According to Cree beliefs, the success of a hunter peaks with age, up to a point. After this peak, a hunter's success would be expected to decline, and his sons or other hunters in the group are thought to inherit part of an older hunter's success. When an old man passes away, some younger people will inherit his animals. The whole process may be considered a cycle, from child, to hunter at his peak, to old man. During this cycle, the amount of animals available remains constant, but the distribution of success varies.

> As a hunter gains experience, he becomes better and better in hunting. He reaches a peak and after that his hunting success goes down. An old man would not be expected to hunt as well as he did when he was at his peak. It is common knowledge that an old man's hunt declines. This often happens after a man reaches 50 or 60. But an old hunter does not worry about his hunting success because he knows he has had his day, that he used to kill many. My uncle was a good trapper, but in his old age he did not catch many. He used to say jokingly that "the game were letting go of him." He would say that he was being ignored by game: the game were leaving him alone. He did not care to kill any. But he set traps anyway. For him, it was a way of life.
>
> When an old man dies, another person takes on from him. It is almost as if that the old man's game is now passed on to a younger person in that group. It is a fundamental belief of the Cree people that a young man would inherit an old man's game.
>
> My father used to catch lots of game. He used to say that once his sons started to hunt, his own hunting success would go down. And in fact, so it happened. My brother, who was an exceptionally successful goose hunter when he was young, now hunts fewer geese. But his sons make up for his losses. It can be said that his four sons inherited part of his catch.

The cycle of hunting success is one of many cyclic phenomena in the Cree worldview. Another one concerns cycles of animal abundance. The cyclic disappearance and reappearance of game animals is thought to be related to the willingness of animals to be hunted. The Cree believe that almost all animals go up and down in abundance, some in shorter cycles and some in longer cycles. For Chisasibi hunters, animals known to disappear and reappear include:

- caribou, which disappeared around the turn of the century and reappeared in the 1980s;
- beaver, which were scarce in the area between about 1930 and 1950 and increased thereafter;
- marten, which declined twice since the turn of the century. In the 1980s it was very scarce in the inland traplines. However, in the coastal traplines it began to reappear in 1982–3;
- porcupine, which were last plentiful in 1960–70 and declined in the 1970s; and

- small game animals—snowshoe hare, rock and willow ptarmigan, spruce and sharp-tailed grouse, which are known to have eight- to ten-year cycles, from one peak of abundance to the next.

The shorter cycles (e.g. the ten-year cycles of hare and ptarmigan) are well known to Western science, but longer cycles such as those of the caribou are not well understood. Many biologists believe that management or lack thereof is responsible for the increase or decrease of caribou. By contrast, the Cree believe that animals will naturally increase or decrease. Those that disappear for a time sooner or later come back by themselves, not as a consequence of management by humans. Disappearing animals such as caribou and marten are said to go under the water or underground. This is thought to be something similar to the disappearance of animals such as ptarmigan, fox, lynx, and snowshoe hares in very cold weather. The belief in the eventual return of disappearing animals is very strong.

My uncle who would have been about 90 [in 1984] missed the caribou. By the time he was old enough to hunt, caribou had already declined. An old man told him not to worry, the caribou would be back some day. And they are back now. Sometimes my uncle did not believe the old men. He asked them, "Where do they go when they disappear?" They answered that it has been known in the past that caribou disappear under the water. There would come a time when they would reappear later. He was at first amazed to hear this, but believed it later on. He came to know that all the animals you see, porcupine, fur animals and others, disappeared from time to time. In his early hunting days, marten were plentiful. He saw them decline and later come back again, all in his lifetime.

He was hunting. He came to a little pond. There were fresh caribou tracks on the new snow. The tracks were leading into the lake. He walked across to the other side of the lake; he thought caribou had swum across. But there were no caribou tracks on the other side. Caribou had submerged. When he went back to the camp, the older men said, "Yes this is how big game and fur animals disappear. But they will someday come back again." A young trapper was checking his muskrat traps in the Sakami River area. He found one of his traps had sprung underwater. He thought it was a muskrat because there was a muskrat den nearby. But instead, he found a marten in his trap. There were no marten tracks in the area; he must have come up under the water. The young trapper was scared. He thought it was unnatural, a bad omen. He returned to the camp [to consult the elders]. The old men reassured him. They said it was not a bad sign, but marten lived under the water, too. I have seen marten tracks coming out of a fishing hole in the ice. The tracks went out of the lake, around a clump of trees, as if the marten was looking for other martens, and back to the lake and into the hole again.

The idea that disappearing animals go underwater or under the land is found in other northern indigenous groups as well. Writing about the eastern Dene who are not related to the Cree, Kendrick *et al.* (2005: 187) say, "The local stories of caribou that 'go underground or underwater' may be a metaphorical reminder of this appearance and disappearance of caribou populations." In the case of the Cree, it is not clear if this was metaphorical language, at least some of the Chisasibi Cree elders in the working group would say that the appearance and disappearance of the caribou was comparable to the effects of an intensely cold period when animals cease to move around. The notion that animals send signs and signals is also found in other groups, for example the Anishinaabe who are related to the Cree (Davidson-Hunt 2006). Among the Anishinaabe, dreams are an extremely important way in which animals and plants communicate with people.

As the Chisasibi CTA working group chose not to discuss dreaming, I am including a narrative from Ella Dawn Green, an Anishinaabe elder from Shoal Lake (Iskatewizaagegan No. 39 Independent First Nation) in northwestern Ontario. The narrative is about medicinal plants that are not there for the taking but may make themselves available to the right people. Knowledge comes through different pathways, including dreams, and one does not know beforehand what a plant may be useful for (Box 5.1).

Obligations of Hunters to Show Respect

Since animals control the hunt, lack of respect for the animals will affect hunting success because animals can retaliate by "returning the discourtesy." The Cree say that the main reason for showing respect to animals is that humans and animals are related, they share the same Creator. Just as one respects other persons, one respects animals. Cree culture is rich with rituals related to respect (Tanner 1979; Preston 2002; Scott 2006). Among the Chisasibi Cree, respect for the animal is shown in several ways:

- the hunter maintains an attitude of humility when going hunting;
- the animal is approached and killed with respect;
- the animal is carried respectfully to camp;
- offerings are made to the animal;
- the meat is butchered according to rules signifying respect;
- the meat is consumed according to rules signifying respect; and
- the remains of the animal are disposed of properly.

> ### Box 5.1 How Medicinal Plant Knowledge Comes to the Anishinaabe
>
> "The Creator put everything on the earth for a reason even if we don't know that reason. How can we decide which bush should stay and which should go? You need to understand how we learn about plants. The way I started learning plants is my aunties, they used to take me out in the bush to show me what kind of plants there are and what kind of plants that we can use for medicine. My mom too, she used to take me out on the lake along the shoreline, and she used to tell me all kinds of plant which I can't remember, and she showed me where to find them. And that was passed on and a lot of these medicines that they showed me and how they are used, they used to tell me that I would be carrying on to the next generation. And it was so important to them for me to learn all this and to keep in mind which plants I am supposed to pick, and there are some poisonous plants that I can't touch.
>
> "And then some of them I received through dreams. Like, I would dream about something, you know. Especially an old lady or an old man would be in my dreams telling me all kinds of things. But after talking to me, like you know it would be a bird or a four-legged, you know those animals that run around and around, that's how they turn when they leave. Dreams, visions . . . visions would be like seeing a bear coming to me and telling me what the purpose of a plant is, you know, giving me that medicine . . . That is how I learned to make medicines for anyone. Another thing I learned, when they have shaking tents, the people in there, the spirits, when they give you medicine, and you are supposed to keep that medicine, it is for you eh, for you to heal. I keep that too because it has already been given to me through shaking tents. That's how I received all these things that I carry, that I carry on, from my aunties, my mom and dad, through dreams and through shaking tents."
>
> *Source*: Ella Dawn Green, Anishinaabe elder, in conversation with Iain Davidson-Hunt (Berkes and Davidson-Hunt 2006: 42).

The rule about an attitude of humility is both important and universal. Hunters should not boast about their abilities. Otherwise, they risk catching nothing because they are being disrespectful of game.

While fishing with a group of people to the south of my area on the James Bay coast, I once boasted that I could catch as many trout as anyone else. It was a good area for speckled trout, and the fishermen were pulling out some 50–60 fish in each of their nets. My net was in the middle of all the other nets. But when I pulled it out, there was only one trout in it! In similar ways, many people have experienced a loss of hunting success after boasting.

The hunter had a cord which he used for carrying black bear. But on this one hunt, he left his cord behind in the camp, laughing and boasting that he could carry any black bear without the cord. He did in fact kill a black bear on that trip. But he found out that he was not able to carry it. [The speaker is saying that this bear was too big for the hunter to carry without the benefit of a rope to tie its limbs over his chest and hips.] The moral of the story is that whatever fun you make of a black bear, this will backfire on you.

The hunter should also maintain an attitude of respect when approaching game. The killing will be done quickly and simply, without mess. The hunter should use a gun appropriate for the size of the animal. For example, a small-bore gun is used for the smaller animals. A hunter wants an animal to look its best. One

Photo 5.1 A moose-hunting camp of the Anishinaabe people, Keeper Lake, Pikangikum, NW Ontario. The hunter should maintain an attitude of respect when approaching game.

Photo: Catie Burlando.

does not want blood all over the place. If a hunter used an oversized gun, for example on a beaver, this would be a transgression.

The Cree see similarity between social relations among humans and those among humans and animals, especially those animals considered particularly powerful and worthy of respect.

> When a hunter visits a camp, he lets it be known that he is a visitor (*maantaau*), a person from another camp. He approaches respectfully and modestly; he announces himself simply, (*nitikushin*) [I am here]. People in the camp come out to greet him as soon as they hear him. When they come out, he has already taken his snowshoes off and put them upright in the snow. People in the camp admire his snowshoes. They say, "These are beautiful snowshoes," they admire the craftsmanship, the good material and design. They note that he is a successful, able hunter.
>
> When a hunter approaches a black bear den in winter, he does not make an exhibition of himself. He announces himself simply and with humility: "I am here." . . . There is similarity between the hunter announcing himself at the camp, and the hunter announcing himself at the bear's den. The hunter shows as much respect to the bear as he shows to people. It is almost as if he is arriving at the den as a visitor, hoping that the bear will accept him.

After every successful hunt, the first thing that the Cree hunter does with the animal is to check the fat content. This is a hunter's "quality control" of the game: the more fat the better, for it shows a healthy animal. With a goose, one pinches the fat layer under the skin (the subcutaneous fat) after removing a handful of feathers from the belly. With a black bear, one cuts the skin in front of the chest, just over the breast bone, to check the fat. This done, the animal is ready to be carried to the camp, and there are rules of respect at this stage as well.

There are proper ways of carrying game. For example, a beaver is normally pulled on its back in the snow. A stick is placed through the nose and a cord is attached to it. However, if there is ice stuck on the back fur, then the hands would be tied, and the animal flipped over and dragged on its front side. Similarly, there are proper ways to carry geese (tied by the necks and draped over the shoulders of the hunter). With black bears, two people can carry a bear with a pole, with the bear's limbs tied. Or a hunter can carry a bear on his back, paws over the shoulder, legs held under the hunter's arms, like a child, and the limbs tied in front over the hunter's chest.

> Carrying a bear has symbolic significance for the hunter. My friend and I killed a black bear. My friend gave me the bear [that is, a gift of respect].

I tried to carry the bear but it was very heavy. I tried to lift it, but I tumbled and fell down, time and again. My friend said, "Now it is really yours." The point is that the human hunter is not all-powerful. Even though I tried hard, the bear prevailed over me. This way, I really earned the bear. It was now truly mine.

Once carried to the camp, offerings may be made to the animal as a show of respect. In the past, offerings were made to all animals, even fish. In the 1980s, offerings were being made only to the more powerful animals such as the black bear. When a hunter makes an offering to animals and to old men, he is, in effect, entering a reciprocal relationship, asking them to give him game. In the practice of Cree hunters of Chisasibi, offerings can be made with tobacco (not indigenous to the subarctic) and with pieces of meat or skin thrown into the fire.

Offerings made to an animal indicates respect. It also means that the hunters are asking the animal to provide game for them. Similarly, offerings can be made to dead men [that is, respected elders]. Offerings to old men in their graves are fairly common, sometimes even to not very old men, and occasionally to women, too.

There was a respected old man who died on the point of a particular lake. He was buried there. When people went by his grave, they would make an offering to him. They rolled tobacco in tree bark and left it there. They were asking the old man to provide game for them in return for the tobacco.

A black bear is brought into camp. Hunters sit in a circle, with the bear in the middle. Someone smokes a pipe beside the bear and makes a gesture of offering the pipe to the bear. Or a piece of tobacco is placed in the bear's mouth as an offering. Once the bear is skinned, a piece of the meat is thrown into the fire. These offerings mean that the hunters are thanking the Provider.

Respect for animals is shown also in the way meat is butchered and distributed. There are special ways to cut every kind of animal, and for different uses of the animal's meat. For example, a loon is butchered differently from a goose. The pattern of cut will be different if a whitefish is going to be smoked as opposed to one that is going to be fresh-boiled. Some of the methods of cutting and preparation are related to showing respect for the animals. For example, when dismembering a goose, women are supposed to cut the wing off the body (and not to break it off). Otherwise, it is said, the husband's luck in the goose hunt will be affected. In butchering a black bear, first the men cut the patterns on the bear. After that, the women skin the bear, and finally the men cut the limbs. There are special cutting patterns especially for the big game.

The owner of the game, say a black bear, decides as he starts to cut it on how to distribute the meat among the families sharing the camp. In the case of a group hunt for a large animal, the general rule is that the "owner" is the person who has made the "crippling shot." He may keep the skin for the fur and may give portions of the meat to others to distribute further. The first hunter may give the bear to a second hunter, and the second hunter may decide to pass the meat to a third. This kind of ritual sharing is considered important for social relations. Commonly, a young hunter would give the meat to one of the old men or old women in the camp, who would then do the honors in distributing it. This signifies deference and respect for the elders. Especially with big game animals, the custom is that an elder would distribute the food, thus showing respect for the animal.

Respect is also shown with the consumption of the game. The major principle is that everything is consumed and there is no waste. It is important that everything that is killed is eaten. Killing for fun or for "recreation" or "sport" without eating it is a transgression. What one kills, one keeps for eating. Young boys who kill small animals, when they are learning to hunt, make a gift of these animals to an old woman who prepares them. The food will then be consumed by the old woman and the boy and symbolically by the whole family. One elder says, "We are done for as a hunting society if we ever reach the point of taking only the haunch of a moose or caribou, as white hunters do."

Traditional Cree cooking uses all parts of the animals. For example, goose feet, necks, and head are eaten; goose fat is rendered or boiled down for later use. Intestines of the bearded seal stuffed with seal blubber are a delicacy for some coastal people. Fish heads are boiled, fish internal organs including liver, eggs, and intestines (but excluding stomach contents and gall bladder) are stir-fried; fish bones are sometimes eaten, pounded into *pimihkaan* (fish pemmican). Blood is used in blood pudding and stews; this is a delicacy. However, there are certain parts of animals that are *not* eaten. For example, caribou brains are not consumed but used in tanning skins. Polar bear liver is not consumed presumably because it is poisonous due to the extremely high content of vitamin A.

It is said that the whiskey jack, or gray jay, hovers about hunting camps, checking to see that nothing is wasted. In the case of some animals, respect is shown by consuming the meat only in the camp presumably because it is a sacred place. For example, black bear meat is eaten only in the camp; one is not allowed to take bear meat as lunch when checking traps and one does not usually take it to the village, not a sacred place. Similarly, lynx is shown respect by consuming the meat within the camp.

Proper disposal is the final stage in showing respect. After the edible parts have been consumed, hunters take proper care of the bones and other remains. The following are hung on trees or placed on top of wooden platforms: all black bear bones, and all skulls (including beaver, lynx, porcupine, muskrat, marten, otter, and mink). The following are returned to water because they are water animals: bones of beaver, otter, mink. There are no general rules for the disposal of the bones of waterfowl species, but some hunters hang the throats (trachea) of geese on trees or camp posts. Dogs are not allowed to eat black bear, beaver, and porcupine meat or bones. Other animal remains, including fish remains, would be buried. Another recommended way of disposing of fish remains is to collect them and place them where scavenger birds can feed on them.

Campsites are to be left tidy and clean. All garbage would be cleaned up and burned before breaking camp. Some of these rules seem to be recent adaptations. Traditionally, the only waste in the camp consisted of animal remains, bones, and wood, which are natural materials that easily go back to nature. In modern life, however, there is also plastic, metal cans, glass, and paper, which create a disposal problem in campsites. Good hunters take special care to burn and/or bury these materials also, so that the young generations will inherit a clean environment.

Importance of Continued Use for Sustainability

It is the animals who control the success of the hunt, and hunters have obligations to show respect to the animals. Another important principle that characterizes Cree worldview is the belief that the continued use of resources is important to achieve a sustainable, productive harvest.

> The tallyman [a senior hunter in charge of a territory, a steward] takes care of a trapline so that the beaver continue to be productive. Taking care of a trapline means not killing too many. A trapper paces himself, killing what he needs, and what can be prepared by the women, so that there is no wastage of meat and fur, and respect for the animals is maintained. He should also make sure that the area is rested [by rotating the sectors of the hunted area]. Normally a trapper should rest parts of his trapline for two or three years but no longer than four years. If he leaves it, say, six or ten years, he is not properly using his area, and the beaver will not be plentiful.

The concept of resting the hunting area is fairly well known. Many (but not all) Cree trappers divide their territory into three or four sectors. They hunt and trap only in one sector at a time, and "rest" the others. Rotation of the hunting territory resembles fallowing in agriculture. Feit (1973, 1986) has shown with another James Bay Cree group that the beaver harvest from a sector rested for two years or more is significantly greater than that from a sector harvested with no rest. The trapper continually observes the environment and monitors the health of the beaver-vegetation system. He observes vegetation changes, beaver tooth marks on cut wood to estimate the age composition of beaver in lodges, and looks for other evidence of overcrowding, such as fighting among the beaver. The Cree see the interaction between beaver and vegetation as a relationship of balance. It is a balance that can flip if the beaver overharvest their food supply. The Cree practice of resting an area, followed by heavy harvesting of beaver, keeps the system from reaching the critical point at which food would be depleted and the balance will be lost. Thus, not only overuse can lead to a drop in productivity, but in the Cree worldview, so does underuse.

> In an area which has not been trapped for a long time, there will be many empty beaver lodges. This may be due to disease because of over-crowding, or it may be due to beavers depleting their food supplies. The trapper knows that in an area which has not been trapped for a long time, various types of beaver food such as aspen would be in low supply.
>
> If there has been a fire, this also affects the beaver. Trappers know that three or four years after a fire the beaver will again begin to inhabit the area. At first, however, they would be eating more of the root foods [underwater bulbs]. The trapper may resume trapping again when the willows are half-grown. This may be some eight to ten years after a fire.

The hunter is always watching the environment, monitoring it for signs and signals. Rotation and resting the land is good practice. The Cree notion of the importance of continued use is superficially similar to that in Western resource management science but probably has different philosophical roots. "Continued use" is not an obligation, in the sense of rules of respect; it is simply good "manage-ment" consistent with the ideas of renewability and animal cycles. The principle that animals control the hunt takes precedence over the principle of continued use:

> From the new camp, the hunter set out the next day with his traps. He was lucky to find beaver lodges, four or five of them, and he was quite happy about that. He sent his son to go even further east the next day. The son checked the traps set the previous day and brought in the beaver. The next day after that, the son checked the last set of traps but had no luck. They waited several days and checked again: still no beaver. He took the traps out, "Let them be, they will increase for the next time," he said. He was not catching anything, and there was a meaning to that. The

beaver did not want to be caught yet. Next fall, he would come back to this area, and maybe then the beaver would be ready to be caught.

The principle of continued use has to be tempered also with common sense and good management. The "manager," in the Cree system, is the senior hunter, called the tallyman. (In Feit's (1986) terminology, the steward.) The senior hunter is the observer of nature, the interpreter of observations, the decision-maker in resource management, and the enforcer of rules of proper hunting conduct. He is also the political leader, ensuring for example that no one goes hungry in the group. There is little doubt that in the old days, the steward was often a spiritual leader as well (see Box 5.2, which is about the Innu who are close relatives of the Cree).

It is the steward's obligation to follow up on the activities of a group that had violated the rules of proper hunting behavior by engaging in unrestrained exploitation.

> The tallyman went to trap a part of his trapline. He had not been there for several years, but he had given permission to another group to trap it a few years previously. These people had reported plenty of beaver at that time. But the trapper knew that there would not be many beaver in that area because these other people had killed too many. He knew this because when these people returned to the village that year, their furs had not been prepared properly. Many of the furs had to be thrown out. They had killed indiscriminately—young, old, every animal. Some of the beaver may even have been trapped out of season. The trapper visited, one after another, lakes and ponds which he knew to be good beaver lakes. There were beaver signs, but these were old signs from before that group's visit. Beaver had declined, had not produced because those trappers had not taken care of that spot. They had done wrong to the game. In such cases, game retaliates. Leave nothing behind—and it affects the later hunt. Bad practice has repercussions for later years.

As the enforcer of community norms, it becomes the steward's obligation to expose "doing wrong to the game." In the process, the steward can initiate social sanction on the guilty parties, shaming them publicly (usually done by the use of humor) and using the example to remind everyone else of the rules.

Conclusions

The general principle that "animals are killed but not diminished" has also been noted by other researchers elsewhere in Cree lands (Tanner 1979; Feit 1986;

Box 5.2 Shamanism Among the Innu (Montagnais) of Labrador

In Innu Culture, What is the Shaman (Kakushapitak)?

Kakushapitak means a person who can see through, who can foretell, who has authority, power. His power lies in using the "shaking tent" (*kushapitakan*) to foretell events, locate animals, and travel through time to learn about families. The shaman masters other techniques to foretell the future such as the chant and drum, the dream, scapulomancy. The shaman is said to be powerful if his predictions, advice, or news are correct. The most powerful shaman is the one who always tells the truth. Some shamans were strong, others weak. The strong shaman was always a great hunter, while the weak ones did not have this skill.

How were Shamans Considered in Everyday Life?

The shaman was a person like anybody else. No particular deference was paid to him. He was respected because he was a great hunter. He played a leadership role like that of a chief today. He knew where to hunt and the group trusted him.

How does the Shaman Transmit his Power?

Ussitshimiush, the sack [medicine pouch] which contains the power, is passed on from generation to generation. For instance, had my great grandfather Toby been a shaman, he would have passed it on to my father who would in turn have passed it to me, Mathieu André. I then could have passed it either to my eldest son or my youngest. If a shaman did not have a son, he would pass it on to his grandson.

How is it that Innu Shamanism has Died Out?

Once the priests arrived, they fought against the ritual. They also prohibited the shaking tent, saying the shaman was helped by the devil, that it was diabolic. The Innu believed that, but I think a superior spirit gave the Innu knowledge of everything that concerns the environment and enables him to act. The old people were afraid of the priests. People say that when old Pukue, one of the great shamans of Sheshatshit, died (and my grandmother witnessed this), his *ussitshimiush*, his sack, was burned. And I think that is one of the reasons why shamanism has disappeared among us.

Source: Nuk André conversation with his father, Mathieu André, an Innu author and elder (André 1989: 5, 6).

Brightman 1993). Is this concept in the sense of "ecologically sustainable use," or is it in the sense of a reincarnation of a "constant supply," so to speak, of animals? In contrast to some other groups of Cree hunters—for example, those in northern Manitoba (Brightman 1993) and the Waswanipi Cree of Quebec (Feit 1986)—the Chisasibi Cree did not articulate the notion of reincarnation of animals.

According to Brightman (1993: 289), the northern Manitoba Cree historically believed that "the numbers of animals available to hunters in the future could be influenced by ceremonial regeneration; the numbers killed or the parts utilized were irrelevant." If Brightman is correct, and the historian Ray's (1975) work also supports that conclusion, the Cree of the 1700s did not associate hunting with depletion. Cree traditional ecological knowledge did not include the consideration of population dynamics of game, and in fact still does not. Brightman (1993) has argued further that the concept of game depletion by overhunting is not aboriginal but represents the influence of Western game management practice. Chapter 6 on caribou examines how the hunting ethic of an aboriginal group itself may change, and Chapter 7 on fisheries analyzes how the Cree seem to be able to manage resources sustainably, given that their management system did not and does not include any accounting by numbers.

Another major difference between Cree views and Western views concerns the nature of "killing." The Cree do not consider the killing of game as an act of violence. The hunter loves the animals he kills, as they sustain his family (Preston 2002). In any case, the animals can only be hunted if they agree to be hunted. Similarly, the Cree have difficulty with the Western notions that hunting involves suffering on the part of the animals, and that the best conservation (as some argue) would mean not hunting the animals at all. To the Cree, if the game want to be left alone, they would let the hunters know. Otherwise, the proper conservation of game does include the hunting and eating of animals. The preservationist ethic is not compatible with Cree conservation: "When you don't use a resource, you lose respect for it." This notion is common to all northern indigenous peoples, and many other indigenous peoples throughout the world, including the Maori (see Chapter 12).

The Chisasibi Cree view of the living environment as a "community of beings" is not a particularly unusual view. Other eastern James Bay groups such as the Cree of Mistassini (Tanner 1979), Waswanipi (Feit 1973, 1986), and Weminji (Scott 2006) have similar views, as do some of the more distant Cree groups in northern Manitoba and Saskatchewan (Brightman 1993). Many other aboriginal groups of North America have similar beliefs as well. For example, writing of the Koyukon of Alaska, a Dene (Athapaskan) group culturally unre-lated to the Cree, Nelson (1982: 218) states that they regard the environment "as a community of entities that are intrinsically supernatural as well as natural. In fact, the strict western conceptual distinction between natural and supernatural would probably make little sense to the Koyukon."

The James Bay Cree worldview, as emerging from this chapter, is consistent with Colorado's (1988) characterization of native science as a holistic and religious perspective grounded in empirical observation. The cosmos has a unity and integrity that is Creator-given, and it is the task of humans to discipline their minds and actions to recognize and understand its workings. The Cree worldview is also consistent with Trosper's (1995) analysis of commonly shared American Indian attitudes of respect toward nature. Trosper argues that there are four commonly (but not universally) held values that are components of *respect*: community (including the "community of beings" view with social obligations and reciprocity); connectedness; concern for future generations (as exemplified by the Iroquois notion of responsibility for the "seventh genera-tion"); and humility. See Box 5.3 about the expression of humility among the Koyukon.

Many of these values are also found in some Western environmental philosophies, for example, in Leopold's (1949) land ethics, as noted by Callicott (1989) and Trosper (1995). However, in Leopold's thought there is no human–nature reciprocity. Rather, it is a one-way street in which it is the humans who are to extend their ethics to include nature; animals have no obligations to nourish humans. Also poorly represented in Western environmental ethics is one of the four components of respect, and one that is of great importance to the Cree: humility. Leopold comes close to the notion of humility by promoting an ethic that reduces humans from superiority to equality: "from

---

Box 5.3 Expressing Humility: The Koyukon of Alaska

"When the river ice breaks up each spring, people speak to it, respect-fully and acknowledging its power. Elders make short prayers, both Christian and traditional Koyukon, asking the ice to drift downstream without jamming and causing floods. By contrast, some years ago, the U.S. Air Force bombed an ice jam on the Yukon River to prevent inundation of communities. Far from approving, some villagers blamed subsequent floods on this arrogant use of physical force. In the end, nature will assert the greater power. The proper role for humans is to move gently, humbly, pleading or coercing, but always avoiding belligerence."

Source: Nelson 1993: 217.

conqueror of the land-community to plain member and citizen of it" (Leopold 1949: 240).

Traditional worldviews of nature are diverse, but many share the belief in a sacred, personal relationship between humans and other living beings. To quote Callicott (1982: 306), "The implicit overall metaphysic of American Indian cultures locates human beings in a larger *social*, as well as physical, environment. People belong not only to a human community, but to a community of all nature as well." This community-of-beings worldview is common not only among American Indians but in many other hunter-gatherer and horticultural peoples around the world (Gadgil and Berkes 1991; Taylor 2005). In general, these beliefs probably go back to the dominant pantheistic tradition before the rise of monotheistic religions (see Box 5.4).

Pantheistic traditions still exist in some contemporary groups such as the James Bay Cree (even though they are now formally Christians), as they once existed in pre-Christian Europe and survived for a time in the Christian mysticism of St. Francis (White 1967). The culture and traditional ethics of the

---

Box 5.4 Iroquois Pantheism

"Animism, which permeates pantheism, involves the theory of the existence of immaterial principle, inseparable from matter, to which all life and action are attributable. In the pantheist view the entire phenomenal world contains godlike attributes: the relations of man to this world are sacramental. It is believed that the actions of man in nature can affect his own fate, that these actions are consequential, immediate and relevant to life. There is, in this relationship, no non-nature category—nor is there either romanticism or sentimentality.

"The Iroquois view is typical of Indian pantheism. The Iroquois cosmography begins with a perfect sky world from which falls the earth mother, arrested by the birds, landing upon the back of a turtle, the earth. Her grandchildren are twins, one good and the other evil. . . . The opposition of these two forces is the arena of life; they can be affected by man's acts in the world of actuality. Consequently all acts—birth and growth, procreating, eating and evacuating, hunting and gathering, making voyages and journeys—are sacramental."

Source: McHarg 1969: 68.

Cree are thus significant not only for their own sake but for linking us with a millennia-old human heritage. A community-of-beings worldview is particularly meaningful today, as it signifies a cosmology in which humans are part of the ecological system. The next two chapters explore in some detail how Chisasibi Cree views of the environment translate into actual human–animal relationships.

CHAPTER 6

A Story of Caribou
and Social Learning

This chapter chronicles how the Cree learned to deal with the variability in caribou numbers and the fact that caribou are depletable. Conservation ethics does not arrive ready-made, it evolves. How it develops is a question of great general interest (Berkes and Turner 2006; Turner and Berkes 2006). The chapter uses historical evidence and contemporary observations of cultural evolution in action to build a picture of social learning. Indigenous hunters have highly unique ways of observing and learning from the environment (Kendrick and Manseau 2008). They are constantly monitoring a number of signals in the environment. If the signs and signals are unusual or out of the ordinary, then they have to be interpreted by people who have suitable experience and wisdom—the elders. In most indigenous societies, the elders manage cross-generational information feedbacks, and make sense of unusual observations and resource intervention outcomes. Elders and stewards provide leadership, carry and transmit knowledge, and sometimes reinterpret new information to help redesign management systems.

Practice is not always true to belief. Philosophers point out that "ethics bear a normative relation to behavior; they do not describe how people actually behave, but rather set out how people ought to behave" (Callicott 1982: 311). For example, the Koyukon people of Alaska often violate their own rules on limiting harvests when they hunt caribou (Nelson 1982). Anyone who has worked in the field knows that rules and ethics are sometimes suspended. One can say about any culture or any group of people that there is always a gap between the ideal practice and the actual. The story of caribou is important in this regard. Cree elders in Chisasibi readily admit that they once overhunted the caribou. However, the events that took place in the community some 70 years later indicate that the Cree hunters as a group had learned from that overhunting experience. The caribou story illustrates how traditional beliefs, such as those described in Chapter 5 about cycles and the return of animals, play out in the real world, and how community-based systems can learn and evolve. It also illustrates the role that traditional stewards and elders play in providing leadership for collective decision-making. It shows why almost all traditional cultures consider elders so important. Elders provide corporate memory for the group, the wisdom to interpret uncommon or unusual events, and they help enforce the rules and ethical norms of the community.

The main issue is the development and application of a conservation ethic in a social group, an issue first raised in Chapter 4. *Conservation ethic*, defined here after Johannes (1994), is the "awareness of one's ability to deplete or otherwise damage natural resources, coupled with a commitment to reduce or eliminate the problem." The hypothesis is that a conservation ethic can develop (1) if a resource is *important, predictable and depletable*, and (2) if it is effectively under the control of the social group in question so that the group can reap the benefits of its conservation (Berkes 1989a).

First, if a resource is superabundant, there is no adaptive advantage in developing a conservation ethic for it, nor a territorial system for its defense. The resource has to be predictable and abundant, and important for the group (see Chapter 3 on territoriality; Dyson-Hudson and Smith 1978; Richardson 1982; Nelson 1982; Berkes 1986a). If the resource is not depletable, it is perfectly logical (and one may argue ecologically adaptive) to kill excess numbers in hunts that are sporadic in space and time. The perturbation of the system can then provide feedback to the resource manager, as well as a store of food. As Nelson (1982: 223) points out in his discussion of Alaska caribou hunting, "a natural response is not to limit harvests intentionally, but the precise opposite—take as much as possible, whenever possible, and store the proceeds for later use."

Second, there is the question of the control of the resource. Societies establish conservation rules and ethics for themselves, not for the benefit of outsiders. The evidence on this question shows that the incursion of outsiders, and the inability of the group to defend an important resource, causes the lifting of rules and conservation ethic (Feit 1986; Berkes 1986a). Once open-access conditions are created, perfectly conservation-minded stewards may well become participants themselves in a "tragedy of the commons" rather than allow the outsiders to take the remaining resource. Such free-for-all depletions of resources seem to have happened in the case of beaver in James Bay in the 1920s, and the overkill of

North American bison at the turn of the century (Berkes *et al.* 1989). In some cases, the condition is reversible: if local controls can be re-established, the group can again reap the benefits of its own restraint, and conservation rules and ethics become operative once again (Feit 1986; Berkes 1989b).

The significance of the caribou case is that the nature of the resource does *not* lend itself well to the development of a conservation ethic. Caribou is indeed one of the most important species of the North American subarctic and Arctic, just as its close relative, reindeer, is important in Northern Scandinavia and Siberia (Tyler *et al.* 2007; Brannlund and Axelsson 2011). They come in very large numbers when they come, but they are unpredictable. As one Dene saying goes, "no one knows the way of the winds and the caribou" (Munsterhjelm 1953: 97). To aboriginal hunters once upon a time, caribou must have seemed superabundant and undepletable, but alas also unpredictable. Furthermore, large herds of caribou migrate long distances and are hunted by different groups of people, making local control, and thus local conservation, all but impossible, except in the cases of small herds of woodland caribou. It is relatively easy to envision the conditions under which a conservation ethic can develop for a range of species important for traditional Amerindians, for example, Pacific salmon (Swezey and Heizer 1993; Gottesfeld 1994), black bear and beaver (Nelson 1982), beaver and moose (Feit 1973, 1986), and Canada goose (Berkes 1982). All of them are predictable resources, or at least their harvest areas are predictable from year to year, and they are depletable over a cycle of relatively few years. Not so in the case of caribou.

"No One Knows the Way of the Winds and the Caribou"

As the most abundant large mammal of Arctic and subarctic North America, caribou (*Rangifer tarandus*) has a special importance in the traditional economy of the aboriginal peoples of tundra and the lichen-woodland zone. Charles Elton, one of the founders of modern ecology, was interested in caribou population dynamics as an illustration of population cycles in subarctic ecosystems. In his classic 1942 book, Elton used the records of missionaries and fur traders to document the decline of the George River caribou herd of the Quebec–Labrador Peninsula at the turn of the century. When abundant, animals of this herd migrate in large numbers, as do barren-ground caribou, but they show physical characteristics that are intermediate between woodland and barren-ground caribou, considered by some biologists as two distinct subspecies.

Elton's (1942) reconstruction indicated that there was a general population decrease after about 1905. The most westerly of the three subpopulations of the George River herd occupied the James Bay and Hudson Bay coast. This subpopulation had started declining earlier, through the 1880s and the 1890s. As the population decreased, the range of the George River herd contracted, and the peripheral range was presumably the first to be abandoned. Sources consulted by Elton mentioned one final large kill in 1914 at Limestone Falls, a major crossing on the Caniapiscau River, which runs north–south and bisects the Quebec–Labrador Peninsula. By 1916, the herd was so reduced that, for the first time in living memory, the caribou did not migrate across the George River, which also runs north–south but is closer to the Atlantic on the Labrador side of the Peninsula.

The George River herd stayed as a small population nestled in the hills of northeastern Labrador, still hunted by the Innu of Labrador. Population surveys as late as the 1950s showed a small herd, perhaps as few as 5,000, and biologists speculated on the reasons for the decline of the herd, citing a variety of possible explanations, including extensive fires in Labrador and climate change, but often emphasizing the key role of aboriginal hunters and the repeating rifle, which had become extensively used in the area at the turn of the century (Banfield and Tener 1958). Then the herd started a rapid increase in the 1960s, with a noticeable expansion of range in the 1970s and the 1980s (see Figure 6.1). Piecing together

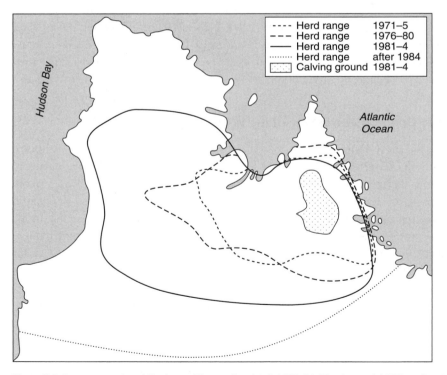

Figure 6.1 Range expansion of the George River caribou herd, 1971–84 (Messier *et al.* 1988), and after 1984 (Couturier *et al.* 1990).

information from aerial surveys, tagging studies with radio collars, observation of tracks, hunters' observations, and kill locations, one could assemble the larger picture of the return of the caribou. The migrations penetrated further and further west and south, in larger and larger numbers, and the caribou started to linger in the more distant areas. The recovery of the George River herd has been dramatic and well documented. The caribou reached a population of some 600,000–700,000 animals, one of the largest *Rangifer* herds in the world by the end of the 1980s, and reoccupied the old range of the herd all the way to the coast of James Bay and Hudson Bay (Jackson 1986; Messier *et al.* 1988; Couturier *et al.* 1990).

Juniper (1979) referred to the George River herd as an "irrupting" population. But was the population change a real cycle? Was it a real recolonization of the former range? Perhaps even more interesting, if the dramatic decline of the caribou at the turn of the century was due to the aboriginal hunter and the improved hunting technology, how then was it possible that the caribou population was increasing with such force in the 1970s and the 1980s, in the presence of greater numbers of aboriginal hunters with even better guns and transportation technology, including roads, trucks, and snowmobiles?

The fact of the matter is, caribou population increases and decreases are a scientific problem yet unresolved. The conventional scope of caribou biology scarcely includes the question of population cycles, simply because no one has a sufficiently long data set. Ten-year cycles of snowshoe hares and lynx lend themselves to scientific analysis, but the multi-generational caribou cycle (if there is a cycle) does not.

Suffice to say that some ecologists think that the fluctuations of caribou numbers are the result of complex and interrelated processes, including the slow growth (50–100 years) of lichens, the winter food of caribou. If conditions are favorable, individual caribou are healthy and have extra energy reserves (fat); the reproduction rate is high and calf mortality low. Under such conditions, caribou numbers can build up quickly by exponential growth. By the time predator numbers catch up, the range may be overgrazed and the caribou not so healthy. The double stress of poor range and high predation may result in the depression of caribou population to low levels. The population remains depressed for a long time, before lichens slowly recover and conditions become favorable to the increase of caribou once more.

The effects of other factors such as hunting pressure, climate change, and fires can add complexity to this general pattern. For example, the effect of heavy hunting during the decline phase can knock down the population even lower, while the same thing during the increase phase merely dampens the fluctuation. Calf survival is an important factor and can be affected by weather (wind and temperature) as well as by predator mortality. Biologists do have an overall model of caribou population changes, based on population surveys, computer simulation studies, and knowledge of other cycling species, but the science of caribou cycles is still uncertain. Many ecologists are reluctant to refer to caribou as a cycling species for the lack of hard data. Western science has simply not recorded a full cycle of increase–decline–increase.

Cree Knowledge of Caribou in Context

In contrast to biologists, aboriginal hunting peoples of Alaska and Northern Canada have experienced many full cycles. For example, the Inuit who live to the north of the Cree above the treeline, believe that there is a natural population cycle in caribou (Milton Freeman, personal communication). To the Cree also, caribou population fluctuations are cyclical, but these are not predictable, periodic cycles. Cree elders' wisdom predicts the return of the caribou but says nothing about its timing, consistent with the Dene notion about the unpredictability of the ways of the caribou. To the Cree, caribou declines and increases are mysterious—but only in part. They are partially explainable in terms of hunter–animal relationships. Declines are related to the ethical transgressions of hunters, as discussed in Chapter 5. Whereas Elton's (1942) data come from biological science and from the records of missionaries and traders, the "data" of the Cree hunter come from culturally transmitted traditional knowledge, stories told by elders, and from the hunter's own day-to-day observations. The caribou are part of the living landscape shared by the Cree and other beings.

However, Cree caribou knowledge is not likely to be as rich as that of the Dene (Northern Athapascans) who occupy the broad swath of the boreal/subarctic from Manitoba to Alaska, and who are among the great experts on caribou. According to Smith (1978), the very social organization of the Dene groups of the central Canadian subarctic can be explained in terms of adaptation to caribou movements. Well positioned groups monitored the possible migration routes. Rules regarding kinship and marriage favored the formation of social links across a broad geographic front, facilitating communication.

> Hunting groups were strategically situated in a long narrow front (of some 1000 km), with relatively shallow depth, near the treeline, from a point west of Hudson Bay to Great Slave Lake. . . . They were thus potentially in contact with all the constituent herds of the Kaminuriak, Beverly and Bathurst populations of caribou. The hunting groups may be viewed as strategically situated reconnaissance patrols for collecting information on caribou movements and intentions. . . . Survival resulted from the spatial placement of regional and local bands and hunting

groups, bound to one another by complex ties of kinship and marriage, which provided a communications network extending through those bands dependent on the caribou.

(Smith 1978: 75, 83)

The spatial arrangement of the bands followed the transition zone from forest to tundra, making it possible for the hunters to exploit either zone. Local band centers were located at fishing lakes to provide a reliable food supply. Periodic excursions to the north of the treeline kept the Dene well-informed of caribou distributions, but the key period for the reconnaissance work was during the caribou fall migration because this is when the Dene could make educated guesses about where the herds would move for the winter. According to the archaeological record, this spatial arrangement had considerable time depth, allowing hunters to accumulate a great many generations of data (Smith 1978).

Box 6.1 provides detail on how this system worked from one group of Dene at the eastern end of Great Slave Lake. They are the Denesoline people (the eastern Dene, also called Chipewyan) now living in the village of Lutsel K'e (formerly Snowdrift). It is based on Parlee *et al.* (2005a) and to some extent on Kendrick *et al.* (2005). The upper panel of Figure 6.2 shows the trails that Denesoline patrols used to spread out from their summer/fall grounds and to move north to meet the caribou. The fall migration movements of the caribou take them from their summer grounds in the tundra, south across the treeline, into their over-wintering grounds. The trails were used also by family groups moving back and forth between alternative hunting camps.

The overall logic of the Denesoline is summarized in Figure 6.2, lower panel. Hunters disperse to intercept the caribou, watching the land and caribou movements. They are observing indicators of the health of the caribou and of the range, while trying to guess the intentions of the caribou. When the patrols encounter the caribou in the fall, the point is not to hunt them but to observe which way they are heading at the crossings, to reduce the uncertainty of *future* hunts from the winter hunting camps when the whole family is present. The key to the system is the use of bifurcation points in the migration path of the caribou, to predict winter distributions and to locate or relocate the camps accordingly.

Being able to observe how the caribou split at bifurcation points is important. When I was involved in the monitoring of impacts of the first of the new diamond mines in the Northwest Territories (IEMA 2011), I talked to Dene elders who wanted to be at the mine site right at the time of the caribou fall migration. They were guessing that the mine would act as a bifurcation point, and they wanted to see how the caribou would respond. Their concern was very practical. If the herds were deflected north of the mine and the new mining road, they would end up in

Box 6.1 How Denesoline Hunters Dealt with Caribou Uncertainty

Denesoline elders of Lutsel K'e say, "The caribou go where they want to go." Yet they had ways of monitoring caribou movements and a strategy for locating their winter hunting camps in a way that minimized uncertainty. In the fall, small groups of hunters organized themselves into reconnaissance parties and moved north to intercept the caribou herds moving south. The fall migrations of the caribou would take them to their overwintering area—but where? The tundra is marked with innumerable caribou tracks from time immemorial. Which of these tracks would the caribou take this year? The Denesoline needed a sophisticated monitoring system to narrow down the possibilities and assure themselves of a winter food supply.

They knew that the large lakes ("big water") limited caribou movements to shorelines and narrows. Caribou avoid large stretches of water and seek narrows where they can cross quickly. These water crossings (*eda*) and other major landscape features around the large lakes are known to the Denesoline as bifurcation points of caribou populations moving south. Like the caribou, hunters traveled along the eskers, other heights of land and shorelines. Use of these landscape features made travel easier and increased the likelihood of encountering caribou. As hunters came within sight of the water crossings, they looked for signs of caribou, and used "waiting places" (*k'a*) to listen and watch for caribou movements on the horizon. Observing caribou movements at the crossings was key to making decisions about where to locate their winter hunting camps. Hunters would watch to see which way the caribou were deflected at these bifurcation points. This enabled them to anticipate where the main caribou populations would most likely end up for the winter. Denesoline hunters observed a number of indicators, including caribou behavior and body condition (fatness), and landscape conditions such as areas rich with reindeer lichen and areas spoiled by fire. These conditions helped shape caribou movements, funneling caribou this way or that way, so that the Denesoline would know where best to establish their camps.

Source: Parlee *et al.* (2005a).

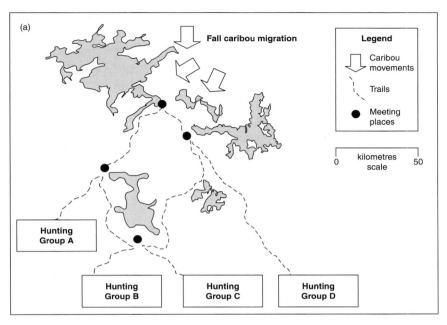

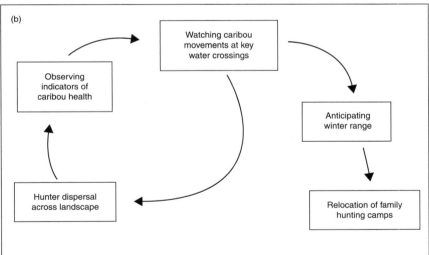

Figure 6.2 Panel A: Hunter organization across the landscape to patrol caribou migrations at key crossings, to be able to anticipate winter range.

Panel B: Denesoline strategy to deal with caribou uncertainty.

Source: Re-drawn from Parlee *et al*. (2005a).

the territory of their northwestern Dene neighbors, the Dogrib. If they were deflected south, more of them would end up in the Denesoline lands.

The reconnaissance system of the Denesoline and other central subarctic Dene is unusual among traditional knowledge and management systems. Because of their network-like organization, they have the ability to collect *synchronic* data (short time-series over a large area), as well as *diachronic* data (long time-series) that is more typical of traditional knowledge systems. The Denesoline example shows that, under certain circumstances, synoptic systems of data collection characteristic of Western scientific systems can also develop among traditional peoples. It is the capability of collecting both synchronic and diachronic information, and making sense of it, that made the Dene the experts on the caribou.

In contrast to the Dene, anthropologists and other Western scholars do not associate eastern James Bay Cree with caribou. Many of their neighbors, the Inuit of Northern Quebec and the Innu (Naskapi and Montagnais) of the eastern part of the Quebec–Labrador Peninsula, are all well-known caribou specialists, although probably not to the same degree as some of the Dene groups. By contrast, the eastern James Bay Cree have seen and hunted the occasional small groups of caribou over the past century, but certainly not the great migrations of caribou. Thus, the notion of "Cree traditional knowledge of caribou" is at odds with the fact that most Chisasibi Cree had never seen a caribou until the 1980s. Caribou herds were last present in the area in the 1910s (Speck 1935: 81; Elton 1942). Records of the Hudson's Bay Company (HBC) from the 1600s to the 1800s indicate that caribou were periodically abundant in the area. It was one of the major food resources of the James Bay Cree in the area north of Eastmain, and a source of irritation to HBC traders because Cree hunters would periodically take off after the caribou instead of concentrating on trapping furs for the HBC (Francis and Morantz 1983: 7).

Hunting grounds of the Chisasibi Cree people are rich in caribou-related place names. Examples include Point Attiquane (Caribou Point) where caribou antlers from ancient hunts may still be found, and Maanikin Lake, *maanikin* being a caribou aggregating device, a corral. The official name of the lake on the map is Lake Darontal, near the much larger Lac Julian. Caribou-related expressions are found in Cree language as well. For example, a late spring snowfall is called *attik-sthaw*, newborn-caribou-footprint-snow. Chisasibi hunting lore is likewise rich with caribou natural history. Examples include, "How do you tell the sex of animals in the herd you are following?" (From the shape of digging marks in snow, "feeding craters" to reach lichens; males and females dig differently.) "How do you tell if there is a really big bull in the group?" (His tracks in the snow would go wide around trees because the big bull takes care not to entangle his large antlers. This is important to know for safety reasons: caribou are not usually dangerous, but Cree hunters are wary of big bulls.)

A traditional winter caribou hunt was a communal affair and targeted not individual animals but groups of caribou. A *maanikin* would be constructed with posts placed like a fence. The fence would get narrower and narrower and force the caribou into a single file. Snares would then be used to tangle up and stop them, and the animals would be dispatched with bows and arrows and spears. To lead the caribou into the corral, the ancient hunters used trees in the general shape of human figures, dotting the land to deflect caribou into the area toward the *maanikin*. The Cree technique is similar to the traditional practices of the Dene of the central subarctic. The Dene used what Smith (1978) calls "chute and pound," made of cut trees with a maze within the pound in which the caribou were caught in snares or speared. A variant was a drift fence that directed caribou along certain paths. The *inukshuk* of the Inuit, built of stone in the shape of human figures, served a similar purpose to the Cree and Dene drift fences, showing that these ethnically distinct groups shared certain traditional practices.

Caribou Return to the Land of the Chisasibi Cree

Chisasibi hunters saw their first large caribou hunt of this century in the winter of 1982–3. According to information from hunters, most of the kills occurred in the far eastern portion of the community hunting area and amounted to some one hundred animals. The following winter, large numbers of caribou appeared further west, in an area accessible by road. In fact, many were right on the road serving a newly constructed hydroelectric dam in the eastern part of the community area. Hunters said "large numbers" were taken, probably several hundreds but the actual kill was unknown, and the hunt was a frenzied affair. The caribou stayed in the area only for a month or so. Chisasibi hunters used the road, bringing back truckloads of caribou. There was so much meat that, as one hunter put it, "people overdosed on caribou." Some people even allowed meat to spoil.

People were excited about the return of the caribou. However, community leaders were concerned, not because of large numbers killed, but because some hunters had been shooting wildly, letting wounded animals get away, killing more than they could carry, wasting meat, not disposing of wastes properly. Chisasibi Cree hunters' code speaks strongly about wastage and calls for burning or burying of animal remains. The leaders were worried that hunters' attitudes and behaviors signaled a lack of respect for the caribou, a serious transgression of the traditional code in which ritual respect ensures that animals will continue to make them-selves available. It is a system of mutual obligations: "show no respect and the game will retaliate" (see Chapter 5).

In the winter of 1984–5, there were almost no caribou on the road. Hunters in trucks waited and waited and many left empty-handed. Those who had the skills to go into the bush and hunt without causing disturbance nevertheless came back with reasonable kills. According to information from hunters, about three hundred caribou were taken, only a fraction of the hunt in the previous year. Back in town, many people were now worried: Had the caribou decided not to come to the Chisasibi hunting grounds after all? The time was right for elders and leaders to do something about their concerns and to draw some lessons from the apparent reluctance of the caribou to come back.

A community meeting was called. Two of the most respected elders stepped forward. Among the Chisasibi Cree, there is no one traditional chief. The elected chief occupies a political position and may change from election to election. The real leadership is a corporate leadership provided by a group of senior hunters and respected elders, as represented in this case by the two elders who came forward. The elders did not voice their concerns and neither did they criticize the hunters who had been breaking the code of ethics. Instead they told a story.

It was the story of the disappearance of the caribou shortly after the turn of the century. Caribou had been declining on the James Bay coast in the latter decades of the century but continued to be plentiful in the Caniapiscau area, near the center of the Labrador Peninsula. This was a great caribou hunting area and a culturally important region where neighboring groups mixed. The Cree of Chisasibi came from the southwest, the Cree of Mistassini came from the south, the Cree of Great Whale came from the northwest, the Naskapi and Montagnais (Innu) of Labrador came from the east, and the Inuit of Ungava Bay came from the north to hunt the great migrating herds of caribou as they crossed the Caniapiscau River.

It was here, in the 1910s, that a disaster occurred, the elders told. Hungry for caribou and equipped with repeating rifles, which had just become widely available, previously respectful hunters became dizzy with newfound power over animals, lost all self-control, and slaughtered the caribou at the crossing points on the Caniapiscau, in an area known as Limestone Falls. Instead of "taking care of the caribou," the hunters killed too many and wasted so much food that the river was polluted with rotten carcasses, the elders told. The following year, the hunters waited and waited, and there were no caribou. None at all. The caribou had disappeared and they were not to be seen for generations.

The elders were now coming to the point of the teaching. The story they were telling was in fact familiar to most, if not all, of the hunters. The slaughter and the subsequent disappearance of the caribou were etched in the collective memory of Chisasibi Cree and had become part of their oral history. But the disappearance of the caribou was not permanent, the elders reminded the hunters. All changes occurred in cycles, and all was not lost. Subsequent to the disaster, the elders continued their story, the wise men had made a prediction: the caribou would once again become plentiful. The caribou would return one day, but the hunters had to take good care of them if the caribou were to stay. It was this prediction that the elders were now retelling, some 70 years later, in Chisasibi in the winter of 1984–5.

By all accounts, the elders' words had a profound effect on the younger hunters. The caribou had indeed come back, true to the old peoples' prediction, validating oral history. However, by violating traditional ethics, were they about to lose the caribou once again?

In the winter of 1985–6, the hunt was carried out very differently. It was a productive hunt and 867 caribou were taken, about two per household, according to the survey done by the Chisasibi Cree Trappers Association (CTA). The CTA had now taken upon itself the responsibility of monitoring the hunt. Overseen by the elders, hunting leaders, and other hunters who make up the membership of the CTA, the hunt was conducted in a controlled and responsible manner, in accordance with traditional standards. There was little wastage, no wild shooting. The harvest was transported efficiently, and wastes from butchering were cleaned up promptly. The Cree exercised their self-management rights under the James Bay Agreement that had been signed ten years previously. The Cree hunters devised the solutions themselves, and government resource managers were not even involved (Drolet *et al.* 1987).

The caribou kept coming. To the Cree it seemed that the caribou were responding to the restoration of proper hunting ethics and respect. They were moving much deeper into the Chisasibi area. Some of the largest numbers were seen halfway between the coast and the eastern limit of the Chisasibi community hunting area. Hunters were ecstatic. In the spring of 1986, caribou were seen right on the James Bay coast for the first time in living memory. Some hunters were passing up the chance to hunt the small, scattered groups of caribou near the coast, until the caribou re-established themselves; instead, the hunters concentrated on the larger aggregations of caribou to the east. By 1990, hunters' observations of tracks showed that caribou had reached the sea all along the James Bay coast, re-establishing the former range of the 1900s. Their observations were consistent with the results of surveys carried out by government biologists (see Figure 6.1).

How did these remarkable changes come about? What was going through the minds of the people? My own field notes from Chisasibi summarize the events of the three years after the restoration of hunting ethics and provide a closer took at the dynamics of traditional knowledge and ethics in action.

A Gathering of the Hunters

The scene: a small meeting room that doubles as the office of the Cree Trappers Association (CTA) in the large building that functions as Chisasibi's administrative center and shopping mall. Topographic maps cover the walls, with the boundaries of Chisasibi's family hunting/trapping territories shown in black lines and the location of last winter's bush radio locations marked with red pins (radios rented from the CTA, one per territory, for safety and communication). Other maps mark the floodlines from the James Bay hydroelectric project and the location of the gravel roads, and the extra-wide (three meter) winter trails being built for the hunters for winter travel. An old man sits in the far corner, playing with what seems to be the pieces of an old bush radio.

The meeting of the Chisasibi CTA does not quite start at the announced hour, but no one seems to mind. We are on "Indian time"; even the band meeting earlier that week had started an hour late. People are dribbling into the meeting room until all the chairs are full (about 20) and there is little room to sit on the floor (another 20 or so). A couple more chairs are brought in as a few particularly respected elders enter the room. The head of the CTA does have an agenda for the meeting but the speakers often digress. There are no knee-slapping jokes but much good-humored banter and a great deal of laughter, as members discuss a variety of issues, from the price of beaver pelts to the upcoming spring goose hunt.

A few remain serious. There is a list of topics to be discussed and decided upon and someone has to make sure that the agenda is covered. Discussion is democratic and freewheeling. Experts and the elders speak relatively little. Some of the younger hunters tend to speak more. All speakers receive a respectful hearing. No one interrupts the speaker, and no one is cut short, not even those who are off-topic. Halfway though the meeting, a smiling man brings a large bag of pop drinks and chocolate bars for all to share. A stack of checks is distributed from the last fur auction. Someone brings a photocopy of an anti-trapping letter to the editor of the Montreal *Gazette*. This generates some heated discussion. The topic soon shifts to something more cheerful: increasing caribou numbers. By now, caribou have become just another discussion item for the hunters. The people of Chisasibi have adjusted to a new life with caribou, as my field notes tell the rest of the story.

Winter of 1985–6

The most celebrated issue is the continuing increase in caribou numbers. This winter Chisasibi hunters obtained far more caribou than moose and black bear, the other big game animals of the area. Caribou tracks are running east–west. Two years ago, the herds were still far inland. This year, big hunts are taking place halfway to the coast. Reports are coming in from Mistassini to the southeast interior and from Wemindji to the south. For the first time, north coast (north of Chisasibi on the James Bay coast) hunters are reporting that, not only are the caribou coming, but they are staying longer, right into the spring. Not so yet on the south coast. But SH (initials of a person) reports large numbers southeast of Eastmain, the Cree village at the mouth of Eastmain River. Somehow the caribou must have crossed southward across the chain of hydroelectric reservoirs on La Grande River. Old GB jokes that he shot his "first caribou" at age 72, three years ago. (The humor is that "the first hunt" for various species is a rite of passage normally enjoyed by an adolescent hunter.) GL mentions that some of the hunters in the Cape Jones area are refraining from hunting, so that the herds would not be disturbed and scared off. He himself shot two caribou last winter near the coast, at the "Old-Man-with-the-Knife" Lake, just north of the Roggan River, which is an old caribou site according to elders. Elders' information is reliable, he chuckles with satisfaction.

A visit with DS brings out an engrossing tale. DS's father, 77 years old, had never seen a caribou in his hunting area on the north coast of James Bay. The caribou had disappeared in DS's grandfather's time, when his grandfather was in "his prime," in his thirties or forties. The grandfather had been a real caribou expert and had had a great deal of knowledge about the caribou, which he passed on to DS's father, and his father unto him. (GL adds an aside, oral history easily reaches back one hundred years, he says.) DS continues. This winter for the first time, a large group of caribou, about 50, was seen in his territory. They made a lazy circle, first swinging east, then south, and then clockwise back to the coast. They looked like they were checking out the territory. Not feeding very much. Just looking like they were getting to know the land. They were in precisely the area where his grandfather said caribou were last seen before they disappeared. I finally ask: were you hunting or just watching? DS looks serious and lost in his thoughts. He shakes his head, no, he did not shoot any, just followed them and watched them. The previous year he saw just a few, did not kill any then, either. Now this year they have doubled. Maybe next year they will increase again and get settled into the area. Then he will take some.

Winter of 1986–7

Caribou numbers keep on increasing. There are more now on the James Bay coast. They come with the first snow. In November, they appear in the area north of Chisasibi. In December, there is a large migration northward, through Cape Jones and Long Island, where James Bay meets Hudson Bay. They are pursued by wolves. According to the hunters' informal monitoring network, this is the first report of large wolf numbers. One caribou GL got this week had a gash on his leg. The Cree do not normally see many wolves. When they do, they consider it an omen and consult the elders for an interpretation.

Among the north coast families, the SN are still not hunting the caribou on their territory; they are hunting the wolves, though, plenty of them. Some of the other families are hunting the caribou. GL's group got 13 on a weekend hunt. Many of the hunters went for the large ones, with big antlers. He got two himself, selected them carefully, one medium-sized female to give away and a smaller one for home. He presented the first one to an old man (to honor him, to signify respect). Hunters noted large fat deposits on the caribou, indicating healthy animals and good feeding conditions. After all, the lichen in that area has been growing undisturbed for almost a century now.

I find SB and his dad with rolled-up sleeves, processing caribou skins. First, they scrape off the inner skin and fat, then they shave off the hair using the blade of an old hockey skate. Then they soak the skin, then they wash it in a solution of brains, a widely used Cree recipe for tanning. SB took five caribou this winter, gave one away. He is feeding two families, and experimenting with the skins. His brother JB smiles; they are experiencing full use, he says, from the hunt to skin processing—the full life cycle of caribou tradition.

In January, the northward migrating herd appeared right at the Hudson Bay town of Great Whale (Poste de la Baleine) for the first time. This is a mixed town of Cree and Inuit, and everyone was surprised to see caribou so close—eye to eye, as one puts it. They got up one morning to see caribou just outside their windows. Only last year, they were going all the way to Lake Minto for their caribou, an air charter distance. But now the caribou are here and you can approach them. The people maintain self-control, however, and every household takes a couple but there is no wild shooting and no waste. The chief of Great Whale reports that they had to chase the caribou off the town dump, and off the town's airstrip! He is proud that the people kept their composure. Someone in Chisasibi relates a Great Whale Inuit belief: When you are hunting caribou at a crossing point, never take the first three caribou in the lead. They lead the herd. Instead, you take the ones at the end. If you leave the ones in the front, they will bring the caribou back the same way next year.

Winter of 1987–8

Now all family groups on the coast are hunting. The caribou are so abundant this spring that they scared off the geese and disrupted the spring goose hunt. Many caribou stay near the coast over the winter. There are some even on Fort George Island, the former village site of Chisasibi. However, there are also signs for the first time that not all is well. Quite a few caribou are found dead in the eastern part of the community territory. Government biologists on the co-management board (the Hunting, Fishing, and Trapping Coordinating Committee established under the James Bay Agreement) ask the Cree representatives for their opinion. Some of the dead caribou seem to have been killed by wolves. The Cree think the wolves do not always eat what they kill. Hunters also notice that fat deposits in the caribou are less than they were in the previous years. The Cree request through the co-management board that the government start taking measures to control the access of non-natives into the area and to tighten the regulation of sport hunters. In the meantime, both the government of Quebec and the government of Newfoundland and Labrador are entertaining proposals for a commercial caribou hunt of the George River herd.

Lessons for the Development of a Conservation Ethic

No doubt the caribou on Cree lands will decline again some day, and the eternal cycle will continue. When I visited Wemindji (just south of Chisasibi) in 2005 and 2006, the caribou were so abundant and easy to hunt that they were being taken for granted, much like packaged meat in the local supermarket (but much cheaper). The story told in this chapter unfolded over a six-year period. I was not a participant in the development of the hunt and the redesign of the caribou management system but merely a bystander and a witness who happened to be present at the right time and the right place. I was, after all, studying mainly the Cree fishery, not caribou. But I was engaged in participatory research, living and eating with the people of Chisasibi, socializing in the community, going on fishing and hunting trips, and learning about traditional knowledge and practice by doing as well as listening. I was therefore exposed to the holistic picture of the hunting economy and ethics.

This chapter does not claim to provide a detailed scholarly analysis of the events around the caribou case. It merely tells a story and suggests a likely way in which a conservation ethic may have developed or changed on the basis of historical experience and social learning. As far as the Crees were concerned, the disappearance of the caribou in the 1910s was unambiguously linked to the last, big, wasteful hunt. The slaughter was not merely an aboriginal myth; it can be located in historical time through the records that Elton (1942) used. The lesson of the transgression, once learned, survived for 70 years in Cree oral history, and it was revived precisely in time to redesign the hunting system when the caribou returned. Had there been government intervention to regulate the Chisasibi caribou hunt, it could not possibly have had as much impact on the hunters as did the teachings of the elders (Drolet *et al.* 1987). The lesson delivered (not to kill too many and not to waste) came right at the heels of the validation of the elders' prediction that the caribou would return one day, and it was too powerful to take lightly, even for the most skeptical young hunter.

The caribou story debunks the "noble savage" myth. The ethics described in Chapter 5 represent the ideal. The Cree hunter's actual behavior can and does deviate from the ideal and the ethical. However, it can also be self-corrected. Self-control is a strong social value among the Cree (Preston 1979, 2002), and the community provides the support, and the necessary social coercion, to help the hunter remain ethical. Even more significant, ethics itself develops—through making mistakes and learning from mistakes. The Cree caribou case has lessons, for example, for the controversy over indigenous residents in protected areas in the Amazon. In response to conservation purists who want to exclude people from protected areas, Holt (2005) argues that people should have the political space to learn from their own mistakes and develop their own conservation ethics. But how does such conservation come about? Tukano shamans acting as ecosystem doctors is one such mechanism (Chapter 3).

In the Cree case, the key role in this dynamic social learning process is played by the holders of the knowledge and the values: the elders. Cree society relies on oral history, and the elders span the generations to provide information feedbacks. What makes elders "wise"? Certainly, not all old people have wisdom, and some people in their fifties may be considered elders. "Elder" is not an age designation but a social position among the Cree and many other indigenous groups. In my opinion, the "wisdom" in the present case is in the elders' timing (they waited for a whole year after the transgression until people were likely to be receptive to their message), their choice of message (the well-known story of the caribou over-kill at Limestone Falls), and their effective use of myth (the ancient prophecy that the caribou will always return but the hunters have to maintain the code of respect).

The starting hypothesis in this chapter was that a conservation ethic can develop if a resource is important, predictable, and depletable, and if it is effec-tively under the control of the social group in question so that the group can reap the benefits of conservation. Choosing caribou as the example made the task chal-lenging. The caribou are important, but the remaining prerequisites (predictability, depletability, control) for the development of a conservation ethic are not easily met. The caribou are certainly not predictable, necessitating the development of ways to reduce uncertainty (Box 6.1). You have to be able to guess where the main populations are likely to be. But once they return to a particular area, certain distributional and behavioral aspects of caribou make them predictable, as discov-ered by the hunter who verified for his own satisfaction that the caribou were in precisely the area where his grandfather said they were last seen. On the question of depletability, however, information is still missing until it is supplied by histor-ical experience and social learning, so there is now a compelling reason to limit harvests. Note that the Cree are not unusual in this regard (Nelson 1982). The Chipewyan (Dene) also did not have a prohibition against waste as long as caribou were considered super-abundant (Heffley 1981; Nelson 1982).

Finally, the question of control comes up explicitly in 1987–8 when there is a threat that the caribou resource will be opened up to uncontrolled numbers of outsiders. It is interesting to note that the Chisasibi Cree do not see neighboring aboriginal groups as a problem. In fact, they are constantly exchanging information with them (Wemindji, Eastmain, Great Whale and Mistassini Cree, the Innu, and the Inuit) to keep track of large-scale caribou movements. Sport hunters, however, are not part of this network and are not in the sphere of a conservation ethic that is recognizable to the Cree. Hence, starting in 1988, the Cree take political steps to safeguard "their" resources from outsiders.

Lessons for Management Policy and Monitoring

In addition to issues of conservation ethic, the caribou story in this chapter has some very interesting lessons on the question of environmental monitoring, and it has some implications for management policy. First, I discuss monitoring and second, return to the issue of uncertainty and its implications for the management of reindeer, caribou's Eurasian relative.

Consistent with the findings of other studies on large mammal management of northern indigenous hunters (Winterhalder 1983; Feit 1987; Kendrick *et al.* 2005; Kendrick and Manseau 2008), the story in this chapter suggests that the Cree and Dene systems for caribou hunting monitor some of the same information base as does Western science—geographic distributions, migration patterns and their change, individual behavior, sex and age composition of the herd, fat deposits in caribou, the presence/absence and effect of predators, and range conditions such as lichen abundance and effects of fire. Of these indicators, the fat content of the caribou seems to receive relatively more attention by the indigenous experts than by biologists.

This finding may be significant because there is evidence that some other traditional management systems also monitor fat content. According to discussions in a traditional knowledge workshop in Labrador, September 1997 (Manseau 1998), every indigenous group represented around the table knew about and used caribou fat monitoring. The groups included the Inuit of Northern Quebec, Inuit of Labrador, and the Innu of Labrador. It is known that indigenous hunters belonging to a number of different groups in Alaska and the Northwest Territories also monitor caribou fat content (Kofinas *et al.* 2003). As documented in some detail by Kofinas (1998), three indicators based on the monitoring of body fat (back fat, stomach fat, and marrow) top the list of some nine indicators of a healthy caribou, as used by the aboriginal hunters of the Porcupine Caribou Herd at the Alaska–Yukon border.

As a rule of thumb, the monitoring of fat content for caribou management makes a great deal of sense because it provides an index of health of both the individual animal and the herd. Fat as indicator integrates the effects of a number of environmental factors, such as environmental stresses and range conditions, acting on the caribou population. It is therefore not surprising that the monitoring of caribou fat is not merely an area-specific bit of local knowledge but rather a *principle of traditional ecological knowledge* widely applicable across the full range of caribou distribution from Labrador to Alaska.

How widely is the principle applicable? Kofinas *et al.* (2003) developed a protocol for community-based monitoring of caribou body condition applicable in all the areas where caribou are found. Different from local monitoring programs in which indigenous people may be employed to carry out monitoring designed by scientists, the protocol by Kofinas and colleagues aims for community-based monitoring in which the logic and methodology are derived from traditional ecological knowledge. Such approaches may be applicable to other areas and other species as well. For example, the Rakiura Maori of New Zealand monitor and record the fatness of sooty shearwater (a seabird) chicks that they harvest (Lyver 2002; Moller *et al.* 2004).

What the Cree and other indigenous peoples monitor has many similarities to scientific monitoring in terms of the information-base used. At the same time, it is fundamentally different from Western science which often gives priority to quantitative measures, and uses population models for management decision-making. The Cree system, by contrast, neither produces nor uses quantitative measures. Rather, it uses a qualitative mental model that provides hunters with an indication of the *population trend over time*, along with the relative health of the animals. This qualitative model reveals the direction (increasing/decreasing) in which the population is headed, and the fatness trend of the animals. It does not require the quantitative estimation of the population size itself for making decisions.

Such traditional knowledge is complementary to Western scientific knowledge, and not a replacement for it. Monitoring fat content alone will not lead to good management decisions, for example, in the case of predator-limited (as opposed to range-limited) caribou populations, and in the case of a caribou population affected, say, by two or three successive bad winters (Anne Gunn, personal communication). On the other hand, exclusive reliance on biological population survey data will not necessarily lead to good management decisions either. There are several cases in the Canadian North and Alaska, with caribou and other wildlife, in which the results of biological censuses misled management decisions and were subsequently corrected by the use of other biological perspectives *and* traditional knowledge of indigenous groups (Freeman 1989, 1992). Such cases illustrate the complementarity of traditional and Western knowledge at a practical level, and highlight the need for conceptual pluralism in resource and ecosystem management.

A final point about management concerns uncertainty and adaptive management. "No one knows the way of the winds and the caribou," probably because the arctic/subarctic ecosystems which are the home of the caribou are themselves unpredictable. This chapter discussed how Dene hunters cope with caribou uncertainty. Research from Scandinavia is establishing that the Saami people have also developed ways of dealing with uncertainty, in this case, it is the uncertainty of the environment in which the reindeer live.

For Saami reindeer herders, a "beautiful herd" is one that has high levels of diversity with respect to age, sex, color, body types, and temperament of the animals. Even apparently non-productive animals have particular roles that contribute to the well-being of the herd as a whole (Tyler *et al.* 2007). This is of course the opposite of the ideal of homogeneity of a pure-bred herd of livestock developed by selection for the requirements of modern high-yield production systems. The traditional management system with high levels of diversity is interpreted as an adaptation to reducing vulnerability to unfavorable and unpredictable environmental conditions. For example, Saami herders speak of the importance of the large males for breaking through crusts of ice on the accumulated snow cover to get at lichens below; without these large males, the whole herd may starve (Tyler *et al.* 2007).

However, agronomists consider adult males unproductive, and the Saami have been under pressure from government authorities to drastically reduce the proportion of adult males and move to the ideal of homogenous, pure-bred livestock. But domestic reindeer live and feed in the open. They fend for themselves and need to cope with environmental variability and uncertainty, especially in an age of climate change in which the frequency of extreme weather events (see Chapter 8) is increasing, including unseasonable rain that leads to crusting on ice. "The increased proportion of females in herds reflects agronomists' translation of modern high yield production practices to reindeer pastoralism. The reduced heterogeneity of herds represents a reversal of the traditional approach; its consequences . . . remain largely unknown" (Tyler *et al.* 2007: 197).

By trial and error over the centuries, Dene hunters and Saami pastoralists have found ways to deal with environmental uncertainties. However, their traditional knowledge systems, adaptive management in the scientific terminology, remain obscure to non-indigenous authorities. In the case of indigenous Canadian caribou hunters, there have been controversies between hunters and government authorities over caribou numbers (Freeman 1989). In the case of indigenous

Photo 6.1 A Saami herder checks snow profile for crusting and other features before he lets his reindeer herd move. The reindeer must break through crusts of ice in the snow cover to reach lichens which are their food. The Saami have a rich vocabulary of snow terms (see Chapter 3). The measurements (snow depth and ground temperature) are collected for the government; the herder himself notes snow depth only on a three-point scale (see Chapter 9, on fuzzy logic). Kautokeino, Finnmark County, Norway.

Photo: Fikret Berkes.

Norwegian reindeer herders, there have been controversies between the Saami and government authorities over reindeer management strategies (Tyler *et al.* 2007). How can we approach the dilemma of finding common ground between Western science and indigenous knowledge?

The next chapter examines this question using a different resource system, the fishery. In the fishery of the Cree people of Chisasibi, there are scientific data that can be used to interpret Cree practices and their management outcomes. Are quantitative population models necessary to manage fisheries? Or are there alternative ways of managing fisheries that rely mainly on contextual information, the reading of environmental signals, and qualitative mental models that provide information on trends in abundance and availability?

CHAPTER 7

Cree Fishing Practices as Adaptive Management

The Cree fishery in James Bay is an example of a traditional system that can provide ecological and resource management insights. This chapter describes the unique characteristics of the fishery: its adaptability, flexibility, use of environmental signals or feedbacks, and its ability to conserve ecological resilience. These characteristics suggest that traditional systems may in some ways be analogous to Adaptive Management with its nonlinear, multi-equilibrium concept of ecosystem processes and its emphasis on uncertainty, resilience, and feedback learning. The chapter ends with the exploration of some of the implications of the case for the broader issue of fisheries management, not only for other areas of North America (Langdon 2006) but also internationally.

When I started working with the Chisasibi fishery in 1974, my original intent was to study the impacts of the giant James Bay hydroelectric project on the Cree fishery. (Impacts included the destruction of the fishery but for different reasons than experts initially thought—but that is another story; see Berkes 1981a, 1988a.) As time went by, I became more and more interested in traditional knowledge and Cree fishing practices. I found that extensive local knowledge existed on distributions, behavior, and life cycles of fish simply because such information was essential for productive fishing, as any fisher knows, and was at one time essential to survival. Chisasibi fishers knew, for example, that in spring the best catches of whitefish were obtained following the melting ice edge in bays; fishers knew where the pre-spawning aggregations were in August, and they knew that in

September whitefish was best harvested over a sand-gravel bottom at certain depths of water. Whereas most ethnobiologists busied themselves with the identification of species and the recording of aboriginal classification systems, this was only a minor interest for me. The boreal/subarctic was, in any case, a species-poor environment. Thus, my initial traditional knowledge emphasis was on the natural history of fish and fishing. But as I started to gain an understanding of the local system, my interests quickly turned to resource management.

As with many northern aboriginal groups, fish are a staple resource for the Cree of James Bay. They say one can rely on fish even when other resources fail or become unavailable. Unlike many of the other animal resources, the Cree take their fish almost for granted, and no rituals and ceremonies involving fish are found in contemporary Chisasibi (formerly known as Fort George). Nevertheless, there is respect for the fish. The principle that animals are in control of the hunt (see Chapter 5) holds also for fish. A fisher does not boast about his or her fishing. It is believed that boasting brings retaliation from the fish—they stop making themselves available. As well, one does not waste fish; one does not abuse fish by swearing at them or by "playing" with them; and one eats what one catches. The Cree are horrified at the thought of catch-and-release fishing practices commonly used in sport fisheries elsewhere in North America.

Most of the Chisasibi Cree fishery takes place in medium- and large-sized lakes, in the estuaries of rivers, and on the James Bay coast. The major fishing technique used in the estuary and on the coast involves setting short (50-meter) gill nets of various mesh sizes from 7-meter, outboard equipped canoes. Smaller paddle canoes, sometimes outboard equipped, are used in lakes and rivers. Other fishing techniques include hand-drawn seines at the base of rapids on the La Grande River, rod and reel, and traditional baited set lines for the larger predatory fish. Fishing seasons are part of the seasonal cycle of harvesting activities, and they are signaled by biophysical events in the landscape such as the spring ice breakup in the river and change of color of the vegetation in September. Fishers know how to recognize and respond to a variety of environmental feedbacks that signal what can be fished where and when. Master fishers or stewards provide leadership.

The Chisasibi fishery in 1974 was a subsistence fishery in which people fished for their own needs. There was no competition from commercial fisheries (Chisasibi was too far from markets and there never had been a commercial fishery), and there was minimal competition from sport fisheries. In isolated areas of Canada, subsistence fisheries are not regulated by government, unlike commercial fisheries, which do come under government regulation. The conventional scientific management systems for subarctic commercial fisheries in Canada have employed some combinations of the following tools: the type of fishing gear used, restrictions on gill-net mesh size, minimum fish size, season closures, and the

Photo 7.1 Hand-drawn seine at the first rapids, La Grande River near Chisasibi. This technique is one of several fishing methods used. In the right season, it was the preferred method for obtaining large harvests of cisco and whitefish, until a hydroelectric dam was built just upstream of the site.

Photo: Fikret Berkes.

prohibition of fishing at times and places when fish are spawning. Catch quotas are common, and maximum sustainable yield calculations based on population dynamics of the stock have also been used in the larger fisheries. The Chisasibi fishery being a subsistence fishery, I knew at the time I started my work that none of the above measures would be in effect. What I did not know was that the Cree had a system of their own.

The Chisasibi Cree System of Fishing

At first, the ways of the Chisasibi fishery seemed fairly simple. There were two basic strategies: small-mesh gill nets were used within commuting distance of the village (about a 15-kilometer radius) and a mix of larger-mesh gill nets were used further away. The most distant locations were visited rarely, perhaps once every ten years or more, and were fished mainly with large mesh sizes (Berkes 1981b; Berkes and Gonenc 1982). Hunters follow the traditional rule-of-thumb of rotating family hunting areas ideally over a cycle of four years (Feit 1973). Within these areas, fishing lakes would also be rotated, fished one year and then rested for a number of years before being fished again. However, the overall system is actually more complicated than that, as some fishing areas may be used several times per season, with rests in between, and distant lakes less than once every ten years. Thus, we have characterized the fishery as multiple-scale, in both space and time (Berkes 1998; Berkes *et al.* 2000).

Most of my fishery research took place near the village, where small-mesh (2½ in. or 63.5 mm) gill nets caught mostly the smaller-sized cisco (*Coregonus artedii*) and the larger-mesh ones (3½ in. or 88.9 mm and larger) mostly the larger-sized whitefish (*C. clupeaformis*). All of this was relatively easy to document after I had accumulated about two years of catch data based on the Cree fishery, traveling with the fishers to their customary locations and recording their catches. Selectivity of the smaller gill net was striking: it caught almost ten times more cisco than whitefish, while the larger gill nets caught five times more whitefish than cisco (see Table 7.1). I was unable to establish, however, if the fishers caught more cisco near the village because they used small nets or because there were more cisco than whitefish in the area. My question was soon answered.

As I got ready to use my own experimental nets, the accompanying Cree fisher who knew my concern but whom I had not asked for help, provided on his own initiative the perfect design for a field experiment. He fished two replicates of two paired nets, one 2½ in. and the other 3 in., side by side for nine consecutive days just across the river from the village (see Table 7.2). The experiment settled the question: there were very few whitefish at that location at that season. Even though the 3 in. net caught relatively more whitefish than did the 2½ in. net, the smaller net provided a higher catch per unit of effort, by a factor of two. There was no sense in using 3 in. or larger nets at that *particular* location and season, although the 3 in. net caught equal numbers of cisco and whitefish in the near-village fishery when all areas and seasons were averaged out (see Table 7.3). To make sure that my generalization held, I had to check and account for seasonal and for year-to-year variations in the catch per unit of effort (Berkes 1981b).

Table 7.1 Selectivity of different mesh sizes of gill nets for whitefish and cisco

Net, in.	No. of net sets	Whitefish		Cisco		Ratio of whitefish to cisco
		No.	Avg. wt., g	No.	Avg. wt., g	
2½	219	273	250	2,536	250	1:9.3
3	86	130	563	192	378	1:1.5
3½ and 4	30	102	694	22	552	4.6:1

Source: Berkes (1977).

Table 7.2 Catch per unit of effort with paired 2½ inch versus 3 inch gill nets

	Catch per net set, g	
	2½ in.	3 in.
Whitefish	110	227
Cisco	1,211	649
Total fish	3,164	1,439
No. of net sets	18	18

Source: Berkes (1977).

Table 7.3 Catch per net set for the four mesh sizes of gill nets in the near-village fishery *versus* away

		Near village, kg	Away from village, kg
2½ in. nets:	Whitefish	0.3	1.6
	Cisco	2.9	1.4
	Total catch	4.8	6.6
3 in. nets:	Whitefish	0.7	2.2
	Cisco	0.9	0.7
	Total catch	2.6	5.5
3½ in. and 4 in. nets:	Whitefish	1.0	2.9
	Cisco	0.1	0.6
	Total catch	2.1	7.8

Source: Berkes (1977).

I still was not sure, however, if the 2½ in. net actually *maximized* the catch per unit of effort in the area near the village. Could one use an even smaller net and get an even higher catch, even though the individual fish would be rather small? Just where were the limits of the system? Since the accompanying Cree fisher seemed to have no interest in carrying out *that* field experiment, I ended up using my own nets. The experiment did not last very long. With a 2 in. net, I found myself catching immature cisco, good numbers perhaps but definitely immature fish of the 20–25 cm size group. By contrast, the 2½ in. net had been catching 25–30 cm fish, four to five years old and mostly mature. My catches with the 2 in. net did not escape the attention of other fishers. Over the course of a day, several canoes drifted over to my nets, fishers looked at the size of the fish, measured the mesh with two fingers thrust in, muttered and shook their heads in disapproval. I had been in the village less than a year and already I was finding out what social sanctions were like. At first I defended my experiment as "science," but by the end of the second day, I had pulled out all the nets. (I discovered some months later that Cree had some stock phrases to ridicule fishers who used smaller nets than those dictated by custom: for example, one would say, "his nets are so small, he cannot put his penis through it.")

However, the system of socially enforced minimum mesh size for cisco did not conserve whitefish, a larger species. A mesh size of 2½ in. was taking immature whitefish; this was perhaps an explanation for the scarcity of whitefish in the waters near the village. Paradoxically, however, the apparent depletion of whitefish in that area but not elsewhere suggested an indigenous solution to the classical dilemma of a multi-species fishery. In Western resource management theory and practice, the curves of yield against fishing effort and against mesh size are different for each species. That is, it is always difficult to choose a mesh size because different species of fish grow and mature at different sizes. It is therefore impossible to harvest more than one species at the optimum level for each (Gulland 1974). In commercial fisheries, the choice of mesh size and other harvesting strategies often represents a compromise, and the overall results are rarely ideal.

What I was observing in the Chisasibi Cree traditional fishery was a management solution with a clear choice: away from the village, the effort was primarily directed at one larger-sized, highly desirable species, whitefish. Near the village, however, the effort was primarily directed against another, cisco, which was also a desirable species but matured at a smaller size and was probably able to withstand a higher fishing pressure. I still had to check whether this strategy *worked* and that the harvest was sustainable over a period of time.

I found that the productivity (measured as the catch per unit of effort) of the Chisasibi fishery as a whole compared favorably with other whitefish fisheries in the Canadian North (Berkes 1977). I also documented the number of reproductive year-classes in the near-village fishery based on essentially one population (or unit stock) of each of the two major species that inhabited the lower La Grande River and its estuary. The cisco had four reproductive year-classes, 4, 5, 6, 7, and a few of 8-year-old fish; the whitefish had three year-classes, 6, 7, 8, and a few of 9-year-olds (Berkes 1979). This many year-classes signaled a healthy cisco population but a somewhat overfished whitefish population, consistent with the earlier analysis. But what really made a convincing argument for sustainability was the comparison of my Chisasibi data with the results of a long-forgotten survey from the 1920s (Dymond 1933). Sampled 50 years apart in the same waters, Dymond's whitefish and cisco had exactly the same number of age-classes as mine, and the age-specific sizes were similar (Berkes 1979). Just to make sure, I checked my age and growth data against that of government researchers working on the James Bay hydroelectric project environmental impact study and satisfied myself that my biological data were reliable (Berkes 1981b).

By now, I was beginning to get a sense of the Chisasibi fishery as a managed system. The fishers used recognizable management strategies; the harvest was productive and sustainable. By knowing when and where to set the nets, the fishers exercised considerable selectivity over their harvest. In the near-village fishery, the fishers selected for cisco and against suckers (fish that people did not like to eat but used as dog food and trapping bait), and the selectivity could be documented by comparing the subsistence catch against biological samples, year after year (see Figure 7.1) (Berkes 1987a).

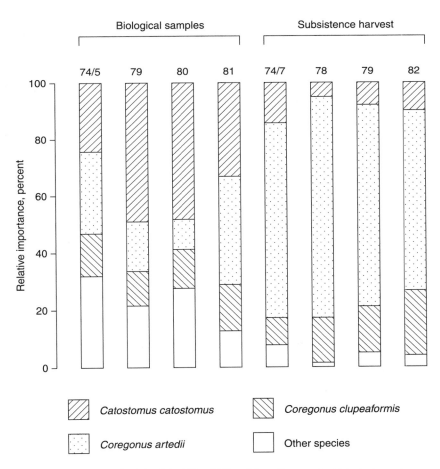

Figure 7.1 Fish species selectivity of the Chisasibi Cree fishery. Compare the biological samples against the subsistence fishery composition, showing selectivity for cisco (*C. artedii*) and whitefish (*C. clupeaformis*) and against suckers (*C. catostomus*).

Source: Modified from Berkes (1987a).

As well, I was beginning to understand the fundamental ways in which a subsistence fishery differed from a commercial fishery. People fished for their needs and there was no incentive to create a surplus. During the seasons when the fish were abundant, as in spring and fall in the La Grande estuary, two small nets were sufficient to catch enough for the needs of an average extended family. But in midsummer, the mean catch per net set decreased to about half of that in the spring months. Fishers compensated for this by setting about twice as many nets so that the daily harvest remained constant (see Table 7.4). The marginal effort required to manage an extra net was relatively low. One extra net took only about half an hour to set and minutes to check. In fact, people could set many more nets if they wanted to, but they did not. Their objective was to catch what they needed, about 10 kilograms per day in the case of the extended family (three nuclear families), documented in Table 7.4. The narrow range in the table indicates that "getting what you need" is indeed a fine art. Ten kilograms of fish was enough food for the family, and they could still provide smoked fish to their exchange network of relatives and friends. To harvest more would have meant to give away more. But since there was no lack of fish in the community, fish would likely be wasted—a transgression.

Being a product of Western scientific training, I was reluctant for a long time to refer to the Cree fishery as a "management system." The conventional wisdom is that if a group of traditional people *seemed* to be managing their resources sustainably, this can probably be explained on the basis of too few people and too "primitive" a technology to do damage to the resource. Well, the apparent productivity and sustainability of the Chisasibi fishery *could not* be explained simply on the basis of small population and inefficient technology. If fisheries management is defined as controlling how much fish is harvested, where, when, of what species, and of what sizes (Gulland 1974: 1), then the Chisasibi

Table 7.4 Relationship between fishing effort and catch per net set for one fishing group setting nets near village

	June	August	October	November
Total fish catch, kg	140	84	60	44
Number of net sets	32	39	14	8
Catch per net set, kg	4.4	2.2	4.3	5.5
Number of days	12	9	7	4
Net sets per day	2.67	4.33	2.00	2.00
Catch per day, kg	11.7	9.3	8.6	11.0

Source: Berkes (1977).

fishers were managing their fishery. Gulland commented that fisheries rarely achieved all of the above management objectives. It seemed therefore that Chisasibi fishers did better than most fishery managers by the very criteria of Western fishery management science.

Subarctic Ecosystems: Scientific Understanding and Cree Practice

Part of the reason many scientists have difficulty with the notion of traditional management concerns the question of information needs for resource management. The conventional wisdom in fish and wildlife management is that detailed population data are needed for management. According to this view, natural history types of information, including species identifications, life cycles, distributions, habits, and behavior—the kinds of information at which traditional peoples are experts—are necessary but insufficient for the needs of management. Indeed, Chisasibi Cree fishers lacked quantitative information, that is, they did not have data on the population dynamics of the harvested species. Not only that, the fishers openly disapproved of the kind of research biologists did to gather population information: sampling immature fish, and tagging fish to determine the range of the stock and to obtain population estimates by marking and recapturing.

To the Cree, these practices were disrespectful of the animals; they violated rules regarding wastage and about playing with fish. As for the biologists' objectives of "controlling" fish populations and "predicting" sustainable yields, the Cree thought that these were immodest aims of apparently immature people playing god, given that the success of fishing depended on whether the fish were willing to be caught, and the maintenance of an attitude of respect and humility by the fisher.

All of this highlighted a paradox in the research of traditional management systems: how do some of these societies do such a good job of managing resources, given that the very notion of management is inconsistent with their worldviews? In the case of the Chisasibi fishery, part of the answer lies with the traditional Cree understanding of the subarctic aquatic ecosystem. But Cree understanding of ecosystems is not articulated in the abstract; it is only reachable through their practices in the concrete (Lévi-Strauss 1962; Preston 1975). We will therefore switch to a Western ecological discourse on subarctic ecosystems before going back to describing the practice of the Cree fishery.

It is well known that subarctic ecosystems are characterized by low species diversity, high year-to-year variability in the biophysical environment, large population fluctuations or cycles, and generally low biological productivity. However, it is also known that fish population assemblages in unfished or lightly fished subarctic lakes are characterized by a large biomass of old (as much as 50- to 60-year-old) and large-sized fish, analogous, as Johnson (1976) pointed out, to the large biomass of trees in tropical forest ecosystems. The biological reason for the high biomass of such species as whitefish and lake trout (*Salvelinus namaycush*) is a matter of some scientific controversy, but the simplest explanation seems to be that proposed by Power (1978). Growth rates of individual fish in the subarctic are relatively rapid until maturity, but after maturity growth rates gradually slow down. Mortality rates decline rapidly through early life and stabilize at a low level once the fish has reached a large size. The combination of this growth and mortality pattern produces a population with many small, few intermediate-sized, and many large fish, hence the unusual bimodal (two-peaked) population length–frequency distributions often observed.

The presence of many large fish in an unfished or lightly fished northern lake gives the misleading impression of high ecosystem productivity. Since primary productivity (plant productivity) is low in the subarctic, fish productivity is low as well. Actual fish production in the estuaries in James Bay (the most productive part of the aquatic ecosystem) was calculated to be 0.3 to 1.3 kg/ha/yr; in the lakes it was even lower (Berkes 1981b). By contrast, in temperate coastal areas, lagoons, and lakes, common values are in the order of 50–100 kg/ha/yr. Those large, old subarctic lake fish only *seem* to be abundant; in fact, they take a very long time to renew themselves. A trophy-sized lake trout, likely to be over 50 years of age, is almost a nonrenewable resource! According to some studies in lakes of Canada's Northwest Territories, the production-to-biomass ratio of species such as whitefish is about 1:10. That is, as a rule-of-thumb, only about one-tenth (or less) of the fish biomass can be harvested each year on a sustainable basis for a given body of water.

However, even a fishing intensity that low could result in the removal of many of the old and large fish. This is not necessarily a bad thing, since the removal of such fish (and lowered competition for food) would result in higher survivorship, increased growth rates, and earlier maturation of the younger individuals of the same species. Analogous to harvesting a forest, such thinning of fish populations triggers increased productivity. This phenomenon is known to scientists and managers as "population compensatory responses" (Healey 1975) and occurs with all living resources. This is the Western scientific counterpart of the Cree notion that continued proper use of resources is essential for sustainability (see Chapter 5).

As the rate of exploitation of such a fish population increases, at a certain point the population is not going to be able to compensate for the loss of large individual fish and will eventually decline. Species will differ with respect to when this point is reached. For example, lake trout has a limited biological ability to respond to exploitation. Whitefish seem to have relatively greater ability, but species such as cisco, which mature at a smaller size, are better adapted to withstand high exploitation rates. These differences among species have been used to explain, for example, how the fish species composition of the Great Lakes has historically changed from one dominated by large, old, slow-growing, and late-maturing species such as sturgeon (*Acipenser fulvescens*) to one dominated by small, fast-growing, and early maturing fish such as yellow perch (*Perca flavescens*) (Regier and Baskerville 1986).

The two basic fishing strategies of the Chisasibi Cree could be interpreted in this light. Small-mesh gill nets used near the village are consistent with the relative abundance of cisco, a smaller species that matures earlier than does whitefish. The use of larger-mesh nets further away in water bodies exploited intermittently is consistent with the maintenance of populations of older and larger fish. Since the Cree do not use ecological formulations to articulate management choices, their system can only be inferred through their practices.

Three Cree Practices: Reading Environmental Signals for Management

Three readily observed sets of management practices provide insights into the "secrets" of the Cree system. The first is about concentrating fishing effort on aggregations of fish. The second concerns rotational or pulse fishing, with short periods of intensive effort with rest periods in between. The third involves the use of a mix of gill-net mesh sizes. All three practices are unusual by the standards of commercial, nontraditional fisheries. However, a number of fisheries ecologists have pointed out the merits of pulse fishing in northern commercial fisheries (Johnson 1976). I discuss each in turn.

The concentration of effort, when and where the prey is abundant, is probably typical of many subsistence systems. Subsistence fishers cannot afford to waste time and effort if they are not catching many. If the return from fishing is poor as compared to that from other subsistence activities, the Chisasibi Cree fisher will very quickly leave his nets and pick up his gun. Because they need to feed their families and because they have limited amounts of equipment, fishers select settings in which fish are easy to catch. Thus, groups of fishers will concentrate, year after year, on the same spawning or pre-spawning aggregations, and on feeding, migrating, and overwintering concentrations of fish, at specific times and places.

An example of such a site is the First Rapids of La Grande River where (until dams were built), large numbers of cisco in pre-spawning aggregations could be obtained in August at the foot of the rapids (Berkes 1987a). There is a high

Photo 7.2 Chisasibi Cree harvesting fish. The Cree optimize catches by rotational or pulse fishing, whereby fishing effort is concentrated on one area at a time, followed by a long period of rest for the area between pulses.

Photo: Fikret Berkes.

premium on fishers' knowledge about the timing and locations of fish concentrations where the catch per unit of effort is known from experience to be high. Fishers of the more traditional families who spend part of the year on the land know the most suitable fishing areas in every bay or lake within the family territory. Given long travel distances, extensive knowledge of the terrain is also essential. This is particularly true on the shallow and indented James Bay coast where the navigator of the canoe needs to know the configuration of the shoreline at different phases of the tide.

The second management practice, pulse fishing, involves fishing a productive area intensively for a short length of time, and then relocating somewhere else.

For example, I recorded the activities of one family fishing group that concentrated its effort in a small inlet, perhaps 100 m by 400 m at low tide, on the James Bay coast not far from the village. They removed a total of 34 kg of fish between June 7 and 12. The initial catch per net set was 6.4 kg, and the final, 2.2 kg, suggesting that a large part of the fishable stock had been removed over that brief period. The group then located their nets elsewhere but indicated that the inlet was a traditional site for the family and that they would be back the following year. Fishing areas may be recognized as traditional but this does not imply that other community members cannot fish there. Stewards do regulate access and effort through their leadership but do not normally limit the access of others into fishing areas. Fishing effort is deployed flexibly and opportunistically, and the initial success of one group seems to encourage others to converge upon an area. For example, on May 24, right after ice breakup in another inlet on the James Bay coast, a fishing group set five nets and obtained 40.8 kg of fish. By May 27, there were about 20 nets in the inlet, but as the catch per net declined to about 2.8 kg, the nets were relocated somewhere else (Berkes 1977).

Pulse fishing and fishing area rotation seemed to be taking place over multiple time scales. In the intensively fished area near the village, a good spot would be fished at least once a year, but further away, less frequently (Berkes 1977). Further away from the village, in areas that are hunted and fished extensively (as opposed to intensively), a hunter/fisher may use a particular lake once or so every few years. Why do people use pulse fishing and rotation? Clearly, the practice optimizes the catch per unit of effort. In the case of extensively used lakes, the practice also helps maintain a population of large-sized fish in the system. The samples available from the more remote fishing locations show good catches of whitefish of 50–55 cm. Since my samples were not many, however, I wanted to make sure that my findings were not due to chance. Checking unpublished length–frequency data of fish harvested by two other Cree groups, the Mistassini and Waswanipi, I could ascertain that whitefish were indeed at about 50–55 cm and the lake trout 50–60 cm in the more distant, extensively fished lakes, with 40–50 cm whitefish in lakes closer to the communities (Berkes 1981b). Each of the data sets showed a scatter of sizes; it seemed that the Cree fisheries took a range of sizes (and ages) and that there were clearly many big ones, especially in the more remote areas.

The third Cree management practice, the use of a mix of gill-net mesh sizes, was responsible for the harvest of a range of whitefish sizes in the Chisasibi fishery and, one can assume, in Mistassini and Waswanipi as well. The range of sizes was initially puzzling: if large fish were available, why not take the largest only? After all, that is what commercial fisheries did in the North. Large fish were what the market wanted and there was pressure on the fisher to produce a standard product. Working and living with Cree subsistence fishers revealed a different set of values and priorities. First of all, fishers would say they "used whatever nets they had," denying any conceptual design in management but affirming practice. Second, large fish and small fish (even of the same species) tasted different and were used for different purposes. For example, a cisco or a small whitefish could be cooked on a stick over open fire. Large whitefish could be boiled, smoked (traditional), or pan-fried (nontraditional). A large white sucker (*Catostomus commersoni*) would be smoked; a small one would merely be trap bait. There was a need for a variety of things and certainly no pressure to produce a standardized commodity to meet the specifications of a commercial product.

The primary mechanism that drove all three management practices (effort concentration, pulse-fishing, and the use of a mix of gill-net mesh sizes) was the fishers' reading of the catch per unit of effort. It was the key environmental signal monitored by the Cree; it shaped the decisions regarding what nets to use, how long to keep fishing, and when to relocate. But the Chisasibi fishers monitored other environmental signals as well. They noted and took into account the species composition of the fish coming out of their nets, the size, the condition or fatness (considered very important as a signal of health), and the sex and reproductive condition of the fish. As well, they observed the fish and noted any unusual patterns in behavior and distributions. The conduct of the fishery was guided by the need for different food products, social obligations to contribute to community exchange networks, and the conservation imperatives of "getting what you need" and minimizing waste.

A Computer Experiment on Cree Practice and Fish Population Resilience

Fishery biologists and managers have for years observed a troubling trend in Northern Canadian commercial lake fisheries for whitefish and lake trout. A lightly fished lake seemingly full of large-sized fish would be selected for commercial fishery development. Exploitation would start with large-mesh gill nets but productivity would soon decline. Healey (1975) has argued, for example, that the use of large gill-net mesh sizes (5½ in. or 139.7 mm) in the Great Slave Lake has led to the selective removal of older year-classes of whitefish, thus reducing population resilience but without triggering population compensatory responses such as increased growth rates and earlier maturity. His argument, therefore, suggested the use of smaller mesh sizes. However, in several cases in which smaller mesh nets have been used, populations have inexplicably collapsed (Healey 1975).

After several experiences of this kind, biologists came up with the explanation that in many cases the collapse was related to a combination of two things.

First, because of the removal of the largest fish, population would come to depend on a small number of reproductive year-classes. Second, if there was poor spawning success for two or more years in a row, for example, due to unusual weather or water conditions, then the population could collapse. That is, the simplification of the age-class structure left populations predisposed or vulnerable to collapse if reproduction was poor. Alternatively, one might say that the presence of many reproductive year-classes in the population was an insurance against the variability of the physical environment that in some years results in complete reproductive failure. It conferred resilience.

I have been using the example of whitefish in subarctic lakes, but the underlying ecological principle has wider applicability. Ecologists interested in evolution start with the assumption that life cycle characteristics of a species must reflect adaptations for improving the chances of survival of that species in its particular environment. The presence of many year-classes of large and slow-growing fish presumably represents a life-cycle adaptation to fluctuations in the ecosystem. In fact, multiple spawning in fish populations elsewhere has been shown to be of adaptive value in dampening the effects of environmental variability, especially those effects leading to poor reproductive success for two or more years in a row (Murphy 1968). Some authors have questioned the supposed fragility of northern ecosystems, pointing out that these ecosystems have a high degree of ecological resilience (Dunbar 1973), defined here as the ability of an ecosystem to absorb perturbations and yet retain its structure and function (Holling *et al.* 1995; Gunderson and Holling 2002). Multiple reproductive year-classes is likely to be a major mechanism for ecological resilience, especially for long-lived fish species.

Intuitively it seemed to me that the Cree practice of using a mix of mesh sizes was a potential solution to the management dilemma of conserving resilience. Hence I proposed a testable hypothesis based on Chisasibi Cree traditional ecological knowledge and management: *Harvest more year-classes at a lower rate by the use of a mix of different mesh sizes* (as opposed to the selective harvest of the oldest year-classes at a higher rate by the use of a single large mesh size); *this would stimulate population compensatory responses without reducing the reproductive resilience of the population* (Berkes 1979). The problem with the hypothesis was that it was all but impossible to test with a field experiment, given the 50-year life span of the northern whitefish. Many descriptive mathematical models in ecology develop and test hypotheses by quantifying processes intuitively known to practitioners. Thus a logical alternative to a 50-year field experiment was a computer experiment (Berkes and Gonenc 1982).

First, we modeled mortality and growth rates in a hypothetical whitefish population. We showed that under certain assumptions, a characteristic bimodal length–frequency distribution is obtained. How such a peculiar distribution comes about can be shown mathematically through the summation of overlapping size-classes of older fish, using any long-lived species that has low growth rates and low mortality rates after first maturity (see Figures 7.2 and 7.3). The population modeled in Figure 7.3 postulates relatively few intermediate-sized (20–40 cm) fish, and an abundance of big fish with a mode at about 50–55 cm representing an accumulation of many old and slow-growing year-classes. The figure also helps illustrate that the fish in these northern lakes are available as easily harvestable large units, not because the populations are highly productive but because they consist of many years of accumulated production. It is a useful way to visualize the appropriateness of a fishing strategy in which one can bank one's food supply by not fishing any one lake year after year but pulse-fishing as needed. "Fish as staple" is not a matter of faith; those fishers *know* that the large fish are in the bank for tomorrow's needs. When they go to rarely fished areas, they set their largest mesh nets (5 and 5½ in.) *because* they are expecting large fish.

Second, we modeled the effect of a single large mesh size on this hypothetical unfished population (see Figure 7.4). Using the known coefficients of selectivity

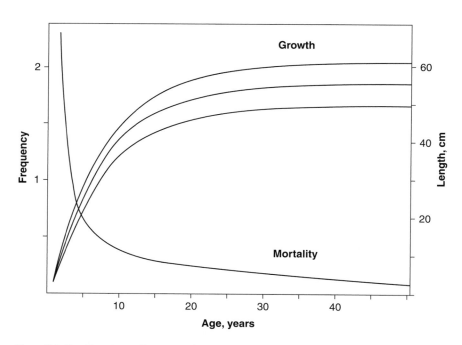

Figure 7.2 Growth and mortality curves of a model lake whitefish population. Intervals on the growth curve indicate ± 1 SD. Equations for curves in Berkes and Gonenc (1982).

Source: Berkes and Gonenc (1982).

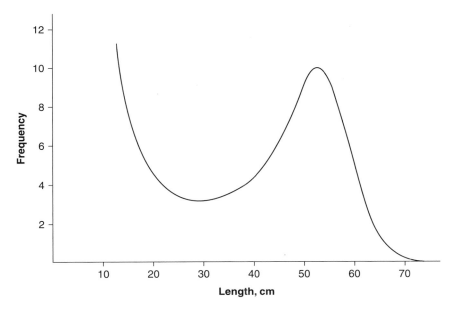

Figure 7.3 Length–frequency structure of a model whitefish population, as calculated from the growth and mortality curves in Figure 7.2.

Source: Berkes and Gonenc (1982).

of gill nets for whitefish, it can be shown that the use of a single large mesh size is indeed efficient in maximizing short-term yields because a large biomass is initially available to 5½ and 5 in. nets, which are the mesh sizes actually used in newly developing northern commercial fisheries. However, a 5½ in. net can result in the depletion of fish over 50–55 cm, depending on the intensity of fishing. Figure 7.4 can also be used to visualize the results of liberalizing mesh size regulations in a hypothetical commercial fishery from 5½ in. (moderate intensity resulting in the depletion of fish over 55 cm), to 5 in. (depletion of fish over 50 cm), and to 4½ in. (depletion of fish over 45 cm).

Third, we modeled the effect of a mixed mesh size strategy to illustrate what population thinning as practiced by Chisasibi fishers may actually look like (Figure 7.5). If the fishery used 3, 3½, 4, 4½, 5, and 5½ in. nets simultaneously, and if the heights of selectivity curves were similar, the length–frequency distribution of the residual population was very similar in shape to that of the original unfished population (see Figure 7.5). This conclusion holds for low and intermediate levels of fishing intensity. We also tried out a number of other combinations of mesh sizes and different assumptions of selectivity and found the outcomes to be basically similar (Berkes and Gonenc 1982).

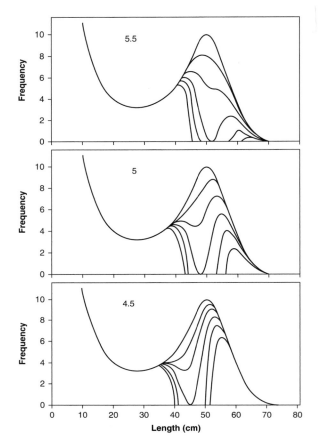

Figure 7.4 The change in length–frequency structure of a model whitefish population when fished with single mesh sizes. Contour lines represent different fishing intensities.

Source: Berkes and Gonenc (1982).

To summarize, the computer experiment illustrates that the thinning of populations by the use of a mix of mesh sizes conserves population resilience, as compared to the wholesale removal of the older age groups by a single large mesh size. Hence the use of a mix of mesh sizes is more compatible with the natural population structure than the use of a single large mesh size alone. Using a traditional Cree-style fishing strategy, many reproductive year-classes remain in the population even after fishing. At the same time, the reduction of the overall population density increases productivity by stimulating growth rates and earlier maturation in the remaining fish and helps the population renew itself.

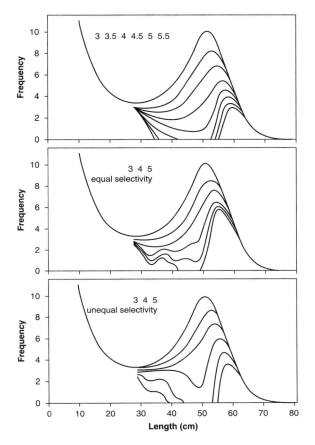

Figure 7.5 The change in length–frequency structure of a model whitefish population
when fished with a mix of mesh sizes. Contour lines represent different fishing intensities.

Source: Berkes and Gonenc (1982).

Traditional Knowledge Systems as Adaptive Management

The Chisasibi Cree fishing system is as different as can be from the biological
management system applicable to boreal/subarctic commercial fisheries. As regulated by government, commercial fisheries tend to be managed on the basis of
gear and mesh size restrictions, season and area closures (as during spawning),
and catch quotas. By contrast, Cree subsistence fishers use the most effective gear
available, the mix of mesh sizes that gives the highest possible catch per unit of
effort by area and by season, and they deliberately concentrate on aggregations
of the most efficiently exploitable fish. In short, the subsistence fishery is a

conventional resource manager's nightmare; it violates just about every conservation tool dear to the heart of government managers and biologists.

At the same time, those practices that seem to contribute to the sustainability of Chisasibi fisheries do not seem to be much appreciated by the conventional Western management system: switching fishing areas according to the declining catch per effort; rotating fishing areas; using a mix of mesh sizes to thin out populations; keying harvest levels to needs; having a system of master fishers/stewards who regulate access and effort; and having a land-use system in which resources are used under principles and ethics agreed upon by all. Does it work? The computer experiment helps understand how and why the Cree fishery is adaptive (Berkes and Gonenc 1982), but perhaps a stronger argument is the apparent sustainability of the age-class structure of the two major species over a 50-year period (Berkes 1979). The Cree fishery is difficult to assess using the standards of conventional fisheries management, but there is one kind of Western resource management science that provides a good fit with a traditional system such as that of the Cree.

Adaptive Management has been discussed widely since Holling's 1978 book, and a number of researchers have pointed out the similarities of Adaptive Management with traditional systems. One of the first was Winterhalder (1983) who noted the relevance of one of the central ideas of Adaptive Management to subarctic hunters: how to manage when much is unknown, some things are uncertain, and the unexpected must be acknowledged. He pointed out that Cree-Ojibwa hunters of northern Ontario were experts in using resources in an environment characterized by uncertainty and novelty, and that their foraging strategies used adaptive flexibility, consistent with Holling's models. A second researcher to make the connection was McDonald (1988: 70) who compared conventional and Adaptive Management systems, with special attention to the Arctic, and concluded that "the adaptive management process potentially provides a methodological framework in which resource scientists and indigenous peoples can work together."

Such a framework seems indeed feasible because, in many ways, there is a remarkable convergence between Adaptive Management and traditional ecological knowledge and management systems. We see in the Cree fishery system that there is learning by doing, a mix of trial-and-error and feedback learning, and social learning with elders and stewards in charge. Like Adaptive Management, there is no dichotomy between research and management in the Cree system. The Cree assume that they cannot control nature or predict yields; they are managing the unknown, as in Adaptive Management. Although the Cree would not use these terms, their thinking is nonlinear and multi-equilibrium. They are used to an unpredictable, ever-changing environment, and they are experts in using resources at different scales of space and time. As in Adaptive Management, the Cree hunter-fisher has respect for complexity and uses practices that conserve ecosystem resilience.

Obviously, there are differences between the two systems as well. Adaptive Management can and does incorporate deliberate experimentation, use of advanced technology (e.g. computer simulations), and reductionistic thinking. Gunderson *et al.* (1995) have in mind large management agencies, not local indigenous institutions, when they talk about social and institutional learning. Management policies can be systematically treated as experiments from which resource managers can learn. The differences are real. But the Cree fisher is also quite capable of conceiving and carrying out field experiments, as in the case of species selectivity of gill nets (see Table 7.2). The Cree do not have formal management policies but they certainly have customary practices that, like the policies of management agencies, can change dramatically, as seen in the case of the caribou. The Cree do not have formal management agencies, but they do have informal institutions in which elders and stewards provide leadership, carry and transmit knowledge, and sometimes reinterpret new information to redesign management systems, again as in the case of the caribou. Traditional management can be reinterpreted as Adaptive Management. Alternatively, Adaptive Management can perhaps be considered a rediscovery of traditional management.

Lessons from Fisher Knowledge

The long-term study of the fishery in Chisasibi is unusual in the literature because subsistence fisheries rarely receive attention, even though they are important in many parts of the world. Also unusual, the Cree fishery shows that it is possible to manage a fishery, in the full sense of scientific fishery management (controlling how much fish is harvested, where, when, and of what species and sizes), completely in the absence of quantitative data and population models.

Cree fishers do have detailed traditional ecological knowledge, including the kind of knowledge that any fisher in any environment needs: when and where to find the fish. But Cree fishers' knowledge extends well beyond that. Fraser *et al.* (2006) showed how the knowledge of the Cree fishers of Mistassini inspired the testing of a hypothesis in evolutionary biology. According to the Cree, there are two kinds of brook trout (*Salvelinus fontinalis*) in Lake Mistassini that they consider to be the same species but clearly different in terms of body shape, color, and behavior. The Cree have observed that the two kinds of trout undertake reverse migrations, that is, one kind migrates into Lake Mistassini to spawn, while the other swims upriver from the Lake to spawning areas. Starting from this observation, Fraser *et al.* (2006) were able to establish that the two kinds of trout were genetically distinct and hypothesized that they represented the post-glacial colonization of Lake Mistassini from two different sources.

Just as Johannes (1981) showed that Pacific Island fishers' knowledge of lunar spawning was richer than that of biologists at that time, fisher knowledge of distinct fish populations is often richer than textbook fish biology. Gallagher (2002) apprenticed himself to Anishinaabe-Metis commercial fishers of Lake Nipigon, north of Lake Superior, to study the unusual forms of lake trout (*Salvelinus namaycush*) reported by them. He found that the three kinds of lake trout that the fishers recognized had distinct coloration, geographic distribution, and depth preferences. Further, he obtained some DNA evidence that they were genetically different as well, possibly corresponding to different stocks of lake trout colonizing Lake Nipigon after glaciation from different source areas.

This kind of detailed knowledge can help local decision-making, but it can also contribute to regional-level planning. The Mekong Basin in Southeast Asia supports one of the world's most biodiverse and productive inland fisheries. It is also one of the most difficult fisheries to manage because of regional conflicts. Valbo-Jorgensen and Poulsen (2001) used fisher knowledge as a research tool to produce integrated maps of the migration routes of some of the major fish species of the Basin across six countries. As well, they collected life history and catch information, allowing the identification of several life history strategies used by clusters of species. In an area of high biodiversity, such a finding provides a way for dealing with complexity.

The logic of such approaches is simple: where biological data do not exist and are not likely to become available soon, fisher knowledge provides a feasible alternative for information needs. This is also the logic of Johannes's (1998) "dataless" management: it is feasible to manage fisheries in the vast expanse of Oceania using a combination of fisher knowledge and a network of marine protected areas, in the absence of biological data of the conventional kind.

However, fisher-generated management information is more than low-cost, second-best data. There is an even more important reason for involving fishers in management and using fisher knowledge. When fishers are involved in the conservation and management of a fishery, they are more likely to take ownership of it. There are many examples of this. The local association of fishers and a Brazilian regional NGO, Mamiraua, developed a monitoring technique for the threatened giant Amazon fish, *pirarucu* (*Arapaima gigas*). The method relies on the ability of fishers to count the fish and even to recognize individual *pirarucu* from the way they rise to the surface to gulp air (many Amazon fish breathe air). The method correlates well with the usual biological mark-and-recapture population estimates, and costs much less. More importantly, it empowers fisher organizations to make management decisions and creates a stewardship ethic. The method has spread across the Amazon Basin and resulted in increased *pirarucu* populations in many areas (Castello 2003; Castello *et al.* 2009).

Local experts using a resource seem to find appropriate rules-of-thumb and local practices and principles to manage the resource. We are still discovering deceptively simple but wonderfully elegant indigenous management practices, such as tidal pulse fishing in Alaska (Langdon 2006). This chapter provided one detailed example (the Chisasibi Cree subsistence fishery) in which the fishers rely on many kinds of observations—but few practices seem to explain much of the documented outcome. Similarly, caribou hunters in Chapter 6 seem to use many kinds of observations but rely heavily on one index, the fatness of the animal, which integrates a number of environmental factors. This conclusion suggests that traditional ecological knowledge and management systems may hold some lessons on how to reduce complexity, and how to deal with complex systems. This theme is going to be picked up again in Chapter 9. But first, we need to explore in some more detail indigenous ways of knowing: how local experts get to know what they know. This is difficult to do with well-established hunting and fishing systems. But climate change, the subject of the next chapter, is a new experience, and provides a good opportunity to examine indigenous ways of making observations and making sense of these observations, as part of the process of knowing.

CHAPTER 8

Climate Change and Indigenous Ways of Knowing

Are there ways of speaking of global issues such as climate change that accord weight to culturally specific understandings as well as to the universalistic frameworks of science?

(Cruikshank 2001)

Since about 2000, there have been a large number of studies to understand indigenous knowledge and views on climate change, most of them from Arctic North America. This flurry of activity is perhaps surprising; an authoritative 1995 book on climate change in the North does not mention even one study on indigenous knowledge related to this topic. The explanation for such a spectacular burst of activity probably has to do with the increased appreciation of indigenous knowledge and the ability of indigenous peoples to bring their views to the attention of an international audience. But it also has to do with the urgency of recent observations.

Residents of the Circumpolar North have been witnessing disturbing environmental changes. Weather has become difficult to predict, as expressed by one Alaska elder with the evocative phrase, "the earth is faster now" used as the title of the book by Krupnik and Jolly (2002). Northerners started witnessing severe climatic and ecological changes in the 1990s, consistent with global climate change models predicting that the largest average temperature increases would be over the polar regions (ACIA 2005).

The previous two chapters dealt with learning (Chapter 6 on caribou and social learning) and adaptation (Chapter 7 on fishing and adaptive management). This chapter provides a different approach to learning and adaptation. It is about indigenous knowledge, not in the sense of cognitive "knowledge" of climate change that comes fully formed, to be transmitted from one generation to the next. But rather, it is about knowledge as process, "weather-related knowledge, consisting in a sensitivity to critical signs in the environment and an intuitive understanding of what they mean for the conduct of practical tasks" (Ingold and Kurttila 2000: 192). It is knowledge that undergoes continual generation and regeneration as people interact with the environment, observing, learning, and adapting.

Thus, the chapter first aims to illustrate the distinction between knowing, the process and knowledge, the thing known, using the example of Inuit observations and understandings of climate change. This is the distinction between static knowledge as "content" versus indigenous ways of perceiving, understanding, and interpreting the environment (Ingold 2000; Preston 2002; Turner 2005). Climate change is an excellent way to explore the distinction because there is no pre-knowledge of it; indigenous experts do not know what to expect, the outcome of change. What they do know is what to look for and how to look for what is important.

Second, the chapter deals with issues in research methodology. The study of indigenous ways of knowing requires the development of new models of community-based research to understand the dynamics of knowledge construction. As Davidson-Hunt and O'Flaherty (2007: 293) put it, "Working from the premise that knowledge is a dynamic process—that knowledge is contingent upon being formed, validated and adapted to changing circumstances—opens up the possibility for researchers to establish relationships with indigenous peoples as co-producers of locally relevant knowledge."

Scholars involved in "sustainability science" have been developing such participatory, place-based approaches to understand issues of global environmental change (Kates et al. 2001). Such issues are intractable by conventional scientific methods because of their complexity. Research on these problems requires a process by which researchers and local stakeholders interact to define important questions, relevant evidence, and convincing forms of argument—in effect, the co-production of knowledge. Place-based models are needed because understanding the dynamic interaction between nature and society requires case studies situated in particular places and cultures (Kates et al. 2001).

Third, the chapter shows what the findings of such collaborative research might look like, and illustrates what indigenous experts are able to deduce from their observations. It includes the changes that the Inuit observe, from the alteration of species distributions to the thawing of permafrost. However, the case study is not simply a documentation of local knowledge by outsiders; rather, it is about the dialogue regarding what is being observed.

For example, when the details of Inuit observations on changes in sea ice exceeded the ability of the original team of researchers to understand the local experts, the team brought in a sea ice expert. When the Inuit found two species of Pacific salmon in their nets in northern Beaufort Sea, they saved the specimens and alerted the biologists who subsequently published the findings (Babaluk *et al.* 2000). Following the lead of the Inuit also meant that the findings were prioritized according to Inuit cultural values, and not scientific ones. For example, the Inuit reported kinds of impacts that scientists and outsiders could hardly imagine: caribou meat under controlled fermentation spoiling because of temperature increase. One of the impacts of climate change from the Inuit point of view was that the lack of sea ice in summer months made some people "lonely for the ice"—because the ice is such a central feature of their life. From a southern point of view, it is too easy to assume that the Inuit should only be happy for any climate warming.

Indigenous Ways of Knowing and New Models of Community-based Research

Place-based research requires working with indigenous peoples and other rural groups, and taking their knowledge seriously. This is not so easy to achieve. Miller and Erickson (2006) noted that many global environmental assessments that started in the 1990s and earlier, including the Intergovernmental Panel on Climate Change (IPCC), the granddaddy of global climate change studies, were strictly scientific efforts and made no mention of indigenous knowledge. By contrast, two of the more recent environmental assessments, the Millennium Ecosystem Assessment (MA 2005) and the Arctic Climate Impact Assessment (ACIA 2005), an offshoot of IPCC, were designed to include scientific *and* indigenous epistemologies. Given the role of the Arctic as "the canary in the coal mine," ACIA explicitly sought to bring in the insights of the people who lived there, and bridge scientific and indigenous epistemologies (Miller and Erickson 2006).

Carrying out place-based research requires a major shift in scientific philosophy and planning, as well as in our view of knowledge—away from expert-knows-best science and toward accepting local and traditional knowledge as a partner and complement. As discussed in Chapter 1, the conflict between science and traditional knowledge is to an important extent related to claims of authority over knowledge. In the Western positivist tradition, there is only one kind of science—Western science. Knowledge and insights that originate outside institutionalized Western scholarship are not easily accepted, and some scientists tend to dismiss understandings that do not fit their own.

Many scientists tend to be skeptical of traditional knowledge, including climate-related knowledge. For example, Cruikshank (2001) points out that Athapascan and Tlingit elders' beliefs in a sentient "land that listens" and glaciers *who* may be offended by human disrespect, do not fit well with the narratives of geophysical science. And yet indigenous stories about glaciers of the St. Elias Mountains where Alaska, Yukon, and British Columbia meet, provide an understanding of the dramatic geophysical upheavals during the late eighteenth and nineteenth centuries (Cruikshank 2005).

How can climate change research be carried out with indigenous knowledge holders without taking this knowledge out of its cultural context (Nadasdy 1999; McGregor 2004)? How can the researcher avoid the trap of treating indigenous knowledge as just another information set from which data can be extracted to plug into scientific frameworks? How can both indigenous and scientific kinds of knowledge be used together respectfully?

First, traditional knowledge and Western science need not be thought of as opposites. Rather, it is useful to emphasize the potential complementarities of the two, and to look for points of agreement rather than disagreement. The use of traditional knowledge contributes to conceptual pluralism, and expands the range of approaches and information sources needed for problem solving (Berkes and Folke 1998). In the area of climate change research, Riedlinger and Berkes (2001) suggested that traditional knowledge can expand the range and richness of the information available, in both space and time scale (Figure 8.1). Based on research carried out in the Arctic, they further suggest that indigenous knowledge and science could be brought together through five areas of convergence, that is, potential areas of collaboration and communication. These relate to the use of traditional knowledge (1) as local-scale expertise; (2) as a source of climate history and baseline data; (3) in formulating research questions and hypotheses; (4) as insight into impacts and adaptation in Arctic communities; and (5) for long-term, community-based monitoring (Table 8.1).

Second, we can develop new models of community-based research to help achieve real collaboration in these potential areas of convergence and capture local observations accurately—but in a way that incorporates their worldview and values as well. The "decolonizing methodology" of Maori educator and scholar Linda Tuhiwai Smith provides a starting point. Smith (1999: 28) argues that colonial power relations have disconnected indigenous peoples from "their histories, their landscapes, their languages, their social relations and their own ways of thinking, feeling and interacting with the world." Researchers working with indigenous people should strive to use decolonizing methodologies that reverse the effects of colonization.

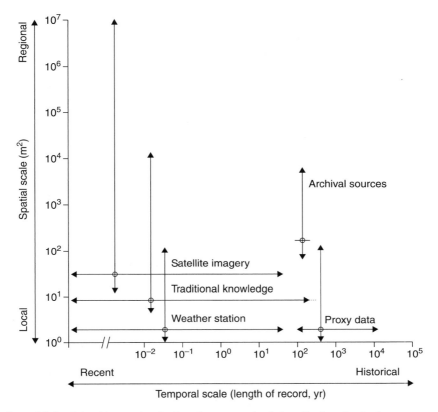

Figure 8.1 Spatial and temporal scales to various approaches to investigating climate change.
Source: Adapted from Riedlinger and Berkes (2001).

Such approaches have been explicitly used by Arctic climate researcher Leduc (2007; 2011) who set out to share scientific understandings with the Inuit, rather than "mining" Inuit knowledge, and used Smith's approach to establish a dialogue that provides space for the Inuit to respond to the science of climate change.

Other Arctic climate researchers have used a variety of participatory research methodologies (Thorpe *et al.* 2001; Krupnik and Jolly 2002; Oozeva *et al.* 2004). For example, the various chapters of Krupnik and Jolly (2002) document the use of creative ways of building and elaborating participatory modes of research in which indigenous peoples are not the "objects" of research but equal partners. These include the use of planning workshops, daily diary entries, participant observation, elder–youth camps, and expert-to-expert interviews. There certainly is more than one way to structure collaborative research that does justice to both indigenous and scientific knowledge (Smith 1999; Cruikshank 2005; Davidson-Hunt and O'Flaherty 2007).

Table 8.1 Five convergence areas that can facilitate the use of traditional knowledge and Western science, in the context of Arctic climate change research

Local-scale expertise	The integrity of traditional knowledge at the local scale has been promoted in discussions of traditional knowledge in the North. Climate change will be first noticeable through biophysical changes in sea ice, wildlife, permafrost, and weather. These changes will not go unnoticed at the local scale in Inuit communities.
Climate history	Traditional knowledge can provide insight into past climate variability, providing an essential baseline against which to compare change. Climate history is embedded in Inuit history of wildlife populations, travels, extreme events, and harvesting records.
Research hypotheses	Traditional knowledge can contribute to the process of formulating scientific hypotheses as another way of knowing and understanding the environment. Collaboration at the initial stage of research expands the scope of inquiry and establishes a role for communities in research planning.
Community adaptation	Traditional knowledge lends insight into adaptations to changes, explaining them in the context of livelihoods and community life. How are communities responding to change? What are the social, economic, and cultural limits to adaptation in northern communities?
Community-based monitoring	Traditional knowledge reflects a cumulative system of environmental monitoring and observation. Monitoring projects have the potential to bridge the gap between science and traditional knowledge by providing a collaborative process.

Source: Riedlinger and Berkes (2001).

Inuit Observations of Climate Change Project

Figure 8.2 is one way to structure collaborative research that can create a partnership of indigenous knowledge and Western science. The figure is based on the Inuit Observations of Climate Change project (Ford 2000; Berkes and Jolly 2001; Riedlinger and Berkes 2001; Nichols *et al.* 2004). There are a number of general features of the partnership arrangement sketched in the figure. The project created a forum in which the agendas of the partners were made transparent and common objectives negotiated. Research aims, approaches, and rules of conduct were all determined jointly. The research process had both a science and a local knowledge component, with provision for the two to learn from one another. There was continuous feedback to the community in the form of preliminary results, and to the research team in the form of revised approaches and verification. The results

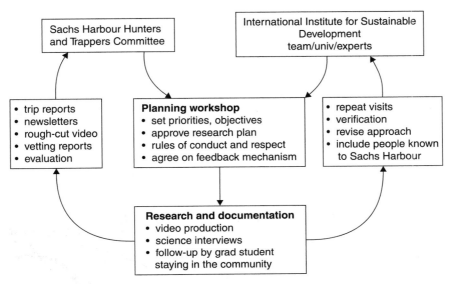

Figure 8.2 A partnership model to combine indigenous and Western knowledge: The Inuit Observations of Climate Change study.

were shared as agreed upon and the findings were deposited with the community in culturally appropriate ways. The community vetted publications, and the local experts received credit for their contributions, as a way of acknowledging their authority over their knowledge.

The project was conducted in Sachs Harbour on Banks Island in the Canadian western Arctic (Figure 8.3), home of the Inuvialuit people who are the descendants of the Inupiat of Alaska, and Mackenzie Delta and central Canadian Arctic people. Sachs Harbour is the smallest (some 30 households) of the six communities in the self-governing Inuvialuit Region where native land claims were settled in 1984.

The people of Sachs Harbour became concerned in the 1990s that environmental changes in their area were making hunting difficult and creating safety problems. In 1998, the community invited the International Institute for Sustainable Development (IISD) to produce a video to document local observations of climate change. The intent was to educate southern people and policymakers, and to explore the potential contributions of Inuvialuit knowledge to climate change research. The second objective was subsequently expanded by the addition of University of Manitoba personnel to the original IISD team.

The video "Sila Alangotok: Inuit Observations on Climate Change" was produced in 2000 and simultaneously launched in The Hague, Netherlands, at the United Nations Climate Change Sixth Conference of the Parties, in Ottawa and in Sachs Harbour (IISD 2000). The observations of Sachs Harbour hunters and

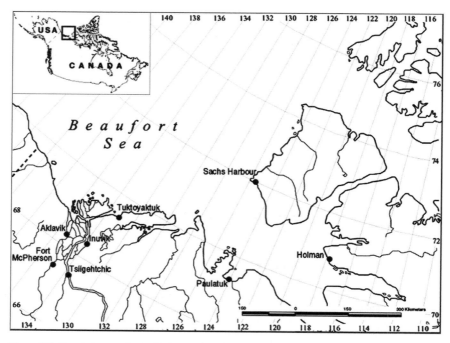

Figure 8.3 The study area: Sachs Harbour on Banks Island, Northwest Territories.

elders were remarkably consistent in providing tangible evidence of climate change. The changes observed in the 1990s were said to be without precedent and outside the range of variation that the Inuvialuit considered normal. The changes reported involved a range of observation on the extent, thickness and the kind of sea ice, the timing and intensity of weather events, fish and wildlife distributions, permafrost and soil erosion. A summary of the findings of local observations of climate change may be summarized under five headings: physical environmental change; predictability of the environment; travel safety on land and ice; access to resources; and changes in animal distributions and condition (Table 8.2).

The community identified changes in sea ice as the top priority for further investigations, and named 16 elders and community members to serve as experts on sea ice. Using the semi-directed interview approach (Huntington 1998), the experts were invited to share their observations and knowledge. They identified several themes considered most critical: diminishing amounts of multi-year ice; the increasing distance from shore of the multi-year ice; changes associated with first-year ice including thinning; changes in timing of sea ice break-up and freeze-up; sea ice travel; and winds and storms. These themes served as the basis for the interview guide (Table 8.3).

Photo 8.1 Checking char nets in Sachs Harbour, Banks Island, Northwest Territories, Canada. Changing patterns of sea ice distribution, break-up and freeze-up times, and changing seasonality have impacted subsistence harvests. Char has been (so far) relatively unaffected.

Photo: Fikret Berkes.

Table 8.2 Environmental changes impacting subsistence activities in Sachs Harbour

1 Physical environmental change:
- Multi-year ice no longer comes close to Sachs Harbour in summer
- Less sea ice in summer means that water is rougher
- Open water is now closer to land in winter
- More rain in summer and fall, makes travel difficult
- Permafrost is no longer solid in places
- Lakes draining into the sea from ground melting and slumping
- Loose, soft snow (as opposed to hard-packed) makes it harder to travel

2 Predictability of the environment:
- It has become difficult to tell when ice is going to break up on rivers
- Arrival of spring has become unpredictable
- Difficult to predict weather and storms
- There are "wrong" winds sometimes
- More snow, blowing snow, and whiteouts

3 Travel safety on land and ice:
- Too much broken ice in winter makes travel dangerous
- Unpredictable sea ice conditions make travel dangerous
- Less multi-year ice means traveling on first-year ice all winter, less safe
- Less ice cover in summer means rougher, more dangerous storms at sea

(Continued)

Table 8.2 Continued

4 Access to resources:
- It is more difficult to hunt seals because of lack of multi-year ice
- In winter, cannot go out as far when hunting because of lack of firm ice cover
- Harder to hunt geese because the spring melt occurs so fast
- Warmer summers and more rain mean more vegetation and food for animals

5 Changes in animal distributions and condition:
- Less fat on the seals
- Observe fish and bird species never before seen
- Increase in biting flies; never had mosquitoes before
- Seeing fewer polar bears in the fall because of lack of ice
- More of species known as least cisco caught now

Source: Adapted from Riedlinger and Berkes (2001) and Berkes and Jolly (2001).

Table 8.3 The interview guide for follow-up questions to Sachs Harbour elders on sea ice

Themes	Follow-up questions
Multi-year ice	Changes in abundance of multi-year ice?
	Has there always been multi-year ice every year (in the harbour)?
	Are there years where multi-year ice has not appeared?
First-year ice and ice features	Is the pack ice moving? Is it further away/closer to shore?
	Is it smaller (is there less) in the summer?
	Where do pressure ridges normally form?
	Are there changes in pressure ridges (location, shape, size)?
	What direction (orientation) do they normally take?
Seasons	Changes in break-up dates?
	Changes in consolidation (freeze-up) dates?
	When do these seasons normally occur?
	How do you define your seasons? Ice movement?
	Harvesting/animal migrations? How many seasons?
Hunting and ice travel	What are ideal conditions for seal hunting?
	Where and how do you hunt and travel across the ice?
	Has the timing of the hunt changed?
	Has the hunt changed? If so, how?
Winds andstorm events	How often does it storm?
	Is hail new to the community?
	Are rainstorms more/less common? Are they more or less severe? Do they last a long time?
	Have wind patterns changed?
	Are winds becoming stronger/weaker? When do these events normally occur?

Source: Nichols *et al.* (2004).

The consensus view of the respondents regarding sea ice changes is illustrated in Figure 8.4 for the fall–winter season. A similar figure was prepared for the spring–summer season as well (Nichols *et al.* 2004) but is not shown here. Figure 8.4 shows that the Inuvialuit focus on the relationships of a number of variables. They do not make a distinction between biological variables, physical variables and human variables. The sum total of changes in sea ice and associated relationships produces a remarkably holistic view of the changes, a mental model of the sea ice environment and the impact of climate change on it.

Sachs Harbour experts were consistent in their observations regarding multi-year ice (ice that has survived a minimum of two summer seasons, important as a source of drinkable water and habitat for certain wildlife) and ice thickness and abundance (Table 8.4). The observations were also consistent regarding ice breakup and freeze-up dates, which are important for travel, access to game, and safety. There was also strong agreement that winds were stronger or that there were more windy days. However, most experts thought the prevailing wind directions had not changed or had changed only slightly (Nichols *et al.* 2004).

Studies elsewhere in the Arctic have confirmed that Inuit observations of sea ice can provide important clues on climate change. We all observe and remember

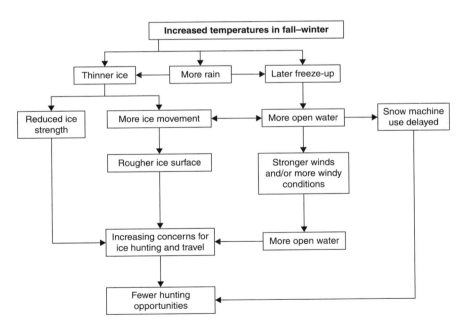

Figure 8.4 Seasonal changes in sea ice and associated relationships in fall–winter, as observed by the people of Sachs Harbour.

Source: Redrawn from Nichols *et al.* (2004).

Table 8.4 Abundance and distribution of multi-year and first-year sea ice, according to local experts in Sachs Harbour

Respondent	Multi-year abundance	Multi-year distribution	First-year ice thickness	Overall ice abundance
A		Further out	Thinner	Less
B		Further out	Thinner	Less
C	Less	Further out	Thinner	Less
D	Less	Further out	Thinner	Less
E	Less		Thinner	Less
F	Less	Further out	Thinner	
G				
H	Less	Further out	Thinner	
I	Less	Further out	Thinner	Less
J	Less	Further out	Thinner	Less
K	Less	Further out	Thinner	Less
L	Less	Further out	Thinner	Less
M	Less	Further out		Less
N	Less	Further out	Thinner	Less
O	Less	Further out	Thinner	Less
P	Less		Thinner	Less

Source: Nichols *et al.* (2004).

certain things that are important to us. For the Inuit, sea ice is at the top of the list of things that are important. In the case of climate change research, sea ice is an excellent area for partnership. Laidler (2006) points out that Inuit and scientific perspectives on sea ice may indeed be the ideal complement. The Inuit provide insights and local observations; science can provide synoptic perspectives. The Inuit have noticed this too and started supplementing their knowledge with Western science and technology. Unpredictable sea ice conditions create vulnerability (Laidler *et al.* 2009). Many Inuit communities have taken to using satellite maps and remote sensing images to help them figure out, for example, unusual patterns of ice break-up and the potential dangers that come with this. Not all communities use new knowledge equally. In Igloolik, which is an island surrounded by often dangerous sea ice, satellite images are routinely used (Laidler *et al.* 2009). By contrast, hunters in Tuktoyaktuk and Aklavik say they do not normally need it or use it, except for polar bear hunting. Hunters of Sachs Harbour seem to be somewhere in between (Berkes and Armitage 2010).

A Convergence of Findings

Many studies published since about 2000 show that the findings of the project at Sachs Habour are not unique (Krupnik and Jolly 2002; Gearheard *et al.*

2006: Krupnik *et al.* 2010; Leduc 2011). However, the more recent studies are showing more depth and detail (Laidler *et al.* 2009; Pearce *et al.* 2009), and indicating that climate change may actually be impacting food security (Ford and Berrang-Ford 2009). Some of the most detailed documentations of local change and impacts of climate change are coming from coastal northern indigenous peoples. But there are other studies too from northern inland locations such as Central Asia and Northern Asia (Crate 2008; Crate and Nuttall 2009; Marin 2010), and from indigenous people from various other parts of the world (Salick and Ross 2009).

What makes indigenous peoples such acute observers? In fact, northern peoples have a good record of noticing environmental change often before the science of it is known. A case in point is a phenomenon known as "Arctic haze," a yellowish air mass affecting large areas. In the 1970s, northern indigenous people began to notice and complain that visibility in the Arctic was not as good as it had been historically. When the phenomenon was finally investigated in the 1980s, it was found to be sulphate aerosol. Subsequent studies found the mechanism: sulfate released into the atmosphere from northern industries was trapped under a circumpolar winter high and then carried around the pole. This led to research on long-range transport of Arctic ecosystem contaminants (Schindler and Smol 2006).

Regarding climate change, some of the earliest observations of what was regarded as abnormal weather came from the boreal/subarctic of central Canada in the 1980s, and from the Hudson Bay and James Bay area in the 1990s. But these earlier reports were vague and did not have much impact on the outside world. It is likely that the observers themselves were initially not very clear about what they were noticing. Participatory research and co-production of knowledge has helped to make sense of the observations, especially when the changes are confounded by many factors. A case in point comes from a study in James Bay, eastern subarctic Canada.

Migratory geese are a major food source of the Cree people on the eastern James Bay coast. But they have been declining on the coast since the 1970s. The overall population numbers of the geese (mainly the Canada goose, *Branta canadensis*) have been healthy, so the issue is not one of overhunting or some other cause of overall population decline. A regional traditional ecological knowledge study by McDonald *et al.* (1997) found that when you add up all the local observations of Cree and Inuit communities around James and Hudson Bay, there appears to have been a major shift of goose flyways from the coast to the inland. The most logical explanation was that the James Bay hydroelectric project, by creating a string of reservoirs inland, had attracted the geese away from the coast.

When Peloquin (2007) started his community-based research project with the Wemindji Cree of eastern James Bay, he hoped to explore the various factors affecting goose distributions. He did not anticipate that climate change would be a major factor. However, the Wemindji Cree considered that the inland shift of the goose flyway was not a simple cause–effect matter. There were factors of human disturbance on the coast, including the use of helicopters, factors related to the new road network, and impacts of the James Bay hydroelectric project (Peloquin and Berkes 2009). But there was also the factor of climate change impacting the habitat of the geese and the environment of the goose hunter. As quoted by Peloquin:

> The weather has been changing a lot since the late 1970s. [It's] not as cold in the wintertime, and after freeze-up you have to wait a long time before you can travel on the ice. And people say the ice is not as thick as it used to be, even out in the Bay. In late February I put out my fish nets, five kilometres from here, I was surprised that the ice was very thin, it was only 10 inch thick where it used to be about 3–4 feet thick. It makes it easier for digging a hole in the ice.
>
> (Peloquin 2007: 99)

The decrease in thickness made it more dangerous to travel on the sea ice at the start of the spring goose hunt. The Cree thought spring was arriving too early and too fast, with rapid snow melt and ice break up. One Cree hunter said, "when the geese arrived [in Blackstone Bay, an important hunting area] there was no snow, only ice." There were other indicators of change. One hunter reported having seen a sea gull in March, which was exceptionally early.

> In the past, say 25–30 years, it would not be unusual to travel by snowmobile as late as 15th of May, whereas nowadays the ice is often too thin for such travel as early as mid-April.
>
> My father used to come back on May 20th, by snowmobile. Now the rivers break up at the end of April, third week of May on the coast.
>
> It's the same inland, it's warmer there too. In the summer too, sometimes it's very hot for a few days, and it can change very rapidly. It changes faster than it used to.

These changes made activities more hazardous and weather predictions difficult. They directly impacted goose availability: early spring and ice break-up, as well as warm weather, were all seen as key in the changes in the goose hunt:

It's too warm, it's not good for the geese, they fly right through (. . .) it's probably why the geese change their patterns.

In the fall, we used to travel on the ice in November. Nowadays, it's often only safe after the new year.

Freeze-up takes longer, we must wait a long time before going on ice (in the fall), and then in the spring ice goes out really fast, too fast.

The Cree think that these changes influenced other biophysical processes that in turn impacted the goose through a series of indirect, climate-induced changes. One of these factors involved the crop of black crowberries (*Empetrum nigrum*). The geese feed on these on their way south in the fall. Hunters reported that with the summers being too warm, these berries "bake" under the sun. By September when the geese start coming back, the berries are all dried out and hard. This was seen as contributing to the geese not stopping and not being available for harvest. Figure 8.5 is a mental model of the various

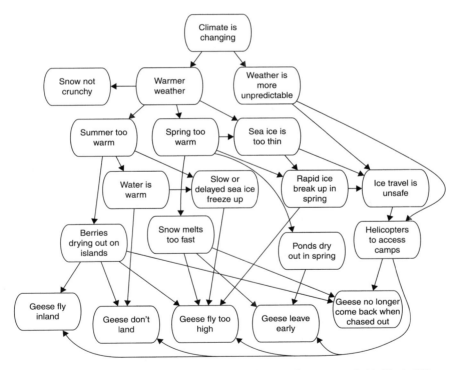

Figure 8.5 Climate-related drivers of change impacting the goose hunt, as reported by Wemindji Cree hunters of James Bay.

Source: Peloquin (2007).

climate-related factors impacting the Wemindji goose hunt. Although there are also factors not related to climate change, it is interesting to note some of the similarities of this model to that produced by the elders of Sachs Harbour (Figure 8.4).

Significance of Local Observations and Place-based Research

Global climate models are used not to predict weather but to indicate slow mean change of average weather. These models have evolved over the years, and are being further improved both in terms of resolution and through the inclusion of new physical parameters. They consist of an atmospheric component coupled with ocean and sea ice models, and a land surface component. They are built on the physical principles that are thought to govern the climate system and are tested against recent climate data.

There is little doubt that these models are important and useful; they have indicated, for example, that climate change effects may be expected to be particularly pronounced in Alaska and the Canadian western Arctic, projections consistent with the actual observations (Krupnik and Jolly 2002). There is an imbalance, however, in the way the models have dominated climate change discourse. Can global climate change models provide the whole answer?

There are two points that can be made regarding this question: (1) global models, without local observations of change, are limited in their explanatory power; and (2) models, as indicators of average change, provide a poor indication on social and ecological impacts of change, which is not so much about mean change but about extreme events and loss of predictability.

Regarding the explanatory power of models, environmental change is a complex systems problem. Complex systems cannot be analyzed at any one level alone. One of the major lessons of complex adaptive systems thinking is that complex systems phenomena, such as climate change, occur at multiple scales (Levin 1999). There are feedbacks across different levels, both geographically (local, regional, global) and in terms of social organization (individual, household, community) (Berkes and Jolly 2001). No single level is the "correct" one for analysis. Climate change cannot be understood at the global level alone, just as it cannot be understood at the local level alone. Since there is coupling between different levels, the system must be analyzed simultaneously across scale.

How can indigenous observations and traditional knowledge be used to help with the problem? Projects involving multiple communities and examining indigenous observations at regional as well as local levels are very significant in this regard because they provide insights at multiple levels (McDonald *et al.* 1997; Krupnik and Jolly 2002; Oozeva *et al.* 2004). Also important are interactive meetings that bring together local experts and scientific experts to try to make sense of patterns of change. This approach was used successfully in the Hudson Bay Bioregion project, which was one of the first documentations of indigenous observations indicating large-scale environmental change (McDonald *et al.* 1997). Such observations at multiple levels and the sharing of knowledge between local experts and scientists complement the findings of global change models, and help fill in the missing parts of the environmental change story.

Regarding the question of impacts, global models indicating *average change* are limited in their capacity to capture major social and ecological impacts. Extreme weather events have disproportionately large impacts. Hence, the study of impacts cannot aim merely at documenting gradual mean change but need to take into account extreme weather events as well. Some of the global climate models include observed and projected changes on parameters such as higher maximum/minimum temperatures and precipitation. This is useful but insufficient because the *actual impacts* of extreme weather occur on the ground, at regional and local levels.

The importance of these local/regional extreme events on Arctic wildlife populations is well known to ecologists and anthropologists. Ice and snow can restrict the availability of forage for caribou and musk-ox, and extreme events such as winter ice storms can cause mass starvation. On the human side, the importance of extreme weather events is well known in many parts of the world through floods, ice storms, tornadoes, and hurricanes. In the Arctic, several chapters in the Krupnik and Jolly (2002) volume provide examples on the importance of extreme events, both in terms of impacts and in terms of causing adaptation problems. Something as simple as warm spells in mid-winter can disrupt entire regional economies by interrupting transportation on ice roads, as has happened in Canada's North over the last decade. Warm spells can also interfere with the local economy by interrupting hunters' travel over ice and by causing safety problems.

Analyzing the issue of human impacts further, the findings indicate that there may be three related phenomena, as observed at the local level by the indigenous peoples of the Arctic: weather is *more variable*, weather is *less predictable*, and there is an increased frequency of *extreme weather events* (Krupnik and Jolly 2002; Fox 2003). The overall effect of these three related changes is potentially very serious for indigenous peoples' lifestyles, nutrition and safety, as shown also in the Sachs Harbour study. The issue of predictability is of special concern, as discussed further below.

Indigenous Knowledge and Adaptation

Local knowledge can supplement the explanatory power of global climate change models, and provide grounded information on the actual impacts. Local responses to the impacts, in turn, provide insights about adaptations. In the Inuit Observations of Climate Change project, we developed an approach that involves (1) observing and analyzing the actual response of the community to climate change, (2) evaluating these observations in the light of the adaptive strategies known to exist in that society, and (3) using these two streams of findings to generate insights about the ability of the people of Sachs Harbour to absorb the change, learn from it and live with it (Berkes and Jolly 2001).

Although climate change is affecting subsistence activities at Sachs Harbour, many of the impacts have been absorbed by the flexibility of the seasonal cycle and short-term adjustments. These adjustments, or coping strategies, relate to modifying subsistence activity patterns (i.e. changing when, where, and how hunting and fishing occur), and trying to minimize risk and uncertainty (Table 8.5).

Table 8.5 Short-term or coping responses to enviornmental change in Sachs Harbour *versus* Inuit cultural practices and long-term adaptations

---

Short-term or coping responses to environmental change at Sachs Harbour

- Modifying the timing of harvest activity to compensate for changing ice break-up and freeze-up dates, and timing of animal migrations
- Modifying the location of harvest activity, as necessitated by changes in ice and snow cover and consequent changes in modes of transportation and travel routes
- Adjusting the mix of species harvested, taking advantage of increased abundance of some species and the appearance of new species
- Minimizing risk and uncertainty, by monitoring river ice and sea ice conditions more closely and limiting risky travel for less accomplished hunters and navigators

---

Cultural practices and adaptive responses to the Arctic environment

- Mobility of hunting groups; seasonal settlements; group size flexibility with grouping and regrouping of self-supporting economic units
- Flexibility of seasonal cycles of harvest and resource use, backed up by oral traditions to provide group memory
- Detailed local environmental knowledge (traditional knowledge) and related skill sets for harvesting, navigating, and food processing
- Sharing mechanisms and social networks for mutual support and risk minimization; high social value attached to sharing and generosity
- Inter-community trade along networks and trading partnerships, to deal with regional differences in resource availability

---

Source: Berkes and Jolly (2001).

These coping strategies are consistent with known Inuit adaptations to living in an uncertain and highly variable environment. The Arctic is an environment in which biological production is relatively low, resources are patchy, and resource availability is unpredictable. These conditions favor small groups and a high degree of mobility and a great deal of flexibility in seasonal cycles. Mobile groups did not always follow the same sequence of hunting locations or rely on the same complex of resources. They took into account unpredictability, harvesting what was available when it was available. Species could be switched opportunistically; for example, a good spring harvest of ringed seals might compensate for a late snow goose migration.

Making a living in Arctic ecosystems requires detailed local environmental knowledge and related skill sets. The unpredictable nature of resource availability creates incentives for individuals to master a diversity of hunting and fishing skills and accumulate knowledge on various species. Competence on the land (survival skills) is highly valued, allowing individuals to exercise a great degree of personal autonomy. However, at the same time, food sharing was very important among the traditional Inuit, as with many aboriginal peoples. Inuit food sharing often went beyond the immediate social group; the Inuit tended to have complex networks of social relationships, and exchanges were based on these extensive networks, including networks that included other communities. The most prestigious families were those who always had food to share. These cultural practices are considered to be long-term adaptive responses to the Arctic environment (Table 8.5).

The people of Sachs Harbour do not see themselves as victims of a climate change drama. Rather, they see themselves as part of the solution. As with many Inuit groups, the people of Sachs Harbour see themselves as resourceful and adaptable. Their coping strategies are based on time-tested Inuit adaptations to the Arctic environment. Many of these adaptive mechanisms are still viable. The first one (mobility) is no longer operative because of the settlement of people into permanent villages, but the other four clusters of adaptations are viable, and the last one (intercommunity trade) is probably more important now than it has ever been.

The flexibility of seasonal cycles of harvest and resource use provides the resilience needed to cope with increased variability and unpredictability and adapt to change. We infer resilience from the diversity of short-term responses to changing patterns of game availability and access. Cultural values that emphasize harvesting what is available and acting opportunistically no doubt facilitate the observed coping strategies. Detailed knowledge base and experience is needed to come up with these coping strategies, and sharing makes sure that the community as a whole is viable. Maintaining traditional Inuit values (*Inuit Qaujimajatuqangit* or IQ) is important to make sure that the adaptation is viable (Thorpe *et al.* 2001;

Wenzel 2004). Sharing requires the persistence and reinforcement of cultural values that favor generosity, reciprocity, and communitarianism, and discourage hoarding and individualism.

The Sachs Harbour case is informative in studying how societies adapt to climate change. One set of responses is short-term; these are the coping mechanisms. The Inuit are experts at living in highly variable environments, and the ability to switch species and adjust the "where, when, and how" of hunting have enabled them to cope with climate change so far. Cultural adaptations of indigenous peoples to living in the highly variable Arctic environment confer resilience to the impacts of environmental change—but up to a limit. Further impacts of climate change will challenge both coping and adaptive responses by making the environment even more variable and thus less predictable.

In the long-run, the two kinds of responses are not distinct. Coping responses and adaptive strategies are continuous along the temporal scale; today's coping strategy once established will become tomorrow's adaptive strategy (Berkes and Jolly 2001). The range and extent of both the short-term and long-term responses define the resilience of the community in the face of change. If these responses are impaired, the population will become vulnerable to change.

Conclusions

The case of climate change shows that traditional environmental knowledge is constantly evolving. The people of Sachs Harbour and Wemindji do not have prior or "traditional" knowledge of climate change. What they have is sensitivity to critical signs and signals from the environment that something unusual is happening. In the case of Sachs Harbour, the people had already decided that the unusual change could be labeled climate change, before they invited the team of outsiders to document their observations. In the case of Wemindji, climate change is one of a complex mix of factors that included the impact of a large hydroelectric development project (Peloquin and Berkes 2009). In both cases, community-based, participatory research resulted in the co-production of knowledge and helped the communities to make sense of change and empower themselves to deal with it. In both cases, the communities do not see themselves as victims; they see themselves as being in control of their destiny.

What are the processes by which traditional ecological knowledge evolves? How does social learning occur? Having sensitivity to signs and signals from the environment is one of the starting points. A group of people needs to be closely connected to their environment to know what the "normal" signs and signals are like. Thus, they would be capable of assessing change when those signs and signals are beyond the expected range of variation and therefore *not* normal. In both Sachs Harbour and Wemindji cases, people are constantly making reference to previous times to be able to make that assessment.

Social learning in the context of adaptation to environmental change is an area that has been receiving much attention. As a starting point, empowerment of communities is important, as this gives them the confidence in their own knowledge and ways of knowing, and dealing with their own problems. In some cases, co-management arrangements help provide such empowerment (Armitage *et al.* 2011). However, empowerment and the use of decolonizing methodologies (Leduc 2011) by themselves may not be sufficient to solve problems. In issues such as climate change, a knowledge partnership is often needed, as none of the parties has full understanding of changes. Observations and understandings from several levels (local, regional and global) have to be brought together. Such knowledge co-production (Davidson-Hunt and O'Flaherty 2007) can serve as a trigger or mechanism for learning and adaptation. Social learning goes beyond individual learning and may be situated within wider social networks (Olsson *et al.* 2004). These learning networks or communities of learning (Robson *et al.* 2009) seem to be common in situations where indigenous knowledge and Western knowledge are brought together for problem-solving.

The chapter illustrates that place-based research and local observations have a crucial role to play in research on environmental change. Such approaches to climate change are not model-driven but are culture-specific, historically informed, and geographically rooted. They take scale into account. A major lesson of complexity theory is that scale is important; local and regional levels have to be addressed simultaneously with the global level. Traditional environmental knowledge is key to understanding environmental change at the local level.

Partnership approaches are needed at this local level, as opposed to expert-knows-best science, creating knowledge through the interaction of scholars and stakeholders. The importance of such interactions, and the creation of "communities of learning" are proving increasingly important to co-produce knowledge for problem-solving (Davidson-Hunt and O'Flaherty 2007; Iverson and McPhee 2008; Robson *et al.* 2009). The larger issue is that civil science produced by non-specialists and stakeholders is a valid input into decision-making for complex environmental problems. There are no "designated" experts on such problems; researchers need to interact with stakeholders to define the key questions, to participate in the research, and to interpret the findings (Kates *et al.* 2001).

Returning to the question of the adequacy of global models showing average change, one can say that these models are not very useful in informing adaptation strategies. My own observations and discussions with local indigenous experts in various parts of the North over the years indicate that the issue of predictability is of prime importance in its own right. Northern land-based livelihoods depend on the peoples' ability to predict the weather ("is the storm breaking so I can get out?"), "read" the ice ("should I cross the river?"), judge the snow conditions ("could I get back to the community before nightfall?"), and predict animal movements and distributions. A hunter who cannot make the right decisions cannot remain a hunter for long.

Impacts of environmental change are stripping northern hunters of their considerable knowledge, predictive ability, and self-confidence in making a living from their resources. This may ultimately leave them as strangers on their own land. Northern peoples are experts on adapting to conditions that outsiders consider difficult, but it is a question of the speed and magnitude of change, in relation to how fast people can learn and adapt. Rapid change requires rapid learning, and unpredictability superimposed on change interferes with the ability to learn.

Even though indigenous knowledge does not have the techniques and quantitative tools at the disposal of Western science, some systems of indigenous knowledge seem to have developed ways to deal with complexity (Gadgil *et al.* 1993). Climate change is both a local and a global phenomenon, and provides a suitable example with which to pursue complex systems issues, the theme of Chapter 9. Any insights from indigenous wisdom in this regard are of huge potential interest, given the difficulties of Western science in dealing with complex environmental problems such as climate change.

Complex Systems, Holism, and Fuzzy Logic

Indigenous knowledge is said to be holistic in the way it deals with the world. Environmental systems are complex systems, showing a number of characteristics not seen in simple systems, such as scale, uncertainty, self-organization and nonlinear dynamics (Levin 1999). The idea of scale is key to understanding ecosystems. Ecosystems are nested systems, for example, with a small watershed inside a larger one and so on. In ecosystems, there is scaling in time as well as space, for example, there are fast and slow processes (e.g. growth of an annual plant versus the growth of a forest). Such scaling in space and time makes ecosystems extremely difficult to predict and control. Uncertainty results from the unstable and unpredictable relationships among the variables in these multi-scale systems. Hence, managing ecosystems and dealing with multi-scale environmental problems, such as climate change, create huge problems.

Our conventional positivist science assumes a single tangible reality that can be fragmented into independent variables, allowing reductionism and the possibility of time and context-free generalizations (Kuhn 2007). These assumptions work best when systems are bounded and control is possible, as in a laboratory setting. Western science-based societies have tended to simplify ecosystems in order to manage them; monocultures look very different from traditional agroforestry systems (Chapter 4). As well, Western science-based societies often dampen the natural variability of ecosystems in an attempt to increase and stabilize resource production—but at the cost of impairing the functioning of renewal cycles and resilience of ecosystems (Holling 1986; Gunderson and Holling 2002; Chapin *et al.* 2009).

The knowledge and practices of some rural and indigenous societies are of significance in this context. Even though indigenous knowledge does not have the quantitative tools and approaches at the disposal of Western science and technology, some local and indigenous systems have developed ways to deal with complexity. Chapters 4 to 8 contain many examples of this. Of course we know that many ancient societies have ruined their natural environments (Krech 1999; Diamond 2005), but other societies have co-existed with their ecosystems for a long time. The accumulation of evidence, especially since the 1990s, indicates that some indigenous groups have resource-use practices that suggest a sophisticated understanding of ecological relationships and dynamics. In particular, many of these examples seem to show an understanding of the key relationships on the land as a whole, that is, a holistic as opposed to a reductionistic view.

Even though our understanding of indigenous ways of knowing and knowledge systems is still rudimentary, the picture that is beginning to come into focus indicates that some traditional societies have experience in reading environmental variables to deal with ecological complexity. But it is difficult to see how these indigenous approaches might work. How do they do it?

This is the subject of the present chapter. First I discuss rules-of-thumb that cut across complexity. Some of these rules produce indicators that can be used in environmental monitoring. Next I expand on practices that seem to show complex systems thinking. This is followed by two sections that build a theory of indigenous knowledge and complexity. The first, based on the knowledge and practice of Caribbean fishers of Grenada, treats local knowledge as a fuzzy logic expert system. The second, based on Inuit observations of Arctic ecosystem contamination, provides a fuzzy logic analysis of indigenous knowledge.

Rules-of-thumb: Cutting Complexity Down to Size

Since the 1970s, Indian ecologist Madhav Gadgil has been studying human cultural adaptations to ecosystems. He noticed that locally developed conservation practices of rural and tribal populations in India did not rely on multiple regulations as one often finds in the West. Rather they relied on rules-of-thumb, simple prescriptions based on a historical and cultural understanding of the environment. These were often backed up by religious belief, ritual, taboos, and social conventions.

In the area of biodiversity conservation, for example, there seemed to be four rules-of-thumb used in various indigenous societies in India and elsewhere. These were:

1 the total protection of certain selected habitats (e.g. sacred forests and other customary sanctuaries);

2 the total protection of certain species of animals or plants (e.g. taboo species);

3 prohibitions concerning vulnerable stages in the life history of certain species (e.g. hunting taboos in south India for fruit bats at daytime roosts); and

4 practices of monitoring of populations and their habitat.

(Gadgil *et al.* 1993)

Of these rules-of-thumb, the first one, with sacred forests or groves (Ramakrishnan *et al.* 1998), and the second, with taboo species (Colding and Folke 2001) are probably the best-known and documented practices. But potentially there are a great many possibilities of folk knowledge encapsulating a rule or practice that reduces complexity and makes it possible to solve a problem. Consider for example the Andean ethnoclimatology case in Chapter 2 on rainfall prediction based on a rule of thumb, the visibility of the Pleiades star cluster (Orlove *et al.* 2002). Or consider the Maori rule-of-thumb that solved a disease problem afflicting *ti*, an indigenous tree species: "*ti* needs to be part of a vegetation complex, rather than all alone in a paddock" (Box 9.1).

Box 9.1 Maori Rule-of-thumb Saves the Cabbage Tree

The cabbage tree or *ti* (*Cordyline* spp.) on the North Island of New Zealand started dying for an unknown reason in the mid-1980s. As the decline worked its way south, the New Zealand Department of Conservation commissioned a report on Maori knowledge of the condition. The report noted the Maori observation that *ti* "need to be part of a vegetation complex, rather than all alone in a paddock" (J. Williams and T. Chrisp, unpublished manuscript). Some months later, scientists isolated the passion vine hopper as the disease-carrying vector. The hopper does not fly more than 1.5 m above ground and is inhibited by surrounding vegetation that also protects *ti* against accidental damage to the lower trunk. The response of *ti* to injury is to grow another head at the injury site, and it is only at the base of a leafy growth that the hopper can penetrate the cortex and exchange fluids (P. Simpson, personal communication). Hence, the cabbage tree can be protected from disease simply by growing other vegetation around it.

Source: Moller *et al.* (2004: 4).

Such prescriptions in the form of rules-of-thumb have the advantage of turning complex decisions into rules that can be remembered easily and enforced locally through social means. Traditional reef and lagoon tenure systems in Asia-Pacific (Chapter 4), with their taboo areas, taboo species, and ritually announced opening and closing dates for permissible harvests, also operate under the same logic (Johannes 2002a).

The First Salmon ceremony practiced by many indigenous groups in the Pacific Northwest of North America may have provided a rule-of-thumb by instituting a simple rule for opening the fishery. In these tribes, people were not free to fish when migrating salmon appeared in the river. They had to wait for the First Salmon ceremony to start fishing (Swezey and Heizer 1993). Many tribes relied on families who were the designated salmon watchers, and on runners who would communicate up the river the news about the approaching salmon. A ritual leader would make the decision after conferring with the people watching the salmon swimming up the river. Presumably he made a qualitative assessment of a sufficient number of spawners escaping upstream before the fishery was declared open and the event marked by a ceremony.

Obviously the First Salmon ceremony is important in its own right for cultural reasons. However, the ecological function attributed to it is consistent with cultural values encoded in stories and rituals about respecting salmon, allowing creatures to reproduce, not interfering with the leaders in migration, and reciprocal obligations of humans and non-human beings in general (Williams and Hunn 1982; Swezey and Heizer 1993; Turner and Berkes 2006). Can an indigenous system, led by an experienced leader with an understanding of salmon ecology, produce results similar to one achieved by biological management? It can be argued that opening the fishery, after a qualitative assessment of an adequate escapement of spawners, is analogous to a biological management system with population models, counting fences, daily data management, and harvest quota enforcement—but without the whole research infrastructure, quantitative data needs, and associated costs.

Intrigued by the possibilities, I decided to ask the experts if a simple, qualitative observational system could function like current management. Taking advantage of a trip to Oregon (a hotspot of indigenous salmon knowledge), I met with some tribal biologists. Could one actually do a qualitative visual assessment of salmon swimming upstream? Absolutely yes, they said. In fact, the current management does something very similar but uses more intrusive techniques to force salmon through a human-made opening; a counting fence. The tribal biologists did use biological techniques themselves and relied on numbers to open and close the fishery. But many of them thought that the traditional qualitative assessment and the use of the First Salmon ceremony for management purposes were perfectly feasible.

On a subsequent visit to Oregon, I met up with Frank Lake who provided more detail on how the First Salmon ceremony could work in management, its cultural significance, and the prospects for strengthening tribal resource management (Lake 2007). The First Salmon ceremony is still practiced by the Karuk people on Klamath River in northwestern California. There are sites where the river narrows and the migrating salmon can be visually assessed.

As described by Frank Lake (personal communication), Ishi-Pishi Falls is an important traditional fisheries site for the Karuk people near the town of Somes Bar. There is a mountain on the edge of the Karuk village of *Ka'timin* (*Ka* = upper,

Photo 9.1 Site of the Karuk traditional fishery, Ishi-Pishi Falls, Klamath River, NW California. Karuk families use the shadow of the Au'witch (Sugar Loaf) mountain as it crosses over the falls to designate fishing days and to access dip-netting sites.

Photo: Frank Lake.

Timin = falls), the center of the Karuk World. The mountain is called *Au'witch*, also known as the "Sugar Loaf" on American maps. During the fishing season, Karuk families use the shadow of the mountain as it crosses over the falls, to designate fishing days and to access dip-netting sites. Certain families had fish harvesting rights that were inherited, traded, and/or shared with others during times of abundant salmon and other fish runs (Lake, personal communication). Contemporary Karuk use of Ishi-Pishi Falls include traditional fishing for lamprey eels, salmon and steelhead (Senos *et al.* 2006).

Community-based Monitoring and Environmental Change

The basic idea behind local monitoring of the environment is simple. The proximity of the users to the resource confers an ability to observe the environment in detail, and in some cases monitor day-to-day changes. Indigenous hunters (Chapter 6) and fishers (Chapter 7) are not alone in their ability to observe detail. Many farmers, naturalists, sport hunters and fishers who spend time on the land also have this ability.

In the mid-1970s I was involved in the conservation of the Mediterranean monk seal (*Monachus monachus*), said to be the rarest mammal in Europe. After some time in the field, it became clear that a team of researchers could spend weeks or months on the coast and never see one *Monachus*. So we started to work with fishing communities. We met with Turkish Aegean small-scale fishers in the community teahouse and mapped *Monachus* sightings, using community consensus. We visited many fishing villages, repeating the mapping process, and used records from adjacent communities to verify one another (Berkes *et al.* 1979).

When we first presented our findings at a conservation conference, we received a great deal of criticism for not doing proper science and relying on fishers' information. (Surely not trustworthy!) Well, the proof of the pudding is in the eating. Some 30 years later, *Monachus* still survives in the Turkish Aegean in roughly the same numbers as in the 1970s. The network of conservation areas for *Monachus* in Turkey is based on the maps we produced from the original monitoring information from the fishers (Monachus Guardian 2011).

There are many monitoring networks in the world, most of them conservation oriented, that use the collective observational powers of naturalists and other citizens, to keep annual records of species numbers and population sizes, to detect changes over time. Some of these networks can be large and specialized. For example, the COASST (2011) network based at the University of Washington, trains monitoring volunteers to record the details of dead sea-birds and make other observations over large areas of the US Pacific coast.

As people with detailed understanding of the environment and an accumulation of observations over generations, indigenous groups have a special place in community-based monitoring. As well, it is becoming clear that many indigenous groups have developed their own traditional monitoring based on their own ways of knowing (Kofinas *et al.* 2002; Heaslip 2008; Castello *et al.* 2009). Most traditional monitoring methods used by indigenous peoples are rapid, low-cost, and easily comprehensible assessments made by the harvesters themselves as they hunt, fish, and gather forest products, or take animals on the grazing range. Hence, most of the known methods for monitoring populations are based on some aspect of observations related to harvesting (Table 9.1). The harvest rate or the catch per unit of effort (CPUE) assessment is probably the most widely used and practical population monitoring index for customary resource users, as detailed in Chapter 7 on Cree fisheries.

A second general method of traditional monitoring is the use of body condition or the fat index, discussed in Chapter 6 on caribou. As noted, many indigenous groups across the range of caribou populations use a fat index. Some of these assessments are based on the appearance and gait of the live animal (e.g. rump fat) before it is selected for harvesting, and others are made during butchering as a retrospective assessment, e.g. marrow fat (Kofinas *et al.* 2003). Caribou is not the only species monitored this way; Cree hunters regularly check the body condition of animals they harvest, from fish to geese. However, North America is not the

Table 9.1 Traditional methods to monitor populations and their health

Method	Description
Catch per unit of effort	Harvest success, or catch rate, usually per unit of time, or time and effort spent
Body condition index	Pre- or post-harvest observation of fat in body parts of many kinds of animals
Breeding success	Number of young per adult or per nest, or the ratio of young to adults in a population
Population density sensing	Qualitative assessment using "feel, see, touch, smell, hear and taste"
Noting unusual patterns	Detecting change by noting extremes (strange distributions, rare occurrences, breeding failure, unexpected behavior, etc.)
Observations of species mixes	Presence or absence of desirable or undesirable species or assemblages
Communal hunts	Collective information gathering by sweeping a large area with the participation of many harvesters

Source: Adapted from Moller *et al.* (2004).

only area where body condition is checked. Maori birders, and no doubt a great many other indigenous groups, also check body condition (Moller *et al.* 2004).

Other methods of traditional monitoring include observations of the numbers of young, an index of future harvests. Hunters, fishers, and gatherers are often experts in forming impressions of the level of abundance of the harvested species by using their various senses. Some indigenous hunters can make abundance estimates from the density of animal tracks. Some Cree hunters can assess the size of resting goose populations at night from the level of noise they make and the intensity of their smell. Maori sometimes refer to sensing their environment through "touch, feel, and sight" (Moller *et al.* 2004). And, of course, "eyeballing" numbers of birds, game, and fish, is very common, as in the migrating salmon example.

Indigenous hunters and fishers are constantly observing and qualitatively assessing a large number of variables, including many of the variables that are normally studied by biologists. Table 9.1 does not list the full set of these variables; rather, the table lists some of the variables known to be preferentially used by various groups, possibly as a way of dealing with complexity. For example, the fat index integrates the combined effects of a number of environmental variables so that monitoring one simple index gives information on a number of variables. The point is not that traditional knowledge provides a low-cost option to carry out scientific monitoring. Many variables happen to be assessed by both kinds of knowledge, but the logic of the two systems is not necessarily the same.

One major difference between the two kinds of monitoring is that indigenous monitoring seems to use indicators that go beyond biophysical systems and assess human–environment relationships. Berkes *et al.* (2007) re-examined the *Voices from the Bay* document (McDonald *et al.* 1997) for various references to signs and signals, in an attempt to capture Cree and Inuit notions of indicators of a healthy environment and indicators of problems. Four clusters of factors were found: the concept of respect as the starting point; followed by concepts of healthy human–environment relations; signs and signals of wellness; and signs and signals of problems.

These indicators are not necessarily generalizable to other areas and contexts, but they are consistent with indigenous notions of healthy relations with the environment and other living beings, and the principles of respect and reciprocity with humans and non-human beings. These notions inform how indigenous people see the environment, and how the health of the land and the health of the people are connected (Parlee *et al.* 2005b). Other studies are consistent with this reading of *Voices from the Bay* in indicating that many indigenous peoples see respect and proper environmental relations as setting the context for the reading of the more "biological" indicators such as the fat index (Manseau *et al.* 2005b; Parlee *et al.* 2005b).

If indigenous monitoring has its own rules and logic, what are the prospects for designing community-based monitoring systems that do not merely use local technicians for scientific monitoring, but are based on traditional ecological knowledge? There is a great deal of international interest on community-based monitoring. However, the rapidly evolving literature is ambiguous on this issue. Many of the experiences seem more focused on knowledge integration than on pursuing monitoring based on traditional ecological knowledge (Aswani and Lauer 2006a, 2006b; Steinmetz *et al.* 2006; Chalmers and Fabricius 2007; Goldman 2007).

Moving beyond knowledge integration and the notion of traditional ecological knowledge being only locally relevant, Kofinas *et al.* (2003) made the argument that community-based monitoring based on traditional ecological knowledge and using the caribou fat index can be applicable over large regions. Likewise, evidence on climate change research from Sachs Harbour, Wemindji and elsewhere (Krupnik and Jolly 2002; Gearheard *et al.* 2006; Berkes and Armitage 2010) shows that indigenous observations are consistent, robust, and generalizable over large geographic areas.

The Hudson Bay bioregion project provides additional evidence that local and traditional environmental knowledge is relevant for monitoring, not only local changes but region-wide, large-scale environmental changes. The project documented what communities said about changes occurring in their environment following the La Grande development, combined these local observations into a regional whole, and used this information as a baseline in the face of additional hydroelectric development. The report made a holistic assessment of all observed changes, including those that seem to be related to contaminants and to climate change, as well as to hydroelectric development. In many cases, it was difficult to disentangle the effects of these three major drivers of change (McDonald *et al.* 1997). This finding is consistent with the evolving view about impacts of globalization that various factors interact to produce "global change" that has its own characteristics (Young *et al.* 2006).

To summarize, local and indigenous community-based monitoring systems often assess some of the same environmental variables as science. However, they are different from scientific monitoring in a number of significant ways. First, the assessment is qualitative; they neither produce nor use quantitative measures. Second, they include value judgments regarding which measures are relatively more important. The measures chosen tend to be integrated and readily observable, as in the caribou fat index or the catch per unit of effort in fishing. Third, the signs and signals of environmental health, or the lack of it, tend to include what may be called contextual variables, for example, the healthy functioning of rules of respect, sharing, reciprocity, and the various interrelationships. The ability of rural and indigenous groups to read their environments and to respond to environmental signals is relatively well known (Berkes and Folke 1998; Berkes et al. 2000). But, further, the ability of some of these groups to monitor large-scale change, such as climate change, is of considerable global interest (Kofinas et al. 2002; Manseau et al. 2005b).

Complex Systems Thinking

After discussing rules-of-thumb and implications for monitoring, in this section we explore the evidence that complex systems thinking exists in some indigenous groups. A number of traditional societies have ecosystem-like concepts (Chapter 4) and some traditional knowledge and management systems have similarities to Adaptive Management with its emphasis on feedback learning and its treatment of uncertainty that is intrinsic to all ecosystems (Chapters 6 and 7). Further, some traditional societies manage resources at multiple levels, as in Cree fisheries (Chapter 7). Having holistic concepts of the land, and dealing with uncertainty and scale are hallmarks of a complexity approach. But we need to explore further for evidence of an intuitive understanding of a complex adaptive system approach, where traditional knowledge and management systems deal with components and interactions of an integrated whole, and where they show an ability to learn and adjust.

Table 9.2 helps expand on some examples of traditional arrangements that seem to show complex adaptive systems thinking. A classic example is the rice terrace irrigation system in Bali managed by priests. This system called *subak* was briefly disbanded ("modernized") with the arrival of Green Revolution rice varieties and their particular management requirements. But missing the flexible timing of water releases in the priest-designed arrangement, the new system worked badly, and the original system was restored. Lansing (1991) was able to show the logic of *subak* by programming the entire system, hence the title of his book, *Priests and Programmers*. In an extension of the study, Lansing et al. (1998) used a modification of the "Daisyworld model" to include feedbacks between the environment and rice irrigators. Modeling the selection of rice cropping patterns as a process of system-dependent selection (in which selection resulting from feedbacks constantly modifies subsequent selection), Lansing et al. (1998) were able to generate solutions that accurately predicted the observed patterns of rice production.

A second example that uses modeling as an analytical tool comes from the Andean highlands. Flannery et al. (1989) used simulation models to analyze decision-making among the Wamani herders of Peru. Since the llamas were capable of overgrazing, the herders had to limit the numbers of animals. But doing this

Table 9.2 Some examples of local and indigenous systems that show complex adaptive systems thinking and holistic understanding of ecological dynamics

Example and description	Reference
Hindu priests manage a system of "water temples" that regulates use of irrigation water in rice agriculture by villagers in Bali, Indonesia. The system can be formalized as an optimization model.	Lansing (1991); Lansing *et al.* (1998)
A system of gift-giving and reciprocity regulates herd size of llamas and periodically re-establishes human–nature relations among the llama herders of the highlands in Ayacucho, Peru.	Flannery *et al.* (1989)
Heuristic rules of the IF . . . THEN . . . form can be constructed from the practices of north Pacific herring fishers to model their decision-making.	Mackinson (2000, 2001)
Tukano shamans manage both human health and ecosystem health through the rules they enforce in the Amazon forests of Colombia.	Reichel-Dolmatoff (1976)
Among New Guinea highland horticulturalists, a ritual of pig slaughter and tribal warfare, which occurs periodically, regulates resource management and population size.	Rappaport (1984)
Sahelian herders of Africa monitor the state of the pasture to make decisions about rotating grazing areas or relocating the herds, allowing for buffer areas for emergency grazing.	Niamir-Fuller (1990, 1998)
Milpa, the multiple-use cyclic maize-growing system of Mexico, may be characterized as a "cultural script," an internalized plan consisting of a series of routine steps with alternative subroutines and decision nodes.	Alcorn and Toledo (1998)

involved the use of social relations, whereby the Wamani used a complicated set of rules for gift-giving and reciprocity to redistribute the animals.

Mackinson (2000, 2001) used a fuzzy logic approach to model the decision-making of herring fishers of British Columbia, Canada. The model starts by pointing out that local knowledge does not lend itself well to mathematical representation, and develops an alternative way. A fuzzy logic expert system is used to combine scientific information and the knowledge of herring fishers to understand the dynamics of herring shoals. Such non-indigenous examples serve as a reminder that probably very few cases use purely traditional knowledge but incorporate elements of different kinds of knowledge (Begossi 1998; Dove 2002).

The next four examples all use verbal models, rather than mathematical ones. All four have been introduced in earlier parts of the book. Here the emphasis is on holism of the case and complex adaptive systems thinking. The classic example of the Tukano of the Colombian Amazon is an early attempt, along with Rappaport's (1984) Papua New Guinea case, to analyze an indigenous system as a self-regulating, feedback-driven cybernetic system (Reichel-Dolmatoff 1976). The ritual management of the game and human behavior is carried out by the shaman. Species abundances are monitored by random scheduling of hunting excursions, helping the shaman to decide which species need protection. The shaman is not only a healer of individual illness but an ecosystem doctor as well (Chapter 3, Box 3.3).

The Sahelian herders of Africa described by Niamir-Fuller (1990, 1998) are resourceful managers of livestock in a fringe environment with highly variable rainfall. They move their herds with the rains, emulating the seasonal migrations of the great herds of African wildlife. They monitor the state of the pasture to make decisions about rotating grazing areas or relocating the herds. They establish reserves within their annual grazing areas. These reserves provide an emergency supply of forage that serves to buffer drought events and maintain the resilience of both the herds and the herders. Behnke *et al.* (1993), Niamir-Fuller (1998), and Scoones (1999) have all pointed out the flexibility of decision-making in many of these traditional African herding systems as an adaptation to highly variable, non-equilibrium semi-arid ecosystems. They have also pointed out that equilibrium-based prescriptions of scientific range management, with carrying capacity and stocking rate calculations, perform poorly in these ecosystems.

Milpa is one of the better-known systems of shifting cultivation, involving the use of fire and succession management (Chapter 4). As practiced by the Huastec people of eastcentral Mexico's tropical humid forest, *milpa* is well adapted to the multiple use of this kind of ecosystem (Alcorn and Toledo 1998). Following the clearing of land by fire, the regenerating vegetation becomes a sequential harvesting system of crops and non-food products. Many of the regrowth species will eventually become trees that provide firewood, construction materials, dyes, medicines, and other resources. Alcorn and Toledo (1998) characterize *milpa* as a "cultural script," an internalized plan consisting of a series of routine steps with alternative subroutines, decision nodes and room for learning and experimenting. A "maize culture hero" oversees *milpa* and warns people of the consequences of improper practice, assuring social enforcement of codes of good practice.

Together these examples provide a rich set of cases from diverse geographic areas and cultures, and from different resource systems. They show that many indigenous systems build holistic practices upon detailed, locally adapted environmental knowledge. These are integrated systems of people and nature that can be characterized as cybernetic systems amenable to description by the use of optimization models, simulation models, fuzzy logic expert systems, heuristic rules, or cultural scripts.

One of the lessons to emerge from this inquiry is what we might call a non-equilibrium sacred ecology. Indigenous knowledge is often seen as rich in understanding the natural history of ecosystem components but not ecosystem processes (Thomas 2003). The material reviewed here indicates that this is not so. The examples given here, along with other evidence (Alcorn 1989; Berkes *et al.* 2000; Muchagata and Brown 2000) suggest that ecosystem process knowledge is part of the usual complement of indigenous knowledge. In particular, indigenous resource systems seem to rely heavily on disturbance ecology. All succession management such as *milpa*, starts with a disturbance event. Sahelian herders stimulate range regrowth by grazing their animals heavily in one area, before moving on to another. Cree fishers (Chapter 7) harvest one area heavily before rotating.

Thomas (2003) argues that we need to learn from the Hewa of Papua New Guinea whose conservation blueprint is the use of small-scale disturbance. Our conventional conservation blueprint excludes disturbance, and aims for unperturbed, stable systems in a state of equilibrium. "Balance of nature" and equilibrium thinking support the view among some conservationists that the best way to conserve nature is to seek out high biodiversity, supposedly pristine ecosystems, remove all human influences (such as haying, grazing, collection of non-timber forest products, use of fire) and re-establish natural biodiversity by stabilizing ecological processes. Such an approach largely fails. Ecosystems are dynamic and disturbance, including some level of human use and disturbance, has an important role in maintaining ecological processes (Berkes and Davidson-Hunt 2006; Miller and Davidson-Hunt 2010).

At the end of Chapter 4, the argument was made, consistent with the Adaptive Management and ecosystem resilience literature (Gunderson and Holling 2002), that all ecosystems require periodic perturbation for renewal. These ideas challenge conventional resource management science and conventional conservation science with their equilibrium-centered emphasis. The non-equilibrium sacred ecology of some indigenous systems, with their practices of small perturbations, notions of reciprocal obligations, and socially enforced ethics that depend on rituals (such as the First Salmon ceremony) and culture heroes provide an alternative to the conventional view. The next two sections provide two analyses of how these alternatives may be approached.

Local Knowledge and Expert Systems

Rules-of-thumb cut across complexity; cultural scripts help grasp how indigenous knowledge systems might work. Another approach is the use of fuzzy cognitive maps, qualitative models of a system consisting of variables and the relationships among those variables (Özesmi and Özesmi 2004). A related approach is the use of fuzzy logic expert systems.

Sandra Grant studied the local knowledge of the longline fishers of Gouyave, Grenada, and suggested that this knowledge could be described as an expert system. This section borrows heavily from Grant and Berkes (2007). Fisher knowledge in the Caribbean does not often involve multi-generational cultural transmission, and there are only few studies of fisher knowledge (Warner 1997; Gomes *et al.* 1998; Breton *et al.* 2006). Full of incipient systems, the Caribbean provides a suitable setting for the examination of the fisher knowledge generation process. When a new fishing technique is introduced, fisher knowledge is created rapidly as fishers develop the capacity to learn from experience. New knowledge is being generated continuously.

We know that fisher knowledge exists, but we have little idea how a fisher knowledge system actually works. We propose that fishers have an applied knowledge system that can be described as an expert system, "a branch of artificial intelligence, providing theories and methods for automating intelligent behaviour. They are computer programs that use heuristic rules to store knowledge, which is used to infer solutions and help provide assistance in solving complex problems normally handled by human experts" (Mackinson 2001: 534). Expert systems assume that human experts use heuristic rules to store knowledge used in problem-solving and help provide assistance in how problems are solved. The knowledge used for decision-making is not quantitative (as in scientific data) but qualitative and consists of fuzzy sets (Mackinson 2000, 2001).

An expert system has three components (Figure 9.1). The knowledge base is the repository of rules, facts, general cases, exceptions, and relations that can help human decision-makers solve problems. The inference engine is the mechanism for manipulating the encoded knowledge base for making inferences and drawing conclusions, using rules in the form "IF *a certain situation occurs* THEN *a known outcome is likely*" and may contain several conditions linked by AND, OR, or NOT. Finally, the user interface provides the link from the system to the user (Mackinson 2001). The expert system is a useful construct, as it not only allows a description of the ecological and technological knowledge of fishers (the knowledge base), but goes two steps further. It helps understand fishers' decision-support system using IF–THEN rules to find and catch fish (the inference engine), and how fishers use social relationships to access the database of knowledge and decision-support system (the user interface).

The longline fishery in Gouyave, on the west coast of Grenada, began in 1979, introduced by Cuban master fishers. The fishers of the area previously used handlines, beach seines, and fish traps. The fishery developed rapidly through multiple phases (Grant *et al.* 2007) and came to dominate the local economy.

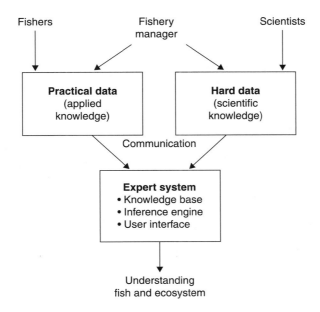

Figure 9.1 A schematic representation of the components of an expert system model for fisher knowledge.

Source: Adapted from Mackinson (2000).

A surface longline is a floating gear that is set and, after a time, retrieved. As used in Gouyave, it can be 10 kilometers long with over 300 baited hooks hanging from droplines. It is used for large pelagic (open water) fish such as yellowfin tuna (*Thunnus albacares*), Atlantic sailfish (*Istiophorus albicans*), and common dolphinfish (*Coryphaena hippurus*). It is one of the more lucrative fisheries in the Caribbean.

Longline fishers have some nine categories of knowledge base with which they find and catch large pelagic fish (Figure 9.2). The diagram should be seen as a simplified schematic, as decision-making is often more complicated than shown here. The process begins with knowing the harvesting and reproductive seasons of fish and the type of bait to be used, its abundance and size availability. Depending on the season and bait, the fishers then choose the most appropriate longline weight type. If weather conditions are favorable, they go fishing. While at sea, the type of bait, fish habits and behavior, and fish movement determine the fishing strategy. They rely on their knowledge of "folk oceanography" (presence/absence of seabirds, seawater color, and current strength and direction) to decide where they actually place the longline. Some of the categories of knowledge are within the control of fishers, while others are not. Fishers control the choice of bait, longline weight, and fishing practice. They can alter the weight of the line and bait type, as available.

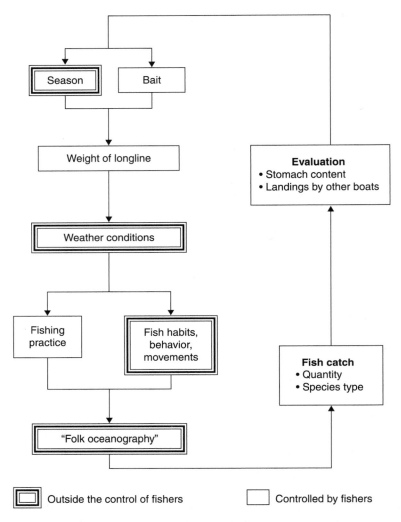

Figure 9.2 A process for fisher decision-making and knowledge production, based on the practice of longline fishers of Gouyave, Grenada.

Source: Adapted from Grant and Berkes (2007).

Thus fishers can experiment with the variables they control, while learning from the variables they cannot (seasons and weather, fish habits and behavior).

Box 9.2 illustrates an expert system built on a multi-layer decision-tree, in the form, IF *a certain situation occurs,* THEN *a known outcome is likely.* Since the goal was to analyze how fishers made decisions around fishing, attributes were typically used in the IF part of the rules, and descriptors in the THEN part. The

---

Box 9.2   An Illustration of Gouyave Longline Fisher Decision-Making Process

IF	Season is December
AND	bait is available—medium and small jack
THEN	prepare light-light longline if birds abundant
AND	seawater colour is blue
AND	current direction N or NW
AND	fish tracking—50 km west
THEN	should catch sailfish
IF	fish catch—sailfish, but a poor catch
AND	other boats were more successful
THEN	evaluate performance—eliminate bait, crew performance, longline, "folk oceanography"
AND	try again

Source: Grant and Berkes (2007: 168).

---

outcomes of these conditions provided feedbacks and opportunities to learn from the process.

At the end of a fishing trip, fishers reflected on their observations and the decision-making process that resulted in their catch for the day. Evaluation involved comparing their fish catch with other boats, and analyzing their performance. If other boats were more successful at catching fish, the fisher often conducted a critical analysis of his performance, often systematically eliminating categories of knowledge that could affect the catch. For example, to eliminate bait as a factor, the fisher investigated the stomach content of the fish caught to see if prey preference was a factor. Often the fisher also sought assistance from others to discuss what could be done to improve his catch, making the necessary adjustments on subsequent trips. This knowledge production process was repeated every time a fisher went on a fishing trip. Confirmation of what they know and new experiences were shared within social groups of Gouyave fishers and networked to become a pool of knowledge.

A Fuzzy Logic Analysis of Indigenous Knowledge

Fuzzy logic appears to be a good fit with indigenous knowledge, and an approach that may help understand, or provide insights, on the question of how local and indigenous knowledge systems may be dealing with complexity. Our emphasis in this section, which borrows heavily from Berkes and Kislalioglu Berkes (2009), is fuzzy logic for observing variables and building mental models (Zadeh 1965, 1973). The section explores the idea that indigenous knowledge is able to deal with ecosystems as complex adaptive systems by using simple prescriptions, consistent with fuzzy logic thinking. Indigenous knowledge pursues holism by considering a large number of variables qualitatively, while Western science tends to concentrate on a small number of variables quantitatively. We use the example of Arctic pollution to illustrate the point.

The Arctic region has been undergoing rapid environmental change in the past few decades. Northern indigenous observations of climate change (Chapter 8) and abnormalities in animals related to Arctic ecosystem contamination are a major concern (Cobb *et al.* 2005). Indigenous observers do not gather quantitative data, but their ways of observing and assessing changes provide insights regarding the way indigenous holism is constructed.

John O'Neil and colleagues (1997) worked with the Inuit of Hudson Bay region in northern Canada and documented how they made sense of the contaminants issue. The major concern was the observation of abnormalities in many animals, focusing on seals. The diagnosis of a sick animal relied on many indicators. The Inuit knew which animals were sick or abnormal. They had a sense of what normal animals should look like, based on their collective experience over many years. They made reference to specific signs that indicated that an animal was not well and should not be eaten: animals with *manimiq* (lumps), discolored bones, abnormal liver, bumps and blueish spots in the intestines, and skinny animals. The Inuit also observed the behavior of the animal, its feeding, swimming, and response to predators, reading signs of wellness continuously and cumulatively (O'Neil *et al.* 1997).

Inuit and other indigenous knowledge holders accumulate such information as a result of many years of observations (analogous to extensive sampling), the sharing of knowledge with other hunters and fishers (data pooling), and forming a collective mental model of what healthy animals would look like. Their "data" on animal health and abnormalities are language-based, rather than numbers-based, and comparisons are performed on perceived ranks (e.g. fat, thin, very thin). The mental processes of data collection, concept formation and retention, and mental model formation among indigenous people follow patterns consistent with the language used, as language shapes terms and concepts. For example, it is well known that the Inuit do not attach much value to numerical precision. They also do not often make simple causal connections, as is often done in positivist science (Kuhn 2007). Rather, they see environmental change and related observations as empirically connected. Systematic generalizations regarding cause–effect relationships are in general avoided and considered "childish," without *ihuma* or sense (Omura 2005).

The fuzzy logic argument is that holistic thinking among the Inuit is possible because precise categorizations and generalizations are avoided. If all the concepts and relationships embedded in a holistic term were to be specified, the whole idea would become unmanageably complex. There seems to be an inverse relationship between the complexity of a system and the degree of precision that can be used meaningfully to describe it. Zadeh (1973: 28) calls this idea the Principle of Incompatibility: "as the complexity of a system increases, our ability to make precise and yet significant statements about its behaviour diminishes until a threshold is reached beyond which precision and significance (or relevance) become almost mutually exclusive characteristics."

Hence, precise quantitative analyses of the behavior of complex systems are not likely to have much relevance to the real world. Indigenous knowledge works in the fuzzy logic sense to the extent that (1) there is a large amount of information, (2) it is collected continuously, and (3) changes are incorporated into the collective mental model as new information flows in. Herein lies the essential similarity of indigenous knowledge and fuzzy logic. The three points above are also the backbone of fuzzy logic models (Box 9.3). In both cases, the analysis of the complex system behavior is carried out, not by using numerically precise data, but by using language-based data that are qualitative and rich.

Fuzzy models rely on language-based information that is converted to simple mathematical expressions that can then be manipulated to make mathematical inferences. For example, in the observations of "skinny seals" or "fat fish," fatness is the linguistic variable and the adjectives are linguistic values. Qualifying terms such as "and," "or," "not" are linguistic connectives. Returning to the example of Inuit observations of unhealthy seals, let us say that experienced hunters among the Inuit of Hudson Bay have been hunting seals (a large sample size) and finding that many of them have abnormalities. Over several hunting seasons (continuous set of observations), hunters have noticed that some seals are thin, some have discolored bones, and some have abnormal livers. After a while, the experienced hunters would begin to formulate an opinion about the general health of the seals.

To put it in fuzzy model terms, the hunters observe seal fatness (variable 1) during the sampling. There is an existing mental model of the various values (different degrees of fatness/thinness) of this variable from experience and the collective memory of experienced hunters and elders. Each seal is evaluated mentally against this tacit model. The seals may be assessed to be generally thinner, and variable 1 is assigned a fatness/thinness value. In fuzzy models, it is assigned a certain weight between 1 and 10. Other variables such as discolored

Box 9.3   Fuzzy Basics

Fuzzy sets were developed as a way to represent the imprecise nature of information in everyday life. In most situations, precision may be useless ("apply the brakes 25 m before the red light") whereas vague directions consistent with the imprecise nature of data and the capabilities of the human brain can be acted upon ("brake pretty soon"). Practical applications of fuzzy logic in electrical and computer systems include self-monitoring and adjusting "smart" systems that can detect and adjust to changing conditions. All soft computing, including decision-support systems, uses fuzzy logic. Fuzzy logic is a way to deal with uncertainty; it is suitable for concepts and systems that do not have sharply defined boundaries. It is an unusual approach because it breaks with the yes–no binary logic of Cartesian tradition which assumes that every proposition has to be either true or false.

In fuzzy logic, things need not be quantified before they can be considered mathematically. Information is classified into broad groupings, simulating the workings of the human mind. "The premise is that the key elements of human thinking are not numbers, but labels of fuzzy sets, that is, classes of objects in which the transition from membership to non-membership is gradual rather than abrupt" (Zadeh 1973: 28). Fuzzy logic has three main distinguishing features: use of linguistic variables in place of numerical variables; characterization of simple relations between variables by fuzzy conditional statements; and characterization of complex relations by fuzzy algorithms. For example, if "fat, thin, very thin" are values for fatness, then fatness is a linguistic variable. Fuzzy conditional statements in the form of IF *a* THEN *b* are used to build a fuzzy algorithm, an ordered sequence of instructions.

Sources: Bezdec (1992); Zadeh (1965, 1973).

bones (variable 2), condition of liver (variable 3), and so on, are assigned different weights, based on the existing mental model of a healthy seal that is good to eat.

All the relevant variables according to the model are weighted. IF variable *x* has a degree of thinness *a*, THEN the seals are assigned a fuzzy conditional statement. This type of reasoning is used for all the variables specified, and helps evaluate the wellness of the seal for eating. As we saw in the last section about fisher knowledge, several "IF *a* THEN *b*" type statements are used.

There is flexibility since weightings may be changed as observations accumulate. Although not attempted here, fuzzy models are able to quantify (by assigning numerical values or weights) the qualitative judgments of hunters based on their expertise.

The Inuit observations on the fatness/thinness of seals (and other variables) are not quantitative and do not need to be. Fuzzy logic is able to work with the approximate values assigned to the categorizations of fatness/thinness that can be inferred from the language used by the hunters. Fuzzy logic simulates human judgment in making sense of a large number of variables by using weightings and mental models of Inuit experts, and then assigning numerical values to these.

How do the Inuit ways of knowing about contaminant effects compare to the science of toxicology? A major difference between science and indigenous knowledge is that toxicological studies tended to work with a single analytical tool at a time, focusing on one or a small number of indicators. By contrast, indigenous knowledge focuses on a large number of less specific (and probably multi-causal) indicators used simultaneously as a suite. Although scientific approaches seek indicator specificity and produce quantitative studies of a small number of indicators, those based on indigenous knowledge do not produce formalized generalizations. But the use of a broad suite of simple indicators (instead of a few detailed and costly ones) gives the hunting community feedback on many aspects of environmental health, a holistic picture of the environment.

Conclusions

The chapter posed the question of how indigenous knowledge develops holistic approaches. We started with a discussion of rules-of-thumb, indigenous ways of monitoring, and reviewed evidence for complex adaptive systems thinking in indigenous knowledge and practice. Then using the example of a recently developed local knowledge system, we explored how fisher knowledge can be construed as a fuzzy logic expert system (Grant and Berkes 2007). Finally, we focused on fuzzy logic for building collective mental models of the environment, as a way to explain how rules-of-thumb and other simple prescriptions can be used to deal with complexity (Berkes and Kislalioglu Berkes 2009).

The last two sections in particular show that adaptive learning, rather than the knowledge content itself, is important. Both in the Grenada fishers example and the Hudson Bay Inuit example, knowledge production can be viewed as a learning process. The experience with various variables and the evaluation of the outcome over time, iteratively add to the knowledge holders' experience and lead to adaptation. This continuous learning process and the ability to deal flexibly with new situations make the knowledge holders adaptive experts. Again in both cases, knowledge is communal, rather than individual. Communal mental models are built to describe the world and to provide rules that simplify complexity.

It is well known in the theory of complex adaptive systems that complexity can emerge from simple rules (Levin 1999). Conversely, it seems, simple rules are appropriate for dealing with complex adaptive systems. Indigenous knowledge seems to build holistic pictures of the environment by considering a large number of variables qualitatively, whereas science tends to concentrate on a small number of variables quantitatively. It is a tradeoff captured in Zadeh's (1973) principle, which says that an inverse relationship exists between the complexity of a system and the degree of precision that can be used meaningfully to describe it.

The large degree of uncertainty in complex adaptive systems limits the ability to make precise (and yet significant) statements about system behavior. Complex adaptive systems cannot easily be comprehended by the use of conventional science simply because we would be overwhelmed by data and would not even be sure that the data are meaningful. Zadeh's insight was to recognize the nature of this problem and depart from Cartesian duality and precision, ironic for an engineer but perhaps not surprising for a scholar with a cultural background in the East (Azerbaijani/Turkish, Iranian, Russian).

The analysis suggests that Zadeh's solutions are a good fit with indigenous knowledge and its holistic treatment of ecosystem complexity, with the use of rules-of-thumb and broad suites of simple indicators. Fuzzy logic analysis can be applied to other kinds of indigenous knowledge on complex systems problems, for example climate change (Chapter 8). The people of Sachs Harbour were observing a great many variables (Table 8.2) and constantly comparing the recent situation to their mental model of what a healthy environment ought to look like, with its expected range of variation. Similarly, the Sahelian herder probably has a mental model of what a good range looks like, and the practitioners of *milpa* have a mental model of proper practice, to be enforced by the "maize culture hero" as needed.

As studies of Cree harvesters show, indigenous hunters may deal with a surprisingly large number of variables qualitatively (Peloquin and Berkes 2009). Just how many variables indigenous knowledge holders can track, we do not know. We do know that many indigenous knowledge systems converge on a few integrative variables (like the fat index for assessing animal health). In the case of science, the key variables are identified by consensus of the accumulating scientific literature. Generated by such a process, the key variables tend to be few in number. In both the science of environmental toxicology and of climate change, there is a sense that the use of a few indicators, no matter how well chosen, may be inadequate in capturing complexity. The indigenous solution is brilliant in building a holistic understanding by monitoring a large number of variables over a long period of time, accumulating and accessing a large amount of qualitative data, and building a collective mental model of healthy animals and environment.

The holistic picture thus constructed can then be used to assess change, without reducing the observed world into discrete (and quantifiable) variables. Gregory Bateson observed that, "The continuum of nature is constantly broken down into a discontinuum of variables in the act of description" (Bateson and Bateson 1987: 165). The conventional scientific solution has been to quantify a few of the variables, whereas the solution in indigenous knowledge has been to find ways of perceiving the continuum of nature and working with it.

CHAPTER 10

How Local Knowledge Develops:
Cases from the West Indies

The last chapter made the argument that simple rules may be appropriate for dealing with complex systems. But how do we develop the ways to perceive Bateson's continuum of nature, the understandings and the practice of living in a complex system that we call the ecosystem? There are relevant theories in environmental perception and environmental education. But there are no commonly accepted theories of the development or evolution of indigenous knowledge.

The chapter starts with a framework of models, elements, and mechanisms of the development of systems of local and traditional knowledge and practice. After discussing the main points of the framework, I go into examples from the islands of the Eastern Caribbean that provide laboratory-like settings in which the evolution of local knowledge and resource management practice can be studied. Building on the Grenada fisheries case in Chapter 9, this chapter highlights four more Caribbean examples: a mangrove conservation and management project in St. Lucia, tropical forest management in Dominica with local entrepreneur-stewards, the cultivation of edible sea moss after the depletion of wild stocks, and a case of Adaptive Management inspired by traditional, community-based sea urchin resource use.

The chapter focuses on several aspects of the development of local and indigenous knowledge: how new knowledge arises and is elaborated upon, the processes involved, and the distinction between local and traditional knowledge. As well, the chapter discusses the relationship between knowledge/practice and ɩne development of institutions, in particular, commons institutions that provide resource rights and the security of access on which local management systems can be based. Thus the chapter elaborates on Figure 1.1 about levels of analysis of traditional knowledge, making the point that management requires institutions to put into effect empirical knowledge and practice.

As pointed out in the last section, the West Indies, strictly speaking, is one part of the world in which traditional systems do *not* exist. The indigenous populations of the Eastern Caribbean islands, and whatever traditional knowledge and resource management systems they might have had, have almost completely disappeared. The present-day populations of Caribbean islands such as St. Lucia, Dominica, Grenada, Jamaica, and Barbados are, to a large extent, the descendants of the people who were enslaved and brought over from Africa by colonists. Their transformation into independent agricultural communities and into groups of fishers and forest users is relatively new. Thus, the Caribbean islands provide appropriate field experiments in the creation of environmental knowledge, and in the evolution of community-based management systems that use this knowledge.

A Framework for Development of Local and Traditional Knowledge

Table 10.1 discusses three areas: models of knowledge development, elements of knowledge systems, and mechanisms of development of knowledge. The discussion is based partly on a pair of synthesis papers that explored two models of the evolution of conservation practice (Turner and Berkes 2006; Berkes and Turner 2006). One model emphasizes the gradual development of environmental knowledge by a group, leading to increasingly more sophisticated understandings of the ecosystem in which the group lives. Termed here the environmental understanding model, it is based on incremental learning, the concomitant development of belief systems, ways of encoding and communicating this knowledge, and the development of institutions to consolidate it (Turner and Berkes 2006).

The second model, termed here the crisis learning model, emphasizes the importance of resource crises and mistakes in shaping how environmental knowledge and practice, in particular conservation practice, develops. Several authors have pointed out the importance of learning from mistakes in shaping future resource use practices (Berkes and Folke 2002; Holt 2005). Johannes observed that almost all of the basic marine conservation practices were in use in the Pacific centuries ago (Table 4.2). "For the Pacific islanders to have devised and employed deliberate conservation measures, first they had to learn that their natural resources were limited. They could have only done so by depleting them" (Johannes 2002b: 3).

Table 10.1 Development of local and traditional knowledge and practice

Models of development of knowledge and practice	Elements of development of knowledge and practice	Mechanisms of development of knowledge and practice
• Environmental understanding • Crisis learning	• Incremental learning and observations • Development of institutions • Encoding and communication of knowledge • Development of belief systems	• Observing and monitoring • Trial and error experimentation • Learning from other places and times • Knowledge encoded in language and narratives

Source: Adapted from Turner and Berkes (2006); Berkes and Turner (2006).

However, most of the actual depletion events are lost in the mists of time. They are not easy to identify or record. The two that we have been able to trace and analyze are the 1910s caribou overkill (Chapter 6) and the Sanikiluaq (Belcher Islands) caribou disappearance in the 1880s (Nakashima 1991).

The evidence is that the environmental understanding model is the dominant way in which knowledge and practice normally develops. If one examines examples of multi-faceted environment and resource management practices, they are too complex and culturally ingrained to have developed solely in response to crisis learning (Turner and Berkes 2006). However, crises may have triggered some kinds of learning and shaped subsequent practice by impacting environmental ethics and values. This appears to be the case in the caribou overkill example. In the case of the Sanikiluaq caribou disappearance, the impact seems to have been, not on values, but on the direction and speed of learning. The Inuit learned to substitute eider duck (*Somateria molissima*) skins to make parkas. The crisis of the caribou loss must have triggered an intense period of experimenting and rapid learning. Emerging out of that new knowledge and practice was an elaborate system of eider skin parka making, unparalleled in the circumpolar Arctic (Nakashima 1991; Berkes and Turner 2006).

Table 10.1 lists several elements in the development of local and traditional knowledge and practice. Based on the material reviewed in this book, Turner and Berkes (2006) and Turner *et al.* (2000), some of the attributes embodied within traditional ecological knowledge systems include the following four areas. First, there is incremental individual and group learning and elaboration of environmental knowledge as a result of detailed observations and experience of variations in nature. This can lead to a sophisticated understanding of the ecosystem in which they dwell. For example, a natural burn attracting browsing deer and increasing berry production in subsequent years, would provide an incentive for the development of anthropogenic burning (Boyd 1999).

Second, there is the development of institutions that guide practice. By institutions we mean the set of rules actually used or rules-in-use (Ostrom 1990). Such institutions are socially constructed, with normative and cognitive dimensions, thus they embed values (Jentoft *et al.* 1998). Rule sets that define access rights and specify appropriate behaviors are known as tenure systems or commons institutions (Trosper 2002, 2009). Most of the resources used by indigenous and other rural groups are commons (common-property or common-pool resources), defined as a class of resources for which exclusion is difficult and joint use involves subtractability (Berkes *et al.* 1989; Feeny *et al.* 1990).

Thus, there are two requirements for making commons work. The first involves solving the problem of exclusion by means of controlling the access of all potential users by establishing property rights. The second involves solving the problem of subtractability by making and enforcing rules for resource use among the authorized users themselves. Once property rights and resource use rules have been established, both the costs and benefits of any management action will be borne by the same individual or group, thus providing incentive to conserve. There is another kind of institution that Davidson-Hunt and Berkes (2003) and Davidson-Hunt (2006) have called institutions of knowledge. It is about rules that govern the evolution of knowledge in a particular group, by framing the process of creativity, learning, and remembering.

Third, there is a need for creating and perpetuating ways of encoding, communicating, and disseminating knowledge and practice. Stories and teachings are one example of the ways in which understandings of environmental knowledge and practice can be disseminated over space and time. Observations and experiences and guiding principles can be taught and acquired over generations, and spread through stories, ceremonies, and discourse from one community to another (Turner *et al.* 2000; Turner *et al.* 2003). Community gatherings are occasions for reinforcing these values. Social relationships, such as the roles and responsibilities of the leaders in relation to their people, resources, and territories, would also be reinforced at such times. Individuals and groups within a community would hold specialized knowledge (e.g. women's knowledge) to be imparted at appropriate times and places (Turner 2003).

Fourth, there is the concomitant development of belief systems that back up knowledge and practice and consolidate supporting values. Attitudes are socially mediated and directed, and they guide and determine our actions. For example, the notion of respect predominates in many traditional belief systems (Callicott 1994; Atleo 2004). Anderson (1996) argues that environmentally appropriate practices work best when incorporated into belief systems. More broadly, Bateson and Bateson (1987) suggest that the unity of nature (i.e. the re-integration of humans and culture into the ecosystem) might only be comprehended through the kind of metaphors used in religion, or through the sacred. This is the area of belief, cosmology, or worldview; the distinctions are difficult to make (Berkes 2001). But it corresponds to the fourth level of analysis in Figure 1.1.

Table 10.1 lists a number of mechanisms of development of local and traditional knowledge. There is constant learning from the lived experience, the daily observation and monitoring of the environment as in the climate change example (Chapter 8) and the Arctic contaminants example (Chapter 9). This process may be accelerated or moved in new directions through novel events that might be related to crisis learning, as in the caribou overkill event. The climate change example suggests that small crises such as near-accidents because of unexpectedly thin ice, trigger much learning and new interpretations.

Observations and events are put through a cultural filter, through institutions of knowledge, about how the process of learning can occur. This is the culturally correct way in which knowledge can be transmitted, individual competency developed, and observations may become part of the accepted, authoritative knowledge of the group (Davidson-Hunt and Berkes 2003). Not only the observation itself, but interpretations and inferences can be folded into an enriched, elaborate system of knowledge and practice.

To what extent does individual knowledge blend with the knowledge of others? Turner and Berkes (2006: 504) state, "over time, even one lifetime, experiences of others blend with personal knowledge and observations, compounding and accumulating to bring enhanced knowledge and wisdom." Others might point out that what is blended is not so much knowledge as the thing known, but knowledge as the process (Ingold 2000; Neves-Graca 2004). The James Bay Cree are always careful to distinguish what they know first-hand, as opposed to blended knowledge. In the Inuit Observations of Climate Change project (Chapter 8), the Inuvialuit people of Sachs Harbour criticized those who were reporting observations other than their own. Thus, individual knowledge and experience tends to be distinct, but it is enriched by the knowledge of the group, and is shaped by the ways of knowing of the group. The mechanisms in Table 10.1 do not distinguish between individual and group processes.

Observing and monitoring of seasonal changes, animal migrations, plant life cycles, and berry production brings an ability to detect variance from the norm (Lantz and Turner 2003). Many of these observations track dynamic processes such as plant succession (Alcorn 1989). Trial and error experimentation and incremental modification are quite common, as in Cree fisheries. Practices such as selective harvesting of cedar bark (without killing the tree) are likely explainable by such experimentation (Deur and Turner 2005). Harvesting and management of live trees is common in diverse areas of the world, and takes many forms (Turner *et al.* 2009).

Learning from other places and times is less common in systems of local knowledge and more common in traditional knowledge. Technologies, products, and ideas transmitted across boundaries are often traceable linguistically (Turner *et al.* 2003). Learning from animals (e.g. bears "pruning" berry bushes) is common in many indigenous groups (Turner 2005). Knowledge encoded in language and narratives is a prime way of communication and dissemination. Terms embody concepts; symbolic and metaphorical stories pass on traditional teachings.

These four clusters of mechanisms or pathways have been condensed from a set of ten items in Turner and Berkes (2006). Note that most if not all of these mechanisms apply to *traditional* knowledge systems, but fewer items apply to *local* knowledge and practice. For example, "learning from other times" is typical of traditional knowledge but not of local knowledge. This is a point that we develop later as a way to distinguish between traditional and local knowledge. Next we turn to the Caribbean cases to examine in detail the development of local knowledge and practice.

Mangrove Conservation and Charcoal Makers

In 1984, I was starting collaborative research with the Caribbean Natural Resources Institute (CANARI) in the island state of St. Lucia and its partner organizations. I had a chance to see the charcoal-making operation in Mankòtè, the largest mangrove stand on the island and a site identified earlier by CANARI as a priority area for conservation. At that time, Mankòtè seemed to be an unlikely area for either conservation or development. The mangrove area was strewn with garbage. There were hardly any mature trees. Much of the area was covered by thin shoots or branches growing out of stumps of the white mangrove (*Laguncularia racemosa*). In places, the forest floor was covered with recently cut branches from which the charcoal makers had selected the best pieces for their charcoal pits. The charcoal producers themselves were economically marginal rural people and looked about as impoverished as any group on the island.

The Mankòtè mangrove had been once covered with mature trees when it was part of a U.S. military base during World War II. During this period, no one other than the military was allowed in and there was no extractive use; this effectively resulted in conservation. After the base closed down in 1960, the area became open-access public land and was used for a variety of purposes such as seasonal fishing, crabbing, bathing, animal grazing, and as a source of wood for charcoal production and for construction. The area was also used as an unauthorized waste disposal site. Two decades of uncontrolled use had left the mangrove in a highly degraded condition.

When I visited the area again in 1992, the changes were remarkable. The charcoal makers were the same people, but the ragged outfits had been replaced by clean, new work clothes. They looked healthy and self-confident. The charcoal-bagging operation was now an efficient assembly line that produced a uniformly bagged and weighed product ready for the market. The charcoal makers had become well-organized small businessmen. The mangrove forest itself looked different as well. There was very little slash on the forest floor, indicating that charcoal producers had become more selective in cutting branches for their charcoal pits. The coppices on the mangrove stumps looked healthy. There was still a dearth of mature trees, but the forest canopy was fuller and higher; Mankòtè mangrove was on the way to recovery.

What produced these changes was a combination of three factors: the evolution of a local knowledge base and management system over some 25 years; the recognition of charcoal producers' resource use rights; and the work of a nongovernmental organization (NGO) in helping organize the charcoal producers and carrying out an integrated conservation–development project for the benefit of both the people and the mangrove (Renard 1994).

The Mankòtè case is relatively unique among integrated conservation–development projects (projects that aim for conservation while simultaneously producing economic benefits for local people) because a time-series of information was available on three variables to test whether the project was achieving its goals of sustainability: the biological status of the mangrove, the amount of charcoal produced, and the evolution of local knowledge and management among the mangrove users.

Mangrove surveys had been conducted in 1986 before the main project intervention, and again in 1989 and 1992, after intervention. Using standard research techniques, the surveys showed that the density of mangrove stems above a certain size increased significantly from 1986 to 1992. The basal area (the sum of the base areas of all the stems) increased more than fourfold, also a statistically significant change. The mean diameter of the stems did not change much. Therefore, the observed increase in the basal area was the result of improved regeneration and stem density (Smith and Berkes 1993). While mangrove recovery was proceeding, charcoal production statistics showed that charcoal makers continued to make at least as much charcoal. Increased biological regeneration from 1989 to 1992 was particularly significant, as it followed a year of relatively high charcoal production in 1991 (Smith and Berkes 1993). What explains the reversal of the degradation trend and the apparent shift toward sustainability?

Management in Mankòtè is not a traditional system. The first evidence of local management only dates back to the 1980s when CANARI researchers noticed that some charcoal makers rotated their cutting areas. As it developed in the 1980s and the early 1990s, the Mankòtè practice was based on going to a location that had good-sized stems and cutting in zigzagging strips before relocating to a new area. There was no formalized rotation, no known rules of allocation, but simply constant communication and first-comer's rights within the group of users and mutual respect for one another's cutting areas.

Perhaps the most important factor for the improved regeneration in Mankòtè was the result of change in cutting practices. Until about the mid-1980s, harvesters practiced clear-cutting and indiscriminate slashing. A particularly important change occurred in the 1989–92 period. Clear-cutting and slashing were replaced by a practice of selective cutting of the larger stems and avoidance of damage to smaller stems. Cutting was done in such a way that did not kill the stump and allowed coppicing and approximated a two-year rotation. Since charcoal makers obtained their wood by selectively cutting the larger shoots from stumps, the stems actually harvested had usually been growing through longer than a two-year cutting cycle.

What were the conditions behind the change of management practices of the charcoal makers? The explanation, as confirmed by the users, was that the Mankòtè mangrove shifted in the 1980s from an open-access to a communal resource. Wood products that used to be freely open to all potential users were now harvested mainly by an organized community of a limited number of charcoal producers. Improved security of resource use rights precipitated a change in behavior and attitude. Instead of cutting indiscriminately, the security of rights to the resource made it possible to cut with more care and conserve for the long term. Charcoal producers could now count on being able to harvest what they had left behind.

Monitoring of charcoal production has continued, degradation by waste disposal has been stopped, and harvesters have been involved in self-help efforts such as the rehabilitation of drainage in the mangrove wetland (Renard 1994). A draft co-management plan has been prepared by which charcoal makers and government managers are to share management responsibility. But the plan has not been officially adopted, and rights to the mangrove forest have not been formalized. However, the charcoal makers' self-regulation system has continued to evolve. The practice of zigzagging was apparently abandoned in the mid-1990s in favor of preferred areas, each controlled by one harvester. Within each area, the harvester moves from one stand to the next through the season. Charcoal makers have continued to practice selective cutting but have been experimenting with different arrangements for area rotation.

Hudson's (1997) work documents the kind of management-related knowledge that is elaborated by the charcoal makers and transmitted to the new generation: slash piled on top of the stumps prevents regeneration, thus stumps should be left clear; cuts should be made cleanly and at a sharp angle, without creating a jagged surface; and for maximum production, shoots should be harvested by cutting five centimeters above the topmost prop root of the mangrove. Although new biological data are not available to examine whether the recovery of the mangrove has continued, it is believed that the amount of charcoal production has been sustainable, and there has been no apparent decline in mangrove cover.

Dominican Sawyers: Developing Private Stewardship

After half an hour of work with the chain saw, the large *gommier* tree was finally on the forest floor. Now began the more difficult work. After trimming the branches and dividing the trunk into three segments with the help of his assistant and young son, the sawyer started cutting the segments, layer by layer, into planks that would be carried out of the valley by hand. Converting one large *gommier* into planks would take most of the day for the small work group, and they would leave behind only the branches and a large pile of sawdust.

This was participant observation research in Dominica. I was in the field assisting the project in part because I wanted to see first-hand how anyone could turn a *gommier* tree (*Dacryodes excelsa*), a species with exceptionally hard, silica-rich wood, into planks with only a handheld chain saw. The forest was alive with birds. Dominica contains a bird fauna that is the richest for its size of any island in the Caribbean (Evans 1986). This avifauna includes two endemic *Amazona* parrot species that dwell in the cavities of large old trees and are considered endangered. Given that the destruction of tropical forests and the associated loss of biodiversity are among the most serious environmental problems, was the Dominican sawyer part of the problem or part of the solution?

Dominica is often called the "nature island" of the Caribbean, unspoiled by extensive agricultural plantations or by tourism development. It supports the most extensive tropical forest cover of the islands of the Eastern Caribbean. As late as 1985, between two-thirds and three-quarters of the island was still covered by forest, much of it on steep slopes (Evans 1986). The island is only 22 km by 47 km in size, but the rugged interior rises steeply to 1,420 m. It is this ruggedness that has protected the forest cover: agriculture is hard to establish and commercial logging is difficult to carry out. But by the same token, the steep terrain is susceptible to erosion damage when agriculture and logging are attempted on the slopes.

Over the past decades, timber cutting in Dominica has exploited two distinct technologies: (1) mechanized harvesting, using skidders and other heavy equipment and relying on the construction of access roads through the forest; and

(2) teams of sawyers, small-scale harvesters employing chain saws and cutting up logs into planks on site in the forest. The two technologies have very different impacts on the tropical forest ecosystem.

Rugged topography, high rainfall, and lack of roads in the interior make much of the productive forest area inaccessible to mechanized operations, and land capability studies indicate that large-scale timber extraction on a sustainable basis is not feasible (Putney 1989). Attempts at large- and medium-scale timber harvesting in 1902, 1947, 1968, 1977, and 1991 all ended in failure, despite government subsidies, economic incentives, and development grants from external donors. In the meantime, the use of heavy machinery on Dominica's wet and difficult terrain led to soil erosion and compaction, and damage to residual vegetation (Putney 1989).

In contrast to mechanized operations, the sawyers cut individually selected trees and convert logs into planks on site using chain saws. They carry the tree out of the forest on foot, plank by plank. Sawyers can operate in Dominica's rough terrain without the need for access roads, and with little residual effect on soil and vegetation. Sawyers "bring the mill to the tree rather than dragging the tree to the mill," says Putney (1989: 19). The mobility of the sawyers makes it possible to spread the harvesting effort in both space and time. Unlike the more capital-intensive operations, there is little financial pressure on sawyers to extract large volumes of timber per unit area to cover high capital costs. This permits light cuts and greater selectivity and care in harvesting.

Since woodcutting is a traditional occupation in Dominica, sawyers possess local knowledge that allows them to operate in an environment in which large-scale operations fail. They know the terrain, the distribution of tree species, how to access steep areas, and how to cut on steep slopes. Thus, the opportunity and background exist to link modern forest conservation with traditional practice. Historically, small sawyers used pit saws, large handsaws operated vertically by teams of two or three. After Hurricane David in 1979, chain saws became common, as they were necessary for the rapid clearance of the blowdown in the wake of the hurricane. This new technology in turn made it possible to exploit the valuable but hard to cut *gommier*.

The community of sawyers started to organize after Hurricane David and established a cooperative-like organization called Cottage Forest Industries (CFI) in 1987. CFI started with both business development and conservation objectives. For many of the members, livelihood issues were initially the primary concern. However, a survey and group interviews carried out in 1991 showed an interesting transition taking place in the minds of sawyers, from financial concerns to sustainable use. Sawyers did indicate that they were in this line of work because it was a well-paying job in an economy that did not offer many opportunities. They

---

Box 10.1 Dominican Sawyers as an International Model for Tropical Forest Sustainability

There is a growing opinion that conventional timber exploitation and tropical forest conservation are no longer compatible. The Dominica experiment holds the promise that it is possible to create incentive structures for small-scale operations to log sustainably, and it has been receiving international attention (Pearce 1993). The Dominica experiment was taken up by Frank Wadsworth of the U.S. Government's Institute of Tropical Forestry. Recognizing that the development of stewardship requires the incentive of secure resource tenure, the Wadsworth management plan included a government concession to CFI in Dominica's forest reserve in the interior of the island, which the Sawyers started cutting in 1993.

The plan included strict controls regarding which trees can be felled. To maintain species diversity, only a certain number of mature *gommier* were to be selectively cut in any one block, with a harvesting cycle of 45 years. A system of monitoring sites was set up, using birds as indicator species for measuring the health of the ecosystem, in such a way that warning signs can be detected within two or three years. The plan relied in part on "paraforesters": sawyers who were given additional training to allow them to play a central role in harvest management and monitoring not only the timber resource but the forest ecosystem. As quoted by Pearce (1993), "No tropical country has yet managed its forest for sustainable timber production," says the plan. "Dominica's success will literally be a model for the world to follow." But the design encountered a number of problems and was never fully implemented. As of 1998, "there is no organized community of sawyers co-managing the forest," says Yves Renard (personal communication), "We are very far from that."

---

enjoyed being sawyers also because they were their own bosses, took pride in their skills and self-reliance, liked the outdoors, and enjoyed working in a group. However, many sawyers also thought that being a CFI sawyer was more than being a woodcutter; it signified a greater knowledge of the forest and more responsibility for conservation.

How does a sense of stewardship evolve? One of the sawyer leaders observed that when he was younger, all he cared about was cutting and selling the wood. As he got older, his attitude toward the forest started changing. This change was the result of his experience in the forest, and his involvement in public education. CFI holds wood-sawing demonstrations at country fairs. Children would come up to him and ask if he cut large old trees. Would he cut one that had cavities and perhaps nesting parrots? These questions made the tough sawyer/businessman think, and they influenced his role as leader and proponent of selective cutting.

Is the Dominica sawyer case merely an attractive story, or does it have significance beyond the Caribbean? Commercial logging, together with agricultural clearing, is a major cause of tropical deforestation worldwide, and there has been a search for alternatives. The local knowledge-based operations of Dominican sawyers show that it is in fact feasible to create incentive structures for small-scale local woodcutters, operating as associations of small independent businessmen, to use tropical forest resources sustainably. According to a management plan drawn up for Dominica by the Institute of Tropical Forestry, the aim is not merely the sustainability of the timber supply but the sustainability of the entire forest ecosystem and the users as well (see Box 10.1).

Cultivating Sea Moss in St. Lucia

What happens when demands or stresses increase on a resource that produces a small supply or has limited capacity for replenishing itself? Can traditional knowledge help extend the supply? Or alternatively, if demand outstrips the supply and the resource crashes, is there a role for newly developed knowledge? These questions come up in many places and for many kinds of resources. The case of sea moss in St. Lucia provides a field study to pursue these questions in more detail.

Sea moss is the generic term for several species of edible red algae, mostly species of *Gracilaria*, traditionally used in the Caribbean. Sea moss contains polysaccharides that dissolve in boiling water and thicken to form a gel when the solution is cooled. It is a thickening agent traditionally used in many parts of the Caribbean in soups, porridge, and drinks, including a popular brew based on sea moss, milk, and rum.

Collection of sea moss in St. Lucia was traditionally done by hand from wild stocks. The traditional harvesters were people from several communities in three areas of St. Lucia. Harvesting was a seasonal activity, and sea moss collecting was part of a livelihood strategy that combined it with other seasonal activities. This presumably allowed the regeneration of sea moss beds between harvests. With increased demand and rising prices in the 1960s and the 1970s, there was an influx of nontraditional sea moss gatherers into the industry, mostly unemployed or underemployed youths who had no experience in sea moss collecting and who wanted to make quick profits. This created open-access (free-for-all) conditions that swamped any conservation-oriented practices that may have existed and resulted in the depletion of sea moss beds. With no pulsing of harvests to allow for regeneration of *Gracilaria* beds, and with the plants pulled from the substrate together with their holdfasts, natural growth and recruitment was no longer sufficient to maintain the resource. The shallower areas were depleted, leaving only small pockets of sea moss, as in the other depleted areas of the Caribbean, such as Barbados (Smith *et al.* 1986).

Sea moss aquaculture was started in St. Lucia in 1981 by the Department of Fisheries, as a response to declining wild stocks and to create alternative livelihoods for coastal communities based on the sustainable use of natural resources. The first commercial plot was started in 1984. In 1985, CANARI began a program of research and training in sea moss production. Various growing techniques were tested, all with the same basic method of seeding lines by inserting sea moss fronds between strands of rope: the Philippine stake-and-line method, bamboo rafts with floating lines, and most recently, floating longlines of 10 to 15 meters, anchored at each end.

The target group for training initially was fishers, partly because they were presumed to be knowledgeable about marine resources. It turned out that many fishers found the cultural switch to a "grower mentality" difficult. Similarly, wild sea moss gatherers were not attracted to aquaculture, presumably because they were unwilling to make the attitudinal adjustment from the immediate returns from wild harvesting to cultivation, which requires day-to-day work but intermittent returns. Thus, the assumption that resource users most familiar with the marine inshore environment were the people who could most easily adapt to strategies and attitudes associated with a different mode of resource production proved wrong (Renard 1994: 12). The sea moss project then targeted a mixed group (including women) of occupational pluralists, people who divided their time among a variety of cash- and subsistence-oriented activities, as typically found in West Indian rural society.

By the late 1980s, sea moss culture became established as a small-scale industry on the southeast and southwest coasts of St. Lucia. The barriers to further growth were not economic (prices were good) or biological (*Gracilaria* grew well on lines). The impediments included, in addition to the inability or unwillingness of many to adopt aquaculture, the short-term problem of loss to occasional hurricanes, and the long-term problem of insecurity of rights to aquaculture areas. If growers owned the *Gracilaria* lines but could not control the waters and the aquaculture sites, what was there to prevent the cultured sea moss from meeting the same fate as the wild *Gracilaria*?

A number of solutions have been devised in different parts of the world to solve the problem of rights. Many of these involve government recognition of individual or communal rights to productive waters. In many countries, coastal groups have traditional use rights to marine resources (see Chapter 4), and in other countries, lagoons and coastal aquaculture sites are leased to individuals, companies, and cooperatives. The St. Lucia sea moss case is informative because it provides examples of some of the practical problems in making commons work. St. Lucia's Fisheries Act of 1984, section 21, provides for the leasing of "land, including areas of the foreshore or the sea-bed for the purposes of aquaculture."

The government of St. Lucia has demarcated aquaculture plots and encouraged sea moss growers to apply for formal leases. The problem, however, is that applications by growers have not been finalized over a period of more than ten years despite reapplication, and they have no greater legal right to aquaculture areas than before (Berkes and Smith 1995). In the absence of formal rights, growers have come to control their areas through joint supervision of the area with other growers and with government officers. They have to some extent developed a code of practice that resembles those in traditional resource use systems elsewhere, similar to reciprocal help relations, based on the traditional rural Caribbean practice of *koudmen* (reciprocal help).

Rehabilitating Edible Sea Urchin Resources

One of the local delicacies that many of the visitors to the West Indies never get to try is the sea egg—it has been almost totally depleted from the shores of some of the more crowded islands such as Barbados and Martinique. The white-spined sea urchin, *Tripneustes ventricosus*, locally known as sea egg in the Eastern Caribbean, is traditionally harvested by family groups for their own needs and by small-scale producers for the local market. Sea eggs first reproduce at one year of age, live in shallow water sea-grass beds, and are relatively easy to collect by free diving. The species is therefore vulnerable to overharvesting but appears capable of rapid recovery if protected.

The sea egg resource of St. Lucia seems to have been used sustainably until the 1980s. Sea urchins were traditionally collected by family groups and harvesting took place mainly during school vacation months. Parents and children shared the work of collecting and preparing the sea eggs. In the south part of the island, the major harvesting area, the bulk of the harvesting took place traditionally over a two-month period, allowing the resource to recover over the other ten months. However, in recent decades, as demand increased, sea egg collecting increasingly became a commercial venture rather than a family-based activity, attracting young and underemployed people looking for part-time income. Year-round harvesting became the norm in areas where there was no community-based management.

Sea urchin populations in St. Lucia were severely affected by hurricanes in 1979 and 1980. Their recovery by 1983 was followed by uncontrolled harvesting in some areas, driven by strong demand from an external market (Martinique), resulting in severe depletion of stocks. To protect the remaining stocks, the government of St. Lucia prohibited sea urchin collecting in 1987. Year-round harvesting, as was the case in parts of St. Lucia before the ban, not only removes egg-bearing individuals but also results in the destruction of many individuals with unripe gonads. The explanation lies in the biology of the species. Although there are seasonal peaks in reproductive activity, the species produces eggs throughout the year, and hence at least some of the urchins would contain mature gonads at any given time. After the ban, some illegal harvesting continued in certain locations, although the regulation was enforced in other areas.

In 1987 CANARI started a project on sea urchins to determine the size and densities of sea egg populations in three different areas of the St. Lucia coast. The main objectives were to establish the conditions necessary for population recovery, and to formulate guidelines for sea urchin management. Given the government ban, the objectives were timely. The three locations were chosen on the basis of the similarity in ecological conditions. All three had been important traditional harvesting sites. The study also collected information on harvesting and marketing from sea urchin collectors and other people associated with the sea egg industry. The study continued until 1989, and the results were very revealing (Smith and Berkes 1991).

They showed that the traditional community-based management that existed in the coastal village of Laborie, one of the three locations of the study, was as effective as the government ban enforced in the Maria Islands Nature Reserve, one of the other locations of the study. Laborie, located on a small bay, had retained the traditional summer harvest of the sea egg, as practiced at least since the early 1900s. Sea egg collecting was not allowed in the bay at other times of the year, either for local residents or for outsiders. In the case of Maria Islands Nature Reserve, commercial sea egg collecting for the Martinique market had been stopped, in part through pressure from the local media to protect the waters of the reserve. In both locations, peak densities of 5 to 7 urchins per square meter occurred following the peak reproductive season.

By contrast, the sea urchin populations in Aupicon, the third study location, remained very low throughout the study: less than 0.1 urchins per square meter. There was no community management in the Aupicon area and no protected areas. Since there was no enforcement of the general government ban, sea egg collecting in Aupicon effectively remained open-access. But in any case, there were very few adults left and almost no young urchins, even after the peak reproductive season. The results of the study suggested that a necessary condition for sea urchin recovery was the presence of a certain minimum number of adult individuals in the environment. Once the adults had been as completely depleted as in Aupicon, few larvae settled at the site and recovery was not possible (Smith and Berkes 1991).

Sea urchin harvesters were kept informed of the progress of the study during the course of the research. CANARI's results were shared both with the Department of Fisheries and local sea urchin divers. Discussions began on the feasibility of establishing a co-management arrangement that would allow harvesting under controlled conditions. The government ban on harvesting was lifted in 1990 after nearly three years of closure, on three conditions, that the harvesters: observe an agreed starting date of harvest; observe a minimum size limit; and report to the Department of Fisheries when the stock above the minimum size was depleted (so that the harvesting season would be closed). As well, harvest zones would be established and harvesters licensed (Warner 1997).

The sea egg research project provided not only the biological information needed to establish management guidelines, it also revealed the existence of a community-based management system in one of the study locations. It showed the traditional wisdom of a seasonal harvest, followed by a period in which the resource would recover. Given that the sea urchin has a one-year life cycle (but lives to at least three years), such a management practice would not deplete the stock, provided a certain critical number of adults were conserved. This traditional system design, emphasizing the importance of closed seasons and the maintenance of a minimum population density, provided useful guidelines in formulating new government regulations.

As well, part of the innovation in St. Lucia's new sea egg management was the arrangement in which harvesters would become partners with government managers in using feedback from the resource to adjust management regulations flexibly. Rather then relying on set seasons and set quotas, the co-management arrangement was designed to make use of the local knowledge of sea egg harvesters, their ability to monitor the harvestable population size, to determine when the sea egg season would open and when it would be closed. This system, which in effect uses principles of Adaptive Management, has been in place since 1989 but has not operated continuously (Renard 1994; Warner 1997).

Lessons from the Caribbean Cases

These Caribbean cases provide informative examples regarding the creation or development of local knowledge and management systems, not only because the islands of the West Indies are compact, laboratory-like settings but also because they pose development issues similar to those in many areas elsewhere in the world. By contrast, the subjects of the previous chapters, the Cree and the Inuit, semi-isolated societies until the 1970s, are not typical of rural societies of the world. In most regions, including the West Indies, communities do not possess detailed traditional ecological knowledge and time-tested management systems based on this knowledge. More typically, whatever exists of local traditional knowledge and management systems is often overwhelmed by population and resource pressures. And yet, as the Grenada, St. Lucia, and Dominica cases show, new local knowledge and management systems are arising all the time.

The mangrove case indicates that the beginnings of a rotational use system can emerge in two generations, or some 20 to 30 years, although local knowledge of charcoal making and woodcutting is no doubt multi-generational. Similarly, most Dominican sawyers are in possession of local knowledge and skills that are at least three or four generations old, perhaps old enough to be considered traditional. But in this case, there is no locally devised management system comparable to the St. Lucia mangrove case. The sea moss example is unusual in that it shows that a cultural orientation to *cultivation* (as opposed to harvesting from the wild) was more important than actual local knowledge and familiarity with the particular ecological setting (the marine inshore environment). However, sea moss growing is a new occupation, and it is not yet clear what knowledge and skills would be passed on to the next generation; there has not yet been a second generation. By contrast, sea urchin harvesting has a multi-generational background, long enough for the transmission of knowledge and elaboration of workable management strategies.

The examples from St. Lucia and Dominica are not unique in showing the creation and elaboration of local knowledge. Other examples can be given from the Caribbean, even though the area has never been considered to harbor much local-level management. For example, no marine tenure system had been documented from the Eastern Caribbean until the 1980s. In contrast to Oceania where reef and lagoon marine tenure systems abound (see Chapter 4), the lack of such systems in the Eastern Caribbean was thought to be due to the relatively recent history of the postcolonial inhabitants of the area. But detailed studies in the 1980s documented rudimentary territorial systems from the north shore of Jamaica. These systems lacked the sophistication of those from Oceania (Johannes 1978, 2002a) but were real enough to be mapped and to function in limiting access to coral reef fish resources in a generally overfished area (Berkes 1987b).

Fishing communities included individuals with a great deal of local knowledge on the biology and habits of reef fish, some of it culturally transmitted, multi-generational knowledge. The technology used (dugout canoes and fish traps) was of mixed traditional heritage and came from indigenous people (now extinct in Jamaica) and from Africa. Other marine tenure systems have also been documented from the Caribbean. For example, Finlay (1995) studied the beach seine fisheries of Grenada, and showed that there were ten rules for the use of the seining sites, nine of which were universally accepted by all fishers, to ensure equity and to manage conflict.

Study methods similar to those used in Jamaica did not generate information on fishing territories in Barbados, and none was expected. Compared to Jamaica, Barbados has an insignificant shelf and coral reef area. Instead, traditional fishing in Barbados was oriented to the open sea. Before engines became available in the 1950s, Barbados fishers used sail to pursue flying fish within a day's travel of the island, and often risked being blown into the open Atlantic toward Africa. Increasingly greater mechanization allowed the Barbados fishing fleet to increase its range—all the way to Trinidad and Tobago by the early 1980s (Berkes 1987b).

In the process of adopting more sophisticated technology, the fishers no doubt lost some of their skills in reading the weather, wind, and waves. However, they picked up other skills, such as the use of radio within groups of cooperating fishers to search for fish and to communicate information on fish concentrations. (Flying fish is a highly aggregated species.) At the same time, greater mobility on the high seas meant that fishers sharpened their knowledge and interpretation of environmental cues in search of aggregations of fish. Studies by Gomes *et al.* (1998) and Grant and Berkes (2007) in the Eastern Caribbean show that there is a system of knowledge of sea color as an indicator of flying fish and large pelagic species such as dolphin fish. Some of this knowledge corresponds to Western science (oceanography and fisheries) and some of it does not. Some types of knowledge are inconsistent from island to island and are distributed unevenly among fishers of different islands. Grenada longline fishers' knowledge, discussed in Chapter 9, is probably one of the more coherent bodies of open sea fisheries knowledge in the Eastern Caribbean.

Knowledge Development and Institutions

We started by asking how systems of local and traditional knowledge developed. By and large, they develop step-wise by the incremental accumulation and refinement of knowledge. None of the Caribbean cases are explainable using the crisis learning model. But charcoal makers show rapid change in knowledge development and application as soon as their resource rights are secured. Dominican sawyers show a change of attitude toward stewardship as parrot conservation becomes a public issue. The development of longline fishing knowledge in Grenada (Chapter 9; Grant *et al.* 2007) shows a familiar pattern: imported technological knowledge (in this case from Cuba), much trial-and-error experimentation, observation and monitoring of outcomes from the use of different variations of gear technology, bait choice, and the use of oceanographic cues.

The cases show how knowledge and practice are elaborated, but do not provide any examples on the original generation of knowledge. It is not easy to document how knowledge is discovered or generated. There are a few cases of detailed ethnographic studies on the transmission of traditional knowledge (e.g. Ohmagari and Berkes 1997; Athayde *et al.* 2009; Wyndham 2010) but almost nothing on its generation. For example, we do not know how exactly Nakashima's (1991) Belcher Islands Inuit made the first eider-skin parka in the 1880s. We do know that bird skin processing, such as bags made of loon skin, is common across the Arctic, and considerable knowledge of eider ducks probably existed in the Belcher Islands (Nakashima, personal communication).

The case described in Box 10.2 on the generation of original knowledge, is one of the rare exceptions. It is a description of how Danish pound net fishers discovered at the turn of the century that these nets (which are large, fixed trap nets) could be adapted to catch eels, a valuable species in northern Europe. The innovation helped extend the fishing season and lowered equipment costs for commercial fishers, at the same time making it difficult for farmer-fishers to compete against them (Vestergaard 1991).

The Caribbean cases are informative in showing the characteristics of local knowledge systems and how they differ from traditional knowledge (Table 10.1). Regarding elements of knowledge, they show incremental learning and some institutional development, but little or no encoding or communicating of knowledge and no evidence of belief systems to consolidate supporting values.

Box 10.2 Generating Knowledge: A Danish Innovation with Pound Nets

"In 1905 or 1906 two brothers Jensen, from Korsor Island on Seeland had noticed that the little plops they heard at their pound nets in the dark evenings of August came from eels crawling over the side of the nets. It seemed eels entered the pound nets, but left them again. So they tried attaching eel traps (fyke nets) to the head of the pound net, and it worked. . . . From then on, many traditional types of eel traps and weirs gradually gave way to pound nets which would catch other fish as well. The use of traditional eel weirs had mostly been a supplementary activity of farmers with coastal rights. With the advent of the eel pound nets, it was professional fishermen who took another step in the process that separated fishing from farming."

Source: Vestergaard 1991: 159.

Regarding mechanisms, they show observation and monitoring, and learning from other places, as technology in three of the five cases (sawyers, sea moss, longline) came from the outside. They do not show learning from "other times" and knowledge encoded in language and narratives.

Clearly, the single most important difference between local knowledge and traditional knowledge is the time dimension (Turner and Berkes 2006). Many of the Caribbean cases are recent by international standards, for example, in comparison to non-indigenous agriculturalists around the world. Only the sawyers include some individuals whose fathers and grandfathers were sawyers. In the case of the Grenada longliners, knowledge development is so new and so rapid that the fleet includes some boats in which the more knowledgeable son is the captain and the father is a crew member!

There are a few cases in the literature that show different knowledge levels among different groups of local knowledge holders living in the same area. Working with colonists in the Brazilian Amazon, Muchagata and Brown (2000) found that among the most recent colonists, knowledge of local species and soil types developed first. Among the colonists who had been there longer, there was evidence of knowledge of ecological processes and of practices adapted to those processes. Ballard and Huntsinger (2006) worked with experienced (8+ years) and less experienced harvesters of salal, a non-timber forest product used in the floral industry. They examined elements of their knowledge and practice, and found that experienced harvesters practiced a rotational system and multiple species management. Unlike newcomer harvesters, they were knowledgeable about successional processes and how these could be managed to meet harvest goals; they knew about timber management practices and how they affected forest understory species of which salal is one.

The important point here is that new local knowledge is developing all the time, and seasoned local knowledge and practice are turning into traditional systems. Even migrant workers (mostly Latin American immigrants) with no formal resource rights or land tenure, are turning into ecologically sophisticated harvesters of salal in the forests of Washington State in a time frame of only about one decade (Ballard and Huntsinger 2006). This creates an interesting problem. A substantial part of the literature on traditional knowledge is concerned with its disappearance (e.g. Johannes 1978; Chapin 1991; Ruddle *et al.* 1992; Turner and Turner 2008), and such loss of traditional knowledge and culture is no doubt a serious matter. Some traditional systems have indeed disappeared because the people themselves have been overrun or destroyed (e.g. Shipek 1993). But there are two problems with the emphasis on loss.

First, the notion of "culture loss" poses a problem for contemporary anthropological definitions of culture, as a process that continually undergoes change, rather than something that can be damaged or lost (Kirsch 2001). Second, the literature on knowledge loss often ignores its twin: knowledge development. Local knowledge is being created all the time, as cases in this chapter illustrate, and incipient "traditional systems" abound. For example, there is a rich tradition of non-timber forest product use among the Raramuri people of northern Mexico. LaRochelle studied their use of wild green vegetation as food, and found that several of the species were in a state of semi-domestication (as opposed to purely wild-harvested) and that a great deal of agricultural experimentation was going on (LaRochelle and Berkes 2003). Hence a more useful broader perspective would consider *both the creation and the loss* of knowledge in local and traditional systems.

What drives the development of new knowledge? The creation of new knowledge in the globalized world often responds to both local needs and new market opportunities (Ruiz-Perez *et al.* 2004; Sears *et al.* 2007). The knowledge developed may include new uses for local resources, new technologies and new marketing links. It is hybrid knowledge that often incorporates non-traditional knowledge, and aspects of it may not be all that different from formal knowledge (Dove 2002; Wilson 2003). Often, it is livelihood-oriented, as in the case of salal harvesters. This gets us into the area of the potential uses of local and traditional knowledge for economic development and livelihoods, an area that will be discussed further in Chapter 11.

Finally, the Caribbean cases show the central importance of local institutional development in the emergence of knowledge and practice systems. Here we are referring mainly to commons institutions, local rules for access control, and rule-making within the group. The examples in this chapter show that there is a general tendency for self-organization toward community-based management that uses local knowledge. The cases here are consistent with the international literature indicating that local knowledge development is most vibrant when local people are able to make their own management decisions (Hanna 1998; Seixas and Berkes 2003; Acheson 2003; Shukla and Gardner 2006).

The Caribbean examples show that even though the development of local knowledge is a necessary condition for community-based management, it is often not a sufficient condition. Managing resources requires the ability to develop management institutions and not just knowledge (Olsson and Folke 2001; Agrawal 2005). Otherwise, what is to prevent other potential users from taking the mangrove wood conserved by the charcoal makers? Or to prevent other sea egg collectors from poaching on the brood population? Or to prevent cultured sea moss from meeting the same fate as the wild sea moss?

The issue of local institutional development is not specific to individual resources such as mangrove wood, sea egg, or sea moss; nor is it specific to the

West Indies. It is a fundamental issue of resource rights in the use of commons. Over historical time, property rights to resources in many parts of the world have been transformed from communal property (in which access and management rights are controlled by an identifiable group) to open access (a free-for-all in which the resource is accessible to all potential users). In the St. Lucia sea moss and sea egg cases, population and resource pressures have resulted in open access; in other cases, colonialism and the central government's economic policies have created open access (e.g. Johannes 1978; Berkes 1985).

As many studies of commons have made clear (McCay and Acheson 1987; Bromley 1992; Ostrom *et al.* 2002), it is this open-access regime (and not communal ownership) that leads to the *tragedy of the commons*. This is the phenomenon in which the individual offloads costs to society while pursuing private benefits, with disastrous consequences for the resource itself in the long run. Communal resource tenure such as that for sea eggs in Laborie, and individual tenure such as that in sea moss aquaculture, provides entry points for solving the tragedy of the commons in coastal waters.

The issue is of importance for marine protected areas as well. Aswani and Hamilton (2004) investigated the use of indigenous ecological knowledge for marine conservation in the Solomon Islands. They found that there were marked differences among neighboring villages in the region with respect to enforcement of conservation rules, making it necessary to distinguish between villages that held secure tenure (i.e. strong commons rights) from those that did not. Conservation could be implemented only when the local control was strong enough to exclude poaching by neighboring groups. They concluded, "simply put, it is meaningless to implement a management regime in an area, no matter how rich in marine biodiversity, if exclusion of non-members and harvest restriction rules cannot be enforced" (Aswani and Hamilton 2004: 79).

The emergence of coastal aquaculture for sea moss, and the recognition of community rights for sea egg harvesting (as in Laborie) may be seen as a change *back from* open-access *to* communal property or private property (Berkes and Smith 1995). Hence the cases in this chapter provide examples of the various ways in which local knowledge arises, in parallel with the development of resource use systems built on self-interest. The chapter merely considers a small region and a limited time scale. The emergence of local knowledge as an adaptive response has no doubt also operated over larger spatial and temporal scales in environmental history. This is a theme that is developed further in Chapter 11 in the broader context of cultural evolution and the adaptation of traditional systems.

Challenges for Indigenous Knowledge

Did Chief Seattle say, "All things are connected"? More so than many other disciplines, indigenous knowledge has to contend with popular and academic myths about traditional peoples. Making sense of the contradictory evidence and providing a coherent picture of the real significance of traditional ecological knowledge for contemporary issues, such as biodiversity conservation, requires the development of a theory of indigenous knowledge that can account for changes in human–nature relations over time.

The study of traditional ecological knowledge is hampered by the existence of several, often contradictory, myths about traditional peoples. One of these myths (the "Exotic Other"), common among Western environmentalists, is that traditional peoples are close to the land and intrinsically attuned to nature, which makes it possible, in some vague way, to live "in balance" with their environment. They are "ecologically noble savages" (Buege 1996). They can do no wrong. Their photographs decorate the covers of popular magazines and provide lasting images in the education of the general public about traditional ecological knowledge (Linden 1991). As Ellen (1993: 126) puts it, the idea of lost ecological knowledge somehow associated with lost tribes is a view that unmistakably "reproduces the notion of a primitive, exotic Other. It is a view that the anthropologist Edmund Leach described with characteristic foresightedness as 'sentimental rubbish.' "

A second myth (the "Intruding Wastrel") holds humans as unnatural intruders, despoilers of pristine ecosystems, and aliens (Evernden 1993). Primitive peoples are not noble savages but tend to be ignorant, superstitious, careless, and backward. This view questions whether traditional peoples ever lived in "balance with nature," at least not due to any cultural adaptations. They lived as biological populations limited by their resources, at the mercy of natural forces and supernatural beliefs, and certainly not as organized communities with their own knowledge–practice–belief complex to adapt to their environment. Their impact may have been small at a time when their population numbers were small and technology simple enough to be environmentally benign. But they had a tendency, even as primitive hunters many thousands of years ago, to cause environmental damage, as witnessed by ancient extinctions.

A third myth about traditional peoples portrays them in terms of a "Noble Savage/Fallen Angel" duality. They should continue to live as "primitives," lest they become a threat to the very ecosystems in which they live. Ramos (1994) describes cycles of adulation followed by denigration experienced by Brazilian Indians when they started to assert their land rights. As Alcorn (1994: 7) explains further, many northern conservationists (biological preservationists) "wish to keep biodiversity in untouched natural settings free of any human habitation. They see people who live and work there as threats. . . . On the other hand, Northern cultural preservationists wish to see exotic peoples preserved as idealized, superior cultures which live in 'harmony with nature,' untainted by the market economy." When such cultures are contaminated, the people became a threat to their environment and to themselves, as fallen angels who could not do anything right.

These three simplified images of traditional peoples sometimes overlap. It is probably fair to say that just about everyone who has a view about indigenous peoples holds preconceived and often ambiguous notions about them. Many people, including indigenous peoples themselves, may believe parts of one or more of these views, and their thinking may change depending on which groups of traditional people they are thinking about. Are they all incorrect? As with all myths, there are elements of truth at the basis of all three views. On the whole, however, this volume argues that they are myths nonetheless.

The chapter starts by addressing the first myth, and the effort to create and nurture the image of the Exotic Other. It then proceeds to address the second (Intruding Wastrel) by focusing on the question of ancient extinctions, including that of the Paleolithic megafauna, and builds a cultural evolutionary perspective, distinguishing between *invaders* and *natives*. The third myth (Noble Savage/ Fallen Angel) is addressed through the debate concerning the differences between Western and indigenous notions of conservation, and the notion of wilderness. Next, the chapter looks at the evidence on adapting traditional systems to the contemporary context, and its significance for developing sustainable local economies with which indigenous and other resource-dependent rural peoples can make a living in the globalized world. Finally, the chapter examines social learning as a way in which cultural evolution and the evolution of traditional systems proceeds.

Limitations of Indigenous Knowledge and the Exotic Other

Tradition is not always adaptive, and traditional people do not always act as wise stewards of the environment. For example, the caribou story in Chapter 6 illustrates the gap between practice and ideology. When conservation practice in the caribou case was eventually restored, this was explainable in terms of social learning, environmental knowledge, oral history, and healthy indigenous institutions, and not in terms of noble savagery. Johannes and Lewis (1993: 106) observe that "the acceptance of all traditional ecological knowledge as infallible is an extreme position, almost as unfortunate as that of dismissing it. Traditional peoples are not infallible, and some of their misuses of natural resources have been, and are, substantial." Brosius (1997, 1999) has analyzed environmentalist representations of indigenous peoples in Sarawak, and found that outsider accounts and claims of representation are often suspect.

As well, indigenous interpretations may be at odds with Western science. Some traditional knowledge may indeed be incorrect, just as some Western scientific findings are later found to be incorrect. There are several well-known cases in which traditional knowledge has provided correction to Western science (Freeman 1992; Johannes et al. 2000). Some of the examples offered by Johannes and Lewis (1993) of errors or limitations of traditional ecological knowledge include the belief of Torres Strait islanders (between Australia and New Guinea) that marine resources were without limit; beliefs overriding objective observations, as in blaming sorcery for the decline in crop yields or hunting success; misinterpreting fish spawning for defecation, as in the case of some Pacific Island groups; and the indigenous belief in northern Alberta, Canada, that forest windfall areas attract lightning.

In many of the cases of excessive claims of indigenous wisdom, neither indigenous people themselves nor researchers can be held responsible. A case in point is the Chief Seattle story. Did Chief Seattle say, "All things are connected"? "The earth does not belong to man; man belongs to the earth"? Did he call the earth our mother, the rivers our brothers, or the perfumed flowers our sisters? He did not. Those words were not written until the early 1970s (Wilson 1992). Chief Seattle did make a speech in the 1850s in relation to treaties in the Pacific Northwest, but the content and the meaning of his talk have been altered considerably. The Washington Territory was created in 1853, and the governor was responsible, among other things, for settling relations with the Indians. To prepare the way for treaty making on Puget Sound, a gathering of the Duwamish was called in December 1854. The governor explained his plans to conclude treaties, and Chief Seattle of the Duwamish responded with a speech of his own.

The chief's speech made a profound impression on Henry A. Smith, who was one of the listeners. Smith published an account of Chief Seattle's speech in a local newspaper some years later. The speech was re-published several times in the next few decades, and in the 1960s, William Arrowsmith, professor of classics at the University of Texas, modernized the language of the speech. Ted Perry, a writer, also at the University of Texas, who had heard the Arrowsmith version of the speech, decided to use parts of it for the script of a movie with an environmental theme, called *Home*. He paraphrased parts of the speech, and for good measure, added fictional text to bolster the ecological imagery. Visitors to the U.S. pavilion at Expo '74 in Spokane were confronted with yet another version of the speech, this one, an impressively concise and poetic ecological message, based on the script of the movie, *Home*, and of course attributed to Chief Seattle (Wilson 1992). Finally, Rudolf Kaiser, a German anthropologist, let the cat out of the bag in an international conference in 1984 and brought the story to the attention of scholars (Knudtson and Suzuki 1992). The myth itself continued to circulate for many more years.

There are several major differences between Smith's version of the speech and the modern accounts. The main difference, says Wilson (1992), is the development of Chief Seattle as a native ecologist. A sense of love of the land is present in the Smith version: "Every part of this county is sacred to my people. Every hillside, every valley, every plain and grove has been hallowed by some fond memory or some sad experience of my tribe" as quoted by Wilson (1992: 15). But in the modern versions, ecological imagery is pervasive and the text is full of human–nature relationships. The Chief Seattle story is reminiscent of the Eskimo snow terminology hoax in some ways (see Chapter 3). It documents the susceptibility of Western society to embrace exaggerated claims of native ecological knowledge and wisdom (see Box 11.1). This is obviously no fault of indigenous peoples and researchers, but it does underscore the need for traditional knowledge scholars to be ever-vigilant.

Invaders and Natives: A Historical Perspective

In a backlash against excessive claims for the ecological wisdom of indigenous peoples, some researchers have pointed out examples of tribal people and ancient societies who did overexploit local resources (e.g. Diamond 1993, 2005; Krech 1999). For example, researchers are finding in the neotropics large areas of forest with few animals, suggesting severe overhunting (Redford 1992). Kay (1994: 359)

Box 11.1 Manufacturing Mythologies: The Case of Chief Seattle's Speech

"If all the beasts were gone, men would die from a great loneliness of spirit. For whatever happens to the beasts, soon happens to man." These are great words, says science writer Stephen Strauss, but unfortunately Chief Seattle never uttered them; Ted Perry made them up. Strauss goes on to examine why we, as Western society, seem to be so susceptible to the perpetration of such sentimental fallacies. Strauss continues: "The fiction became part of the program called *Home* which aired in 1972. Initially, Mr. Perry said he attributed his fictional musings to Chief Seattle and later told the producer of his ruse. . . . From there the power of urban myth took over. Spurious speech or not, Mr. Perry's sentiments struck a chord. The speech was reprinted and translated widely. And the myth of the myth lives on. . . ."

"What's going on here?" Strauss asks, "particularly when Mr. Perry tells everyone, including [the publishers of] *Brother Eagle, Sister Sky*, that the speech they are promoting as Chief Seattle's is fraudulent. There is a kind of bald-faced re-writing of history in the name of sentimentalized Indian environmentalism. . . . Historical record be damned, says [the publisher]. . . . His company can put any words it wants into the mouth of Chief Seattle because 'we don't have access to [his] actual words.' . . . All that matters is that people believe Chief Seattle uttered the sentiments. 'These words have been attributed to the Chief or to the Chief's intent and have been used by the ecological movement for some time,' he says. But others point out that the issue is really one of the packaging of wisdom. It only has true resonance if it were said by a wise native person. 'It doesn't sound the same if it was produced by a guy named Ted,' says Rick Caldwell, librarian at the Seattle Museum of History and Industry, who regularly demythologizes the speech for the curious."

Source: Strauss 1992.

---

argues that "Native Americans had no effective conservation practices and the manner in which they harvested ungulates [such as elk] was the exact opposite of any predicted conservation practice," presumably related to the idea that "for humans, conservation is seldom an evolutionarily stable strategy."

A number of authors have questioned if claims of indigenous conservation can stand up to scrutiny. For example, Smith and Wishnie (2000) argue that evidence for indigenous conservation is weak if conservation is defined in terms of the two criteria of effect and design. That is, any action or practice "should (a) prevent or mitigate resource depletion, species extirpation, or habitat degradation, and (b) be designed to do so" (Smith and Wishnie 2000: 501). Others have pointed out the issue of waves of species extinctions accompanying migrations of early humans to the Americas and to major and minor islands around the world.

Martin (1973) proposed the hypothesis that Ice Age humans, at that time already proficient hunters, were responsible for the extinction of much of the megafauna (mostly large mammals) in the Americas. Their extinction had previously been explained in terms of Pleistocene glaciation and the shift of climate belts. Martin's provocatively entitled story, "The Discovery of America," begins with the end of the last Ice Age when big game hunters from Siberia crossed over to North America. Finding an unpopulated continent full of big game, the invaders expanded southward. Their exploding populations provided a moving front of death and destruction for the inexperienced prey that they encountered— mammoths, horses, camels, and ground sloths. According to Martin, the coexistence of hunters and megafauna probably lasted no more than ten years in any one area before extinction occurred. This did not give animals time to learn defensive behavior, nor for other adaptations to develop.

Martin's overkill hypothesis provides, certainly no proof, but a plausible model for the extinction of the megafauna. It addresses some of the paradoxes that had puzzled paleontologists for a long time: the almost total absence of kill sites, and sudden (as opposed to gradual) extinctions. For example, the timing of ground sloth extinctions at specific areas coincides almost exactly with the arrival of Stone Age hunters. Even though confounding factors such as climate change indicate that the original model may be simplistic, there is general agreement about the contribution of early Americans to the extermination of many large species (Martin and Klein 1984).

More certain is the role of invaders in bringing about the extinction of many species that once occupied islands such as Madagascar, New Zealand, and Hawaii. Perhaps the clearest cases come from New Zealand and the extermination of flightless moas and many other species of large birds by the ancestors of the Maori. Coinciding with prehistoric human settlement, at least 44 endemic species of land birds became extinct in the past 1,000 years (Steadman 1995). The larger picture in the Pacific indicates a major crisis of extinctions. About 3,500 years before the present, humans arrived in Western Polynesia and Micronesia, reaching virtually all of Oceania by 1,000 years before the present. Detailed island-by-island archaeological studies by Steadman (1995) and others have shown that most species of land birds and populations of seabirds on those islands were exterminated by human activities, not only by hunting but also as a result of habitat change and predation by non-native mammals. The loss of bird biodiversity in the tropical Pacific, largely attributable to pre-European invaders, may exceed 2,000 species and represent a 20 percent reduction worldwide in the number of bird species.

To recap, the overkill hypothesis may be elaborated upon to argue that the development of hunting in Africa led to technologically skilled hunters capable of killing at a distance, unlike other predators. The long coexistence of humans and African wildlife allowed the animals to co-evolve with the human predator, thus limiting extinctions. However, the expansion of these hunters out of Africa brought them into contact with naive animals, those unaccustomed to the human hunter. The hunters had their largest impact on large-sized animals, not only because they targeted them, but also because large animals tend to have relatively few young and low rates of population renewal. If extinctions had been explainable on the basis of Pleistocene climate change alone, both large and small species would have been affected—which is not the case (Owen-Smith 1987).

In terms of the geography of extinctions, the most noticeable impacts of invaders occurred on islands. Species diversity is often lower on islands than the mainland, and the impacts of newly arrived predators are further magnified because there is no place of escape and the native species have evolved in the absence of native predators. Many island animals are relatively easy to kill, and such tameness can also be found today on remote islands and in areas in which there has been no hunting. As well, extinctions on islands are easier to document, especially if they were relatively recent (Steadman 1995). In the case of very large "islands" such as Australia, the evidence is much less clear. There is some evidence that early hunters are associated with the extinction of some large marsupials and birds. But there is also evidence that people may have been present in Australia for thousands of years before the major wave of extinctions, which argues against the simple version of the overkill hypothesis (Bahn 1996).

Just what do these findings signify for traditional ecological knowledge and human ecology in general? They destroy the myth of the Exotic Other, imbued with environmental wisdom, but they do not necessarily support the Intruding Wastrel myth either. It is significant that much of the evidence cited by the critics of indigenous conservation is archaeological or ethnohistoric in nature (Krech 1999; Smith and Wishnie 2000). This suggests that the evolutionary aspects of conservation knowledge and practice should be examined.

A number of human ecologists, notably Dasmann (1988), have pointed out that a distinction must be made between invaders and natives. When humans invade a new and unfamiliar ecosystem, their impact on the environment may be substantial initially. This initial relationship may change as the people develop a knowledge base, learn from their mistakes, and come to terms with the limits of their new environment. Long-settled natives tend to co-evolve with their environment, and they often achieve a level of symbiosis with their environment (Dasmann 1988; Callicott 1994). This is not likely to happen over short periods. A knowledge base takes a long time to develop, and practices based on such knowledge even longer. Practices will be grounded in institutions, as in land and marine tenure systems.

The transition from invader to native is not easy to study and document. Most of the evidence is indirect. For example, the ancestors of the Maori may have exterminated some of the moa and other large land birds, but the contemporary Maori (and many other Pacific island peoples) have well-developed systems of ecological knowledge, practice, and indigenous environmental ethics (Roberts *et al.* 1995; Moller *et al.* 2009; Wehi 2009), indicating that the Maori evidently learned from the experience. Similarly, the ancestors of American Indians may have contributed to the extinction of the American megafauna, but their descendants have some of the most sophisticated systems of ecological ethics (Callicott 1982, 1994). We do not need to resort to Chief Seattle's speech to make the point: the notion that "all things are related and interconnected" does exist in many American Indian cultures, for example, among the Nuu-Chah-Nulth of British Columbia (Atleo 2004).

The relationship of the eastern James Bay Cree to their animals such as beaver (Feit 1986), goose (Berkes 1982; Scott 1986), moose (Feit 1987), black bears (see Chapter 5; Tanner 1979), and caribou (see Chapter 6) all indicate a relationship involving resource stewardship and respect. In contrast to the rapid pace and large magnitude of megafaunal overkill in Martin's (1973) hypothesis, there is no record of even a single species of large mammal extinction in the eastern James Bay since the glaciers covering the area retreated several thousand years ago. To make sense of this contradiction of evidence, we need a theory to explain the transition from invader to native.

Indigenous Peoples as Conservationists?

Much of the debate on traditional peoples can be reduced to one question: are they natural conservationists or not? The myth of the Exotic Other would hold that they are; the myth of the Intruding Wastrel, that they are not. The myth of the Noble Savage/Fallen Angel acknowledges that either case is possible but does not allow for a third choice or nuanced solutions. The question itself is part of the problem; one should instead ask: What kind of conservation?

In the Western tradition, there are two fundamentally different kinds of conservation: "wise use" conservation and preservation (Worster 1977; Norton 1991, 2005; Borgerhoff Mulder and Coppolillo 2005). Modern conservation combines elements of both. It differs from wise use conservation in its rejection of utilitarianism and instrumental values, or nature-as-commodity. It differs from preservationism in its rejection (as unrealistic) of a pure hands-off approach to nature, in the form of extensive wilderness areas unoccupied by humans. Modern conservation seeks to sustain species and ecosystems and has come to focus on biodiversity as an overarching goal. How biodiversity conservation interacts with traditional conservation is one of the major issues of the traditional ecological knowledge field, as the exchange between Redford and Stearman, and Alcorn, discussed below, shows.

Although biodiversity as a concept has its roots in the field of conservation biology, many people other than biologists have claimed standing, especially the indigenous people inhabiting the rain forests of the Amazon Basin (Redford and Stearman 1993; Redford and Mansour 1996). The message from these indigenous peoples and their supporters has been that "tribal land rights and sovereignty must be supported in order to save both indigenous peoples *and the world's remaining natural areas*" (as quoted by Redford and Stearman 1993: 250). But are the agendas of the indigenous peoples consistent with the interests of biodiversity conservation? The authors argue that well-meaning but perhaps overzealous attempts to portray all indigenous peoples as natural conservationists places an unrealistic expectation on native groups to preserve land ceded to them in the same state as they received it. This is happening at a time when many indigenous groups are linked to the market economy and may be compelled to engage in activities that differ in type and intensity from traditional patterns of resource use.

In the indigenous view, according to the authors, preserving biodiversity apparently means preventing large-scale destruction (hydroelectric development, mines, large ranches, and so on) and conserving certain "acceptable" levels of biodiversity. Such a view of biodiversity does not preclude practices of shifting cultivation for the market, small-scale cattle ranching, selective logging for commerce, and subsistence and even commercial hunting. Some of these activities may conserve elements of biodiversity, but not the full range of biodiversity. For example, the activities of rubber tappers in the extractive reserves of Brazil have been shown to alter forest biodiversity. "If the full range of genetic, species, and ecosystem diversity is to be maintained *in its natural abundance* on a given piece of land, then virtually any significant activity by humans must not be allowed. . . . Even low levels of indigenous activity alter biodiversity" (Redford and Stearman 1993: 252). Hence, if an area is expected to meet biodiversity conservation as well as indigenous needs, there are necessarily trade-offs that must be addressed explicitly (Redford and Stearman 1993).

In the view of Alcorn (1993), the indigenous notion of biodiversity conservation as provided by Redford and Stearman ("preventing large-scale destruction") is inadequate and misleading. There are several other elements of indigenous conservation. Many groups demonstrate a concern for maintaining ecological processes and the species that mediate those processes. In many indigenous communities, there are well-respected local experts interested in rare plants. In

Asia and Africa, there are traditions of maintaining sacred forest areas (Gadgil and Vartak 1976; Castro 1990; Dei 1993). Many indigenous groups have community-enforced rules for resource use. Indigenous peoples' goals may not match the narrower conservation goals as indicated by Redford and Stearman, but "they more closely match the broader goals espoused by many conservationists who recognize that most of the world's biodiversity is found, and will continue to be found, in landscapes occupied by people" (Alcorn 1993: 425).

Partnership of conservationists and indigenous peoples, Alcorn continues, offers the best option for achieving conservation. One barrier to such partnerships is the attitude that conservationists are in a position of authority to "cede" rights, "When Redford and Stearman write about indigenous people 'claiming standing' to enter conservation discussions, their statement implicitly acknowledges the problem [that] 'conservationists' are acting as gatekeepers to a discussion table that does not have a place set for those whose homeland's future hangs in the balance" (Alcorn 1993: 426).

The debate between Redford and Stearman, and Alcorn is covered here in some detail because it highlights not only the political dimension of the issue (more on this in Chapter 12) but also the larger question of the difference between Western versus indigenous notions of conservation. Bridging the gap between the two positions in the debate depends on the feasibility of having indigenous peoples as *participants* and co-managers in conservation, instead of either Noble Savages or Fallen Angels. This, in turn, depends on the search for a universal, cross-cultural concept of conservation, if such a thing is possible.

Forcing indigenous conservation into the mold of Western conservation is not likely to work. Dwyer (1994: 91) states the problem succinctly: "The resource management systems of indigenous people often have outcomes that are analogous to those desired by Western conservationists. They differ, however, in context, motive and conceptual underpinnings. To represent indigenous management systems as being well suited to the needs of modern conservation, or as founded in the same ethic, is both facile and wrong." That they are not founded on the same ethic is clear, for example, from Chapter 5 on the Cree Indians. The Cree believe that the use of a resource is necessary for its continued productivity. Use is, in fact, an obligation. Many other examples can be given. The Maori environmental ethic, for instance, is oriented to conservation for human use. Traditional prohibitions are intended to ensure resource productivity, not to safeguard some notion of so-called intrinsic value—simply because there is no human–nature or self–other duality in the Maori worldview (Roberts et al. 1995).

A practical consequence of this is that the Maori conservation ethic of sustainable utilization conflicts with New Zealand's 1987 Conservation Act, which stipulates "preservation" and "setting aside of land" to meet conservation objectives

(Roberts *et al.* 1995). The issue is not merely the political control of land, but from the Maori point of view, the unacceptable notion of conservation driven by the Western concept of a human–nature dichotomy. Such a dichotomy "only serves to further alienate all humans, but particularly Maori, from their land, and thus from their *kaitiaki* [guardianship, stewardship] responsibilities" (Roberts *et al.* 1995: 15).

"Wilderness" and a Universal Concept of Conservation

To appreciate the arguments of Alcorn, Dwyer, and Roberts and her colleagues, it is useful to examine the notion of *wilderness*, which is central to the preservationist school of the two streams of Western thought that make up modern conservation. The preservationist belief holds that there is an inverse relationship between human presence and the well-being of the natural environment. Wilderness areas, enhanced and maintained in the absence of people, are seen as pristine environments similar to those that existed before human interference. According to the 1964 U.S. Wilderness Act, wilderness is a place "where man himself is a visitor who does not remain" (Gómez-Pompa and Kaus 1992a). To examine the idea of wilderness as the basis of a universal concept of conservation, there are two considerations: (1) Does wilderness as a notion stand up to a cross-cultural critique? (2) Is wilderness ecologically real?

For many indigenous peoples and for much of the rest of the non-Western world, including the great Asian religions, the distinction between nature and culture is meaningless. Strict dichotomies, such as nature–culture or mind–nature, are alien to many non-Western traditions. For example, in the symbol for the yin-yang principle in Chinese philosophy, it is considered that there is some yin within the yang and vice versa (Hjort af Ornas 1992). As noted in Chapter 2, the concept of an external environment or nature separate from human society is the basis of the Cartesian dichotomy of mind versus matter, and hence humans versus environment (Bateson 1972: 337).

"Wilderness" is the thought product of a people who see themselves as separate from environment, a value appropriate for a technological–industrial society no longer in direct contact with nature, a value not shared by indigenous cultures and many rural societies of the world (Klein 1994; Selin 2003). For indigenous peoples from the Arctic to the tropics, there is no wilderness but home. Hence, a kind of conservation that is based on preserving wilderness and maintaining the Cartesian dualism between mind and matter, which itself is at the roots of our environmental problem (e.g. Bateson 1972, 1979), cannot provide a universal concept of conservation.

Wilderness as an ecological notion is also questionable. No doubt there are areas that satisfy the usual definitions of wilderness as places free of human presence (Antarctica comes to mind). Many other areas, however, previously considered wilderness turn out to be cultural landscapes (anthropogenic land-scapes) on closer examination (Posey 1998; Thomas 2003; Salick *et al.* 2007; Hunn 2008; Johnson and Hunn 2010). Many apparently pristine areas did in fact support large numbers of people in the past, whose activities influenced what remains today. For example, much of the "wilderness" found by early Europeans in North America, "what Longfellow erroneously referred to as the 'forest primeval,' was in most parts of the continent and in varying degrees a human artifact" (Lewis 1993b: 395).

> Scientific findings indicate that virtually every part of the globe, from the boreal forests to the humid tropics, has been inhabited, modified, or managed throughout our human past. . . . The concept of wilderness as the untouched or untamed land is mostly an urban perception, the view of people who are far removed from the natural environment they depend on for raw resource. The inhabitants of rural areas have different views of the areas that urbanites designate as wilderness, and they base their land-use and resource management practices on these alternative visions. Indigenous groups in the tropics, for example, do not consider the tropical forest environment to be wild; it is their home.
>
> (Gómez-Pompa and Kaus 1992a: 273)

These considerations indicate that wilderness and wilderness preservation cannot be the basis of a universal, cross-cultural concept of conservation. More promising is the notion of *sustainability*, as in the broad-based definition of conservation in *Caring for the Earth*: "the management of human use of organisms or ecosystems to ensure such use is sustainable. Besides sustainable use, conservation includes protection, maintenance, rehabilitation, restoration, and enhancement of populations and ecosystems" (IUCN/UNEP/WWF 1991). This definition has been criticized by preservationists as being too use-oriented, but it represents a trend in conservation thinking that is trying to put humans back into the landscape (McNeely 1994, 1996; Borgerhoff Mulder and Coppolillo 2005). Much effort and thought have been expended to reconcile conservation and local needs. According to some, conservation is achievable by making it an attractive economic choice for people:

> The debate between "sustainable use" of wildlife and "pure preservation" hinges on a very simple economic problem. If peasant farmers in Latin America, Asia and Africa cannot make wildlife pay, then they will destroy the wildlife, plant their crops and bring in their domestic animals. The challenge for planners who care about the earth's wilds is to make wildlife conservation a sensible economic choice for the poor farmers concerned.

Sometimes—not always—that will mean allowing those farmers to kill some of the animals concerned and trade in wildlife products.

(Harland 1993)

A major paradigm change among many Western conservationists is that some kinds of human use are acceptable as part of conservation planning. This has been a debate of over one hundred years in the United States, featuring preservationists versus wise-use conservationists. In the context of indigenous peoples, the debate has a cross-cultural dimension as well. Indigenous practices of conservation differ from Western conservation in context and motive, and it may never be possible (or desirable) to integrate the two but rather to find common ground in sustainability. Perhaps the most useful way to think about indigenous conservation is that it is complementary to Western conservation, not a replacement for it. Indigenous conservation is legitimate in its own right, just as indigenous knowledge is legitimate in its own right. It does not have to be recast in a Western idiom or legitimized through Western science.

Many hunters and fishers behave in the short term as "optimal foragers" maximizing their catch per unit of effort—but within the operative rules in their societies (see Chapter 7; Alvard 1993). Indigenous peoples do not have a concern necessarily with the preservation of *all* the species in their environment (and neither do most non-indigenous peoples). No one has ever documented a "traditional preservation ethic," except perhaps with sacred sites. And it is true that some groups enter into strategic alliances with conservationists mainly for material benefits. The case in point is the group in the Solomon Islands that asked for a supply of chain saws as soon as they were invited into a community-based conservation project (Hviding 2003). Each alliance of indigenous people and conservationists will likely be different, and there will be trade-offs that must be addressed explicitly (Berkes 2007, 2009b).

Conservation cannot be assumed, but it cannot be assumed away either. There is an evolutionary biology argument to the effect that indigenous conservation is improbable because human beings will pursue selfish, short-term interests, and that conservation is seldom an evolutionarily stable strategy, says Kay (1994). However, that argument holds if humans existed and used resources as solitary individuals. But they do not. There is a large commons literature that shows that in indigenous and other resource-dependent rural communities of the world, one almost always finds institutions with rules that serve to limit short-term self-interest and promote long-term group interest. These communities typically exhibit precisely those characteristics that favor conservation: close personal relationships and inter-dependence, social control of "cheating," land use practices informed by many generations of collective experience living within the resources of an area (Hunn *et al.* 2003).

As shown in Chapter 10 in particular, local and traditional knowledge often develops in tandem with commons institutions. In many cases, indigenous peoples' capacity to maintain and to adapt their systems can be enhanced through the defense of their land and resource rights and tenure systems. These protected rights provide incentives to conserve, as shown in many of the Caribbean examples in Chapter 10 and the Aswani and Hamilton (2004) marine protected area case.

The acceptance of indigenous conservation in its own terms would in itself be a major paradigm change in the conservation field. In the dominant positivist paradigm of Western science, conservation professionals assume that they know best. But this style of conservation has neglected the needs and aspirations of local people, their knowledge and management systems, their institutions, and their worldviews. The old ideology attempted to exclude people from nature. The new ideology can start to treat people as part of the landscape to be conserved, to enable local participation in decision-making, and to encourage pluralistic ways of thinking about the world (Pimbert and Pretty 1995; Pretty 2007; Johnson and Hunn 2010).

An example of humans-as-part-of-landscape thinking is provided by the notion of cultural keystone species. Keystone species are those that have key ecological functions (Gadgil *et al.* 1993). Cultural keystone species are those that form the contextual underpinnings of a culture (Cristancho and Vining 2004). Examples include the western red cedar in the Pacific Northwest indigenous cultures of North America (Garibaldi and Turner 2004), caribou for the Dene (Chapter 6), and whitefish for the James Bay Cree (Chapter 7).

There is an accumulation of cases showing what indigenous conservation may look like and the factors impacting it. These cases come from a diversity of cultures and geographic areas, and deal with protected landscapes and agrobiodiversity (Amend *et al.*, 2008), protected landscapes and cultural/spiritual values (Mallarach 2008), sacred dimensions of protected areas (Papayannis and Mallarach 2009), sacred natural sites (Verschuuren *et al.* 2010), and indigenous rights and resource management (Painemilla *et al.* 2010). In addition to these five volumes, a large number of additional studies exist, as cited throughout this volume, that show distinct, practical and yet spiritual, livelihood-oriented notions of indigenous conservation. The interest in indigenous and community-conserved areas (ICCAs) may be considered in this context (Borrini-Feyerabend *et al.* 2004a).

Perhaps most important, accepting indigenous conservation in its own terms may mean abandoning that idea of indigenous people living "in 'harmony with nature,' untainted by the market economy," as Alcorn (1994: 7) put it. Like most people in the world, indigenous and other rural peoples are often engaging with the market economy in an attempt to improve their livelihoods. Conservation of key resources often has the mixed motive of keeping a healthy environment *and* making a living. That is why the Smith and Wishnie (2000) ideal of effect and design criteria to prove indigenous conservation is off the mark. I do not know of any indigenous group that thinks of its land- and resource-use practices as solely designed to achieve conservation; they often think of their practices as achieving conservation *and* securing livelihoods *and* being the right thing to do.

Adapting Traditional Systems to the Modern Context

Can traditional systems be transformed, or be adapted to the contemporary context? How do traditional practices evolve to respond to modern pressures? An examination of change and adaptation in a variety of cases provides an understanding of the limits and capabilities of traditional management systems. Since the area of common interest between Western and indigenous conservation is sustainability, one way of assessing the complementarity of the two systems is to look for examples in which the transformed system or the combined system is sustainable, biologically, economically and culturally. In this section, first I give examples of system transformation. Second, I discuss various efforts to combine systems.

Sustainable transformations of entire systems of people and nature are possible, and have occurred in the past. One of the best known examples is the rise of irrigated rice systems in historic Indonesia (Geertz 1963). A second example comes from the Philippines and shows the steps involved in converting a tropical forest ecosystem into a completely different system. The case in point is the transition from traditional shifting cultivation to irrigated rice production, as studied in Palawan, the Philippines, by Conelly (1992). During the 1950s and the 1960s, settlers in the area produced their rice, the local staple, in long-fallow swidden fields cleared from the forest. By 1970, land was becoming scarce due to population pressure, and by 1980 typical fallow periods had declined from more than ten years to only two to four years, together with declining yields. A widely held theory of agricultural change holds that the adoption of intensive cultivation techniques allows the farmer to support a larger population by increasing the yield per unit area. This growth in carrying capacity, however, will be achieved at the cost of lower labor efficiency (Boserup 1965). Intensive cultivation, as in wet rice agriculture, requires more work than does shifting cultivation; thus, Conelly had to address the question of why the local people did not resist the change.

What Conelly found was that the long-term consequence of the change probably did entail lower labor efficiency (i.e. more work for the farmer) as well as increased carrying capacity. But in the short term, standards of living improved. The reason for this was that farmers did not make the transition directly from long-fallow shifting cultivation to wet rice culture. Rather, they were forced to make the transition from a short-fallow swidden *that had already become unproductive*, to a more intensive form of cultivation that at least fed the population

(Conelly 1992). The example of the Palawan irrigated rice system is fundamentally different from shifting cultivation, *kebun-talun* or *pekarangan* (Chapter 4). It shows that it is possible to convert a tropical forest into a productive rice monoculture. But of course, the forest ecosystem no longer exists; it has been replaced by a different ecosystem. As well, it should be added that such conversions are obviously not going to work everywhere, depending on factors such as soil type.

Efforts to combine elements of traditional systems and contemporary systems are many, and span the broad field of indigenous knowledge from agriculture (Warren *et al.* 1995), agroforestry (Dove 2002) and forestry (Ramakrishnan 2007; Trosper 2007; Parrotta and Trosper 2012), to soil and water conservation (Reij *et al.* 1996) and environmental assessment (Reid *et al.* 2006). They include examples of technological innovation, such as the use of Nishga'a (also spelled Nishga) fish wheels to improve salmon management in the Pacific Northwest. In an effort to improve salmon returns on the Nass River, the local aboriginal management authority, the Nishga'a Fisheries Board, combined traditional and modern biological approaches. Observing that electronic fish sensors can be inaccurate, the Nishga'a devised a fish-counting system that combined the ancient fish wheel technology with modern statistical methods and data analysis. Salmon are sampled at an upriver fish wheel station at which the proportion of tagged fish is used to calculate returns. Reportedly, this procedure provides more accurate and reliable data than those collected by electronic tracking systems (Corsiglia and Snively 1997).

There is a rapidly developing pool of experience in combining traditional approaches with appropriate science and technology. Examples include combining traditional knowledge with geographic information systems (GIS) for marine protected area planning (Aswani and Lauer 2006b); combining traditional knowledge with satellite tracking (Huntington *et al.* 2004); and combining Maori knowledge with biological techniques for harvesting seabirds (Newman and Moller 2005). Robertson and McGee (2003) applied local knowledge to a wetland rehabilitation project in Australia. When historical ecological information proved unavailable, oral history was effectively used for information about changes in the frequency and distribution of flood events over the last 60 years. This is similar to the logic in climate change research in Chapter 8.

Also along these lines, there have been attempts to use scientific weather forecasting and local forecasting together. Roncoli and Ingram (2002) studied the attempts to combine rainfall forecasting methods in Burkina Faso. Scientific forecasts predict the total rainfall at the regional scale, whereas local forecasts stress rainfall duration and distribution, and use a rich set of environmental indicators. Raj (2006) described an initiative to bring scientific rain forecasting to rural villages in India's Tamil Nadu state that has low and unpredictable levels of rainfall. As in Burkina Faso, the regional level forecast supplemented the information available to farmers, but did not displace the very detailed traditions of local rain forecasting based on a great many environmental indicators.

Integrating traditional ecological knowledge and science is often a question of scale (Gagnon and Berteaux 2009). Many examples of knowledge integration and complementarity come from applied areas of conservation. Roth (2004) pointed out that in Thailand, state-based scientific knowledge in protected areas and community knowledge operate at two distinct spatial scales. Thus, viable conservation arrangements require the use of both kinds of knowledge in a partnership of scales. Box 11.2 contains an example of the use of local knowledge of the indigenous Dusun people

---

Box 11.2 Ancestral Ecology for Conservation

As Martin tells the story, Dius Tadong knows a great deal about the tropical forest in his country, Malaysia. After working for several years all over his native island, Borneo, for the Sabah State Forest Authority, he decided to return to his home village, part of the Dusun community. The Dusun are an indigenous group who still depend to a large extent on what nature provides. They live on the edge of the Kinabalu National Park, a large protected area of 753 square kilometers. Tadong works with the villagers to collect and list plants. The project aims at providing better knowledge and use of plant species in protected regions by providing training and assistance.

"In Kinabalu Park," Martin writes, "the first stage consists of drawing up an inventory on the rich flora, believed to include about 4,000 species, starting with plants that are useful to humanity. Studies of medicinal, edible and decorative plants are planned. Dius Tadong continues to cultivate the land, just as the other five plant collectors still work in their villages. They concentrate on palm trees, including those used to make cane, which are of crucial importance to the local population. The trees are used as food and in traditional medicine, as roofing material, to make rope, and in arts and crafts. . . .

"Similar projects are underway elsewhere—in Bolivia, Cameroon, Mexico, Uganda and the Caribbean for instance—in the hope of building ecological awareness based on ancestral knowledge. These projects may turn out to be more rewarding than previous efforts because they are being conducted in cooperation with the local people who know the forest intimately."

Source: Martin 1993: 5.

to build a botanical inventory in a Malaysian national park. Note that the researcher himself is Dusun, and this joint project of UNESCO, the World Wildlife Fund, and Kew Botanical Gardens starts with the useful plants, including locally important cane species. The result is a two-way interaction; local people share their knowledge and the results help community economic development.

Traditional Systems for Building Livelihoods in a Globalized Economy

A different kind of two-way interaction is apparent in the Zulu herbalist case (see Box 11.3). The solution was precipitated by a resource crisis, as the demand for

---

Box 11.3 Zulu Herbalists of South Africa as Essential Ingredients in Plant Conservation

"Squeezed between gritty Umlazi (a black township) and the neighboring Indian township of Chatsworth, a solitary 220-hectare green lung breathes a future into local conservation and the medicinal plant trade. The Durban Parks Department's Silverglen Nature Reserve is home to Umlaas Nursery, South Africa's first and largest medicinal plant nursery, which grows thousands of specimens of 350 plant species commonly used for traditional medicine. . . .

"Plant growing is a matter of science: seeds, bulbs, and cuttings provide sprouts, and high-tech tissue culture generation is done in a Durban Parks Department laboratory. But the nursery's success depends on the arcane knowledge of Zulu herbalists such as Mkhuluwe Cele—heirs to a mystic oral tradition—who identified the important plants disappearing from the wild and explained their uses.

" 'I was caught a number of times by the Natal Parks Board for picking protected plants,' Cele admits with a smile. 'When I saw the plants in Silverglen I felt jealous. After all, I thought, I also had soil and could plant.' Today Cele grows thousands of plants in his own nursery which he started with the help of a grateful Silverglen team. One of Cele's 11 children is learning nursery management and ethnobotany at Silverglen."

Source: Mbanefo 1992: 11, 12.

medicinal plants exceeded the supply. At the time the nursery was established, some species such as the *mathithibala* (*Haworthia* spp.), for warding off evil spirits and purifying the blood, had already disappeared, and conservationists wanted to secure medicinal plants for the future. If the managers had tried to stop overexploitation, they would simply have driven the trade underground. Instead, they involved a local university, obtained funding from a donor agency, and started growing medicinal plants, including the pepperbark tree of northern Zululand, now extremely rare in the wild. Part of the success of the nursery project is in its involvement of traditional herbalists. They contribute their knowledge to the project and, in turn, receive the means of growing their own plants. Their knowledge is returned to the community as well; for example, the nursery instructs gatherers to put mud on a tree's wound when they peel bark, a traditional Zulu practice.

Wild medicinal plants are on the decline everywhere in the world. At the 2001 International Conference on Tropical Ecosystems in Bangalore, India, some of the largest sessions were devoted to the conservation and village-based domestication of tropical medicinal plants. In addition to species and habitat protection, there was a large emphasis on the conservation of ethnobotanical knowledge for rural economic benefits and livelihoods. Agroforestry in general is an area in which there is a great deal of interest, both for ecological and for economic reasons. As we have seen in Chapter 4, the multi-species plantation of crop, non-crop and tree species are practiced in many parts of the world. These systems can be used as the basis for developing additional practices for economic development.

Some of these agroforestry systems are very sophisticated. For example, Armitage (2003) identifies traditional agroecological practices and knowledge frameworks in Sulawesi, Indonesia, that can be used as the basis for Adaptive Management, with a focus on learning, innovation, and flexibility. In another example, Kerala state in India contains a large part of the Western Ghats biodiversity hotspot. Some of this biodiversity is in protected areas, some of it is in community-conserved sacred groves, and some of it is in agroforestry plantations.

Bhagwat *et al.* (2005) examined the diversity of trees, birds, and macrofungi in these three land-use types, and found high levels of biodiversity, comparable to protected areas, in sacred groves and in multi-species plantations. They found no significant differences in the distribution of endemic and threatened birds across the three land-use types. Although endemic trees were more abundant in the forest reserve than in sacred groves, threatened trees were more abundant in sacred groves than in the forest reserve. They concluded that sacred groves maintained by tradition and the multi-functional cultural landscapes produced by centuries-old systems of plantation should be considered an important component of biodiversity conservation strategies (Bhagwat *et al.* 2005, 2008). The multi-species plantations are historically important, and are said to have been sustainable for

500 years; the area includes the Malabar coast that exported black pepper and other spices to medieval Europe.

How do such systems evolve? The *vihambas* of East Africa give a glimpse of the evolution of commercial agroforestry without destroying the original forest cover. The Chagga of Tanzania are a mixture of ethnic groups who settled in the area of the great Kilimanjaro. Different groups contributed their crop species, and over time, a rich mixture of domestic plants inspired a form of land use known as *vihamba*, multi-storey tree gardens characterized by great biodiversity, giving visitors the impression of being in the Garden of Eden (Kuchli 1996). The Chagga are experts in combining many types of plants requiring different amounts of light and having roots of varying depths. *Vihamba* incorporates patches of the original forest where useful species remain standing; other parts of the natural forest are replaced by cultivated species. By the turn of the century, the Chagga were successfully growing coffee as a cash crop, incorporating the shade-tolerant coffee bush into their *vihambas*. Contemporary Chagga farmers cultivate up to 60 different species of trees on an area the size of a football field.

The Chagga case is not an isolated example. Beaucage *et al.* (1997) provide a remarkably similar case of a biologically diverse and productive coffee agroforestry system from the Nahua of the Lower Sierra Norte, Mexico. The fourth most biodiverse country in the world, Mexico is full of traditional management systems and rapidly evolving community-based forestry enterprises. Castillo and Toledo (2001) discussed the ecological sense of a diversity of agroforestry systems in Mexico, showing that commercial use has not compromised biodiversity. Indigenous-controlled, community-based enterprises such as Nuevo San Juan have a track record of over 20 years, producing a diversity of products while at the same time there has been an increase in the total forest cover. Bray *et al.* (2003, 2005) have suggested that community-managed forests of Mexico can serve as a global model for sustainable forest landscapes.

The variety of products and uses in Mexico's forests, along with the India and East Africa agroforestry cases, support the argument made in Chapter 4 that many traditional systems, such as shifting cultivation, *kebun-talun* and *pekarangan*, maintain tropical ecosystem resilience and sustain productive landscapes through the diversity of uses. Some of these uses are subtle. In the Pacific Northwest, for example, indigenous people recognize over 100 species of plants used as famine and survival foods (Turner and Davis 1993). These species are not normally eaten but saved as special foods, alternative foods, emergency foods, hunger suppressants, and thirst quenchers. In parts of Africa, such famine foods are of obvious survival value (Muller and Almedom 2008).

It is not only indigenous people who have this kind of detailed knowledge of plant species use. Rural people in many parts of India (Gadgil *et al.* 2000) and

Turkey also seem to have detailed knowledge of useful plant species. The Anatolian peninsula (Asia Minor), which is a part of Turkey, is a plant biodiversity hotspot. More than 2,000 years ago in Asia Minor, Dioscorides wrote his 5-volume encyclopedia about herbal medicine, and the present-day rural population seems to continue the tradition (Cetinkaya 2006). In the mid-Aegean region of Turkey, Kargioglu and colleagues (2010) report that informants had ethnobotanical uses for 184 out of the 964 species that they identified (19 percent), including food (65 species), animal fodder (111), medicinal (119), and other (70). Ertug (2000) reports that villagers in Melendiz Plain, in close proximity to a Neolithic archaeological site in central Anatolia, recognized 300 plant species as useful. Of these, more than 100 species were considered as edible wild greens. Ertug (2000) indicates that historical continuity may be part of the explanation of the richness of the traditional knowledge of plants, and suggests that her findings provide clues to archaeologists and archaeobotanists, as well as to pharmacologists and botanists.

How many different species of wild greens can one eat? Such redundancy of food species parallels the emerging view of biodiversity as consisting of functionally redundant species that help maintain ecosystem resilience in fluctuating environments (Holling *et al.* 1995; Gunderson and Holling 2002). Some species are more drought-resistant than others, some survive extreme cold well, others recover quickly after fires and so on, each playing a different role in the ecosystem (or in the livelihood system) and the suite of species *together* providing resilience. There is little doubt that all of these traditional uses help maintain high degrees of biodiversity. "Even low levels of [human] activity alter biodiversity" (Redford and Stearman 1993: 252) but these activities can also create small-scale disturbances that facilitate ecosystem renewal cycles, create patchiness and increase species numbers (Chapter 2, Figure 2.1; Chapter 4).

Much of the world's biodiversity depends on the ability of local people to make a living from their environment without destroying the landscape and the biodiversity that it supports, in India, Turkey, Mexico (Toledo *et al.* 2003; Robson and Berkes 2011), and elsewhere (Parrotta and Trosper 2012). Can local and traditional knowledge be used to help accomplish this?

We explored a set of 42 indigenous cases in the United Nations Development Programme (UNDP) Equator Initiative database that had been nominated for the Equator Prize as successful models of integrated conservation–development projects in tropical countries around the world (Berkes and Adhikari 2006). Livelihood needs of the people in rural areas of the tropics can be a threat to biodiversity conservation. However, there have been many experiments in using local resources to create economic opportunities while conserving biodiversity, and these experiments are informative.

The UNDP cases showed a high diversity in the kinds of businesses developed and resources used, often focusing on a mix of resources, rather than a single commodity. They were often set up to provide social dividends to community members; they were *social enterprises*, not based upon utilitarian economic models, but rather a model in which resources provided for much broader goals, economic, environmental, cultural, and political. They provided multiple benefits, including self-determination, cultural revitalization, protection of watersheds and sacred sites, employment, and capacity building (Berkes and Adhikari 2006). Whereas global actors can be opportunistic and transient, "roving bandits" with no attachment to place (Berkes *et al.* 2006), the actors involved in many of the UNDP cases were place-based, with attachment to place and to cultural and environmental values.

Examples included the Comunidad Indigena de Nuevo San Juan project, one of Mexico's community-based forestry enterprises (Castillo and Toledo 2001; Bray *et al.* 2003). The project started with the indigenous group seeking control over its traditional lands as a way to rebuild toward self-governance, and has gained control over 11,000 hectares of forest land in a biodiversity-rich region under collective ownership. The project has set up a multi-faceted social enterprise based on forestry and forest products, ecotourism, agroforestry, and wildlife management. Community benefits from the project have reduced out-migration, helped meet basic needs, eliminated extreme poverty, upgraded medical services, improved the quality of housing, and helped provide residential water, sanitation, and electricity (Orozco-Quintero 2007).

In some of the UNDP cases, indigenous peoples have a form of comparative advantage related to their skills and backgrounds. These included projects dealing with agroforestry products, medicinal plants, ecotourism, and ecological restoration (Berkes and Adhikari 2006). In each of these areas, aboriginal groups have a unique product or service to offer, related to their environment-related skills—skills not easily obtained by non-indigenous people. These comparative advantages are echoed in the smallholder timber management case studied by Sears *et al.* (2007). Using hybrid knowledge, farmers of eastern Amazonia of Brazil have developed a local timber industry. The small-scale development was based in part on local and traditional knowledge of specific kinds of forests and management of ecological processes such as natural regeneration.

This kind of economic development does not seem to result in the loss of traditional knowledge. Although some researchers have linked the loss of local ecological knowledge to the expansion of the market economy, others have found persistence of local ecological knowledge despite major socioeconomic changes. Still others have found that economic integration through local resource-based industries could accelerate the acquisition of local ecological knowledge.

Reyes-Garcia *et al.* (2007) found that participation in wage labor is associated with loss of ethnobotanical knowledge. But economic development based on local resources can take place without eroding local ecological knowledge, and can in fact strengthen it if economic development takes place through activities that keep people on the land and in their culture.

Toward an Evolutionary Theory of Traditional Knowledge

It is important to recognize indigenous resource management systems not as mere traditions but as adaptive responses that have evolved over time. These adaptations may involve the evolution of similar systems in geographically diverse areas (*convergent evolution* in the terminology of evolutionary biologists), as in the case of shifting agriculture found in virtually all tropical areas of the world (Brookfield and Padoch 1994). They may involve the elaboration of one basic model of management into a diversity of variations (what evolutionary biologists call *adaptive radiation*), as one finds, for example, in the reef and lagoon tenure systems of Oceania (Johannes 1978, 2002a). They may involve the co-evolution of prey and predator, or the cultivator and the crop, as in Hawaiian taro and kawa plants (Winter and McClatchley 2009). They may involve the major transformation of the landscape from one productive system to another, as in the Palawan irrigated rice example (Conelly 1992). They may involve the synthesis of several traditions, and current commercial pressures, into a new, sustainable, and beautiful system, as in the *vihambas* of Kilimanjaro (Kuchli 1996). The examples show that adaptive responses can be recreated to solve emerging resource management problems. The Caribbean cases in the last chapter illustrate how societies are constantly self-organizing in various ways to respond to resource management needs.

Two features of these adaptations stand out. The first, alluded to above, is the extraordinary similarity of basic designs shared by different cultures in comparable ecosystems worldwide, coupled with a remarkable diversity in practice even in adjacent areas. For example, Kuchli (1996) comments that the *vihambas* are complex agroforestry systems "without parallel." In fact, that is not true. Indonesian home gardens (*pekarangan*) as described in Chapter 4 share many of the characteristics of the *vihamba*. Neither is the *vihamba* unique as a coffee agroforestry system. Locally developed, diverse, tropical agroforestry systems that include coffee as a cash crop are found, among other places, in Nigeria (Warren and Pinkston 1998), Kenya, New Guinea (Brookfield and Padoch 1994), and Mexico (Beaucage *et al.* 1997; Castillo and Toledo 2001; Toledo *et al.* 2003).

The second feature of these adaptations is that they tend not to proceed in smooth and even steps but rather in fits and starts. The Palawan case is unusual in that it catches the process of transformation of agricultural systems. It shows that change proceeds in discontinuous steps, from long-fallow swidden to short-fallow and then to wet rice culture. The same kind of rapid transformation is also apparent in the way Chisasibi Cree hunters readjusted their caribou hunts in the 1980s (see Chapter 6). The relevant theory in evolutionary biology is *punctuated equilibrium*, which states that evolution does not occur gradually (as Darwin thought) but rather through long periods of relative stability punctuated by periods of rapid change. The renewal of ecosystems and resource management institutions also seems to proceed that way (Gunderson *et al.* 1995; Gunderson and Holling 2002).

The mechanism of the transition from invader to native is likely to proceed in a similar fashion as well. The fortuitous observation of the modification of caribou hunting practice based on experience and oral history, as summarized in Chapter 6, provides insights in this regard. Social learning and cultural evolution based on a gradual accumulation of ecological knowledge and understanding is the major mechanism of the development of traditional ecological knowledge (Chapter 10). But crisis learning may speed up or shape this process towards a new relationship between a group of people and their resources.

Another line of evidence is provided by archaeology. McGovern *et al.* (1988) studied Viking-age colonization of North Atlantic offshore islands by Scandinavian settlers. They found that medieval farming technology brought to the islands by the settlers resulted in soil erosion through pasture mismanagement and forest depletion. The colonists eventually took some measures to correct their mistakes. Many environmental feedback messages, however, were difficult to interpret due to the masking effect of climate change, and the impacts of poor management practices were often difficult to reverse. For example, it was not easy to judge pasture overgrazing until after it had occurred. In this case, learning did not occur rapidly enough (in the period eighth to eleventh century) for adaptation and redesign to proceed, presumably because the message of resource crisis was not clearly received by the population.

These findings suggest that the evolution of traditional knowledge is complicated by many factors. The experience of a resource crisis is important in some cases. But we cannot say if it is a necessary or a sufficient condition for social learning. Signals from the environment have to be received and properly interpreted by the people in question if they are to be successful in adapting to the new circumstances. The development of an appropriate conservation ethic, as part of the belief system or the worldview guiding practice, is another necessary condition. It may also proceed via periods of rapid change punctuating long periods of relative stability. There is insufficient evidence to develop principles regarding the relationship between the ethics and practice of resource management. We may hypothesize, however, that belief or ethics is the *slower variable* in a knowledge–practice–belief complex. One evidence for this is that the Cree Indian trappers of James Bay apparently suspended their conservation *ethics* and changed their *practice* between 1920 and 1930, contributing to the depletion of beaver. After their resource tenure was recognized by law, proper practice was restored after about 1950, based on the same ethic as had existed previously (Feit 1986; Berkes *et al.* 1989).

A conservation ethic may never develop, if the group in question fails to experience a crisis or is unable to interpret it. The Torres Strait islanders constitute a case in point (Johannes and Lewis 1993). This group lives in a particularly productive area in the path of migratory species and is probably unable to receive feedbacks of resource depletion as do many Pacific island peoples, such as those in Palau (Robert Johannes, personal communication). However, the more recent findings of Kwan (2005), that there are some management practices for dugong, may be evidence that Torres Strait islanders have learned some conservation since Johannes' earlier work. The evolution of a conservation ethic over the period of a few decades is not uncommon. Agrawal (2005) documented in some detail the evolution of forest conservation in the Kumaon Hills of northern India, from the 1920s onward, along with the development of local forest management institutions. He found a close relationship between individual behavior, group practice, and the development of codes of behavior through institutions.

In some cases, it is unclear why a conservation ethic fails to develop. Often used as an example (Diamond 2005), a disturbing case is Easter Island, one of the more remote and larger islands of the Pacific, colonized by the ancestors of the Polynesians about 1,500 years before the present. Environmental degradation was gradual but severe, and included the loss of more of the terrestrial biota than in any other island of its size in Oceania. Deforestation of the island was virtually complete by about 550 years before present (Steadman 1995). However, unlike the Easter Islanders, many societies in the Pacific and elsewhere seem to be able to learn from experience and develop appropriate ethics and practices to solve their environmental problems. The major conclusion is the adaptability of most societies and their knowledge systems.

This adaptability is the key ingredient for developing sustainable local economies with which indigenous and other resource-dependent rural peoples of the world can make a living. Much of traditional ecological knowledge is hybrid knowledge, even where the culture retains some semblance of the sacred (Crate 2006) and is shaped by needs and opportunities (Ruiz-Pérez *et al.* 2004). Many experiments are underway in knowledge integration (Reid *et al.* 2006; Davidson-Hunt and O'Flaherty 2007; Woo *et al.* 2007; Ballard *et al.* 2008; Moller *et al.* 2009; Sileshi *et al.* 2009; Knapp *et al.* 2011; Armitage *et al.* 2011). Local and traditional knowledge can serve economic development and livelihoods (Berkes 2007), and appropriate, land-based economic opportunities can serve knowledge development (Reyes-Garcia *et al.* 2007). Experiences in Mexico (Bray *et al.* 2005) and Kerala, India (Bhagwat *et al.* 2005) show that economic development based on local knowledge and biodiversity can be our best bet for an environmentally sustainable future.

CHAPTER 12

Toward a Unity of Mind and Nature

There has been a remarkable growth of international interest in traditional ecological knowledge, and more broadly in indigenous knowledge, since the early 1990s. This trend is reflected in the growth and diversification of the scholarly literature. Indigenous knowledge has been transformed from an esoteric idea in WCED (1987) into a concept taken seriously enough to be mainstreamed in two large international initiatives, the Millennium Ecosystem Assessment (MA 2005; Capistrano *et al.* 2005; Reid *et al.* 2006) and the Arctic Climate Impact Assessment (ACIA 2005). It is significant that the predecessors of these two projects, both products of the 1990s, did not have an indigenous knowledge component (Miller and Erickson 2006). The growth of the indigenous knowledge literature has been accompanied by the differentiation of indigenous knowledge into a range of areas, from ethnobotany (an already established field) to, for example, indigenous land-use studies that in turn has its own diversified literature from Central America, Southeast Asia, Australia, and Canada (Chapter 2).

Along with the diversification of the kinds of indigenous knowledge, there has been a diversification of communication media used for indigenous knowledge. In the mid-1980s when I was assisting the James Bay Cree with their book on good hunting practice for the youth (Bearskin *et al.* 1989), there were few media options available. But if we were to do that project now, we might think of constructing a website, producing a CD-ROM, audiotapes, videotapes, and perhaps an atlas or posters, as well as a book. These new media options allow us to mix and match to find the best fit among kinds of knowledge, the intended audience and the appropriate media type for communicating that knowledge (Bonny and Berkes 2008). The audience itself has diversified as well. In addition to scholars, resource managers, and decision-makers, rural and indigenous communities themselves are using the results of indigenous knowledge research. They are using it for the stewardship of their lands and resources, political voice, cultural preservation, economic development, and education of the youth. The prospects for indigenous knowledge look much brighter than they did in the early 1990s.

The globalization of Western culture has meant, among other things, the global spread of Western ways of environmental and resource management. The remaining pockets of traditional systems probably cannot escape history, but they can transform themselves into diverse and creative hybrid systems that build on traditional ways of knowing, and take advantage of windows of opportunity (e.g. entry into bioeconomy) in a rapidly changing world. They can also inspire new approaches to environmental stewardship, and suggest more participatory and locally grounded alternatives to top-down, centralized environmental management.

During the past century, a diversity of traditional knowledge and practice systems all over the world has been replaced by a monolithic Western resource management science. Until only a few years ago, the spread of modern, rational, scientific resource management was considered a part of "natural progress." The problem is that Western scientific resource management, despite all of its power, seems unable to halt the depletion of resources and the degradation of the environment. Part of the reason for this paradox may be that Western resource management, and reductionist science in general, developed in the service of a utilitarian, exploitive, dominion-over-nature worldview of colonists and industrial developers (Worster 1977; Gadgil and Berkes 1991). Utilitarian sciences were best geared for the efficient use of resources as if they were limitless, consistent with the laissez-faire doctrine still alive in today's neoclassical economic theory. But utilitarianism is ill-suited for sustainability, which requires a new philosophy that recognizes ecological limits and the unity of humans and nature, and strives to satisfy social as well as economic needs.

Perhaps the most fundamental lesson of traditional ecological knowledge is that worldviews and beliefs do matter. Almost all traditional ecological knowledge systems may be characterized as a complex of knowledge, practice, *and belief*. Almost universally, one encounters an ethic of nondominant, respectful human–nature relationship, a sacred ecology, as part of the belief component of traditional ecological knowledge. This is true not only for the Cree people or Australian aboriginal people, but for many other groups as well. For example, the Fijian expressions of spiritual affinity with land, *ne qau vanua* ("the land which supports me and to which I belong") and *na vanua na tamatu* ("the people are the land") (Ravuvu 1987), could have just as easily come from traditional peoples of the Americas, Africa, Australia, or New Guinea (Ballard 1997). The notion of unity of people and land is not absent in Western societies, either. For example, witness the Gaelic greeting, "Where do you belong to?" signifying specific connections to land (Mackenzie 1998).

In general, the idea of identification with nature goes back to the dominant pantheistic (many gods) traditions before the rise of monotheistic (single god) religions. These beliefs existed in pre-Christian Europe and survived for a time in the Christian mysticism of St. Francis (White 1967). They may be found in the Sufi mysticism of Islam, and in Hindu, Buddhist, and Taoist traditions (Callicott 1994; Taylor 2005; Jenkins 2010). Pantheistic religions have all but disappeared, but the worldview associated with them has survived longer, as in the case of the James Bay Cree. The decline of the worldview that identifies with nature seems to be related to the decline of pantheism, as well as to the rise of the modern industrial state with its ethos of control of nature and a utilitarian, depersonalized science.

The science of ecology occupies a unique position. Although much of ecology continues as a conventional reductionistic science, the more holistic approaches in ecology provide a new vision of the earth as an ecosystem of interconnected relationships in which humans are part of the web of life. However, Roszak's (1972: 404) question still remains open: "which will ecology be, the last of the old sciences or the first of the new?" This is not an easy question for ecologists. Many would not be comfortable, for example, with the contention that ecology is "discovering a new version of the 'enchanted world' that was part of the natural mind for most of human history" (Berry 1988). Although Leopold (1949) explained his land ethic in ecological terms, an ethic of ecology has not caught on among ecologists, probably for the simple reason that Western science, by definition, does not include an ethical or belief component.

However, traditional ecological knowledge does, and it is not surprising that many of the alternative thinkers such as Aldo Leopold and Gregory Bateson incorporate a component of value, wisdom, ethics, or belief in environmental stewardship. Norton (2005) points out that ecology cannot be value-neutral when directed at such normative goals as sustainability or resilience. The idea that science should be completed before values are injected into a policy process is obsolete. Norton looks forward to the development of a post-positivist ecology (consistent with Roszak).

This chapter opens with a consideration of the political ecology of traditional knowledge, and continues with a section on its role in the empowerment of indigenous peoples and other marginalized groups dependent on local resources. The main argument is that the use of indigenous knowledge is *political* because it threatens to change power relations between indigenous groups and the dominant society. The chapter then turns to a consideration of traditional knowledge as a challenge to the positivist–reductionist paradigm in Western science, on the basis of the critique of conventional resource management and the development of alternative environmental management approaches in Western science, such as Adaptive Management.

The chapter then discusses making scientific sense of indigenous knowledge, and compares indigenous knowledge with post-positivist approaches. This leads to the question of the potential for integrating traditional ecological knowledge with Western science. The two kinds of knowledge may be best pursued in parallel. Contact points may be provided by certain kinds of holistic Western science, such as complexity and fuzzy logic, consistent with the stewardship of nature, rather than its domination and control. The chapter ends with a recap of some of the main lessons of traditional ecological knowledge: its compelling argument for conceptual pluralism; its inspiration of more participatory, community-based alternatives to top-down resource management; and its potential to inject a measure of ethics into the science of ecology and resource management, thereby restoring the "unity of mind and nature" (Bateson 1979).

Political Ecology of Indigenous Knowledge

Mac Chapin (personal communication) observes that, "In all the discussions of 'indigenous knowledge' there is seldom talk of the wider social, political context. It is not just systems of knowledge that come into play, but social systems that have different ways of going about things: different beliefs and values, different priorities, different decision-making systems." Political ecology is a historical outgrowth of the central questions asked by the social sciences about the relations between human society in its political and cultural complexity, and human-dominated nature. As a field, it differs from political economy, which has tended to reduce everything to social constructions, disregarding ecological relations. Political ecology expands ecological analysis to include culture and politics, in particular, the relations of power (Blaikie 1985; Rocheleau 1995; Scott 1998).

The application of political ecology to indigenous knowledge starts by focusing on the familiar political–economic divisions among the actors (interest groups or stakeholders), "divisions between international, national and local interests; between North and South; between science and politics; official and folk; and power relations at the local level deriving from differences of class, ethnicity and gender" (Blaikie and Jeanrenaud 1996: 1).

The complexity of traditional knowledge issues may be interpreted and made more comprehensible by considering that there exist different actors who relate in different ways to the resource in question; the actors define knowledge, ecological relations, and resources in different ways and at different levels or geographic scales; they bring to bear on these definitions their culture and their experience;

and they will use different definitions in pursuit of their own "projects" or political agendas (Blaikie 1985; Colchester 1994; Robbins 2004).

The controversial issue of intellectual property rights provides a useful example. Some industries and governments have pressed for the extension of intellectual property rights to biological products so they can be patented. Under debate is the issue of privatization (through patenting) of agricultural varieties, individual genes, and biochemical products from natural or bioengineered species. But what about agricultural varieties developed by traditional management systems, or species that have long-established traditional uses?

Such a species is the neem tree (*Azadirachta indica*) that has been used for centuries by traditional doctors and farmers in India. Chemical properties of neem make it suitable for the extraction of a number of medicinal substances and natural pesticides. These properties have been known to Indians for many generations, and scientific research on neem has been carried out by Indian institutions, but these chemical properties have never been patented. In fact, under Indian law, medicinal or agricultural products cannot be patented. However, since 1985, a number of U.S. patents have been registered by U.S. and Japanese firms on neem-based biological products. This has created a bitter controversy, with the Indians charging that multinationals have no right "to expropriate the fruit of centuries of indigenous experimentation" (Shiva and Holla-Bhar 1993). One response in India has been the formation of an alliance of farmers and scientists to develop an alternative form of intellectual property. The *goan samoj*, a village-level collective, would hold "collective intellectual property rights" to assert that knowledge is a social product, subject to local common rights. These would give the community the right to benefit commercially from traditional knowledge (Shiva and Holla-Bhar 1993).

The neem case illustrates the divisions between international, national, and local interests, and between North and South. As well, the case shows that different actors relate in different ways to the resource, define knowledge in different ways and at different geographic scales, and use different definitions in pursuit of their own projects. Laws on intellectual property rights are generally inappropriate for defending local rights. Western legal tools of copyrights and patents cannot readily be used for indigenous knowledge (Brush and Stabinsky 1996; Zerbe 2004). It is not clear what the *goan samoj* or other groups defending local intellectual property rights can do under international law. However, many groups, such as the India-based Honey Bee Network (SRISTI 2011) have been effective on the ground in promoting community interests. In cases where the communal right to benefit commercially from traditional knowledge can be enforced, other kinds of political ecology problems emerge. One might expect equity dilemmas at the local level, as communities are not homogenous entities. There often is a multiplicity of interests and actors within a community who relate to resources in different ways (Agrawal 1997).

A second example is a classic controversy over the use of traditional knowledge in environmental assessment in the Northwest Territories (NWT), Canada. The NWT was the first jurisdiction in Canada to develop policies for the use of traditional knowledge. A report prepared after several years of study by a working group (Legat 1991) was adopted by the NWT government recognizing that "aboriginal traditional knowledge is a valid and essential source of information about the natural environment and its resources, the use of natural resources, and the relationship of people to the land and to each other." The policy was put into effect during an environmental assessment process in 1995 leading to the approval of a major mining project. The government's environmental assessment panel issued a directive to the proponent (BHP Diamonds Inc.) to give traditional knowledge equal consideration with science in assessing the impacts of the proposed mine (Stevenson 1996).

The objections subsequently raised by Howard and Widdowson (1996) to the directive and to its implications touched off a heated public policy debate in Canada about the nature and role of traditional knowledge ("TK"), a debate that attracted several rejoinders and the first news media coverage in this area. Howard and Widdowson (1996) argued that "TK, because of its spiritual component, is a threat to environmental assessment" because "rational understanding of the world is impeded by spiritualism." They talked about how "aboriginal groups obfuscated the Panel's attempts to understand" TK, and how "the aboriginal leadership then went on to argue that TK holders must be involved directly to protect the 'intellectual property rights' of First Nations." They concluded that traditional knowledge is "a cash cow for TK consultants and aboriginal leaders" and "has limited value and little to do with knowledge," and that "interest in TK is politically motivated."

The controversy, which has continued into the 2000s, illustrates the divisions between North (in this case, the aboriginal-dominated NWT government) and South (the dominant Euro-Canadian culture, which has only superficial sympathy for aboriginal concerns and values). As well, the case shows that different actors relate in different ways to the resource and define knowledge in different ways. In fact, by choosing carefully the definition used, one can manipulate ethnic prejudices. Howard and Widdowson (1996) used an NWT government definition of traditional knowledge ("knowledge and values . . . from the land or *from spiritual teachings*," emphasis added by the authors), to make their point that spiritualism was the key issue. This helped portray traditional knowledge as vague and unworthy of serious consideration by the dominant culture, which of course values the "rational" (Berkes and Henley 1997).

The Howard and Widdowson argument is interesting in part because it questions the validity and applicability of traditional knowledge because of its belief component. This assumes that there are other kinds of science that do not have a belief component or a cultural context, a point rejected by philosophers such as Feyerabend

(1987) and Norton (2005). The issue brings to mind Holmes's (1996) observation that Westerners are often unable to understand indigenous values or cosmologies, except as either "myth" or "data." The objection to *spiritualism* is merely an excuse to denigrate traditional knowledge; the real issue is resource management power and legitimacy. This can be deduced from Howard and Widdowson's (1996) objection, not only to the use of traditional knowledge, but also to the devolution of management authority to native groups, as creating a "conflict of interest."

This debate is not an isolated example. A similar debate has raged in New Zealand for a number of years. Dickison (1994: 6) notes: "The idea of a separate indigenous science, practiced by Maori before European settlement and passed on to their descendants, is an appealing one." But, he asks, how does Maori knowledge measure up to the conventional definition of science? "The answer, it seems, is not very well," because "Maori knowledge acquisition was neither objective (relying as it did on religious faith), nor rational (it mixed supernatural with mundane explanations)." Other assessments, as we have seen, indicate that Maori knowledge does "measure up" quite well (Lyver 2002; Mulligan 2003; Moller *et al.* 2004; Newman and Moller 2005; Stephenson and Moller 2009).

If one uses the perspective of such thinkers as Lévi-Strauss (1962) and Feyerabend (1987), the answer, it seems, is that Maori science is science—but *not* Western science. More to the point, Maori science, or any indigenous knowledge system, is not necessarily inconsistent with all of Western science. It is, however, definitely inconsistent with the positivist–reductionist tradition in Western science, and the assumption that the professional expert knows best. There is more to come on this point, after we further explore the use of indigenous knowledge for empowerment and note that the use of traditional knowledge is, after all, often very political.

Indigenous Knowledge and Empowerment

It is often assumed that indigenous peoples have only two options: to return to an ancient and "primitive" way of life, or to abandon traditional beliefs and practices and become assimilated into the dominant society. Increasingly, indigenous groups have been expressing preference for a third option: to retain culturally significant elements of a traditional way of life, combining the old and the new in ways that maintain and enhance their identity while allowing their society and economy to evolve. Local and traditional knowledge is relevant to economic development in part because it confers certain comparative advantages to indigenous groups in initiatives that require specialized knowledge of species, varieties and ecological processes (Berkes and Adhikari 2006). These initiatives may include conservation projects, ecological rehabilitation, ecotourism, and the cultivation of medicinal plants and genetically valuable crop varieties (Laird 2002; Nazarea 2006; Shukla and Gardner 2006).

For indigenous groups in many parts of the world, traditional knowledge has become a symbol for regaining control over their own cultural information. Reclaiming this knowledge has become a major strategy for local re-education and revitalization movements (Kimmerer 2002; Ross and Pickering 2002; Alcorn *et al.* 2003).

Indigenous peoples across North America, Latin America, Northern Europe, South Asia, and Southeast Asia are making similar claims: the right to control their lands and resources as a basis for their local economy; the right to self-determination and self-government; and the right to represent themselves through their own political organizations (Colchester 1994; Smith 1999; Battiste and Henderson 2000). All of these claims have their basis in indigenous peoples' knowledge of and attachment to the land, their traditional knowledge and management systems, and their local institutions. The first two examples described here deal with the use of traditional knowledge for mapping aboriginal land claims, and the third deals with its use for co-management of resources, that is, the sharing of power and responsibility between the government and local users, in this case, the Maori of New Zealand.

Inuit Land Use Maps for Self-Government

Aboriginal land-use studies in the Canadian North have been undertaken since the 1970s mainly to document land claims. The pioneering study that provided inspiration and methodology for many of the subsequent ones was *The Inuit Land Use and Occupancy Project* (Freeman 1976, 2011). Southern researchers and northern knowledge holders collaborated to document Inuit land use in the Canadian Arctic. They detailed how communities understood their environment and dealt with the cultural organization of land use and its social meaning. Composite maps, combining those for different resources and for different time periods, showed that the Inuit used almost all of the Arctic—a land that southerners had always considered "empty." The maps were regarded with disbelief in some circles until the overwhelming evidence of many other mapping studies showed that not only the Inuit but many indigenous groups still use their lands and resources extensively as part of a mixed economic strategy for livelihoods. Riewe's (1992) *Nunavut Atlas* extended the work of Freeman and his colleagues and provided a comprehensive series of land-use maps that were used in land selection by the Inuit as part of a comprehensive claims settlement, the Nunavut Agreement of 1993, leading to the creation of the self-governing Inuit territory of Nunavut in 1999 in the Canadian Eastern Arctic.

Reconstructing Aboriginal Land Ownership in Australia

Early European settlers widely believed that Australian indigenous people did not have territories or boundaries and were "aimless wanderers." But as anthropological, geographic, and linguistic studies demonstrated, especially since the

1970s, Aboriginal groups held communal rights and responsibilities, usually through lineage groups, for distinct areas of land and resources, through the use of ecological and spiritual knowledge (Young 1992; Kalit and Young 1997). Recent land claims legislation, based primarily on the establishment of proof of traditional ownership, has made the issue of Aboriginal territories crucially important both politically and economically. Once land passes into Aboriginal control, mining companies no longer have unimpeded access to it. One of the consequences of increased attention to ownership and boundary issues was that Aboriginal land tenure in Australia was found to be more complex than previously thought. Sutton (1995) brought together a huge amount of information on Aboriginal land use, initially as a critique of some existing maps and analyses of traditional territories. The maps showed that the complexities and multiple layerings often make it impossible to delineate boundaries as simple lines. As well, similar complexities have emerged in the definition of "traditional owners" because of the fluidity of group membership (Sutton 1995; Kalit and Young 1997; Davies 1999). Understanding the complexities of aboriginal land use proved to be important for planning purposes and for implementing co-management with indigenous groups (Ross *et al.* 2009).

Conflicting Worldviews in New Zealand

The Treaty of Waitangi, signed by the English Crown and chiefs of the Maori tribes in 1840, sets out indigenous land rights in New Zealand. The Conservation Act of 1987 directs the Department of Conservation to establish co-management arrangements with the Maori, in accordance with the principles of the Treaty of Waitangi. The problem is that the conservation ethic adopted by the act involves "the preservation and protection of . . . resources for the purpose of maintaining their intrinsic values," whereas the conservation ethic of the Maori is motivated by a different philosophy (Roberts *et al.* 1995: 15). Maori conceptualize humans "as part of a personified, spiritually imbued 'environmental family.' . . . Earth's bounty is considered to be a gift necessitating reciprocity on the part of human users in order to maintain sustainability" and requiring a sense of guardianship (*kaitiaki*) (Roberts *et al.* 1995: 14). The imposition of the Western concept of a dichotomy between humans and nature, and the setting aside of land for preservation, merely serve to alienate Maori from their land and *kaitiaki* responsibilities. Some New Zealand scientists and Maori have jointly developed creative solutions to this impasse, involving the co-management of contentious resources as a means of bridge-building and dialogue between the two cultures (Taiepa *et al.* 1997; Stephenson and Moller 2009). One of the mechanisms developed to signify mutual respect and to safeguard the intellectual property rights of Maori traditional knowledge-holders is the Cultural Safety contract (see Box 12.1).

Box 12.1 Instituting Mutual Respect of Knowledge Systems in New Zealand

The Rakiura Island at the southern tip of New Zealand supports a traditional Maori harvest of the seabird *titi*, or sooty shearwater. It is the last full-scale bird harvest controlled by the Maori, and it is under pressure from some conservation NGOs who allege that *titi* are declining. University researchers have entered into a co-management agreement with the Rakiura Maori to research and monitor *titi* ecology and harvest. A major component of the project is the traditional knowledge of the birders, which is proving to be considerable. University of Otago's Henrik Moller comments: "We are stunned by the long series of data that the birders have recorded and are beginning to reveal to us. One of the *Kaitiaki* (guardians) went to her mother and provided us with a 40-year data score on the fatness and the relative number of *titi* chicks."

A formal "Cultural Safety" contract was drawn up to clarify rules for disclosure and the ownership of information coming out of the study. According to the contract, the Rakiura Maori retain complete ownership of intellectual property rights over traditional knowledge. The scientific data gathered on *titi* ecology and harvests are jointly owned by the University and the Rakiura Maori. The contract guarantees that *titi* population data would be published, whether or not it predicts the sustainability of the resource, thus safeguarding the scientific integrity of the university researchers.

The contract requires university researchers to communicate study results to the Rakiura Maori first. At the end of the ten-year project, there will be a maximum of a one-year delay before the final scientific findings may be submitted for publication. This will give the Rakiura Maori time to meet and formulate their collective response to the final results, before the findings are disclosed to the general public. Interim results of the project will be communicated to the Maori on an ongoing basis by the use of an informal newsletter prepared in nontechnical language. The contract guarantees the *kaitiaki* of the Rakiura Maori full access to research data, the right to submit the data for a second opinion, and the right to see and comment on anything proposed for publication.

Source: Taiepa *et al.* 1997; Moller (personal communication).

Each of the three cases above deals with the use of traditional knowledge for empowerment in different parts of the world. In each case, the use of indigenous knowledge is political because it threatens to change the balance of power between indigenous groups on the one hand *versus* governments, developers, and conventional resource management scientists on the other. Consistent with the cultural importance of indigenous peoples' attachment to land, many of the examples of empowerment deal with land use mapping and land claims. Mapping has become a political process, but is also one of the most innovative and dynamic areas in traditional knowledge research because mapping has stimulated the development of techniques using modern technology such as GIS and remote sensing, and the development of participatory, cross-cultural approaches to the research process itself (Weinstein 1993; Duerden and Kuhn 1998; Murray *et al.* 2008; see Table 2.2 in Chapter 2).

Although cooptation is always a possibility, it is clear that indigenous people are able to use mapping and other tools to their advantage. Indigenous peoples, once empowered to become central actors, do not necessarily play the game according to the rules established by others. For example, Stoffle and colleagues (1990) used Turner's (1988) "index of cultural significance" to map protection priorities for local plant species used by the Paiute and Shoshone Indians and potentially affected by the nuclear waste disposal site to be set up in the Yucca Mountain project in Nevada. Undertakings of this sort, however rigorous their scientific methodology, may still be unacceptable to indigenous worldviews. Turner (1988) herself was not able to convince the Salish people to use the index for prioritizing the importance of plant species. One woman informant simply refused to go along with the exercise, saying "they are all important" (Turner 1988).

The New Zealand case is particularly telling because the controversy is directly on the issue of worldviews. The Maori are asserting the legitimacy of their views of conservation and are willing to reach out to the dominant society by going into partnerships with university researchers. However, the Cultural Safety contract (Box 12.1) is not merely a research protocol; it is used as a tool to share the power of knowledge. Similar cases of conflicting conservation views, accompanied by power struggles, are found in many parts of the world. Cox and Elmqvist (1997: 84), writing about rain forest reserves in Samoa, found that "the principles of indigenous control were unexpectedly difficult to accept by Western conservation organizations who, ultimately, were unwilling to cede decision-making authority to indigenous peoples." These attitudes are changing rapidly as indigenous groups move to control the access of researchers (Mauro and Hardison 2000) and diverse kinds of partnerships develop (Sheil and Lawrence 2004; Woo *et al.* 2007; Pearce *et al.* 2009). Research contracts such as the one with the Maori have become the norm, rather than the exception.

Elsewhere, struggles have been internal as well as external. For example, the Marovo Lagoon Project in the Solomon Islands was undertaken to assert traditional land and marine tenure in the face of development pressures. But the major struggle did not involve outsiders or foreign views. Research results on customary tenure and traditional management institutions were used to resolve internal differences—the differences between those who believed that customary tenure was an impediment to "progress" and development, versus those who saw opportunities to work with, rather than against, customary rights and traditional social institutions (Baines 1991; Baines and Hviding 1993; Hviding 2006).

These examples concentrate on politics, but issues of politics and philosophy in the use of traditional knowledge are often intertwined. The use of indigenous knowledge may threaten to break the monopoly of conventional resource management science on "truth." The next section shifts the focus of inquiry from political ecology to philosophy of science, for a more detailed examination of the extent to which indigenous knowledge systems are consistent with Western science.

Indigenous Knowledge as Challenge to the Positivist– Reductionist Paradigm

Since the early seventeenth century, science has been dominated by positivism (also called logical positivism or rationalism). It is an approach that assumes the existence of a reality driven by immutable laws based on the search for universal truths. The role of science is to discover these truths, with the ultimate aim of predicting and controlling nature. Science consists of value-neutral descriptions of objective events in nature, with the assumption that scientists themselves are detached from the world and operate in a value-free environment (Norton 2005). Positivism uses reductionism, which involves breaking a system into discrete components, analyzing the components, and making predictions on the basis of the analysis of the parts. Knowledge about the world is then synthesized into generalizations and principles independent of context, space, and time (Capra 1996).

I am using the term "positivist–reductionist paradigm" to emphasize the importance of reductionism as a key element of this philosophy. Reductionism, as opposed to the holism of traditional ecological knowledge, is central to the argument in this book. The above summary of the positivist–reductionist paradigm is simplistic to be sure; not too many scientists would subscribe to all the assumptions of the paradigm. But it is also true that the positivist–reductionist approach has dominated conventional resource management and conservation thinking (Berkes and Folke 1998), as seen in the New Zealand case and elsewhere.

In recent decades, ecology has made great strides in understanding and analyzing complexity and natural variability. Ecosystems are increasingly

perceived as being in a state of continuous change, thus necessitating the development of multi-equilibrium thinking and attention to system resilience (Holling
1973; Norberg and Cumming 2008; Chapin *et al.* 2009). Few contemporary ecologists would defend the equilibrium concept, and yet the equilibrium-centered
idea of maximum sustained yield (MSY) and its close relatives are still used in
fisheries, wildlife, and forestry. In the short term, quantitative targets such as MSY
are well-suited for the efficient utilization of fisheries and other resources, as if
stocks were discrete commodities in space and time. However, to the extent that
these assumptions are faulty, the MSY is part of the problem and an impediment
to sustainability in the larger context of the long-term maintenance of healthy
ecosystems (Francis *et al.* 2007).

The point is that both ecology and resource management science, that developed under the conventional and mechanistic worldview, shaped by the utilitarian
premises of the industrial age, "had more to say about the human mission to
extract rather than to conserve" (Worster 1977: 53). The managers who were in
charge of such resource management were not only the technocrats who knew
how to calculate quantitative targets, but they were also the high priests of the
positivist–reductionist paradigm. These managers rejected traditional knowledge
and management systems because they did not fit with the paradigm. Instead, they
were characterized by: embeddedness of knowledge in the local culture; boundedness of local knowledge in space and time; the importance of community; lack of
separation between nature and culture, and between subject and object; attachment to the local environment; and a noninstrumental approach to nature (Banuri
and Apffel Marglin 1993).

The development of a technocratic-bureaucratic class, the separation of the
user from the manager and the governed from the governor were justified in terms
of the rise of the modern state, whose affairs had become too complicated for the
ordinary citizen. In place of traditional management systems, the high priests
enforced a system characterized by disembeddedness; universalism; supremacy
of individualism; nature–culture and subject–object dichotomy; mobility; and an
instrumental, utilitarian attitude toward nature (Banuri and Apffel Marglin 1993;
Norton 2005).

These changes in resource and environmental management science should not
be seen in isolation. Rather, they should be regarded in the larger context of a great
transformation of society and values that characterized the period after the seventeenth century, the period of the Enlightenment. The development of positivist–
reductionist science was closely linked to the emergence of industrialization and
to economic theories of both capitalism and communism. Through the technological domination of the earth, scientists and economists promised to "deliver a more
fair, rational, efficient, and productive life for everyone, themselves above all"

(Worster 1988: 11). Their method was simply to free individual enterprise from the bonds of traditional hierarchy and community, whether the bondage derived from other humans or the earth (Kellert 1997). That meant teaching everyone to treat the earth, as well as each other, with a "frank, energetic self-assertiveness, unembarrassed by too many moral or aesthetic sentiments" (Worster 1988: 11).

In pursuing individual wealth, people were taught to regard land, resources, and their own labor as potential commodities for the market. As explored by Polanyi (1964), this Great Transformation of the scientific–economic system was also linked to a radical transformation of social attitudes. "Everyday dealings of people with nature were altered too, so that ecological relations, deriving as they did from human social relations, also became more destructive as they grew more distant. Just as capitalists organized the new underclass of workers into instruments of profit, so they organized the earth as the raw material for that labor to exploit" (Worster 1988: 12).

In exploring the relationship of traditional knowledge to Western science, these considerations led to the conclusion that indigenous knowledge systems are fundamentally inconsistent with a certain kind of Western science, more specifically, the positivist–reductionist tradition. It is this paradigm that displaced traditional knowledge in the first place, insisting that experts knew best and asserting that users of resources cannot be the managers at the same time. Given its bias for individualism over community, its utilitarian attitude toward nature, and its nature–culture and subject–object dichotomies, it is clear that the positivist–reductionist paradigm holds little promise as a framework for understanding indigenous knowledge or for integrating Western science and other kinds of knowledge.

Many Westerners believe that knowledge has been converging into a coherent whole. Norgaard has used the metaphor of sciences as islands of knowledge, gradually growing and pushing back the sea of ignorance. The belief in the ultimate and final victory of Western science has been accompanied by the belief that all cultures would merge into one "correct" way of thinking about the world, human development and well-being. For example, development economists have typically projected social and economic change in a way that leads all cultures to adopt one correct Western way of thinking. This then justified, for example, policies like exporting "development" to Africa and assimilating indigenous peoples. To the extent that such development and "progress" after the Western pattern have not worked, a re-visioning of the future becomes necessary (Norgaard 1994, 2004).

If our sciences were truly merging, one would expect to find that our growing islands of knowledge would seamlessly come together. What one finds instead is a fundamental questioning of old paradigms in those sciences centrally involved in the management of resources and the environment. For example, the assumptions of neoclassical economics have run into biophysical limits dictated by ecological considerations, and equilibrium-centered supply/demand analyses are providing poor predictions, thus making a paradigm change likely. Both ecology and economics are in a state of flux as post-positivist approaches threaten to take over the old paradigms. There are many challenges to the positivist–reductionist paradigm; indigenous knowledge can be considered as one of them.

Making Scientific Sense of Indigenous Knowledge

Indigenous knowledge is a challenge to the essential question of what constitutes knowledge. Turnbull (1997: 560) argued that when local and indigenous knowledge is probed deeply, "in no case does it come out looking the standard Western notion"; rather, it tends to show a "blend of knowledge, practice, trusted authority, spiritual values, and local social and cultural organization: a knowledge space." The ancient wisdom of many traditional peoples is a good fit with some of the post-positivist approaches to contemporary natural and social sciences—sometimes you have to go back to go forward (Berkes and Folke 2002; Turnbull 2009).

How do the basic assumptions of indigenous knowledge compare with positivist and post-positivist views? Kuhn (2007) discussed complexity as one of the post-positivist approaches and compared it to positivism. Building on the work of Lincoln and Guba (1985), she also compared it to social constructivism (naturalistic research), another post-positivist approach. Using three of the five areas of Kuhn (2007) to distinguish positivist and post-positivist approaches, Table 12.1 summarizes the assumptions of indigenous knowledge versus positivism, social constructivism, and complexity.

Regarding the nature of reality, indigenous knowledge is consistent with social constructivism and complexity in rejecting the positivist assumption of a single tangible reality. Similarly, on the question of generalizations, indigenous knowledge largely agrees with social constructivism and complexity that context-free generalizations or the universal truths that positivism seeks are not generally possible. Most traditions of indigenous knowledge allow generalizations at the level of values, such as the importance of respect and reciprocity, and the idea that humans cannot predict and control nature. Regarding the role of values, social constructivism, complexity, and indigenous knowledge all reject the positivist belief in a value-free science. Most traditions of indigenous knowledge would probably go further than social constructivism and complexity in seeing values as driving the quest for knowledge. As Jim Bourque, a Canadian indigenous leader and the head of a traditional ecological knowledge working group, used to say, "traditional knowledge is all about moral values."

Finally, the other two basic groups mentioned in Kuhn (2007) but not used in Table 12.1, concern the relationship of the knower to the known (epistemology)

Table 12.1 Basic beliefs (axioms) that guide inquiry in positivist and alternative approaches

	The nature of reality	The possibility of generalization	The role of values
Positivism	There is a single tangible reality that can be fragmented into independent variables.	Time- and context-free generalizations are possible, leading to time- and context-free truth statements.	Values do not have a role in inquiry. Inquiry should be value-free.
Social constructivism	There are multiple constructed realities that are best studied holistically.	Only time and context-related working hypotheses are possible.	Inquiry is value-bound. Inquirer expresses values through choice of paradigm guiding the inquiry process, theory guiding data gathering, and treatment processes.
Complexity	Reality is dynamic, self-organizing, and emergent. It is both singular and multiple at the same time.	Only time- and context-related working hypotheses are possible, unless one moves to discussion of very general organizing principles.	Values are inherently implicated in the inquiry process. Often it will be a focus on values that will guide the process toward a satisfying outcome.
Indigenous knowledge	Reality is elusive, subject to constant testing against observations, and to interpretations by those qualified.	Generalizations tend to simplify unknowable interrelationships, and are therefore discouraged, except at the level of basic societal values.	Values are explicit in knowledge. Ways of knowing are informed by values and beliefs, as in "head and heart together" (Dene); "science with a heart" (Maori).

Sources: First two rows based on Lincoln and Guba (1985); third row, Kuhn (2007).

and the possibility of causal linkages. On both points, indigenous knowledge again joins social constructivism and complexity in rejecting the positivist belief that the knower and the known are independent, and the belief that it is possible to distinguish causes from effects.

Indigenous knowledge is not a philosophy of science, at least not formally, and there is not one kind of "indigenous knowledge" but many traditions. Nevertheless, it is interesting to see that indigenous knowledge (based on the considerable wealth of material summarized in this book) comes out so clearly at odds with positivist science. But it is equally interesting that indigenous knowledge is largely consistent with the two post-positivist sciences—social constructivism and complexity—in terms of its axioms. Can post-positivist sciences be used to understand indigenous knowledge and to bridge different knowledge systems?

The alternative post-positivist approaches in environmental management are represented by complexity, systems thinking, and evolutionary approaches. The applied form of this stream is represented by Adaptive Management, in which uncertainty and surprises are an integral part of the anticipated set of responses (Holling 1978). Adaptive Management is fundamentally interdisciplinary and combines historical, comparative, and experimental approaches. Problems are dealt with as systems problems in which the behavior of the system is complex and unpredictable, and causes are usually multiple. Adaptive Management involves multi-equilibrium thinking and attention to system integrity, focusing on ecosystem processes rather than ecosystem products. Ecological relationships are nonlinear in nature, cross-scale in space and time, and have an evolutionary character (Holling *et al.* 1998).

As discussed in Chapters 6, 7, and 8, Adaptive Management is a good match for traditional ecological knowledge, and a potential bridge between Western and indigenous ways of knowing in the area of ecology and resource management (Berkes *et al.* 2000). It is part of the holistic tradition in Western science—not the mainstream tradition, but significant nonetheless. This holistic tradition includes systems theory, gestalt psychology, quantum physics, and ecology (Capra 1996). Systems theory is often equated with complex adaptive systems. Fuzzy logic (not mentioned by Capra) may also be added to the list. Many of these holistic sciences are potentially suitable to provide frameworks for integrating Western and indigenous knowledge.

Chapters 8 and 9 highlight complexity, and Chapter 9 more specifically uses fuzzy logic to understand how the holism of local and traditional systems deals with complexity. The book uses an evolutionary approach (especially in Chapter 10) to build a theory of indigenous knowledge. Local and traditional knowledge is about practice, and that is why it can be protected by protecting *practice*, not by collecting "best practice" cases in a museum sense (Agrawal 1995a, 2002). Building a theory of indigenous knowledge is at odds with the reality that indigenous knowledge is something that one practices. I "do theory" in this book, with humility, for the benefit of Western thinkers who need Western sciences such as complexity theory and fuzzy logic to understand indigenous knowledge. Indigenous knowledge holders themselves do not need the theory; they already practice it.

What indigenous knowledge holders practice is far from the realities of reductionist science, and yet some scientists are willing to listen to traditional knowledge. Trosper and Parrotta (2012) ask: how much of traditional knowledge has become acceptable, and to which scientists? First, they come up with a list of components of traditional knowledge ("all things are connected"; "humans are part of the system" and so on, to "practical experience on land is the main source of knowledge"). Then, they create a "ladder of recognition" by examining which kinds of science accept which components, covering social–ecological systems, resilience theory, sustainability science and ecological economics, and the actor-network theory of Latour (2004). Although the list of sciences of Trosper and Parrotta (2012) is different from that in Table 12.1 there is agreement to the effect that several Western sciences, as well as humanities (Ommer et al. 2008), can in fact understand traditional knowledge or parts of it.

Understanding indigenous knowledge brings with it the question of bridging knowledge systems (Reid et al. 2006). There seems to be good agreement that knowledge partnerships, as in the co-production of climate change knowledge (Chapter 8), and the use of local/traditional knowledge alongside science for practical problem-solving work quite well (Berkes 2009a). As well, Ommer et al. (2008) have shown that the use of narratives, for example, works well in both indigenous knowledge and humanities. Nevertheless, much more needs to be done to explore the ways in which Western and traditional knowledge can be used together—and how much integration is or is not desirable in the first place.

Attempts at integration inevitably come up against the questions of power sharing and decision-making. The cases summarized in this chapter, as well as those in Chapters 2, 10, and 11, indicate that the use of indigenous knowledge can provide both empowerment for local peoples and improvement of the knowledge base for decision-making. However, in many cases, indigenous knowledge has been ignored or dismissed; conversely, there have been other cases in which indigenous peoples have been reluctant to work with Western scientists or to share their knowledge.

As discussed in the context of climate change (Chapter 8) and elsewhere, perhaps the most useful way to think about indigenous knowledge is that it is complementary to Western scientific knowledge, and not a replacement for it. Rooted in different worldviews and unequal in power, Western and traditional knowledge are not easy to combine. It may never be possible or desirable to meld the two, even if Western knowledge is represented by one of the holistic traditions. Each is legitimate in its own right, within its own context; each has its own strengths. The two kinds of knowledge may be pursued separately but in parallel, enriching one another as needed. Several authors have used the metaphor of the Two-Row Wampum to characterize how the two knowledge systems could interact.

Two-Row Wampum is a beaded belt describing a friendship treaty between the Dutch and the Iroquois. The rows of beads on the belt represent Dutch vessels and Iroquois canoes, traveling side by side down "the river of life." The paths of the two kinds of vessels remain separate, but the people on the two kinds of boats are meant to interact and to assist one another as need be (Doubleday 1993; McGregor 2004; Stevenson 2006). Such a relationship comes closest to respecting the integrity of both ways of knowing while maintaining the opportunities for the two kinds of knowledge to enrich one another, as in the case of Arctic Borderlands Ecological Knowledge Co-op (Kofinas *et al.* 2002; Eamer 2006).

Learning from Traditional Knowledge

The explosion of interest in traditional ecological knowledge in recent years reflects the need for ecological insights from indigenous practices of resource use, and the need to develop a new ecological ethic based in part on indigenous wisdom. By treating indigenous ways of knowing as a knowledge–practice–belief complex, we can examine empirical knowledge, practice, institutions, and worldviews, and their dynamics, together. The main lessons of traditional knowledge, as summarized here, fall into three clusters: the first addresses the unity and diversity of indigenous systems; the second, the importance of participatory and community-based resource management; and the third, the ethics of a sacred ecology.

Unity and Diversity of Indigenous Systems

Traditional management systems pose a paradox. On the one hand, they are characterized by an extraordinary similarity of basic designs shared by different cultures in different geographic areas in comparable ecosystems. Examples include shifting cultivation developed by peoples of tropical forests worldwide, and reef and lagoon tenure systems of island peoples dependent on marine resources. On the other hand, they are characterized by a remarkable diversity in practice, even in adjacent areas. For example, in shifting cultivation, the actual crop mix used and the details of practice vary; in reef and lagoon tenure, the set of rules used and the mix of exploitation-control mechanisms differ; and in semiarid-area herding systems, the details of rotation and migration are all fine-tuned to the local environment and vary from one area and group to the next. Also notable is the evidence that rules may be used flexibly and may vary from one year to the

next, using cues from the ecosystem as feedback to adjust for environmental fluctuations, based on an accumulation of traditional knowledge (Berkes *et al.* 2000;
Parlee *et al.* 2006).

Traditional ecological knowledge is considered by some to be merely locally
relevant because it is locally developed. This is a very limited view. Many practices
are common enough to be called principles; these include rotation of exploited
areas and use of territorial systems, as found in different kinds of ecosystems. The
Dene practice of monitoring the fat content of caribou as a qualitative management
measure is found not only in adjacent areas and related cultural groups, but right
across North America from Alaska to Labrador. The use of fat content as a monitoring tool that integrates a range of ecosystem information is also found in seabird
harvesting systems of the Maori of New Zealand, indicating the potential for gener-
ating universal management principles from some locally developed practices.

These findings are consistent with the historical and evolutionary view of
indigenous resource management systems as adaptive responses that have evolved
over time, not as mere traditions. Scholars have paid relatively little attention to the
evolution of traditional knowledge systems, but there is evidence of what evolutionary biologists call convergent evolution, adaptive radiation, co-evolution, and
punctuated equilibrium. Chapter 6 provides evidence that adaptive responses
resulting in a change in management practice and worldview may be explained by
social learning and cultural evolution, sometimes triggered by a resource crisis.
Chapter 10 emphasizes the various mechanisms by which local knowledge is elaborated to become time-tested, multi-generational traditional knowledge. There is
much experimentation and learning in the process.

The lesson for Western science is that we should perhaps be building resource
management systems that are open to alternative ways of thinking. Rather than
being conceptually closed, we need a science compatible with pluralistic ways of
thinking about the world (Miller *et al.* 2008). This requires an explicit recognition
that our multiple models in Western science "do not fit into a single, coherent understanding. . . . Conceptual pluralism is what we have" (Norgaard 1994: 96). This
pluralism can include different ways of knowing, non-Western knowledge about
specific ecosystems as well as non-Western perspectives in interpreting that knowledge. Western science, as a product of Western culture, represents but one cultural
perspective. There are different ways of knowing and no one universal standard for
determining the validity of knowledge. For some, this is no doubt a controversial
view that runs counter to the conventional wisdom of positivist science.

Participatory, Community-based Resource Management

A second lesson from traditional systems concerns the central importance of
community-based processes in the development of practices and rules, and hence

the necessity of incorporating participatory processes into contemporary resource management. There is evidence of a general tendency for community self-organization toward building institutions in parallel with building knowledge for sustainable practice. However, examples such as those in Chapter 10 also show that even though the development of local knowledge is a necessary condition, it is often not a sufficient condition for sustainability.

The fundamental issue is one of defining commons rights for shared resources such as forests, grazing lands, wildlife, and fisheries (Ostrom *et al.* 2002). Over historical time, property rights in resources in many parts of the world have been transformed from communal property (in which access and management rights are controlled by an identifiable group) to open access (free-for-all). Restoring traditional resource tenure can pave the way to establishing property rights in areas in which resource harvesting had previously operated under nonsustainable, open-access conditions. Once property rights and resource use rules have been established, both the costs and benefits of any management action will be borne by the same individual or group, thus providing an incentive to conserve.

Whether rural and traditional peoples practice conservation or not depends more on this fundamental point than on any supposed natural inclination of a group to act as conservers or nonconservers. Illustrations include the development of mangrove conservation in Chapter 10. Traditional peoples, like all peoples, respond to incentives. Self-interest, coupled with social sanctions, is key to biodiversity conservation and sustainable resource use in general. Resource rights, balanced against responsibilities, strengthen the traditional conservation ethic wherever it may exist, together with communal resource management systems that sustain these rights (Berkes 1989a; Trosper 2009; Painemilla *et al.* 2010).

Traditional systems inspire a new resource management science open to the participation of resource users in management, one that uses locally grounded alternatives to top-down centralized resource management (Sherry and Myers 2002; Kendrick 2003). The subsidiarity principle is the general principle here: using as much local-level management as possible; only so much government regulation as necessary. This helps humanize resource management, addressing local needs and taking into account local knowledge, practice, and values. Local participation in decision-making requires capacity building through a knowledge of the land and an understanding of cultural landscapes (Suchet-Pearson and Howitt 2006). Social learning is the key to combining participation with Adaptive Management (Armitage *et al.* 2007), and to building adaptive capacity in the face of social and environmental change (Armitage *et al.* 2011).

The use of traditional knowledge is especially important in the context of indigenous peoples' empowerment. Many aboriginal people, from the Australian outback to the Brazilian Amazon, are raising concerns about resource depletion and are demanding a share in management decisions. The use of traditional knowledge provides a mechanism, a point of entry, to implement co-management and self-government and to integrate local values into decision-making (King 2004; Borrini-Feyerabend *et al.* 2004b; Ross *et al.* 2009). Respect for indigenous knowledge and management systems levels the playing field and helps find a new balance against an expert-dominated positivist science.

Ethics of Sacred Ecology

A third lesson from traditional systems concerns the potential to forge new ethical principles for ecology and resource management. Traditional knowledge has the power to address some of the shortcomings of the contemporary Western knowledge–practice–belief complex, as identified by various scholars: restoring the unity of mind and nature; providing intuitive wisdom for developing awareness of the nonlinear nature of our environment; addressing the problem of a self-identity distinct from the world around us; and restoring a cosmology based on morality toward nature.

Bringing nature and culture together to re-integrate humans back into the ecosystem, or "the unity of mind and nature" in Bateson's metaphorical language, is perhaps the cornerstone of the above list of challenges. Bateson himself did not write about indigenous knowledge, but he certainly did know about indigenous ways of knowing from his own anthropological research in Oceania. His concept of the sacred (Bateson and Bateson 1987: 2) is a good fit with the sacred ecology practiced by many indigenous and other peoples of the world. A fundamental lesson of such sacred ecology is that worldviews are important. Positivist science, despite claims to the contrary, has its own value-laden assumptions. If the notion of "man's dominion over nature" symbolizes the positivist paradigm, the "community-of-beings" worldview symbolizes sacred ecology. Some kinds of ecology accept the latter idea, but much of contemporary ecology uses reductionistic thinking, which is not helpful to the task of uniting mind and nature.

The challenge is to cultivate a kind of post-positivist ecology that rejects the materialist tradition and questions the Newtonian, machine-like view of ecosystems, the one with ecological cycles pictured as giant gears powered by the sun. The indigenous knowledge systems of diverse groups, from the Cree and the Dene of the North American subarctic, to the Maori and the Fijians of the South Pacific, provide an alternative view of ecosystems. This is a view of an ecosystem pulsating with life and spirit, incorporating people who *belong* to that land and who have a relationship of peaceful coexistence with other beings.

In many indigenous views, such a coexistence does not preclude the human use of resources. In Leopold's (1949) land ethics, it is the humans who are to extend *their* ethics to include nature; animals have no obligations toward humans, at least no explicit obligations. By contrast, in James Bay Cree ethics (as outlined in Chapter 5), and in North American Indian ethics in general, the relationship is not one-way, and there is explicit human–nature reciprocity in which animals have obligations to nourish humans in return for respect and other proper behavior (Callicott 1994; Preston 2002).

Some authors reject indigenous peoples' ethics as human-centric and use-oriented and confuse it with utilitarianism. Many systems of indigenous ethics not only include human–nature reciprocity but are deeply moral. This point sharply distinguishes most indigenous ethics from utilitarianism, which is characterized by an amoral approach to commodification of nature. In building new ecological ethics, traditional ecological knowledge bridges the gap between utilitarianism as a kind of human-centric ethics, and biocentric ethics. A series of ideas in environmental ethics, including Leopold's land ethics, deep ecology, Gaia, topophilia/love of land, sense of place, bioregionalism, and biophilia/love of living beings, has explored the personal meaning and sacred dimensions of ecology that have been missing from scientific ecology. The knowledge–practice–belief complex of many indigenous traditions incorporates wisdom that has implicitly or explicitly inspired many of these ideas about the centrality and beauty of the larger whole and the place of humans in it.

References

Acheson, J. M. 1975. "The lobster fiefs": economic and ecological effects on territoriality in the Maine lobster industry. *Human Ecology* 3: 183–207.

Acheson, J. M. 2003. *Capturing the Commons. Devising Institutions to Manage the Maine Lobster Industry.* Lebanon, NH: University Press of New England.

ACIA. 2005. *Arctic Climate Impact Assessment.* Cambridge: Cambridge University Press. [online]: http://www.acia.uaf.edu

Adoukonou-Sagbadja, H., A. Dansi, R. Vodouhe, and K. Akpagana. 2006. Indigenous knowledge and traditional conservation of fonio millet (*Digitaria exilis, Digitaria iburua*) in Togo. *Biodiversity and Conservation* 15: 2379–95.

Agrawal, A. 1995a. Indigenous and scientific knowledge: some critical comments. *Indigenous Knowledge and Development Monitor* 3(3): 3–6.

Agrawal, A. 1995b. Dismantling the divide between indigenous and scientific knowledge. *Development and Change* 26: 413–39.

Agrawal, A. 1997. *Community in Conservation: Beyond Enchantment and Disenchantment.* Gainesville, FL: Conservation and Development Forum Discussion Paper.

Agrawal, A. 2002. Indigenous knowledge and the politics of classification. *International Social Science Journal* 173: 287–97.

Agrawal, A. 2005. *Environmentality.* Durham, NC: Duke University Press.

Ahmed, M., A. D. Capistrano, and M. Hossain. 1997. Experience of partnership models for the co-management of Bangladesh fisheries. *Fisheries Management and Ecology* 4: 233–48.

Alcorn, J. B. 1984. *Huastec Mayan Ethnobotany.* Austin, TX: University of Texas Press.

Alcorn, J. B. 1989. Process as resource. *Advances in Economic Botany* 7: 63–77.

Alcorn, J. B. 1990. Indigenous agroforestry strategies meeting farmers' needs. In *Alternatives to Deforestation* (A. B. Anderson, ed.). New York: Columbia University Press, 141–51.

Alcorn, J. B. 1993. Indigenous peoples and conservation. *Conservation Biology* 7: 424–6.

Alcorn, J. B. 1994. Noble savage or noble state? Northern myths and southern realities in biodiversity conservation. *Ethnoecológica* 2(3): 7–19.

Alcorn, J. B. and V. M. Toledo. 1998. Resilient resource management in Mexico's forest ecosystems: the contribution of property rights. In *Linking Social and Ecological Systems* (F. Berkes and C. Folke, eds). Cambridge: Cambridge University Press, 216–49.

Alcorn, J. B., J. Bamba, S. Maisun, I. Natalia, and A. G. Royo. 2003. Keeping ecological resilience afloat in cross-scale turbulence: an indigenous social movement navigates change in Indonesia. In *Navigating Social–Ecological Systems* (F. Berkes, J. Colding, and C. Folke, eds). Cambridge: Cambridge University Press, 299–327.

Alegret, J. L. 1995. Co-management of resources and conflict management: the case of the fishermen's *confreries* in Catalonia. MARE Working Paper No. 2. Aarhus, Denmark: Aarhus University.

Alexiades, M. N. (ed.) 2009. *Mobility and Migration in Indigenous Amazonia*. New York and Oxford: Berghahn.

Alvard, M. S. 1993. Testing the "ecologically noble savage" hypothesis: interspecific prey choice by Piro hunters of Amazonian Peru. *Human Ecology* 21: 355–87.

Amarasinghe, U. S., W. U. Chandrasekara, and H. M. P. Kithsiri. 1997. Traditional practices for resource sharing in an artisanal fishery of a Sri Lankan estuary. *Asian Fisheries Science* 9: 311–23.

Amend, T., J. Brown, A. Kothari, A. Phillips, and S. Stolton (eds) 2008. *Protected Landscapes and Agrobiodiversity Values*. Gland: IUCN and GTZ.

Anadón, J. D., A. Giménez, R. Ballestar and I. Pérez. 2009. Evaluation of local ecological knowledge as a method for collecting extensive data on animal abundance. *Conservation Biology* 23: 617–625.

Anderson, E. N. 1996. *Ecologies of the Heart: Emotion, Belief, and the Environment*. New York: Oxford University Press.

Anderson, E. N. and F. M. Tzuc. 2005. *Animals and the Maya in Quintana Roo*. Tucson, AZ: University of Arizona Press.

Anderson, M. K. 2005. *Tending the Wild: Native American Knowledge and the Management of California's Natural Resources*. Berkeley, CA: University of California Press.

Anderson, M. K. and M. G. Barbour. 2003. Simulated indigenous management: a new model for ecological restoration in national parks. *Ecological Restoration* 21: 269–77.

André, N. 1989. Shamanism among the Montagnais. *Rencontre* 10(3): 5–6.

Arctic Borderlands Ecological Knowledge Co-op. 2011. [online]: http://www.taiga.net/coop/index.html

Ari, Y., A. Soykan, F. Caki, D. Tokdemir, and D. Aykir. 2005. Cultural ecology of Kaz Mountain National Park. Scientific and Technical Research Council of Turkey, Project No. Caydag—103Y105. Balikesir, Turkey.

Armitage, D. 2003. Traditional agroecological knowledge, adaptive management and the socio-politics of conservation in Central Sulawesi, Indonesia. *Environmental Conservation* 30: 79–90.

Armitage, D., F. Berkes, and N. Doubleday (eds). 2007. *Adaptive Co-management: Collaboration, Learning, and Multi-Level Governance*. Vancouver: University of British Columbia Press.

Armitage, D., F. Berkes, A. Dale, E. Kocho-Schellenberg, and E. Patton. 2011. Co-management and the co-production of knowledge: learning to adapt in Canada's Arctic. *Global Environmental Change* 21: 995–1004.

Arnakak, J. 2002. Incorporation of Inuit Qaujimanituqangit, or Inuit traditional knowledge into the Government of Nunavut. *The Journal of Aboriginal Economic Development* 3: 33–39.

Aswani, S. 1997. Troubled waters in south-western New Georgia, Solomon Islands. *Traditional Marine Resource Management and Knowledge Information Bulletin* 8: 2–16.

Aswani, S. and R. J. Hamilton. 2004. Integrating indigenous ecological knowledge and customary sea tenure with marine and social science for conservation of bumphead parrotfish (*Bolbometopon muricatum*) in the Roviana Lagoon, Solomon Islands. *Environmental Conservation* 31(1): 69–82.

Aswani, S. and M. Lauer. 2006a. Benthic mapping using local aerial photo interpretation and resident taxa inventories for designing marine protected areas. *Environmental Conservation* 33: 263–73.

Aswani S. and M. Lauer. 2006b. Incorporating fishers' local knowledge and behaviour into geographical information systems (GIS) for designing marine protected areas in Oceania. *Human Organization* 65: 80–101.

Athayde, S. F., A. Kalabi, K. Y. Ono and M. N. Alexiades. 2009. Weaving power: displacement and the dynamics of basketry knowledge amongst the Kaiabi in the Brazilian Amazon. In *Mobility and Migration in Indigenous Amazonia* (M. N. Alexiades, ed.). New York: Berghahn, 249–70.

Atleo, E. R. (Umeek). 2004. *Tsawalk: A Nuu-chah-nulth Worldview*. Vancouver: University of British Columbia Press.

Babaluk, J. A., J. D. Reist, J. D. Johnson, and L. Johnson. 2000. First records of sockeye (*Oncorhynchus nerka*) and pink salmon (*O. gorbuscha*) from Banks Island and other records of Pacific salmon in Northwest Territories, Canada. *Arctic* 53: 161–4.

Bahn, P. G. 1996. Further back down under. *Nature* 383: 577–8.

Baines, G. B. K. 1989. Traditional resource management in the Melanesian South Pacific: a development dilemma. In *Common Property Resources* (F. Berkes, ed.). London: Belhaven, 273–95.

Baines, G. B. K. 1991. Asserting traditional rights: community conservation in Solomon Islands. *Cultural Survival Quarterly* 15(2): 49–52.

Baines, G. and E. Hviding. 1993. Traditional environmental knowledge for resource management in Marovo, Solomon Islands. In *Traditional Ecological Knowledge: Wisdom for Sustainable Development* (N. M. Williams and G. Baines, eds). Canberra: Centre for Resource and Environmental Studies, Australian National University, 56–65.

Balée, W. 1994. *Footprints of the Forest. Ka'apor Ethnobotany—the Historical Ecology of Plant Utilization by an Amazonian People.* New York: Columbia University Press.

Ballard, C. 1997. It's the land, stupid! The moral economy of resource ownership in Papua New Guinea. In *The Governance of Common Property in the Pacific Region* (P. Larmour, ed.). Canberra: Australian National University, 47–65.

Ballard, H. L. and L. Hunstinger. 2006. Salal harvester local ecological knowledge, harvest practices and understory management on the Olympic Peninsula, Washington. *Human Ecology* 34: 529–47.

Ballard, H. L., M. E. Fernandez-Gimenez, and V. E. Sturtevant. 2008. Integration of local ecological knowledge and conventional science: a study of seven community-based forestry organizations in the USA. *Ecology and Society* 13(2): 37. [online]: http://www.ecologyandsociety.org/vol13/iss2/art37/

Banfield, A. F. W. and J. S. Tener. 1958. A preliminary study of the Ungava caribou. *Journal of Mammalogy* 39: 560–73.

Banuri, T. and F. Apffel Marglin (eds). 1993. *Who Will Save the Forests?* London: United Nations University/Zed Books.

Barnston, G. 1861. Recollections of the swans and geese of Hudson's Bay. *Canadian Naturalist and Geologist* 6: 337–44.

Barreiro, J. 1992. The search for lessons. *Akwe:kon Journal* 9(2): 18–39.

Barrera-Bassols, N. and V. M. Toledo. 2005. Ethnoecology of the Yucatec Maya: symbolism, knowledge and management of natural resources. *Journal of Latin American Geography* 4: 9–41.

Barsh, R. L. 1997. Fire on the land. *Alternatives Journal* 23(4): 36–40.

Basso, K. H. 1972. Ice and travel among the Fort Norman Slave: folk taxonomies and cultural rules. *Language in Society* 1: 31–49.

Bateson, G. 1972. *Step to an Ecology of Mind.* New York: Ballantine.

Bateson, G. 1979. *Mind and Nature: A Necessary Unity.* New York: Dutton.

Bateson, G. and M. C. Bateson. 1987. *Angels Fear: Towards an Epistemology of the Sacred.* New York: Bantam Books.

Battiste, M. and J. (Sa'ke'j) Youngblood Henderson. 2000. *Protecting Indigenous Knowledge and Heritage.* Saskatoon: Purich Publishing.

Bearskin, J., G. Lameboy, R. Matthew, J. Pepabano, A. Pisinaquan, W. Ratt, and D. Rupert. 1989. *Cree Trappers Speak* (compiled and ed. by F. Berkes). Chisasibi, Quebec: Cree Trappers Association's Committee of Chisasibi and the James Bay Cree Cultural Education Centre.

Beaucage, P. and Taller de Tradición Oral del Cepec. 1997. Integrating innovation: the traditional Nahua coffee-orchard (Sierra Norte de Puebla, Mexico). *Journal of Ethnobiology* 17: 45–67.

Begossi, A. 1998. Resilience and neo-traditional populations: the *caicaras* (Atlantic forest) and *caboclos* (Amazon, Brazil). In *Linking Social and Ecological Systems* (F. Berkes and C. Folke, eds). Cambridge: Cambridge University Press, 129–57.

Begossi, A., N. Hanazaki, and N. Peroni. 2000. Knowledge and the use of biodiversity in Brazilian hot spots. *Environment, Development and Sustainability* 2: 177–93.

Begossi, A., N. Hanazaki and J. Y. Tamashiro 2002. Medicinal plants in the Atlantic Forest (Brazil): knowledge, use and conservation. *Human Ecology* 30: 281–299.

Begossi, A., S. V. Salivonchyk, L. G. Araujo *et al.* 2011. Ethnobiology of snappers (*Lutjanidae*): target species and suggestions for management. *Journal of Ethnobiology and Ethnomedicine* 7: 11.

Behnke, R. H., I. Scoones, and C. Kerven (eds). 1993. *Range Management at Disequilibrium: New Models of Natural Variability and Pastoral Adaptation in African Savannas.* London: Overseas Development Institute.

Belcher, B., M. Ruiz-Pérez, and R. Achdiawan. 2005. Global patterns and trends in the use and management of commercial NTFPs: implications for livelihoods and conservation. *World Development* 33: 1435–52.

Berkes, F. 1977. Fishery resource use in a subarctic Indian community. *Human Ecology* 5: 289–307.

Berkes F. 1979. An investigation of Cree Indian domestic fisheries in northern Quebec. *Arctic* 32: 46–70.

Berkes, F. 1981a. Some environmental and social impacts of the James Bay hydroelectric project, Canada. *Journal of Environmental Management* 12: 157–72.

Berkes, F. 1981b. Fisheries of the James Bay area and northern Quebec: a case study in resource management. In *Renewable Resources and the Economy of the North* (M. M. R. Freeman, ed.). Ottawa: Association of Canadian Universities for Northern Studies/Man and the Biosphere Program, 143–60.

Berkes, F. 1982. Waterfowl management and northern native peoples with reference to Cree hunters of James Bay. *Musk-Ox* 30: 23–35.

Berkes, F. 1985. Fishermen and the "tragedy of the commons." *Environmental Conservation* 12: 199–206.

Berkes, F. 1986a. Common property resources and hunting territories. *Anthropologica* 28: 145–62.

Berkes, F. 1986b. Chisasibi Cree hunters and missionaries: humour as evidence of tension. In *Actes du Dix-Septième Congrès des Algonquinistes* (W. Cowan, ed.). Ottawa: Carleton University Press, 15–26.

Berkes, F. 1987a. Common property resource management and Cree Indian fisheries in subarctic Canada. In *The Question of the Commons* (B. J. McCay and J. M. Acheson, eds). Tucson, AZ: University of Arizona Press, 66–91.

Berkes, F. 1987b. The common property resource problem and the fisheries of Barbados and Jamaica. *Environmental Management* 11: 225–35.

Berkes, F. 1988a. The intrinsic difficulty of predicting impacts: lessons from the James Bay hydro project. *Environmental Impact Assessment Review* 8: 201–20.

Berkes, F. 1988b. Environmental philosophy of the Cree people of James Bay. In *Traditional Knowledge and Renewable Resource Management in Northern Regions* (M. M. R. Freeman and L. Carbyn, eds). Edmonton: Boreal Institute, University of Alberta, 7–21.

Berkes, F. (ed). 1989a. *Common Property Resources: Ecology and Community-Based Sustainable Development*. London: Belhaven.

Berkes, F. 1989b. Cooperation from the perspective of human ecology. In *Common Property Resources: Ecology and Community-Based Sustainable Development* (F. Berkes, ed.). London: Belhaven, 70–88.

Berkes, F. 1992. Success and failure in marine coastal fisheries of Turkey. In *Making the Commons Work* (D. W. Bromley, ed.). San Francisco, CA: Institute for Contemporary Studies Press, 161–82.

Berkes, F. 1993. Traditional ecological knowledge in perspective. In *Traditional Ecological Knowledge: Concepts and Cases* (J. T. Inglis, ed.). Ottawa: Canadian Museum of Nature and the International Development Research Centre, 1–9.

Berkes, F. 1998. Indigenous knowledge and resource management systems in the Canadian subarctic. In *Linking Social and Ecological Systems* (F. Berkes and C. Folke, eds). Cambridge: Cambridge University Press, 98–128.

Berkes, F. 2001. Religious traditions and biodiversity. *Encyclopedia of Biodiversity*, Vol. 5. San Diego, CA: Academic Press, 109–20.

Berkes, F. 2007. Community-based conservation in a globalized world. *Proceedings of the National Academy of Sciences* 104: 15188–15193.

Berkes, F. 2009a. Indigenous ways of knowing and the study of environmental change. *Journal of the Royal Society of New Zealand* 39: 151–6.

Berkes, F. 2009b. Community conserved areas: policy issues in historic and contemporary context. *Conservation Letters* 2: 19–24.

Berkes, F. 2011. Restoring unity: the concept of social-ecological systems. In *World Fisheries: A Social-Ecological Analysis* (R. E. Ommer, R. I. Perry, K. Cochrane, and P. Cury, eds). Oxford: Wiley-Blackwell, 9–28.

Berkes, F. and M. MacKenzie. 1978. Cree fish names from eastern James Bay, Quebec. *Arctic* 31: 489–95.

Berkes F. and T. Gonenc. 1982. A mathematical model on the exploitation of northern lake whitefish with gill nets. *North American Journal of Fisheries Management* 2: 176–83.

Berkes, F. and A. H. Smith. 1995. Coastal marine property rights: the second transformation. In *Philippine Coastal Resources Under Stress* (M. A. Juinio-Menez and G. F. Newkirk, eds). Quezon City: University of the Philippines, 103–13.

Berkes, F. and H. Fast. 1996. Aboriginal peoples: the basis for policy-making towards sustainable development. In *Achieving Sustainable Development* (A. Dale and J. B. Robinson, eds). Vancouver: University of British Columbia Press, 204–64.

Berkes, F. and T. Henley. 1997. Co-management and traditional knowledge: threat or opportunity? *Policy Options* March: 29–31.

Berkes, F. and C. Folke (eds). 1998. *Linking Social and Ecological Systems: Management Practices and Social Mechanisms for Building Resilience*. Cambridge: Cambridge University Press.

Berkes, F. and D. Jolly. 2001. Adapting to climate change: social-ecological resilience in a Canadian western Arctic community. *Conservation Ecology* 5: 18. [online]: http://www.consecol.org/vol5/iss2/art18

Berkes, F. and C. Folke. 2002. Back to the future: ecosystem dynamics and local knowledge. In *Panarchy: Understanding Transformations in Human and Natural Systems* (L. H. Gunderson and C. S. Holling, eds). Washington, DC: Island Press, 121–46.

Berkes, F. and T. Adhikari. 2006. Development and conservation: indigenous businesses and the UNDP Equator Initiative. *International Journal of Entrepreneurship and Small Business* 3: 671–90.

Berkes, F. and I. J. Davidson-Hunt. 2006. Biodiversity, traditional management systems, and cultural landscapes: examples from the boreal forest of Canada. *International Social Science Journal* 187: 35–47.

Berkes, F. and N. J. Turner. 2006. Knowledge, learning and the evolution of conservation practice for social-ecological system resilience. *Human Ecology* 34: 479–94.

Berkes, F. and M. Kislalioglu Berkes. 2009. Ecological complexity, fuzzy logic and holism in indigenous knowledge. *Futures* 40: 6–12.

Berkes, F. and D. Armitage. 2010. Co-management institutions, knowledge and learning: adapting to change in the Arctic. *Etudes/Inuit/Studies* 34: 109–31.

Berkes, F., H. Anat, M. Esenel, and M. Kislalioglu. 1979. Distribution and ecology of *Monachus monachus* on Turkish coasts. In *The Mediterranean Monk Seal* (K. Ronald and R. Duguy, eds). Oxford: Pergamon Press, 113–27.

Berkes, F., D. Feeny, B. J. McCay, and J. M. Acheson. 1989. The benefits of the commons. *Nature* 340: 91–3.

Berkes, F., P. J. George, R. J. Preston, A. Hughes, J. Turner, and B. D. Cummins. 1994. Wildlife harvesting and sustainable regional native economy in the Hudson and James Bay Lowland, Ontario. *Arctic* 47: 350–60.

Berkes, F., C. Folke, and M. Gadgil. 1995a. Traditional ecological knowledge, biodiversity, resilience and sustainability. In *Biodiversity Conservation* (C. Perrings, K.-G. Maler, C. Folke, C. S. Holling, and B.-O. Jansson, eds). Dordrecht: Kluwer, 281–99.

Berkes, F., A. Hughes, P. J. George, R. J. Preston, B. D. Cummins, and J. Turner. 1995b. The persistence of aboriginal land use: fish and wildlife harvest areas in the Hudson and James Bay Lowland, Ontario. *Arctic* 48: 81–93.

Berkes, F., J. Colding, and C. Folke. 2000. Rediscovery of traditional ecological knowledge as adaptive management. *Ecological Applications* 10: 1251–62.

Berkes, F., J. Colding and C. Folke (eds). 2003. *Navigating Social-Ecological Systems: Building Resilience for Complexity and Change*. Cambridge: Cambridge University Press.

Berkes, F., T. P. Hughes, R. S. Steneck *et al.* 2006. Globalization, roving bandits and marine resources. *Science* 311: 1557–8.

Berkes, F., M. Kislalioglu Berkes, and H. Fast. 2007. Collaborative integrated management in Canada's North: the role of local and traditional knowledge and community-based monitoring. *Coastal Management* 35: 143–62.

Berkes, F., G. P. Kofinas, and F. S. Chapin, III. 2009. Conservation, community and livelihoods. In *Principles of Ecosystem Stewardship* (F. S. Chapin, III, G. P. Kofinas and C. Folke, eds). New York: Springer, 129–47.

Berlin, B. 1973. Folk systematics in relation to biological classification and nomenclature. *Annual Review of Ecology and Systematics* 4: 259–71.

Berlin, B. 1992. *Ethnobotanical Classification: Principles of Categorization of Plants and Animals in Traditional Societies*. Princeton, NJ: Princeton University Press.

Berlin, B., D. E. Breedlove, and P. H. Raven. 1974. *Principles of Tzeltal Plant Classification: An Introduction to the Botanical Ethnography of a Mayan-Speaking People of Highland Chiapas*. New York: Academic Press.

Berry, T. 1988. *The Dream of the Earth*. San Francisco, CA: Sierra Club Books.

Bezdec, J. 1992. Fuzzy models—what are they and why? *Transactions on Fuzzy Systems* 1: 1–5.

Bhagwat, S., C. Kushalappa, P. Williams, and N. Brown. 2005. The role of informal protected areas in maintaining biodiversity in the Western Ghats of India. *Ecology and Society* 10: 8. [online]: http://www.ecologyandsociety.org/vol10/iss1/art8/

Bhagwat, S. A., K. J. Willis, H. C. B. Birks and R. J. Whittaker. 2008. Agroforestry: A refuge for tropical biodiversity? *Trends in Ecology & Evolution* 23: 261–7.

Bhagwat, S. A., N. Dudley and S. R. Harrop. 2011. Religious following in biodiversity hotspots: challenges and opportunities for conservation and development. *Conservation Letters* 4: 234–40.

Bielawski, E. 1992. Inuit indigenous knowledge and science in the Arctic. *Northern Perspectives* 20(1): 5–8.

Bird, D. W., R. B. Bird, and C. H. Parker. 2005. Aboriginal burning regimes and hunting strategies in Australia's western desert. *Human Ecology* 33: 443–64.

Bird, R. B., D. W. Bird, B. F. Codding, C. H. Parker, and J. H. Jones. 2008. The "fire stick farming" hypothesis: Australian aboriginal foraging strategies, biodiversity, and anthropogenic fire mosaics. *Proceedings of the National Academy of Sciences* 105: 14,796–801.

Bishop, C. A. and T. Morantz (eds). 1986. Who owns the beaver? Algonquian land tenure reconsidered. Special issue of *Anthropologica* 28(1 & 2).

Bjorkan, M. and M. Qvenild. 2010. The biodiversity discourse: categorisation of indigenous people in a Mexican bio-prospecting case. *Human Ecology* 38: 193–204.

Blackburn, T. C. and K. Anderson (eds). 1993. *Before the Wilderness: Environmental Management by Native Californians*. Menlo Park, CA: Ballena Press.

Blaikie, P. 1985. *The Political Economy of Soil Erosion in Developing Countries*. Harlow: Longman.

Blaikie, P. and S. Jeanrenaud. 1996. Biodiversity and human welfare. Geneva: United Nations Research Institute for Social Development (UNRISD) Discussion Paper No. 72.

Boas, F. 1934. *Geographical Names of the Kwakiutl Indians*. New York: Columbia University Press.

Bocco, G. 1991. Traditional knowledge for soil conservation in Central Mexico. *Journal of Soil and Water Conservation* 46: 346–48.

Bonny, E. and F. Berkes. 2008. Communicating traditional environmental knowledge: addressing the diversity of knowledge, audiences and media types. *Polar Record* 44: 243–53.

Borgerhoff Mulder, M. and P. Coppolillo. 2005. *Conservation: Linking Ecology, Economics, and Culture*. Princeton, NJ: Princeton University Press.

Borrini-Feyerabend, G. 1996. *Collaborative Management of Protected Areas: Tailoring the Approach to the Context*. Gland, Switzerland: IUCN (International Conservation Union).

Borrini-Feyerabend, G., A. Kothari, and G. Oviedo. 2004a. *Indigenous and Local Communities and Protected Areas*. Gland, Switzerland: World Commission on Protected Areas/IUCN (International Conservation Union).

Borrini-Feyerabend, G., M. Pimbert, M. T. Farvar, A. Kothari, and Y. Renard. 2004b. *Sharing Power. Learning-by-Doing in Co-management of Natural Resources Throughout the World*. Tehran: IIED and IUCN/CEESP, and Cenesta.

Boserup, E. 1965. *The Conditions for Agricultural Growth: The Economics of Agrarian Change Under Population Pressure*. Chicago, IL: Aldine.

Boyd, R.T. (ed.). 1999. *Indians, Fire and the Land in the Pacific Northwest*. Corvallis, OR: Oregon State University Press.

Brannlund, I. and P. Axelsson. 2011. Reindeer management during colonization of Sami lands: a long-term perspective of vulnerability and adaptation strategies. *Global Environmental Change* 21: 1095–105.

Brascoupe, S. 1992. Indigenous perspectives on international development. *Akwe:kon Journal* 9(2): 6–17.

Bray, D. B., L. Merino-Perez, P. Negreros-Castillo, G. Segura-Warnholtz, J. M. Torres-Rojo, and H. F. M. Vester. 2003. Mexico's community-managed forests as a global model for sustainable landscapes. *Conservation Biology* 17: 672–7.

Bray, D. B., L. Merino-Pérez, and D. Barry (eds.) 2005. *The Community Forests of Mexico: Managing for Sustainable Landscapes*. Austin: University of Texas Press.

Breton, Y., D. Brown, B. Davy, M. Haughton, and L. Ovares (eds). 2006. *Coastal Resource Management in the Wider Caribbean: Resilience, Adaptation, and Community Diversity*. Ottawa: International Development Research Centre.

Brightman, R. A. 1993. *Grateful Prey: Rock Cree Human–Animal Relationships*. Berkeley, CA: University of California Press.

Brokensha, D., D. M. Warren, and O. Werner (eds). 1980. *Indigenous Knowledge Systems and Development*. Washington, DC: University Press of America.

Bromley, D. W. (ed.). 1992. *Making the Commons Work*. San Francisco, CA: Institute for Contemporary Studies Press.

Bronowski, J. 1978. *The Origins of Knowledge and Imagination*. New Haven, CT and London: Yale University Press.

Brook, R. K. and S. M. McLachlan. 2008. Trends and prospects for local knowledge in ecological and conservation research and monitoring. *Biodiversity Conservation* 17: 3501–12.

Brookfield, H. and C. Padoch. 1994. Appreciating agrodiversity: a look at the dynamism and diversity of indigenous fanning practices. *Environment* 36(5): 6–11, 37–45.

Brosius, J. P. 1997. Endangered forest, endangered people: environmentalist representations of indigenous knowledge. *Human Ecology* 25: 47–69.

Brosius, P. 1999. Analyses and interventions: anthropological engagements with environmentalism. *Current Anthropology* 40: 277–309.

Brosius, J. P. 2001. Local knowledges, global claims: on the significance of indigenous ecologies in Sarawak, East Malaysia. In *Indigenous Traditions and Ecology* (J. A. Grim, ed.). Cambridge, MA: Harvard University Press, 125–57.

Brown, F. and Y. K. Brown (compilers). 2009. *Staying the Course, Staying Alive: Coastal First Nations Fundamental Truths: Biodiversity, Stewardship and Sustainability*. [online]: http://www.biodiversitybc.org

Brown, J. and A. Kothari. 2011. Traditional agricultural landscapes and community conserved areas: an overview. *Management of Environmental Quality* 22: 139–53.

Brown, J. E. (recorder and ed.). 1953. *The Sacred Pipe: Black Elk's Account of the Seven Rites of the Oglala Sioux*. Norman, OK: University of Oklahoma Press.

Brush, S. and D. Stabinsky. 1996. *Valuing Local Knowledge: Indigenous People and Intellectual Property Rights*. Washington, DC: Island Press.

Bruun, O. and A. Kalland (eds). 1995. *Asian Perceptions of Nature: A Critical Approach*. London: Curzon Press.

Bryan, J. 2011. Walking the line: participatory mapping, indigenous rights and neoliberalism. *Geoforum* 42: 40–50.

Buege, D. J. 1996. The ecologically noble savage revisited. *Environmental Ethics* 18: 71–88.

Butler, C. 2004. Researching traditional ecological knowledge for multiple uses. *Canadian Journal of Native Education* 28: 33–47.

Butz, D. 1996. Sustaining indigenous communities: symbolic and instrumental dimensions of pastoral resource use in Shimshal, Northern Pakistan. *Canadian Geographer* 40: 36–53.

Byg, A., J. Salick and W. Law. 2010. Medicinal plant knowledge among lay people in five eastern Tibet villages. *Human Ecology* 38: 177–91.

Cajete, G. 2000. *Native Science: Natural Laws of Interdependence*. Santa Fe, NM: Clear Light Publishers.

Callicott, J. B. 1982. Traditional American Indian and Western European attitudes toward nature: an overview. *Environmental Ethics* 4: 293–318.

Callicott, J. B. (ed.). 1989. *In Defense of the Land Ethic: Essays in Environmental Philosophy*. Albany, NY: State University of New York Press.

Callicott, J. B. 1994. *Earth's Insights: A Survey of Ecological Ethics from the Mediterranean Basin to the Australian Outback*. Berkeley, CA: University of California Press.

Callicott, J. B. 2008. The new new (Buddhist?) ecology. *Journal for the Study of Religion, Nature and Culture* 2: 166–82.

Camou-Guerrero A., V. Reyes-Garcia, M. Martinez-Ramos, and A. Casas. 2008. Knowledge and use value of plant species in a Rarámuri community: a gender perspective for conservation. *Human Ecology* 36: 259–72.

Capistrano, D., C. Samper K., M. J. Lee, and C. Raudsepp-Hearne (eds). 2005. *Ecosystems and Human Well-being: Multiscale Assessments, Vol. 4*. Washington DC: Millennium Ecosystem Assessment and Island Press. [online]: http://www.maweb.org/en/Multiscale.aspx

Capra, F. 1982. *The Turning Point*. New York: Simon & Schuster.

Capra, F. 1996. *The Web of Life*. New York: Anchor Books, Doubleday.

Castello, L. 2003. A method to count pirarucu *Arapaima gigas*: fishers, assessment, and management. *North American Journal of Fisheries Management* 24: 379–89.

Castello, L., J. P. Viana, G. Watkins *et al.* 2009. Lessons from integrating fishers of Arapaima in small-scale fisheries management at the Mamirauá Reserve, Amazon. *Environmental Management* 43: 197–209.

Castillo, A. and V. M. Toledo. 2001. Applying ecology to the Third World. *BioScience* 50: 66–76.

Castro, P. 1990. Sacred groves and social change in Kirinyaga, Kenya. In *Social Change and Applied Anthropology* (M. Chaiken and A. Fleuret, eds). Boulder, CO: Westview Press, 277–89.

Ceci, L. 1978. Watchers of the Pleiades: Ethnoastronomy among native cultivators in northeastern North America. *Ethnohistory* 25: 301–17.

Cetinkaya, G. 2006. Medicinal and aromatic plants in Koprulu Canyon National Park, Turkey. *Biodiversity* 7: 31–6.

Chalmers, N. and C. Fabricius. 2007. Expert and generalist local knowledge about land-cover change on South Africa's Wild Coast: can local ecological knowledge add value to science? *Ecology and Society* 12(1): 10. [online]: http://www.ecologyandsociety.org/vol12/iss1/art10

Chambers, R. 1983. *Rural Development: Putting the Last First*. London: Longmans.

Chapin, F. S. III, G. P. Kofinas and C. Folke (eds) 2009. *Principles of Ecosystem Stewardship: Resilience-based Resource Management in a Changing World*. New York: Springer-Verlag.

Chapin, M. 1988. The seduction of models: Chinampa agriculture in Mexico. *Grassroots Development* 12(1): 8–17.

Chapin, M. 1991. Losing the way of the Great Father. *New Scientist* 131(1781): 40–4.

Chapin, M. and B. Threlkeld. 2001. *Indigenous Landscapes. A Study in Ethnocartography*. Arlington, VA: Center for the Support of Native Lands.

Chapin, M., Z. Lamb, and B. Threlkeld. 2005. Mapping indigenous lands. *Annual Review of Anthropology* 34: 619–38.

Chapman, M. D. 1985. Environmental influences on the development of traditional conservation in the South Pacific region. *Environmental Conservation* 12: 217–30.

Chapman, M. D. 1987. Traditional political structure and conservation in Oceania. *Ambio* 16: 201–5.

Christianty, L., O. S. Abdoellah, G. G. Marten, and J. Iskandar. 1986. Traditional agroforestry in West Java: the *pekarangan* (homegarden) and *kebun-talun* (annual-perennial rotation) cropping systems. In *Traditional Agriculture in Southeast Asia* (G. G. Marten, ed.). Boulder, CO: Westview, 132–58.

Christy, F. T. 1982. Territorial use rights in marine fisheries: definitions and conditions. Rome: FAO Fisheries Technical Paper No. 227.

Clement, D. 1995. *La Zoologie des Montagnais*. Paris: Editions Peters.

COASST. 2011. Coastal Observation and Seabird Survey Team. Seattle, WA: University of Washington [online]: http://depts.washington.edu/coasst

Cobb, D., M. Kislalioglu Berkes, and F. Berkes. 2005. Ecosystem-based management and marine environmental quality indicators in northern Canada. In *Breaking Ice* (F. Berkes, R. Huebert, H. Fast, M. Manseau, and A. Diduck, eds). Calgary: University of Calgary Press, 71–93.

Colby, B. N. 1966. Ethnographic semantics: a preliminary survey. *Current Anthropology* 7: 3–17.

Colchester, M. 1994. Salvaging nature: indigenous peoples, protected areas and biodiversity conservation. Geneva: UNRISD Discussion Paper No. 55.

Colding, J. 1998. Analysis of hunting options by the use of general food taboos. *Ecological Modelling* 110: 5–17.

Colding, J. and C. Folke. 1997. The relation between threatened species, their protection, and taboos. *Conservation Ecology* 1(1): 6. [online]: http://www.consecol.org/vol1/iss1/art6

Colding, J. and C. Folke. 2001. Social taboos: "invisible" systems of local resource management and biological conservation. *Ecological Applications* 11: 584–600.

Collier, R. and D. Vegh. 1998. Gitxsan mapping workshop. Crossing Boundaries: 7th Conference of the International Association for the Study of Common Property, June. Vancouver, British Columbia.

Colorado, P. 1988. Bridging native and western science. *Convergence* 21: 49–70.

Conelly, W. T. 1992. Agricultural intensification in a Philippine frontier community: impact on labor efficiency and farm diversity. *Human Ecology* 20: 203–23.

Conklin, H. C. 1957. Hanunoo agriculture. Report of an integral system of shifting cultivation in the Philippines. Rome: FAO Forestry Development Paper No. 5.

Cordell, J. 1995. Review of Traditional Ecological Knowledge (N. M. Williams and G. Baines, eds). *Journal of Political Ecology* 2: 43–7.

Cordova, V. F. 1997. Ecoindian: a response to J. Baird Callicott. *Ayaangwaamizin: The International Journal of Indigenous Philosophy* 1: 31–43.

Corsiglia, J. and G. Snively. 1997. Knowing home. *Alternatives Journal* 23(3): 22–7.

Costa-Pierce, B. A. 1987. Aquaculture in ancient Hawaii. *BioScience* 37: 320–30.

Costa-Pierce, B. A. 1988. Traditional fisheries and dualism in Indonesia. *Naga* 11(2): 34.

Coulthard, S. 2011. More than just access to fish: the pros and cons of fisher participation in a customary marine tenure (*padu*) system under pressure. *Marine Policy* 35: 405–412.

Couturier, S., J. Brunelle, D. Vandal, and G. St.-Martin. 1990. Changes in the population dynamics of the George River caribou herd, 1976–87. *Arctic* 43: 9–20.

Cox, M., G. Arnold, and S. Villamayor Tomás. 2010. A review of design principles for community-based natural resource management. *Ecology and Society* 15(4): 38. [online]: http://www.ecologyandsociety.org/vol15/iss4/art38

Cox, P. A. and T. Elmqvist. 1997. Ecocolonialism and indigenous-controlled rainforest preserves in Samoa. *Ambio* 26: 84–9.

Crate, S. A. 2006. *Cows, Kin and Globalization: An Ethnography of Sustainability.* Lanham, MD: AltaMira.

Crate, S. A. 2008. Gone the bull of winter? *Current Anthropology* 49: 569–95.

Crate, S. A. and M. Nuttall (eds). 2009. *Anthropology and Climate Change.* Walnut Cree, CA: Left Coast Press.

Cristancho, S. and J. Vining 2004. Culturally defined keystone species. *Human Ecology Review* 11: 153–64.

Crona, B., and Ö. Bodin. 2006. What you know is who you know? Communication patterns among resource users as a prerequisite for co-management. *Ecology and Society* 11(2): 7. [online]: http://www.ecologyandsociety.org/vol11/iss2/art7

Cronon, W. 1983. *Changes in the Land: Indians, Colonists, and the Ecology of New England.* New York: Hill & Wang.

Cruikshank, J. 1995. Introduction: changing traditions in northern ethnography. *The Northern Review* 14: 11–20.

Cruikshank, J. 1998. *The Social Life of Stories. Narrative and Knowledge in the Yukon Territory.* Lincoln, NB: University of Nebraska Press and Vancouver: University of British Columbia Press.

Cruikshank, J. 2001. Glaciers and climate change: perspectives from oral traditions. *Arctic* 54: 377–93.

Cruikshank, J. 2005. *Do Glaciers Listen? Local Knowledge, Colonial Encounters and Social Imagination.* Seattle, WA: University of Washington Press and Vancouver: University of British Columbia Press.

Cunningham, A. B. 2001. *Applied Ethnobotany: People, Wild Plant Use and Conservation.* London: Earthscan.

Dasmann, R. F. 1988. Towards a biosphere consciousness. In *The Ends of the Earth* (D. Worster, ed.). Cambridge: Cambridge University Press, 277–88.

Davidson-Hunt, I. J. 2003. Indigenous lands management, cultural landscapes and Anishinaabe people of Shoal Lake, Northwestern Ontario, Canada. *Environments* 31(1): 21–42.

Davidson-Hunt, I. J. 2006. Adaptive learning networks: developing resource management knowledge through social learning forums. *Human Ecology* 34: 593–614.

Davidson-Hunt, I. J. and F. Berkes. 2003. Learning as you journey: Anishnaabe perception of social-ecological environments and adaptive learning. *Conservation Ecology* 8(1): 5. [online]: http://www.consecol.org/vol8/iss1/art5

Davidson-Hunt, I. J. and R. M. O'Flaherty. 2007. Researchers, indigenous peoples and place-based learning communities. *Society and Natural Resources* 20: 291–305.

Davidson-Hunt, I. and F. Berkes. 2010. Journeying and remembering: Anishinaabe landscape ethnoecology from northwestern Ontario. In *Landscape Ethnoecology* (L. M. Johnson and E. S. Hunn, eds). New York and Oxford: Berghahn, 222–40.

Davidson-Hunt, I. J., P. Jack, E. Mandamin, and B. Wapioke. 2005. Iskatewizaagegan (Shoal Lake) plant knowledge: an Anishinaabe (Ojibway) ethnobotany of northwestern Ontario. *Journal of Ethnobiology* 25: 189–227.

Davies, J. 1999. More than "us" and "them": local knowledge and sustainable development in Australian rangelands. *Proceedings of the VI International Rangelands Congress*, 61–6.

Davis, A. and J. R. Wagner. 2003. Who knows? On the importance of identifying "experts" when researching local ecological knowledge. *Human Ecology* 31: 463–89.

Davis, A. and K. Ruddle. 2010. Constructing confidence: rational scepticism and systematic enquiry in local ecological knowledge research. *Ecological Applications* 20: 880–94.

Dei, G. J. S. 1992. A Ghanaian town revisited: changes and continuities in local adaptive strategies. *African Affairs* 91: 95–120.

Dei, G. J. S. 1993. Indigenous African knowledge systems: local traditions of sustainable forestry. *Singapore Journal of Tropical Geography* 14: 28–41.

Dekens, J. 2007. Local knowledge on disaster preparedness: a framework for data collection and analysis. *Sustainable Mountain Development* 52: 20–3.

Dene Cultural Institute. 1993. *Traditional Dene Environmental Knowledge: A Pilot Project Conducted in Ft. Good Hope and Colville Lake, NWT, 1989–1993.* Hay River, Northwest Territories: Dene Cultural Institute.

Denevan, W. M., J. M. Treacy, J. B. Alcorn, C. Padoch, J. Denslow, and S. F. Paitan. 1984. Indigenous agroforestry in the Peruvian Amazon: Bora Indian management of swidden fallows. *Interciencia* 9: 346–57.

Denslow, J. S. 1987. Tropical rainforest gaps and tree species diversity. *Annual Review of Ecology and Systematics* 18: 431–51.

De Schlippe, P. 1956. *Shifting Cultivation in Africa: The Zande System of Agriculture.* London: Routledge & Kegan Paul.

Deur, D. and N. J. Turner (eds). 2005. *"Keeping it Living": Traditions of Plant Use and Cultivation on the Northwest Coast of North America.* Seattle, WA: University of Washington Press.

Diamond, J. 1966. Zoological classification system of a primitive people. *Science* 151: 1102–4.

Diamond, J. 1993. New Guineans and their natural world. In *The Biophilia Hypothesis* (S. R. Kellert and E. O. Wilson, eds). Washington, DC: Island Press, 251–71.

Diamond, J. 2005. *Collapse. How Societies Choose to Fail or Succeed.* New York: Penguin Books.

Dickison, M. 1994. Maori science? *New Zealand Science Monthly* May: 6–7.

Dominguez, P., F. Zorondo-Rodriguez and V. Reyes-Garcia. 2010. Relationships between religious beliefs and mountain pasture uses: a case study in the high Atlas mountains of Marrakech, Morocco. *Human Ecology* 38: 351–62.

Doubleday, N. C. 1993. Finding common ground: natural law and collective wisdom. In *Traditional Ecological Knowledge: Concepts and Cases* (J. T. Inglis, ed.). Ottawa: Canadian Museum of Nature and the International Development Research Centre, 41–53.

Dove, M. R. 1993. A revisionist view of tropical deforestation and development. *Environmental Conservation* 20: 17–24.

Dove, M. 2002. Hybrid histories and indigenous knowledge among Asian rubber smallholders. *International Social Science Journal* 173: 349–59.

Drolet, C. A., A. Reed, M. Breton, and F. Berkes. 1987. Sharing wildlife management responsibilities with native groups: case histories in Northern Quebec. *Transactions of the 52nd North American Wildlife and Natural Resources Conference*, 389–98.

Dubos, R. 1972. *A God Within.* New York: Scribner.

Dudley, N., L. Higgins-Zogib and S. Mansourian. 2008. The links between protected areas, faiths, and sacred natural sites. *Conservation Biology* 23: 568–77.

Duerden, F. and R. G. Kuhn. 1998. Scale, context and the application of traditional knowledge of the Canadian North. *Polar Record* 34: 31–8.

Duffield, C., J. S. Gardner, F. Berkes, and R. B. Singh. 1998. Local knowledge in the assessment of resource sustainability: case studies in Himachal Pradesh, India, and British Columbia, Canada. *Mountain Research and Development* 18: 35–49.

Dunbar, M. J. 1973. Stability and fragility in Arctic ecosystems. *Arctic* 26: 179–85.

Dwyer, P. D. 1994. Modern conservation and indigenous peoples: in search of wisdom. *Pacific Conservation Biology* 1: 91–7.

Dymond, J. R. 1933. Biological and oceanographic conditions in Hudson Bay. 8. The Coregonine fishes of Hudson and James bays. *Contributions to Canadian Biology and Fisheries* 8 (NS) No. 28: 1–12.

Dyson-Hudson, R. and E. A. Smith. 1978. Human territoriality: an ecological assessment. *American Anthropologist* 80: 21–41.

Eamer, J. 2006. Keep it simple and be relevant: the first ten years of the Arctic Borderlands Ecological Knowledge Co-op. In *Bridging Scales and Knowledge Systems* (W. V. Reid, F. Berkes, T. Wilbanks, and D. Capistrano, eds). Washington, DC: Island Press, 185–206. [online]: http://www.maweb.org/documents/bridging/bridging.10.pdf

Edwards, S. E. and M. Henrich. 2006. Redressing cultural erosion and ecological decline in a far North Queensland aboriginal community (Australia): the Aurukun ethnobiology database project. *Environment, Development and Sustainability* 8: 569–83.

Ellen, R. 1993. Rhetoric, practice and incentive in the face of the changing times. In *Environmentalism: The View from Anthropology* (K. Milton, ed.). London and New York: Routledge, 126–43.

Ellen, R. (ed.) 2007. *Modern Crises and Traditional Strategies: Local Ecological Knowledge in Island Southeast Asia.* New York and Oxford: Berghahn.

Ellen, R. F. and P. Harris. 2000. Introduction. In *Indigenous Environmental Knowledge and its Transformations* (R. F. Ellen, A. Bicker and P. Parkes, eds). Amsterdam: Harwood, 213–51.

Ellen, R. F., P. Parkes, and A. Bicker (eds). 2000. *Indigenous Environmental Knowledge and its Transformations: Critical Anthropological Perspectives*. Amsterdam: Harwood.

Elton, C. 1942. *Voles, Mice and Lemmings: Problems in Population Dynamics*. London: Oxford University Press.

Emery, A. R. 1997. *Guidelines for Environmental Assessment and Traditional Knowledge. A Report from the Centre of Traditional Knowledge to the World Council of Indigenous People*. Ottawa: Centre for Traditional Knowledge.

Engel, J. R. and J. G. Engel (eds). 1990. *Ethics of Environment and Development*. London: Belhaven.

Ericksen, P. and E. Woodley. 2005. Using multiple knowledge systems in sub-global assessments: benefits and challenges. In *Ecosystems and Human Well-being: Multiscale Assessments, Vol. 4*. Washington, DC: Millennium Ecosystem Assessment and Island Press, 85–117. [online]: http://www.maweb.org/en/Multiscale.aspx

Ertug, F. 2000. An ethnobotanical study in central Anatolia, Turkey. *Economic Botany* 54: 155–82.

Evans, L. S. 2010. Ecological knowledge interactions in marine governance in Kenya. *Ocean & Coastal Management* 53: 180–191.

Evans, P. H. G. 1986. Dominica multiple land use project. *Ambio* 15: 82–9.

Evernden, N. 1993. *The Natural Alien: Humankind and Environment*, 2nd edn. Toronto: University of Toronto Press.

Eyzaguirre, P. B. and O. F. Linares (eds.) 2004. *Home Gardens and Agrobiodiversity*. Washington DC: Smithsonian.

Fairhead, J. and M. Leach. 1996. *Misreading the African Landscape: Society and Ecology in a Forest-Savanna Mosaic*. Cambridge: Cambridge University Press.

Fals-Borda, O. 1987. The application of participatory action-research in Latin America. *International Sociology* 2: 329–47.

Fathy, H. 1986. *Natural Energy and Vernacular Architecture*. Chicago, IL: University of Chicago Press.

Fazey, I, J. A. Fazey, J. G. Salisbury *et al.* 2006. The nature and role of experiential knowledge for environmental conservation. *Environmental Conservation* 33: 1–10.

Feeny, D., F. Berkes, B. J. McCay, and J. M. Acheson, 1990. The tragedy of the commons: twenty-two years later. *Human Ecology* 18: 1–19.

Feit, H. A. 1973. Ethno-ecology of the Waswanipi Cree; or how hunters can manage their resources. In *Cultural Ecology* (B. Cox, ed.). Toronto: McClelland & Stewart, 115–25.

Feit, H. A. 1986. James Bay Cree Indian management and moral considerations of fur-bearers. In *Native People and Resource Management*. Edmonton, Alberta: Society of Professional Zoologists, 49–65.

Feit, H. A. 1987. North American native hunting and management of moose populations. *Swedish Wildlife Research Vitlrevy Suppl.* 1: 25–42.

Feit, H. A. 1991. Gifts of the land: hunting territories, guaranteed incomes and the construction of social relations in James Bay Cree society. *Senri Ethnological Studies* 30: 223–68.

Felt, L. F. 1994. Two tales of a fish: the social construction of indigenous knowledge among Atlantic Canadian salmon fishers. In *Folk Management in the World's Fisheries* (C. L. Dyer and J. R. McGoodwin, eds). Niwot: University Press of Colorado, 251–86.

Feyerabend, P. 1987. *Farewell to Reason*. London: Verso.

Fienup-Riordan, A. 1990. *Eskimo Essays*. New Brunswick, NJ and London: Rutgers University Press.

Finlay, J. A. 1995. Community-level sea use management in the Grenada beach seine fishery. Master's thesis, University of the West Indies, Cave Hill, Barbados.

Flannery, K. V., J. Marcus, and R. G. Reynolds. 1989. *The Flocks of the Wamani: A Study of Llama Herders on the Punas of Ayacucho, Peru*. San Diego, CA: Academic Press.

Ford, J. D. and L. Berrang-Ford. 2009. Food security in Iglooloik, Nunavut: an exploratory study. *Polar Record* 45: 225–36.

Ford, N. 2000. Communicating climate change from the perspective of local people: a case study from Arctic Canada. *Journal of Development Communication* 1(11): 93–108.

Fox, J. 2002. Siam mapped and mapping in Cambodia: boundaries, sovereignty, and indigenous conceptions of space. *Society and Natural Resources* 15: 65–78.

Fox, S. 2003. When the weather is *uggianaqtuq*: Inuit observations of environmental change. CD-ROM. Boulder, Colorado: Cartography Lab, Geography, University of Colorado.

Francis, D. and T. Morantz. 1983. *Partners in Furs: A History of the Fur Trade in Eastern James Bay 1600–1870*. Montreal: McGill-Queens University Press.

Francis, R. C., M. A. Hixon, M. E. Clarke, S. A Murawski, and S. Ralston. 2007. Ten commandments for ecosystem-based fisheries scientists. *Fisheries* 32: 217–33.

Fraser, D. J., T. Coon, M. R. Prince, R. Dion, and L. Bernatchez. 2006. Integrating traditional and evolutionary knowledge in biodiversity conservation: a population level case study. *Ecology and Society* 11: 4. [online]: http://www.ecologyandsociety.org/vol11/iss2/art4

Freeman, M. M. R. 1970. The birds of Belcher Islands, NWT, Canada. *The Canadian Field-Naturalist* 84: 277–90.

Freeman, M. M. R. (ed.). 1976. *Report of the Inuit Land Use and Occupancy Project*. 3 vols. Ottawa: Department of Indian and Northern Affairs.

Freeman, M. M. R. 1984. Contemporary Inuit exploitation of the sea-ice environment. In *Sikumiut: "The People Who Use the Sea Ice."* Ottawa: Canadian Arctic Resources Committee, 73–96.

Freeman, M. M. R. 1989. Gaffs and graphs: a cautionary tale in the common property resource debate. In *Common Property Resources: Ecology and Community-Based Sustainable Development* (F. Berkes, ed.). London: Belhaven, 92–109.

Freeman, M. M. R. 1992. The nature and utility of traditional ecological knowledge. *Northern Perspectives* 20(1): 9–12.

Freeman, M. M. R. 1993a. The International Whaling Commission, small type whaling, and coming to terms with subsistence. *Human Organization* 52: 243–51.

Freeman, M. M. R. 1993b. Traditional land users as a legitimate source of environmental expertise. In *Traditional Ecological Knowledge: Wisdom for Sustainable Development* (N. M. Williams and G. Baines, eds). Canberra: Centre for Resource and Environmental Studies, Australian National University, 153–61.

Freeman, M. M. R. 2011. Looking back – and looking ahead – 35 years after the Inuit land use and occupancy project. *The Canadian Geographer* 55: 20–31.

Freeman, M. M. R. and L. N. Carbyn (eds). 1988. *Traditional Knowledge and Renewable Resource Management in Northern Regions*. Edmonton: Boreal Institute for Northern Studies, University of Alberta.

Freeman, M. M. R., Y. Matsuda, and K. Ruddle (eds). 1991. Adaptive Marine Resource Management Systems in the Pacific. Special Issue of *Resource Management and Optimization* 8(3/4): 127–245.

Friedman, J. 1992. Myth, history and political identity. *Cultural Anthropology* 7: 194–210.

Gadgil, M. 1987. Diversity: cultural and biological. *Trends in Ecology and Evolution* 2: 369–73.

Gadgil, M. and V. D. Vartak. 1976. The sacred groves of Western Ghats in India. *Economic Botany* 30(2): 152–60.

Gadgil, M. and R. Thapar. 1990. Human ecology in India: some historical perspectives. *Interdisciplinary Science Reviews* 15: 209–23.

Gadgil M. and F. Berkes. 1991. Traditional resource management systems. *Resource Management and Optimization* 8: 127–41.

Gadgil, M. and R. Guha. 1992. *This Fissured Land: An Ecological History of India*. Delhi: Oxford University Press.

Gadgil, M., F. Berkes, and C. Folke. 1993. Indigenous knowledge for biodiversity conservation. *Ambio* 22: 151–6.

Gadgil, M., P. R. Seshagiri Rao, G. Utkarsh, P. Pramod, and A. Chhatre. 2000. New meanings for old knowledge: the People's Biodiversity Registers programme. *Ecological Applications* 10: 1251–62.

Gagnon, C. A., and D. Berteaux. 2009. Integrating traditional ecological knowledge and ecological science: a question of scale. *Ecology and Society* 14(2): 19. [online] http://www.ecologyandsociety.org/vol14/iss2/art19

Galaty, J. G. and D. L. Johnson (eds). 1990. *The World of Pastoralism: Herding Systems in Comparative Perspective*. New York: Guilford Press.

Gallagher, C. 2002. Traditional knowledge and genetic discrimination of Lake Nipigon lake trout stocks. Master's Thesis, University of Manitoba, Winnipeg.

Garibaldi, A. and N. Turner. 2004. Cultural keystone species: implications for ecological conservation and restoration. *Ecology and Society* 9: 1. [online]: http://www.ecologyandsociety.org/vol9/iss3/art1

Gearheard, S., W. Matumeak, I. Angutikjuak *et al.* 2006. "It's not that simple": a collaborative comparison of sea-ice environments, their uses, observed changes, and adaptations in Barrow, Alaska, USA, and Clyde River, Nunavut, Canada. *Ambio* 35: 203–11.

Geertz, C. 1963. *Agricultural Involution: The Process of Ecological Change in Indonesia*. Berkeley, CA: University of California Press.

Gelcich, S., T. P. Hughes, P. Olsson *et al.* 2010. Navigating transformations in governance of Chilean marine coastal resources. *Proceedings of the National Academy of Sciences* 107: 16,794–9.

Geniusz, W. M. 2009. *Our Knowledge is Not Primitive. Decolonizing Botanical Anishinaabe Teachings*. Syracuse: Syracuse University Press.

Ghimire, S., D. McKey, and Y. Aumeeruddy-Thomas. 2005. Heterogeneity in ethnoecological knowledge and management of medicinal plants in the Himalayas of Nepal: implications for conservation. *Ecology and Society* 9: 6. [online]: http://www.ecologyandsociety.org/vol9/iss3/art6

Giarelli, G. 1996. Broadening the debate: The Tharaka participatory action research project. *Indigenous Knowledge and Development Monitor* 4(2): 19–22.

Glacken, C. 1967. *Traces on the Rhodian Shore: Nature and Culture in Western Thought from Ancient Times to the End of the Eighteenth Century*. Berkeley, CA: University of California Press.

Goffredo, S, F. Pensa, P. Neri, A. Orlandi *et al.* 2010. Unite research with what citizens do for fun: "recreational monitoring" of marine biodiversity. *Ecological Applications* 20: 2170–87.

Goldman, M. 2007. Tracking wildebeest, locating knowledge: Maasai and conservation biology understandings of wildebeest behaviour in Northern Tanzania. *Environment and Planning D* 25: 307–31.

Gomes, C., R. Mahon, W. Hunte, and S. Singh-Renton. 1998. The role of drifting objects in pelagic fisheries in the southeastern Caribbean. *Fisheries Research* 34: 47–58.

Gómez-Pompa, A. and A. Kaus. 1992a. Taming the wilderness myth. *BioScience* 42: 271–9.

Gómez-Pompa, A. and A. Kaus. 1992b. Letters. *BioScience* 42: 580–1.

González, N., F. Herrera, and M. Chapin. 1995. Ethnocartography in the Darién. *Cultural Survival Quarterly* winter: 31–3.

Gottesfeld, L. M. J. 1994. Conservation, territory and traditional beliefs: an analysis of Gitksan and Wet'suwet'en subsistence, northwest British Columbia. *Human Ecology* 22: 443–65.

Gould, S. J. 1980. *The Panda's Thumb*. New York and London: Norton.

Grant, S. and F. Berkes. 2007. Fisher knowledge as expert system: a case from the longline fishery of Grenada, the Eastern Caribbean. *Fisheries Research* 84: 162–70.

Grant, S., F. Berkes, and J. St. Louis. 2007. A history of change and reorganization: the pelagic longline fishery in Gouyave, Grenada. *Gulf and Caribbean Research* 19(2): 141–8.

Grenier, L. 1998. *Working with Indigenous Knowledge: A Guide for Researchers*. Ottawa: International Development Research Centre.

Grim, J. A. (ed.). 2001. *Indigenous Traditions and Ecology. The Interbeing of Cosmology and Community*. Cambridge, MA: Harvard University Press.

Groenfelt, D. 1991. Building on tradition: indigenous irrigation knowledge and sustainable development in Asia. *Agriculture and Human Values* 8: 114–20.

Gulland, J. A. 1974. *The Management of Marine Fisheries*. Bristol: Scientechnica.

Gunderson, L. H. and C. S. Holling (eds). 2002. *Panarchy: Understanding Transformations in Human and Natural Systems*. Washington, DC: Island Press.

Gunderson L. H., C. S. Holling, and S. S. Light (eds). 1995. *Barriers and Bridges to the Renewal of Ecosystems and Institutions*. New York: Columbia University Press.

Gwich'in Elders. 2001. *More Gwich'in Words About the Land*. Inuvik, Northwest Territories: Gwich'in Renewable Resource Board.

Haggan, N., B. Neis, and I. G. Baird (eds). 2006. *Fishers' Knowledge in Fisheries Science and Management*. Paris: UNESCO Publishing.

Hanna, S. S. 1998. Managing for human and ecological context in the Maine soft shell clam fishery. In *Linking Social and Ecological Systems* (F. Berkes and C. Folke, eds). Cambridge: Cambridge University Press, 190–215.

Hardesty, D. L. 1977. *Ecological Anthropology*. New York: Wiley.

Harland, D. 1993. Letters. *Time* June 14.

Hart, E. and B. Amos. 2004. *Learning About Marine Resources and Their Use through Inuvialuit Oral History*. Inuvik, Northwest Territories: Inuvialuit Cultural Resource Centre.

Healey, C. 1993. The significance and application of TEK. In *Traditional Ecological Knowledge: Wisdom for Sustainable Development* (N. M. Williams and G. Baines, eds). Canberra: Centre for Resource and Environmental Studies, Australian National University, 21–6.

Healey, M. C. 1975. Dynamics of exploited whitefish populations and their management with special reference to the Northwest Territories. *Journal of the Fisheries Research Board of Canada* 32: 427–48.

Heaslip, R. 2008. Monitoring salmon aquaculture waste: the contribution of First Nations' rights, knowledge, and practices in British Columbia, Canada. *Marine Policy* 32: 988–96.

Heckler, S. (ed.) 2009. *Landscape, Power and Process: Re-evaluating Traditional Environmental Knowledge*. Oxford and New York: Berghahn.

Heffley, S. 1981. The relationship between North Athapaskan settlement patterns and resource distribution. In *Hunter-Gatherer Foraging Strategies: Ethnographic and Archeological Analyses* (B. Winterhalder and E. A. Smith, eds). Chicago, IL: University of Chicago Press, 126–47.

Heywood, V. H. (executive ed.). 1995. *Global Biodiversity Assessment*. Cambridge, U.K.: United Nations Environmental Program and Cambridge University Press.

Hjort af Ornas, A. 1992. Cultural variation in concepts of nature. *GeoJournal* 26: 167–72.

Holling, C. S. 1973. Resilience and stability of ecological systems. *Annual Review of Ecology and Systematics* 4: 1–23.

Holling, C. S. (ed.). 1978. *Adaptive Environmental Assessment and Management*. London: Wiley.

Holling, C. S. 1986. The resilience of terrestrial ecosystems: local surprise and global change. In *Sustainable Development of the Biosphere* (W. C. Clark and R. E. Munn, eds). Cambridge: Cambridge University Press, 292–317.

Holling, C. S., D. W. Schindler, B. W. Walker, and J. Roughgarden. 1995. Biodiversity in the functioning of ecosystems: an ecological synthesis. In *Biodiversity Loss* (C. Perrings, K.-G. Maler, C. Folke, C. S. Holling, and B.-O. Jansson, eds). Cambridge: Cambridge University Press, 44–83.

Holling, C. S., F. Berkes, and C. Folke. 1998. Science, sustainability and resource management. In *Linking Social and Ecological Systems: Management Practices and Social Mechanisms for Building Resilience* (F. Berkes and C. Folke, eds). Cambridge: Cambridge University Press, 342–62.

Holmes, L. 1996. Elders' knowledge and the ancestry of experience in Hawai'i. Ph.D. dissertation, University of Toronto.

Holt, F. L. 2005. The catch-22 of conservation: indigenous peoples, biologists and cultural change. *Human Ecology* 33: 199–215.

Hoole, A. and F. Berkes. 2010. Breaking down fences: recoupling social-ecological systems for biodiversity conservation in Namibia. *Geoforum* 41: 304–317.

Howard, A. and F. Widdowson. 1996. Traditional knowledge threatens environmental assessment. *Policy Options* Nov.: 34–6.

Hudson, B. 1997. A socio-economic study of community-based management of mangrove resources of St. Lucia. Master's thesis, University of Manitoba, Winnipeg.

Hughes, J. D. 1983. *American Indian Ecology*. El Paso, TX: University of Texas Press.

Hunn, E. 1993a. What is traditional ecological knowledge? In *Traditional Ecological Knowledge: Wisdom for Sustainable Development* (N. M. Williams and G. Baines, eds). Canberra: Centre for Resource and Environmental Studies, Australian National University, pp. 13–15.

Hunn, E. 1993b. The ethnobiological foundation for TEK. In *Traditional Ecological Knowledge: Wisdom for Sustainable Development* (N. M. Williams and G. Baines, eds). Canberra: Centre for Resource and Environmental Studies, Australian National University, 16–20.

Hunn, E. S. 1999. The value of subsistence for the future of the world. Cultural memory and sense of place. In *Ethnoecology: Situated Knowledge/Located Lives* (V. D. Nazarea, ed.). Tucson, AZ: University of Arizona Press, 23–36.

Hunn, E. S. 2008. *A Zapotec Natural History*. Tucson: University of Arizona Press.

Hunn, E. S. and J. Selam. 1990. *Nch'i-Wana "The Big River": Mid-Columbia Indians and their Land*. Seattle, WA: University of Washington Press.

Hunn, E. S., D. R. Johnson, P. N. Russell, and T. F. Thornton. 2003. Huna Tlingit traditional environmental knowledge, conservation, and the management of a "wilderness" park. *Current Anthropology* 44: S79–S103.

Hunt, C. 1997. Cooperative approaches to marine resource management in the South Pacific. In *The Governance of Common Property in the Pacific Region* (P. Larmour, ed.). Canberra: Australian National University, 145–64.

Huntington, H. P. 1998. Observations on the utility of the semi-directive interview for documenting traditional ecological knowledge. *Arctic* 51: 237–42.

Huntington, H. P. 2000. Using traditional ecological knowledge in science: methods and applications. *Ecological Applications* 10: 1270–4.

Huntington, H. P., R. S. Suydam, and D. H. Rosenberg. 2004. Traditional knowledge and satellite tracking as complementary approaches to ecological understanding. *Environmental Conservation* 31: 177–80.

Hutchings, J. 1998. Discarding, catch rates and fishing effort in Newfoundland's inshore and offshore cod fisheries: analytical strengths and weaknesses of interview-based data. Workshop on Bringing Fishers' Knowledge into Fisheries Science and Management, May 1998, St. John's, Newfoundland.

Hviding, E. 1990. Keeping the sea: aspects of marine tenure in Marovo Lagoon, Solomon Islands. In *Traditional Marine Resource Management in the Pacific Basin: An Anthology* (K. Ruddle and R. E. Johannes, eds). Jakarta: UNESCO/ROSTSEA, 7–44.

Hviding, E. 2003. Contested rainforests, NGOs, and projects of desire in Solomon Islands. *International Social Science Journal* 178: 539–53.

Hviding, E. 2006. Knowing and managing biodiversity in the Pacific islands: challenges of environmentalism in Marovo Lagoon. *International Social Science Journal* 187: 69–85.

IEMA 2011. Independent Environmental Monitoring Agency. A Public Watchdog for Environmental Monitoring of Ekati Diamond Mine. [online]: http://www.monitoringagency.net

IISD 2000. *Sila Alangotok: Inuit Observations of Climate Change*. Video: 42 minutes. Winnipeg: International Institute for Sustainable Development.

Ingold, T. 2000. *The Perception of the Environment: Essays in Livelihood, Dwelling and Skill*. New York: Routledge.

Ingold, T. 2006. Rethinking the animate, re-animating thought. *Ethnos* 71: 9–20.

Ingold, T. and T. Kurttila. 2000. Perceiving the environment in Finnish Lapland. *Body and Society* 6: 183–96.

Inuit Circumpolar Conference. 1992. Development of a program for the collection and application of indigenous knowledge. Presented at the United Nations Conference on Environment and Development (UNCED), Rio de Janeiro.

Irvine, D. 1989. Succession management and resource distribution in an Amazonian rain forest. In *Resource Management in Amazonia: Indigenous and Folk Strategies* (D. A. Posey and W. L. Balée, eds). New York: New York Botanical Garden, 223–37.

Ishigawa, J. 2006. Cosmovisions and environmental governance: the case of in situ conservation of native cultivated plants and their wild relatives in Peru. In *Bridging Scales and Knowledge Systems* (W. V. Reid, F. Berkes, T. Wilbanks and D. Capistrano, eds). Washington, DC: Island Press, 207–24. [online]: http://www.maweb.org/documents/bridging/bridging.11.pdf

IUCN (International Conservation Union). 1986. *Tradition, Conservation and Development*. Occasional Newsletter of the Commission on Ecology's Working Group on Traditional Ecological Knowledge. No. 4.

IUCN/UNEP/WWF 1991. *Caring for the Earth: A Strategy for Sustainable Living*. Gland, Switzerland: International Conservation Union.

Iverson, J. O. and R. D. McPhee. 2008. Communicating knowledge through communities of practice: exploring internal communicative processes and differences among CoPs. *Journal of Applied Communication Research* 36: 176–99.

Jackson, L. 1986. World's greatest caribou herd mired in Quebec–Labrador boundary dispute. *Canadian Geographic* 105(3): 25–33.

Jantsch, E. 1972. *Technological Planning and Social Futures*. London: Cassell.

Janzen, D. 1986. The future of tropical ecology. *Annual Review of Ecology and Systematics* 17: 305–6.

Jenkins, W. (ed.) 2010. *The Spirit of Sustainability. Volume l. Encyclopedia of Sustainability*. Great Barrington, MA: Berkshire.

Jentoft, S., B. J. McCay, and D. C. Wilson. 1998. Social theory and fisheries co-management. *Marine Policy* 22: 423–36.

Johannes, R. E. 1978. Traditional marine conservation methods in Oceania and their demise. *Annual Review of Ecology and Systematics* 9: 349–64.

Johannes, R. E. 1981. *Words of the Lagoon: Fishing and Marine Lore in the Palau District of Micronesia*. Berkeley, CA: University of California Press.

Johannes, R. E. (ed.). 1989. *Traditional Ecological Knowledge: A Collection of Essays*. Gland, Switzerland: International Conservation Union (IUCN).

Johannes, R. E. 1994. Pacific island peoples' science and marine resource management. In *Science of the Pacific Island Peoples* (J. Morrison, P. Geraghty, and L. Crowl, eds). Suva, Fiji: Institute of Pacific Studies, University of the South Pacific, 81–9.

Johannes, R. E. 1998. The case for data-less marine resource management: examples from tropical nearshore fisheries. *Trends in Ecology and Evolution* 13: 243–46.

Johannes, R. E. 2002a. The renaissance of community-based marine resource management in oceania. *Annual Review of Ecology and Systematics* 33: 317–40.

Johannes, R. E. 2002b. Did indigenous conservation ethics exist? *Traditional Marine Resource Management and Knowledge Information Bulletin* 14: 3–7.

Johannes, R. E. and W. MacFarlane. 1991. *Traditional Fishing in the Torres Strait Islands*. Hobart: Commonwealth Scientific and Industrial Research Organization.

Johannes, R. E. and H. T. Lewis. 1993. The importance of researchers' expertise in environmental subjects. In *Traditional Ecological Knowledge: Wisdom for Sustainable Development* (N. M. Williams and G. Baines, eds). Canberra: Centre for Resource and Environmental Studies, Australian National University, 104–8.

Johannes, R. E., P. Lasserre, S. W. Nixon. J. Pliya, and K. Ruddle. 1983. Traditional knowledge and management of marine coastal systems. *Biology International*, Special Issue 4.

Johannes, R. E., M. M. R. Freeman, and R. J. Hamilton. 2000. Ignore fishers' knowledge and miss the boat. *Fish and Fisheries* 1: 257–71.

Johnsen, D. B. 2009. Salmon, science, and reciprocity on the Northwest Coast. *Ecology and Society* 14: 43. [online]: http://www.ecologyandsociety.org/vol14/iss2/art43

Johnson, L. 1976. Ecology of Arctic populations of lake trout, *Salvelinus namaycush*, lake whitefish, *Coregonus clupeaformis*, Arctic char, *S. alpinus*, and associated species in unexploited lakes of the Canadian Northwest Territories. *Journal of the Fisheries Research Board of Canada* 33: 2459–88.

Johnson, L. M. 1999. Aboriginal burning for vegetation management in northwest British Columbia. In *Indians, Fire and the Land in the Pacific Northwest* (R. Boyd, ed.). Corvallis, OR: Oregon State University Press, 238–54.

Johnson, L. M. and E. S. Hunn (eds.) 2010. *Landscape Ethnoecology*. New York and Oxford: Berghahn.

Johnson, M. (ed.). 1992. *Lore: Capturing Traditional Environmental Knowledge*. Ottawa: Dene Cultural Institute and International Development Research Centre.

Juhé-Beaulaton, D. 2008. Sacred forests and the global challenge of biodiversity conservation: the case of Benin and Togo. *Journal for the Study of Religion, Nature and Culture* 2: 351–372.

Juniper, I. 1979. Problems in managing an irrupting caribou herd. Proceedings of the Second International Caribou Symposium, Roros, Norway, 722–4.

Kalit, K. and E. Young. 1997. Common property conflict and resolution: Aboriginal Australia and Papua New Guinea. In *The Governance of Common Property in the Pacific Region* (P. Larmour, ed.). Canberra: Australian National University, 183–208.

Kalland, A. 1994. Indigenous knowledge—local knowledge: prospects and limitations. In *Arctic Environment: A Report on the Seminar on Integration of Indigenous Peoples' Knowledge*. Copenhagen: Ministry of the Environment/The Home Rule of Greenland, 150–67.

Kaneshiro, K. Y., P. China, K. N. Duin *et al.* 2005. Hawai'i's mountain-to-sea ecosystems: social-ecological microcosms for sustainability science and practice. *EcoHealth* 2: 349–60.

Kargioglu, M., S. Cenkci, A. Serteser, M. Konuk and G. Vural. 2010. Traditional uses of wild plants in the middle Aegean region of Turkey. *Human Ecology* 38: 439–50.

Kassam, K-A. S. 2009. *Biocultural Diversity and Indigenous Ways of Knowing*. Calgary: University of Calgary Press.

Kassam, K.-A., M. Karamkhudoeva, M. Ruelle, and M. Baumflek. 2010. Medicinal plant use and health sovereignty: findings from the Tajik and Afghan Pamirs. *Human Ecology* 38: 817–29.

Kates, R. W., W. C. Clark, R. Corell *et al.* 2001. Sustainability science. *Science* 292: 641–2.

Kay, C. E. 1994. Aboriginal overkill: the role of native Americans in structuring western ecosystems. *Human Nature* 5: 359–98.

Keesing, R. M. 1989. Creating the past: custom and identity in the contemporary Pacific. *Contemporary Pacific* 1: 19–42.

Keith, R. F. and M. Simon. 1987. Sustainable development in the northern circumpolar world. In *Conservation with Equity* (P. Jacobs and D. A. Munro, eds). Cambridge: International Union for the Conservation of Nature and Natural Resources, 209–25.

Kellert, S. R. 1997. *Kinship to Mastery: Biophilia in Human Evolution and Development*. Washington, DC: Island Press.

Kellert, S. R. and E. O. Wilson (eds). 1993. *The Biophilia Hypothesis*. Washington, DC: Island Press.

Kendrick, A. 2003. Caribou co-management in northern Canada: fostering multiple ways of knowing. In *Navigating the Dynamics of Social-Ecological Systems* (F. Berkes, J. Colding and C. Folke, eds). Cambridge: Cambridge University Press, 241–67.

Kendrick, A. and M. Manseau. 2008. Representing traditional knowledge: resource management and Inuit knowledge of barren-ground caribou. *Society and Natural Resources* 21: 404–18.

Kendrick, A., P. O'B. Lyver and the Lútsël K'é Dëne First Nation. 2005. Dënesôline (Chipewyan) knowledge of barren ground caribou (*Rangifer tarandus groenlandicus*) movements. *Arctic* 58: 175–91.

Kimmerer, R. W. 2000. Native knowledge for native ecosystems. *Journal of Forestry* 98(8): 4–9.

Kimmerer, R. W. 2002. Weaving traditional ecological knowledge into biological education: a call for action. *BioScience* 52: 432–8.

Kimmerer, R. W. and F. K. Lake. 2001. The role of indigenous burning in land management. *Journal of Forestry* 99(11): 36–41.

King, L. 2004. Competing knowledge systems in the management of fish and forests in the Pacific Northwest. *International Environmental Agreements: Politics, Law and Economics* 4: 161–77.

Kirsch, S. 2001. Lost worlds: environmental disaster, "culture loss," and the law. *Cultural Anthropology* 42: 167–98.

Klee, G. (ed.). 1980. *World Systems of Traditional Resource Management*. London: Edward Arnold.

Klein, D. R. 1994. Wilderness: a Western concept alien to Arctic cultures. *Arctic Institute of North America, Information North* 20(3): 1–6.

Knapp, C. N. and M. Fernandez-Gimenez. 2008. Knowing the land: a review of local knowledge revealed in ranch memoirs. *Rangeland Ecology and Management* 61: 148–55.

Knapp, C. N. and M. E. Fernandez-Gimenez. 2009. Knowledge in practice: documenting rancher local knowledge in Northwest Colorado. *Rangeland Ecology and Management* 62: 500–9.

Knapp, C. N., M. Fernandez-Gimenez, E. Kachergis, and A. Rudeen. 2011. Using participatory workshops to integrate state-and-transition models created with local knowledge and ecological data. *Rangeland Ecology and Management* 64: 158–70.

Knudsen, S. 2008. Ethical know-how and traditional ecological knowledge in small scale fisheries on the Eastern Black Sea Coast of Turkey. *Human Ecology* 36: 29–41.

Knudtson, P. and D. Suzuki. 1992. *Wisdom of the Elders*. Toronto: Stoddart.

Kofinas, G. P. 1998. The costs of power sharing: community involvement in Canadian porcupine caribou co-management. Ph.D. thesis, University of British Columbia, Vancouver.

Kofinas, G. with the communities of Aklavik, Arctic Village, Old Crow and Fort McPherson. 2002. Community contributions to ecological monitoring: knowledge co-production in the U.S.–Canada Arctic Borderlands. In *The Earth is Faster Now* (I. Krupnik and D. Jolly, eds). Fairbanks, AK: Arctic Research Consortium of the United States, 54–91.

Kofinas, G., P. Lyver, D. Russell, R. White, A. Nelson, and N. Flanders. 2003. Towards a protocol for community monitoring of caribou body condition. *Rangifer*, Special Issue No. 14: 43–52.

Kothari, A. 1996. India's protected areas: the journey to joint management. *World Conservation* 2(96): 8–9.

Kothari, A. 2006. Community-conserved areas: towards ecological and livelihood security. *Parks* 16: 3–13.

Kovach, M. 2009. *Indigenous Methodologies: Characteristics, Conversations and Contexts*. Toronto: University of Toronto Press.

Krech, S. III 1999. *The Ecological Indian: Myth and History*. New York: Norton.

Krupnik, I. and D. Jolly (eds). 2002. *The Earth Is Faster Now: Indigenous Observations of Arctic Environmental Change*. Fairbanks, AK: Arctic Research Consortium of the United States.

Krupnik, I., W. Walunga (Kepelgu) and V. Metcalf (eds). 2002. *Akuzilleput Igaqullghet. Our Words Put to Paper*. Washington, DC: Arctic Studies Center, Smithsonian Institution.

Krupnik, I., C. Aporta, S. Gearhard, G. J. Laidler and L. Holm Nielsen (eds.) 2010. *SIKU: Knowing Our Ice. Documenting Inuit Sea Ice Knowledge and Use*. New York: Springer.

Kuchli, C. 1996. Tanzania: a second Garden of Eden. *People and the Planet* 5(4): 20–1.

Kuhn, L. 2007. Why utilize complexity principles in social inquiry? *World Futures* 63: 156–75.

Kuhn, T. S. 1970. *The Structure of Scientific Revolutions*, 2nd edn. Chicago, IL: University of Chicago Press.

Kwan, D. 2005. Traditional use in contemporary *ailan* (island) ways: the management challenge of a sustainable dugong fishery in Torres Strait. *Senri Ethnological Studies* 67: 281–302.

Laidler, G. J. 2006. Inuit and scientific perspectives on the relationship between sea ice and climate: the ideal complement? *Climatic Change* 78: 407–44.

Laidler, G. J., J. D. Ford, W. A. Gough *et al.* 2009. Travelling and hunting in a changing Arctic: assessing Inuit vulnerability to sea ice change in Igloolok, Nunavut. *Climatic Change* 94: 363–397.

Laird, S. (ed.). 2002. *Biodiversity and Traditional Knowledge*. London: Earthscan.

Lake, F. 2007. Co-evolution of people, salmon and place. Paper presented at the Pathways to Resilience Conference, Oregon State University and Oregon Sea Grant, Portland, April 2007.

Langdon, S. J. 2006. Tidal pulse fishing. In *Traditional Ecological Knowledge and Resource Management* (C. R. Menzies, ed.). Lincoln, NE: University of Nebraska Press, 21–46.

Lansing, J. S. 1987. Balinese water temples and the management of irrigation. *American Anthropologist* 89: 326–41.

Lansing, J. S. 1991. *Priests and Programmers*. Princeton, NJ: Princeton University Press.

Lansing, J. S., J. N. Kremer, and B. B. Smuts. 1998. System-dependent selection, ecological feedback and the emergence of functional structure in ecosystems. *Journal of Theoretical Biology* 192: 377–91.

Lantz, T. C. and N. J. Turner. 2003. Traditional phenological knowledge (TPK) of aboriginal peoples in British Columbia. *Journal of Ethnobiology* 23: 263–86.

LaRochelle, S. and F. Berkes. 2003. Traditional ecological knowledge and practice for edible wild plants: biodiversity use by the Raramuri in the Sierra Tarahumara, Mexico. *International Journal of Sustainable Development and World Ecology* 10: 361–75.

Latour, B. 2004. *Politics of Nature: How to Bring Sciences into Democracy*. Cambridge, MA: Harvard University Press.

Lauer, M. and S. Aswani. 2009. Indigenous ecological knowledge as situated practices: understanding fishers' knowledge in the Western Solomon Islands. *American Anthropologist* 111: 317–29.

Leach, M. 1994. *Rainforest Relations: Gender and Resource Use Among the Mende of Gola, Sierra Leone*. Edinburgh: Edinburgh University Press.

Leach, M. and R. Mearns (eds). 1996. *The Lie of the Land: Challenging Received Wisdom on the African Environment*. London: The International African Institute.

Leacock, E. B. 1954. The Montagnais "hunting territory" and the fur trade. Menasha, WI: American Anthropological Association, Memoir No. 78.

Leduc, T. B. 2007. Sila dialogues on climate change: Inuit wisdom for a cross-cultural interdisciplinarity. *Climatic Change* 85: 237–50.

Leduc, T. B. 2011. *Climate, Culture and Change: Inuit and Western Dialogues with a Warming North*. Ottawa: University of Ottawa Press.

Lee, K. N. 1993. *Compass and Gyroscope: Integrating Science and Politics for the Environment*. Washington DC: Island Press.

Lee, R. B. and I. Devore (eds). 1968. *Man the Hunter*. Chicago, IL: Aldine.

Legat, A. (ed.). 1991. Report of the Traditional Knowledge Working Group. Yellowknife: Department of Culture and Communications, Government of the Northwest Territories.

Legat, A., S. A. Zoe, and M. Chocolate. 1995. The importance of knowing. In *NWT Diamonds Project Environmental Impact Statement*, Vol. 1, Apps. Vancouver: BHP Diamonds Inc.

Lejano, R. P. and H. Ingram 2007. Place-based conservation: lessons from the Turtle Islands. *Environment* 49(9): 19–26.

Lemelin, R. H., M. Dowsley, B. Walmark *et al.* 2010. *Wabusk* of the Omushkegouk: Cree-polar bear (*Ursus maritimus*) interactions in Northern Ontario. *Human Ecology* 38: 803–15.

Leopold, A. 1949. *A Sand County Almanac*. Reprinted 1966. Oxford: Oxford University Press.

Lévi-Strauss, C. 1962. *La pensée sauvage*. Paris: Librarie Plon. (English translation: 1966. *The Savage Mind*. Chicago, IL: University of Chicago Press.)

Levin, S. A. 1999. *Fragile Dominion: Complexity and the Commons*. Reading, MA: Perseus Books.

Lewis, H. T. 1973. *Patterns of Indian Burning in California: Ecology and Ethnohistory*. Ramona, CA: Ballena Press.

Lewis, H. T. 1989. Ecological and technological knowledge of fire: Aborigines versus park managers in northern Australia. *American Anthropologist* 91: 940–61.

Lewis, H. T. 1993a. Traditional ecological knowledge: some definitions. In *Traditional Ecological Knowledge: Wisdom for Sustainable Development* (N. M. Williams and G. Baines, eds). Canberra: Centre for Resource and Environmental Studies, Australian National University, 8–12.

Lewis, H. T. 1993b. In retrospect. In *Before the Wilderness: Environmental Management by Native Californians* (T. C. Blackburn and K. Anderson, eds). Menlo Park, CA: Ballena Press, 389–400.

Lewis, H. T. and T. A. Ferguson. 1988. Yards, corridors and mosaics: how to burn a boreal forest. *Human Ecology* 16: 57–77.

Lewis, J. (Wuyee Wi Medeek). 2004. Forests for the future: the view from Gitxaala. *Canadian Journal of Native Education* 28: 8–14.

Lincoln, Y. and E. Guba. 1985. *Naturalistic Inquiry*. London: Sage.

Lind, A. W. 1938. *An Island Community: Ecological Succession in Hawaii*. Chicago, IL: University of Chicago Press.

Linden, E. 1991. Lost tribes, lost knowledge. *Time* 138(12): 44–56 (Sept. 23).

Linnekin, J. 1983. Defining tradition: variations on the Hawaiian identity. *American Ethnologist* 10: 241–52.

Lobe, K. and F. Berkes. 2004. The padu system of community-based fisheries management: change and local institutional innovation in south India. *Marine Policy* 28: 271–81.

Louis, P. R. 2007. Can you hear us now? Voices from the margin: using indigenous methodologies in geographic research. *Geographical Research* 45: 130–39.

Lovelock, J. E. 1979. *Gaia: A New Look at Life on Earth*. London and New York: Oxford University Press.

Ludwig, N. A. 1994. An Ainu homeland: an alternative solution for the Northern Territories/Southern Kuriles imbroglio. *Ocean and Coastal Management* 25: 1–29.

Lugo, A. 1995. Management of tropical biodiversity. *Ecological Applications* 5: 956–61.

Lutz, J. S. and B. Neis (eds.) 2008. *Making and Moving Knowledge*. Montreal and Kingston: McGill-Queen's University Press.

Lyver, P. 2002. The use of traditional environmental knowledge to guide sooty shearwater (*Puffinus griseus*) harvests by Rakiura Maori. *Wildlife Society Bulletin* 30: 29–40.

MA. 2005. *Millennium Ecosystem Assessment Synthesis Report*. Chicago, IL: Island Press.

Maass, A. and R. L. Anderson. 1986. *. . . and the Desert Shall Rejoice: Conflict, Growth, and Justice in Arid Environments*. Malabar, FL: Krieger.

Mabry, J. B. (ed.). 1996. *Canals and Communities: Small-Scale Irrigation Systems*. Tucson, AZ: University of Arizona Press.

McCay, B. J. and J. M. Acheson (eds). 1987. *The Question of the Commons: The Culture and Ecology of Communal Resources*. Tucson, AZ: University of Arizona Press.

McClanahan, T. R., H. Glaesel, J. Rubens, and R. Kiambo. 1997. The effects of traditional fisheries management on fisheries yields and the coral-reef ecosystems of southern Kenya. *Environmental Conservation* 24: 105–20.

M'Closkey, K. 2002. *Swept Under the Rug: A Hidden History of Navajo Weaving*. Albuquerque, NM: University of New Mexico Press.

McDonald, M. 1988. An overview of adaptive management of renewable resources. In *Traditional Knowledge and Renewable Resource Management in Northern Regions* (M. M. R. Freeman and L. N. Carbyn, eds). Edmonton: Boreal Institute, University of Alberta, 65–71.

McDonald, M., L. Arragutainaq, and Z. Novalinga (compilers). 1997. *Voices from the Bay: Traditional Ecological Knowledge of Inuit and Cree in the Hudson Bay Bioregion*. Ottawa: Canadian Arctic Resources Committee and municipality of Sanikiluaq.

McGovern, H., G. F. Bigelow, T. Amorosi, and D. Russell. 1988. Northern islands, human error and environmental degradation. *Human Ecology* 16: 225–70.

McGregor, D. 2004. Traditional ecological knowledge and sustainable development: towards co-existence. In *In the Way of Development. Indigenous Peoples, Life Projects and Globalization* (M. Blaser, H. A. Feit, and G. McRae, eds). London and New York: Zed Books, 72–91.

McGregor, D., W. Bayha, D. Simmons. 2010. "Our Responsibility to Keep the Land Alive": voices of northern indigenous researchers. *Pimatisiwin: A Journal of Aboriginal and Indigenous Community Health* 8: 101–23.

McGregor, S., V. Lawson, P. Christophersen *et al.* 2010. Indigenous wetland burning: conserving natural and cultural resources in Australia's world heritage-listed Kakadu National Park. *Human Ecology* 38(6): 721–9.

McHarg, I. L. 1969. *Design with Nature*. Garden City, NY: Doubleday/Natural History Press.

Mackenzie, F. 1998. "Where do you belong to?" Land and the construction of community in the Isle of Harris, Outer Hebrides, Scotland. Crossing Boundaries: 7th Conference of the International Association for the Study of Common Property, June 1998, Vancouver, British Columbia.

Mackinson, S. 2000. An adaptive fuzzy expert system for predicting structure, dynamics and distribution of herring shoals. *Ecological Modelling* 126: 155–78.

Mackinson, S. 2001. Integrating local and scientific knowledge: an example in fisheries science. *Environmental Management* 27: 533–45.

McNeely, J. A. 1994. Lessons from the past: forests and biodiversity. *Biodiversity and Conservation* 3: 3–20.

McNeely, J. A. 1996. Conservation—the social science? *World Conservation* 2(96): 2.

McNeely, J. A. and D. Pitt (eds). 1985. *Culture and Conservation*. London: Croom Helm.

Maffi, L. (ed.). 2001. *On Biocultural Diversity: Linking Language, Knowledge and the Environment*. Washington, DC: Smithsonian Institution Press.

Maffi, L. 2005. Linguistic, cultural and biological diversity. *Annual Review of Anthropology* 29: 599–617.

Maffi, L. and E. Woodley 2010. *Biocultural Diversity Conservation. A Global Sourcebook*. London: Earthscan.

Magga, O. H. 2006. Diversity in Saami terminology for reindeer, snow and ice. *International Social Science Journal* 187: 25–34.

Majnep, I. and R. Bulmer. 1977. *Birds of My Kalam Country*. London: Oxford University Press.

Mallarach, J.-M. (ed.) 2008. *Protected Landscapes and Cultural and Spiritual Values*. Gland, Switzerland: IUCN, GTZ and Obra Social de Caixa Catalunya.

Malmberg, T. 1980. *Human Territoriality*. The Hague: Mouton.

Manseau, M. (ed.). 1998. Traditional and Western Scientific Environmental Knowledge. Workshop Proceedings. Goosebay, Labrador: Institute for Environmental Monitoring and Research.

Manseau, M., B. Parlee and G. B. Ayles. 2005a. A place for traditional ecological knowledge in resource management. In *Breaking Ice* (F. Berkes, R. Huebert, H. Fast, M. Manseau, and A. Diduck, eds). Calgary: University of Calgary Press, 141–64.

Manseau, M., B. Parlee, L. Bill, A. Kendrick, and Rainbow Bridge Communications (producers) 2005b. Watching, listening, learning, understanding changes in the environment: community-based monitoring in northern Canada. Video. In *Breaking Ice* (F. Berkes, R. Huebert, H. Fast, M. Manseau and A. Diduck, eds). Calgary: University of Calgary Press.

Marin, A. 2010. Riders under storms: contributions of nomadic herders' observations to analysing climate change in Mongolia. *Global Environmental Change* 20: 162–76.

Marles, R., C. Clavelle, L. Monteleone, N. Tays, and D. Burns. 2000. *Aboriginal Plant Use in Canada's Northwest Boreal Forest*. Vancouver: University of British Columbia Press.

Marlor, C. 2010. Bureaucracy, democracy and exclusion: why indigenous knowledge holders have a hard time being taken seriously. *Qualitative Sociology* 33: 513–31.

Martin, G. 1993. Dius Tadong: Ancestral ecology. *UNESCO Sources* 50: 5.

Martin, G. J., C. I. Camacho Benavides, C. A. Del Campo García *et al.* 2011. Indigenous and community conserved areas in Oaxaca, Mexico. *Management of Environmental Quality* 22: 250–66.

Martin, L. 1986. "Eskimo words for snow": a case study in the genesis and decay of an anthropological example. *American Anthropologist* 88: 418–33.

Martin, P. S. 1973. The discovery of America. *Science* 179: 969–74.

Martin, P. S. and R. G. Klein (eds). 1984. *Quaternary Extinctions*. Tucson, AZ: University of Arizona Press.

Mathew, S. 1991. Study of territorial use rights in small-scale fisheries: traditional systems of fisheries management in Pulicat Lake, Tamil Nadu, India. Rome: FAO Fisheries Circular No. 890.

Mathias-Mundy, E. and C. M. McCorkle. 1995. Ethnoveterinary medicine and development—a review of the literature. In *The Cultural Dimension of Development* (D. M. Warren, L. J. Slikkerveer, and D. Brokensha, eds). London: Intermediate Technology Publications.

Mauro, F. and P. D. Hardison. 2000. Traditional knowledge of indigenous and local communities: international debate and policy initiatives. *Ecological Applications* 10: 1263–9.

Mayr, E. 1963. *Animal Species and Evolution*. Cambridge, MA: Belknap Press of Harvard University Press.

Mbanefo, S. 1992. Medicine men. *World Wide Fund for Nature, WWF News* 76: 11–12.

Menominee Tribal Enterprises. 2011. [online]: http://www.mtewood.com

Menzies, C. R. 2004. Putting words into action: negotiating collaborative research in Gitxaala. *Canadian Journal of Native Education* 28: 15–32.

Menzies, C. R. (ed.). 2006. *Traditional Ecological Knowledge and Resource Management*. Lincoln, NE: University of Nebraska Press.

Messier, F., J. Huot, D. Le Henaff, and S. Luttich. 1988. Demography of the George River caribou herd: evidence of population regulation by forage exploitation and range expansion. *Arctic* 41: 279–87.

Miller, A. M. and I. Davidson-Hunt. 2010. Fire, agency and scale in the creation of aboriginal cultural landscapes. *Human Ecology* 38: 401–14.

Miller, A. M., I. J. Davidson-Hunt and P. Peters 2010. Talking about fire: Pikangikum First Nation elders guiding fire management. *Canadian Journal of Forestry Research* 40: 2290–301.

Miller, C. and P. Erickson. 2006. The politics of bridging scales and epistemologies. In *Bridging Scales and Knowledge Systems* (W. V. Reid, F. Berkes, T. Wilbanks, and D. Capistrano, eds). Washington, DC: Island Press, 297–314. [online]: http://www.maweb.org/documents/bridging/bridging.16.pdf

Miller, T. R., T. D. Baird, C. M. Littlefield *et al.* 2008. Epistemological pluralism: reorganizing interdisciplinary research. *Ecology and Society* 13: 46. [online] http://www.ecologyandsociety.org/articles/2671.html

M'Lot, M. and M. Manseau. 2003. Ka isinakwak askiy: using Cree knowledge to perceive and describe the landscape of the Wapusk National park area. *The National Parks and National Historic Sites of Canada Research Links* 11: 1, 4–6.

Moller, H., F. Berkes, P. O. Lyver, and M. Kislalioglu. 2004. Combining science and traditional ecological knowledge: monitoring populations for co-management. *Ecology and Society* 9: 2. [online]: http://www.ecologyandsociety.org/vol9/iss3/art2

Moller, H., P. O'B. Lyver, C. Bragg *et al.* 2009. Guidelines for cross-cultural participatory action research partnerships: a case study of a customary seabird harvest in New Zealand. *New Zealand Journal of Zoology* 36: 211–41.

Monachus Guardian. 2011. [online]: http://www.monachus-guardian.org

Moorehead, R. 1989. Changes taking place in common-property resource management in the Inland Niger Delta of Mali. In *Common Property Resources* (F. Berkes, ed.). London: Belhaven, 256–72.

Morauta, L., J. Pernetta, and W. Heaney (eds). 1982. *Traditional Conservation in Papua New Guinea: Implications for Today.* Port Moresby, Papua New Guinea: Institute for Applied Social and Economic Research.

Morseth, C. M. 1997. Twentieth-century changes in beluga whale hunting and butchering by the Kanigmiut of Buckland, Alaska. *Arctic* 50: 241–55.

Muchagata, M. and K. Brown. 2000. Colonist farmers' perceptions of fertility and the frontier environment in eastern Amazonia. *Agriculture and Human Values* 17: 371–84.

Muir, C., D. R. Rose and P. Sullivan. 2010. From the other side of the knowledge frontier: indigenous knowledge, social-ecological relationships and new perspectives. *The Rangeland Journal* 32: 259–65.

Muller, J. and A. M. Almedom. 2008. What is "famine food"? Distinguishing between traditional vegetables and special foods for times of hunger/scarcity (Boumba, Niger). *Human Ecology* 36: 599–607.

Mulligan, M. 2003. Feet to the ground in storied landscapes: disrupting the colonial legacy with a poetic politics. In *Decolonizing Nature: Strategies for Conservation in a Post-colonial Era* (W. M. Adams and M. Mulligan, eds). London: Earthscan, 268–89.

Munsterhjelm, E. 1953. *The Wind and the Caribou.* New York: Macmillan.

Murphy, G. I. 1968. Pattern of life history and the environment. *American Naturalist* 102: 391–403.

Murray, G., B. Neis, C. T. Palmer, and D. C. Schneider. 2008. Mapping cod: fisheries science, fish harvesters' ecological knowledge and cod migrations in the northern Gulf of St. Lawrence. *Human Ecology* 36: 581–98.

Murray, S. O. 1982. The dissolution of classical ethnoscience. *Journal of the History of Behavioral Sciences* 18: 163–75.

Nabhan, G. P. 1985. *Gathering the Desert.* Tucson, AZ: University of Arizona Press.

Nabhan, G. P. 2000a. Native American management and conservation of biodiversity in the Sonoran Desert bioregion. In *Biodiversity and Native America* (P. E. Minnis and W. J. Elisens, eds). Norman, OK: University of Oklahoma Press, 29–43.

Nabhan, G. P. 2000b. Interspecific relationships affecting endangered species recognized by O'odham and Comcaac cultures. *Ecological Applications* 10: 1288–95.

Nadasdy, P. 1999. The politics of TEK: power and the "integration" of knowledge. *Arctic Anthropology* 36: 1–18.

Naess, A. 1989. *Ecology, Community and Lifestyle: Outline of an Ecosophy.* Trans. and ed. D. Rothenberg. Cambridge: Cambridge University Press.

Nakashima, D. J. 1991. The ecological knowledge of Belcher Island Inuit: a traditional basis for contemporary wildlife co-management. Ph.D. thesis, McGill University, Montreal.

Nakashima, D. J. 1993. Astute observers on the sea ice: Inuit knowledge as a basis for Arctic co-management. In *Traditional Ecological Knowledge: Concepts and Cases* (J. T. Inglis, ed.). Ottawa: Canadian Museum of Nature/International Development Research Centre, 99–110.

Nakashima, D. J. 1998. Conceptualizing nature, the cultural context of resource management. *Nature and Resources* 34(2): 8–22.

Natcher, D. C., S. Davis, and C. G. Hickey. 2005. Co-management: managing relationships, not resources. *Human Organization* 64: 240–50.

Natcher, D. C., M. Calef, O. Huntington *et al.* 2007. Factors contributing to the cultural and spatial variability of landscape burning by native peoples of Interior Alaska. *Ecology and Society* 12(1): 7. [online]: http://www.ecologyandsociety.org/vol12/iss1/art7

Nazarea, V. D. 1998. *Cultural Memory and Biodiversity.* Tucson, AZ: University of Arizona Press.

Nazarea, V. D. (ed.). 1999. *Ethnoecology: Situated Knowledge/Located Lives.* Tucson, AZ: University of Arizona Press.

Nazarea, V. D. 2006. Local knowledge and memory in biodiversity conservation. *Annual Review of Anthropology* 35: 317–35.

Neihardt, J. G. 1932 *Black Elk Speaks*. Lincoln, NE and London: University of Nebraska Press.

Neis, B. 1992. Fishers' ecological knowledge and stock assessment in Newfoundland. *Newfoundland Studies* 8: 155–78.

Neis, B. 2005. A need for historical knowledge for using current knowledge. *Common Property Resources Digest* No. 75: 5–7.

Neis, B., L. Felt, D. C. Schneider, R. Haedrich, J. Hutchings, and J. Fischer. 1996. Northern cod stock assessment: what can be learned from interviewing resource users? Department of Fisheries and Oceans, Atlantic Fisheries Research Document No. 96/45.

Nelson, R. K. 1969. *Hunters of the Northern Ice*. Chicago, IL: University of Chicago Press.

Nelson, R. K. 1982. A conservation ethic and environment: The Koyukon of Alaska. In *Resource Managers: North American and Australian Hunter-Gatherers* (N. M. Williams and E. S. Hunn, eds). Washington DC: American Association for the Advancement of Science, 211–28.

Nelson, R. 1993. Searching for the lost arrow: physical and spiritual ecology in the hunter's world. In *The Biophilia Hypothesis* (S. R. Kellert and E. O. Wilson, eds). Washington, DC: Island Press, 201–28.

Netting, R. M. 1981. *Balancing on an Alp: Ecological Change and Continuity in a Swiss Mountain Community*. Cambridge: Cambridge University Press.

Netting, R. M. 1986. *Cultural Ecology,* 2nd edn. Prospect Heights, IL: Waveland Press.

Neves-Graca, K. 2004. Revisiting the tragedy of the commons: ecological dilemmas of whale watching in the Azores. *Human Organization* 63: 289–300.

Newman, J. and H. Moller. 2005. Use of mātauranga (Māori traditional knowledge) and science to guide a seabird harvest: getting the best of both worlds? *Senri Ethnological Studies* 67: 303–21.

Newsome, A. 1980. The eco-mythology of the red kangaroo in central Australia. *Mankind* 12: 327–34.

Niamir, M. 1990. Herders' decision-making in natural resources management in arid and semiarid Africa. Rome: FAO Community Forestry Note No. 4.

Niamir-Fuller, M. 1998. The resilience of pastoral herding in Sahelian Africa. In *Linking Social and Ecological Systems: Management Practices and Social Mechanisms for Building Resilience* (F. Berkes and C. Folke, eds). Cambridge: Cambridge University Press, 250–84.

Nichols, T., F. Berkes, D. Jolly, N. B Snow, and the Community of Sachs Harbour 2004. Climate change and sea ice: local observations from the Canadian western Arctic. *Arctic* 57: 68–79.

Norberg, J. and G. S. Cumming (eds.) 2008. *Complexity Theory for a Sustainable Future*. New York: Columbia University Press.

Norgaard, R. B. 1994. *Development Betrayed: The End of Progress and a Coevolutionary Revisioning of the Future*. London and New York: Routledge.

Norgaard, R. B. 2004. Learning and knowing collectively. *Ecological Economics* 49: 231–41.

Norton, B. 1991. *Toward Unity Among Environmentalists*. New Haven, CT: Yale University Press.

Norton, B. G. 2005. *Sustainability. A Philosophy of Adaptive Ecosystem Management*. Chicago, IL: University of Chicago Press.

Nyamweru C. and E. Kimaru. 2008. The contribution of ecotourism to the conservation of natural sacred sites: a case study from coastal Kenya. *Journal for the Study of Religion, Nature and Culture* 2: 327–50.

Odum, E. P. 1971. *Fundamentals of Ecology*, 3rd edn. Philadelphia, PA: Saunders.

O'Flaherty, R. M., I. J. Davidson-Hunt, and M. Manseau. 2008. Indigenous knowledge and values in planning for sustainable forestry: Pikangikum First Nation and the Whitefeather Forest Initiative. *Ecology and Society* 13(1):6. [online]: http://www.ecologyandsociety.org/vol13/iss1/art6

Ohmagari, K. and F. Berkes. 1997. Transmission of indigenous knowledge and bush skills among the Western James Bay Cree women of subarctic Canada. *Human Ecology* 25: 197–222.

Oldfield, M. L. and J. B. Alcorn (eds). 1991. *Biodiversity: Culture, Conservation and Ecodevelopment*. Boulder, CO: Westview Press.

Olsson, P. and C. Folke. 2001. Local ecological knowledge and institutional dynamics for ecosystem management: a study of Lake Racken watershed, Sweden. *Ecosystems* 4: 85–104.

Olsson, P., C. Folke, and F. Berkes 2004. Adaptive co-management for building resilience in social-ecological systems. *Environmental Management* 34: 75–90.

Ommer, R. E., H. Coward, and C. C. Parrish. 2008. Knowledge, uncertainty and wisdom. In *Making and Moving Knowledge* (J.S. Lutz and B. Neis, eds.). Montreal and Kingston: McGill-Queen's University Press, 20–41.

Omura, K. 2005. Science against modern science: the socio-political construction of otherness in Inuit TEK (traditional ecological knowledge). *Senri Ethnological Studies* 67: 323–44.

O'Neil, J., B. Elias, and A. Yassi. 1997. Poisoned food: cultural resistance to the contaminants discourse. *Arctic Anthropology* 34: 29–40.

Ontario Ministry of Natural Resources. 1994. *A Proposal for an Environmental Information Partnership in the Moose River Basin.* Kapuskasing, Ontario: Moose River Basin Project.

Oozeva, C., C. Noongwook, G. Alowa, and I. Krupnik. 2004. *Watching Ice and Weather Our Way.* Washington DC: Arctic Studies Center, Smithsonian Institution.

Orlove, B. S. and S. B. Brush. 1996. Anthropology and the conservation of biodiversity. *Annual Reviews of Anthropology*, 25: 329–52.

Orlove, B. S., J. C. H. Chiang, and M. A. Cane 2000. Forecasting Andean rainfall and crop yield from the influence of El Niño on Pleiades visibility. *Nature* 403: 69–71.

Orlove, B. S., J. C. H. Chiang and M. A. Cane 2002. Ethnoclimatology in the Andes: a cross-disiplinary study uncovers a scientific basis for the scheme Andean potato farmers traditionally use to predict the coming rains. *American Scientist* 90: 428–435.

Ormsby, A. A. and S. A. Bhagwat. 2010. Sacred forests of India: a strong tradition of community-based natural resource management. *Environmental Conservation* 37: 1–7.

Orozco-Quintero, A. M. 2007. Self-organization, linkages and drivers of change: strategies for development in Nuevo San Juan, Mexico. Winnipeg, MB: Master's Thesis, University of Manitoba.

Ostrom, E. 1990. *Governing the Commons: The Evolution of Institutions for Collective Action.* Cambridge: Cambridge University Press.

Ostrom, E., T. Dietz, N. Dolsak, P. C. Stern, S. Stonich, and E. U. Weber (eds). 2002. *The Drama of the Commons.* Washington, DC: National Academy Press.

Owen-Smith, N. 1987. Pleistocene extinctions: the pivotal role of megaherbivores. *Paleobiology* 13: 351–62.

Özesmi, U. and S.L. Özesmi. 2004. Ecological models based on people's knowledge: a multi-step fuzzy cognitive mapping approach. *Ecological Modelling* 176: 43–64.

Painemilla, K. W., A. B. Rylands, A. Woofter and C. Hughes (eds). 2010. *Indigenous Peoples and Conservation: From Rights to Resource Management.* Arlington, VA: Conservation International.

Palsson, G. 1982. Territoriality among Icelandic fishermen. *Acta Sociologica* 25(supplement): 5–12.

Pandey, D. N. 1998. *Ethnoforestry: Local Knowledge for Sustainable Forestry and Livelihood Security.* Udaipur and New Delhi: Himanshu Publications.

Papayannis, T. and J.-M. Mallarach (eds). 2009. *The Sacred Dimension of Protected Areas.* Gland, Switzerland: IUCN.

Parlee, B., M. Manseau, and Lutsel K'e Dene First Nation. 2005a. Using traditional knowledge to adapt to ecological change: Denesoline monitoring of caribou movements. *Arctic* 58: 26–37.

Parlee, B., F. Berkes, and the Teetl'it Gwich'in Renewable Resources Council 2005b. Health of the land, health of the people: a case study on Gwich'in berry harvesting from northern Canada. *EcoHealth* 2: 127–37.

Parlee, B., F. Berkes, and Teetl'it Gwich'in Renewable Resources Council 2006. Indigenous knowledge of ecological variability and commons management: a case study on berry harvesting from northern Canada. *Human Ecology* 34: 515–28.

Parrotta, J. A. and R. L. Trosper (eds). 2012. *Traditional Forest-Related Knowledge: Sustaining Communities, Ecosystems and Biocultural Diversity.* New York: Springer.

Pawluk, R. R., J. A. Sandor, and J. A. Tabor. 1992. The role of indigenous soil knowledge in agricultural development. *Journal of Soil and Water Conservation* 47: 298–302.

Pearce, F. 1993. Living in harmony with forests. *New Scientist* 23 September: 11–12.

Pearce, T., J. D. Ford, G. J. Laidler *et al.* 2009. Community collaboration and climate change research in the Canadian Arctic. *Polar Research* 28: 10–27.

Peloquin, C. 2007. Variability, change and continuity in social-ecological systems: insights from James Bay Cree cultural ecology. Winnipeg, MB: Master's Thesis, University of Manitoba.

Peloquin, C. and F. Berkes. 2009. Local knowledge, subsistence harvests, and social-ecological complexity in James Bay. *Human Ecology* 37: 533–45.

Peluso, N. L. 1995. Whose woods are these? Counter-mapping forest territories in Kalimantan, Indonesia. *Antipode* 27 (4): 383–406.

Pepper, D. M. 1984. *The Roots of Modern Environmentalism.* London: Croom Helm.

Peroni, N., A. Begosi, and N. Hanazaki. 2008. Artisanal fishers' ethnobotany: from plant diversity use to agrobiodiversity management. *Environment, Development and Sustainability* 10: 623–37.

Pesek, T., M. Abramiuk, N. Fini *et al.* 2010. Q'eqchi' Maya healers' traditional knowledge in prioritizing conservation of medicinal plants: culturally relative conservation in sustaining traditional holistic health promotion. *Biodiversity Conservation* 19: 1–20.

Pieroni, A. and L. L. Price (eds). 2006. *Eating and Healing. Traditional Food as Medicine.* New York: Haworth Press.

Pilgrim, S. and J. Pretty (eds). 2010. *Nature and Culture. Rebuilding Lost Connections.* London: Earthscan.

Pimbert, M. P. and J. N. Pretty. 1995. Parks, people and professionals. Geneva: United Nations Research Institute for Social Development (UNRISD) Discussion Paper No. 57.

Pimbert, M. P. and B. Gujja. 1997. Village voices challenging wetland management policies. *Nature and Resources* 33: 34–42.

Poffenberger, M., B. McGean, and A. Khare. 1996. Communities sustaining India's forests in the twenty-first century. In *Village Voices, Forest Choices* (M. Poffenberger and B. McGean, eds). Delhi: Oxford University Press, 17–55.

Polanyi, K. 1964. *The Great Transformation.* Boston, MA: Beacon Press. (Original edn 1944.)

Polunin, N. V. C. 1984. Do traditional marine "reserves" conserve? A view of Indonesian and New Guinean evidence. *Senri Ethnological Studies* 17: 267–83.

Posey, D. A. 1985. Indigenous management of tropical forest ecosystems: the case of the Kayapo Indians of the Brazilian Amazon. *Agroforestry Systems* 3: 139–58.

Posey, D. A. 1998. Diachronic ecotones and anthropogenic landscapes in Amazonia: contesting the consciousness of conservation. In *Advances in Historical Ecology* (W. Balée, ed.). New York: Columbia University Press, 104–17.

Posey, D. A. (ed.). 1999. *Cultural and Spiritual Values of Biodiversity.* Nairobi: UNEP and Intermediate Technology Publications.

Posey, D. A. and W. L. Balée (eds). 1989. *Resource Management in Amazonia: Indigenous and Folk Strategies.* New York: New York Botanical Garden.

Posey, D. A. and G. Dutfield. 1996. *Beyond Intellectual Property: Toward Traditional Resource Rights for Indigenous Peoples and Local Communities.* Ottawa: International Development Research Centre.

Posey, D. A. and G. Dutfield (principal writers). 1997. *Indigenous Peoples and Sustainability: Cases and Actions.* Utrecht: International Books/IUCN (International Conservation Union).

Power, G. 1978. Fish population structure in Arctic lakes. *Journal of the Fisheries Research Board of Canada* 35: 53–9.

Preston, R. J. 1975. Cree Narrative: Expressing the Personal Meanings of Events. Ottawa: National Museum of Man Mercury Series, Canadian Ethnology Service Paper No. 30, National Museum of Canada.

Preston, R. J. 1979. The development and self control in the eastern Cree life cycle. In *Childhood and Adolescence in Canada* (K. Ishwaran, ed.). Toronto: McGraw-Hill, 83–96.

Preston, R. J. 2002. *Cree Narrative. Expressing the Personal Meanings of Events,* 2nd edn. Montreal and Kingston: McGill-Queen's University Press.

Preston, R. J., F. Berkes, and P. J. George. 1995. Perspectives on sustainable development in the Moose River Basin. Papers of the 26th Algonquian Conference, pp. 378–93.

Pretty, J. 2007. *The Earth Only Endures: On Connecting with Nature and Our Place in it.* London: Earthscan.

Pretty, J., W. Adams, F. Berkes *et al.* 2009. The intersections of biological diversity and cultural diversity: towards integration. *Conservation & Society* 7(2): 100–12.

Pruitt, W. O. 1960. Animals in the snow. *Scientific American* 202(1): 60–8.

Pruitt, W. O. 1978. *Boreal Ecology.* London: Edward Arnold.

Pruitt, W. O. 1984. Snow and living things. In *Northern Ecology and Resource Management* (R. Olson, F. Geddes, and R. Hastings, eds). Edmonton: University of Alberta Press, 51–77.

Pullum, G. 1991. *The Eskimo Vocabulary Hoax and Other Irreverant Essays on the Study of Language.* Chicago, IL: University of Chicago Press.

Putney, A. D. 1989. Getting the balance right. *World Wildlife Fund Reports* June/July: 19–21.

Raffles, H. 2002. Intimate knowledge. *International Social Science Journal* 173: 325–35.

Raj, R. 2006. Harmonizing traditional and scientific knowledge systems in rainfall prediction and utilization. In *Bridging Scales and Knowledge Systems* (W. V. Reid, F. Berkes, T. Wilbanks, and D. Capistrano, (eds). Washington, DC: Island Press, 225–39. [online]: http://www.maweb.org/documents/bridging/bridging.12.pdf

Ramakrishnan, P. S. 1992. *Shifting Agriculture and Sustainable Development: An Interdisciplinary Study from North-Eastern India.* Paris: UNESCO/Parthenon.

Ramakrishnan, P. S. 2007. Traditional forest knowledge and sustainable forestry: a north-east India perspective. *Forest Ecology and Management* 249: 91–9.

Ramakrishnan, P. S., K. G. Saxena and U. M. Chandrashekara (eds). 1998. *Conserving the Sacred for Biodiversity Management.* New Delhi: Oxford and IBH Publishing.

Ramakrishnan, P. S., K. G. Saxena, and K. S. Rao (eds). 2006. *Shifting Agriculture and Sustainable Development of North-Eastern India: Tradition in Transition.* New Delhi: Oxford and IBH Publishing.

Ramos, A. 1994. From Eden to limbo: the construction of indigenism in Brazil. In *Social Construction of the Past: Representation as Power* (G. C. Bond and A. Gillam, eds). London: Routledge, 74–88.

Rappaport, R. A. 1979. *Ecology, Meaning and Religion.* Richmond, CA: North Atlantic Books.

Rappaport, R. A. 1984. *Pigs for the Ancestors: Ritual in the Ecology of a New Guinea People*, 2nd edn. New Haven and London: Yale University Press.

Ravuvu, A. D. 1987. *The Fijian Ethos.* Suva, Fiji: Institute of Pacific Studies, University of the South Pacific.

Ray, A. J. 1975. Some conservation schemes of the Hudson's Bay Company, 1821–50. *Journal of Historical Geography* 1: 49–68.

Redford, K. H. 1992. The empty forest. *BioScience* 42: 412–22.

Redford, K. H. and C. Padoch (eds). 1992. *Conservation of Neotropical Forests: Working from Traditional Resource Use.* New York: Columbia University Press.

Redford, K. H. and A. M. Stearman. 1993. Forest-dwelling native Amazonians and the conservation of biodiversity. *Conservation Biology* 7: 248–55.

Redford, K. H. and J. A. Mansour (eds). 1996. *Traditional Peoples and Biodiversity Conservation in Large Tropical Landscapes.* Arlington, VA: America Verde/The Nature Conservancy.

Redman, C. 1999. *Human Impacts on Ancient Environments.* Tucson, AZ: University of Arizona Press.

Regier, H. A. 1978. *A Balanced Science of Renewable Resources with Particular Reference to Fisheries.* Seattle, WA and London: Washington Sea Grant and University of Washington Press.

Regier, H. A. and G. L. Baskerville. 1986. Sustainable redevelopment of regional ecosystems degraded by exploitive development. In *Sustainable Development of the Biosphere* (W. C. Clark and R. E. Munn, eds). Cambridge: Cambridge University Press, 75–103.

Reichel-Dolmatoff, G. 1976. Cosmology as ecological analysis: a view from the rain forest. *Man* 11(NS): 307–18.

Reid, R. S. and J. E. Ellis. 1995. Impacts of pastoralists in South Turkana, Kenya: livestock-mediated tree recruitment. *Ecological Applications* 5: 978–92.

Reid, W. V., F. Berkes, T. Wilbanks, and D. Capistrano (eds). 2006. *Bridging Scales and Knowledge Systems: Linking Global Science and Local Knowledge in Assessments.* Washington DC: Millennium Ecosystem Assessment and Island Press. [online]: http://www.maweb.org/en/Bridging.aspx

Reij, C., I. Scoones, and C. Toulmin (eds). 1996. *Sustaining the Soil: Indigenous Soil and Water Conservation in Africa.* London: Earthscan.

Renard, Y. 1994. *Community Participation in St. Lucia.* Washington, DC: Panes Institute, and Vieux Fort, St. Lucia: Caribbean Natural Resources Institute.

Reyes-Garcia, V., V. Valdez, T. Huanca, W. R. Leonard and T. McDade. 2007. Economic development and local ecological knowledge: a deadlock? Quantitative research from a native Amazonian society. *Human Ecology* 35: 371–7.

Richards, P. 1985. *Indigenous Agricultural Revolution: Ecology and Food Production in West Africa.* London: Hutchinson.

Richardson, A. 1982. The control of productive resources on the Northwest coast of North America. In *Resource Managers: North American and Australian Hunter-Gatherers* (N. M. Williams and E. S. Hunn, eds). Washington, DC: American Association for the Advancement of Science, 93–112.

Riedlinger, D. and F. Berkes. 2001. Contributions of traditional knowledge to understanding climate change in the Canadian Arctic. *Polar Record* 37: 315–28.

Riewe, R. 1991. Inuit use of the sea ice. *Arctic and Alpine Research* 23: 3–10.

Riewe, R. (ed.). 1992. *Nunavut Atlas.* Edmonton: Canadian Circumpolar Institute and the Tungavik Federation of Nunavut.

Rist, S. and F. Dahdouh-Guebas. 2006. Ethnosciences—a step towards the integration of scientific and indigenous forms of knowledge in the management of natural resources for the future. *Environment, Development and Sustainability* 8: 467–93.

Robbins, P. 2004. *Political Ecology: A Critical Introduction*. Oxford: Blackwell.

Robbins, P. 2006. The politics of barstool biology: environmental knowledge and power in greater Northern Yellowstone. *Geoforum* 37: 185–99.

Roberts, M., W. Norman, N. Minhinnick, D. Wihongi, and C. Kirkwood. 1995. *Kaitiakitanga*: Maori perspectives on conservation. *Pacific Conservation Biology* 2: 7–20.

Robertson, H. A. and T. K. McGee. 2003. Applying local knowledge: the contribution of oral history to wetland rehabilitation at Kanyapella Basin, Australia. *Journal of Environmental Management* 69: 275–87.

Robinson, L. W. and F. Berkes. 2010. Applying resilience thinking to questions of policy for pastoralist systems: lessons from the Gabra of northern Kenya. *Human Ecology* 38: 335–50.

Robson, J. P. and F. Berkes. 2010. Sacred nature and community conserved areas. In *Nature and Culture: Rebuilding Lost Connections* (S. Pilgrim and J. Pretty, eds). London: Earthscan, 197–216.

Robson, J. P. and F. Berkes. 2011. Exploring some myths of land use change: can rural to urban migration drive declines in biodiversity? *Global Environmental Change* 21: 844–54.

Robson, J. P., A. M. Miller, C. J. Idrobo *et al.* 2009. Building communities of learning: indigenous ways of knowing in contemporary natural resources and environmental management. *Journal of the Royal Society of New Zealand* 39: 173–7.

Rocheleau, D. E. 1991. Gender, ecology, and the science of survival: stories and lessons from Kenya. *Agriculture and Human Values* 8: 156–65.

Rocheleau, D. 1995. Maps, numbers, text and context: mixing methods in feminist political ecology. *Professional Geographer* 47: 458–66.

Roncoli, C. and K. Ingram. 2002. Reading the rains: local knowledge and rainfall forecasting in Burkina Faso. *Society and Natural Resources* 15: 409–27.

Rose, D. B. 2004. *Reports from a Wild Country: Ethics for Decolonization*. Sydney: University of New South Wales.

Rose, D. 2005. An indigenous philosophical ecology: situating the human. *Australian Journal of Anthropology* 16: 294–305.

Ross, A. and K. Pickering. 2002. The politics of reintegrating Australian aboriginal and American Indian indigenous knowledge into resource management: the dynamics of resource appropriation and cultural revival. *Human Ecology* 30: 87–214.

Ross A., K. Pickering, J. Snodgrass, H. D. Delcore and R. Sherman. 2010. *Indigenous Peoples and the Collaborative Stewardship of Nature: Knowledge Binds and Institutional Conflicts*. Walnut Cree, CA: Left Coast Press.

Ross, H., C. Grant, C. J. Robinson, A. Izurieta, D. Smyth and P. Rist. 2009. Co-management and indigenous protected areas in Australia: achievements and ways forward. *Australasian Journal of Environmental Management* 16: 242–52.

Roszak, T. 1972. *Where the Wasteland Ends*. Garden City, NY: Doubleday.

Roth, R. 2004. Spatial organization of environmental knowledge: conservation conflicts in the inhabited forest of northern Thailand. *Ecology and Society* 9 (3): 5. [online]: http://www.ecologyandsociety.org/vol9/iss3/art5

Ruddle, K. 1994a. Local knowledge in the folk management of fisheries and coastal marine environments. In *Folk Management in the World's Fisheries: Lessons for Modern Fisheries Management* (C. L. Dyer and J. R. McGoodwin, eds). Niwot: University Press of Colorado, 161–206.

Ruddle, K. 1994b. A guide to the literature on traditional community-based fishery management in the Asia-Pacific tropics. Rome: FAO Fisheries Circular No. 869.

Ruddle, K. and T. Akimichi (eds). 1984. *Maritime Institutions in the Western Pacific*. Senri Ethnological Studies 17. Osaka: National Museum of Ethnology.

Ruddle, K., and R. E. Johannes (eds). 1985. The Traditional Knowledge and Management of Coastal Systems in Asia and the Pacific. Jakarta: UNESCO.

Ruddle, K. and R. E. Johannes (eds). 1990. *Traditional Marine Resource Management in the Pacific Basin: An Anthology*. Jakarta: UNESCO.

Ruddle, K., E. Hviding, and R. E. Johannes. 1992. Marine resources management in the context of customary tenure. *Marine Resource Economics* 7: 249–73.

Ruiz-Pérez, M., B. Belcher, R. Achdiawan *et al.* 2004. Markets drive the specialization strategies of forest peoples. *Ecology and Society* 9(2): 4. [online]: http://www.ecologyandsociety.org/vol9/iss2/art4

Sable, T., G. Howell, D. Wilson, and P. Penashue. 2006. The Askhui Project:linking Western science and Innu environmental knowledge in creating a sustainable environment. In *Local Science vs. Global Science: Approaches to Indigenous Knowledge in International Development* (P. Sillitoe, ed.). New York: Berghahn Books, 109–18.

Sadler, B. and P. Boothroyd (eds). 1994. *Traditional Ecological Knowledge and Modern Environmental Assessment*. Vancouver: Centre for Human Settlements, University of British Columbia.

Said, E. 1994. *Culture and Imperialism*. New York: Vintage.

Salick, J. and N. Ross. 2009. Traditional peoples and climate change. *Global Environmental Change* 19: 137–39.

Salick, J., A. Amend, D. Anderson *et al.* 2007. Tibetan sacred sites conserve old growth trees and cover in the eastern Himalayas. *Biodiversity and Conservation* 16: 693–706.

Sanford, R. L., J. Saldarriga, K. E. Clark, C. Uhl, and R. Herrera. 1985. Amazon rainforest fires. *Science* 227: 53–5.

Sayles, J. S. and M. E. Mulrennan. 2010. Securing a future: Cree hunters' resistance and flexibility to environmental changes, Wemindji, James Bay. *Ecology and Society* 15: 22. [online]: http://www.ecologyandsociety.org/articles/3828.html

Schaaf, T. and C. Lee (eds). 2006. *Conserving Cultural and Biological Diversity: The Role of Sacred Natural Sites and Cultural Landscapes*. Proceedings of the Tokyo Symposium. Paris: UNESCO.

Schindler, D. W. and J. P. Smol. 2006. Cumulative effects of climate warming and other human activities on freshwaters of arctic and subarctic North America. *Ambio* 35: 160–8.

Schlacher, T. A., S. Lloyd, and A. Wiegand. 2010. Use of local ecological knowledge in the management of algal blooms. *Environmental Conservation* 37: 210–21.

Schmidt, J. J. and M. Dowsley. 2010. Hunting with polar bears: problems with passive properties of the commons. *Human Ecology* 38: 377–87.

Schultes, R. E. 1989. Reasons for ethnobotanical conservation. In *Traditional Ecological Knowledge: A Collection of Essays* (R. E. Johannes, ed.). Gland, Switzerland: International Conservation Union (IUCN).

Schultes, R. E. and S. Reis (eds). 1995. *Ethnobotany: Evolution of a Discipline*. Portland, OR: Timber Press.

Scoones, I. 1999. New ecology and the social sciences: what prospects for fruitful engagement? *Annual Review of Anthropology* 28: 479–507.

Scott, C. 1986. Hunting territories, hunting bosses and communal production among coastal James Bay Cree. *Anthropologica* 28: 163–73.

Scott, C. 1989. Knowledge construction among Cree hunters: metaphors and literal understanding. *Journal de la Société des Américanistes* 75: 193–208.

Scott, C. 2006. Spirit and practical knowledge in the person of the bear among Wemindji Cree Hunters. *Ethnos* 71: 51–66.

Scott, J. C. 1998. *Seeing Like a State: How Certain Schemes to Improve the Human Condition Have Failed*. New Haven: Yale University Press.

Sears, R. R., C. Padoch, and M. Pinedo-Vasquez. 2007. Amazon forestry transformed: integrating knowledge for smallholder timber management in eastern Brazil. *Human Ecology* 35: 697–707.

Seixas, C. and F. Berkes. 2003. Dynamics of social-ecological changes in a lagoon fishery in southern Brazil. In *Navigating Social-Ecological Systems* (F. Berkes, J. Colding, and C. Folke, eds). Cambridge: Cambridge University Press, 271–98.

Selin, H. (ed.). 2003. *Nature across Cultures*. Dordrecht: Kluwer.

Senos, R., F. K. Lake, N. Turner, and D. Martinez. 2006. Traditional ecological knowledge and restoration practice. In *Restoring the Pacific Northwest: The Art and Science of Ecological Restoration in Cascadia* (D. Apostol and M. Sinclair, eds). Washington, DC: Island Press, 393–426.

Shaw, S. and A. Francis (eds). 2008. *Deep Blue: Critical Reflections on Nature, Religion and Water*. London: Equinox.

Sheil, D. and A. Lawrence. 2004. Tropical biologists, local people and conservation: new opportunities for collaboration. *Trends in Ecology and Evolution* 19: 634–38.

Shepard, P. 1973. *The Tender Carnivore and the Sacred Game*. New York: Scribner.

Sheridan, M. J. 2009. The environmental and social history of African sacred groves: a Tanzanian case study. *African Studies Review* 52: 73–98.

Sheridan, M. J. and C. Nyamweru (eds). 2008. *African Sacred Groves*. Athens OH: Ohio University Press.

Sherry, E. and H. Myers. 2002. Traditional environmental knowledge in practice. *Society and Natural Resources* 15: 345–58.

Shipek, F. 1993. Kumeeyay plant husbandry: fire, water, and erosion management systems. In *Before the Wilderness: Environmental Management by Native Californians* (T. C. Blackburn and K. Anderson, eds). Menlo Park, CA: Ballena Press, 379–88.

Shiva, V. 1988. *Staying Alive: Women, Ecology and Development*. London: Zed Press.

Shiva, V. and R. Holla-Bhar. 1993. Intellectual piracy and the neem tree. *The Ecologist* 23(6).

Shukla, S. R. and J. S. Gardner. 2006. Local knowledge in community-based approaches to medicinal plant conservation: lessons from India. *Journal of Ethnobiology and Ethnomedicine* 2: 20 [online]: http://www.ethnobiomed.com/content/2/1/20

Shukla, S. and A. J. Sinclair. 2009. Becoming a traditional medicinal plant healer: divergent views of practicing and young healers on traditional medicinal plant knowledge skills in India. *Ethnobotany Research and Applications* 7: 039–051.

Sileshi, G. W., P. Nyeko, P. O. Y. Nkunika, B. M. Sekematte *et al.* 2009. Integrating ethno-ecological and scientific knowledge of termites for sustainable terminate management and human welfare in Africa. *Ecology and Society* 14: 48. [online]: http://www.ecologyandsociety.org/vol14/iss1/art48

Sillitoe, P. 2002. Contested knowledge, contingent classification: animals in the highlands of Papua New Guinea. *American Anthropologist* 104(4): 1162–71.

Sillitoe, P. (ed.) 2006. *Local Science vs. Global Science: Approaches to Indigenous in International Development*. New York and Oxford: Berghahn.

Silvano, R. A. M. and A. Begossi. 2010. What can be learned from fishers? An integrated survey of fishers' local ecological knowledge and bluefish (*Pomatomus saltatrix*) biology on the Brazilian coast. *Hydrobiologia* 637: 3–18.

Simpson, L. R. 2001. Decolonizing our processes: indigenous knowledge and ways of knowing. *Canadian Journal of Native Studies* 21: 137–48.

Simpson, L. 2005. Traditional ecological knowledge among aboriginal peoples in Canada. In *Encyclopedia of Religion and Nature* (B. R. Taylor, ed.). London and New York: Thoemmes Continuum, 1649–51.

Sirait, M., S. Pasodjo, N. Podger, A. Flavelle, and J. Fox. 1994. Mapping customary land in East Kalimantan, Indonesia: a tool for forest management. *Ambio* 23: 411–17.

Siu, R. G. H. 1957. *The Tao of Science: An Essay on Western Knowledge and Eastern Wisdom*. Cambridge, MA: MIT Press.

Skolimowski, H. 1981. *Eco-Philosophy*. London: Boyars.

Slobodkin, L. B. 1968. How to be a predator. *American Zoologist* 8: 43–51.

Smith, A. H. and F. Berkes. 1991. Solutions to the "tragedy of the commons": sea-urchin management in St. Lucia, West Indies. *Environmental Conservation* 18: 131–36.

Smith, A. H. and F. Berkes. 1993. Community-based use of mangrove resources in St. Lucia. *International Journal of Environmental Studies* 43: 123–31.

Smith, A. H., A. Jean, and K. Nichols. 1986. An investigation of the potential for the commercial mariculture of seamoss (*Gracilaria* spp. *Rhodophycophyta*) in St. Lucia. *Proceedings of the Gulf and Caribbean Fisheries Institute* 37: 4–11.

Smith, E. A. and M. Wishnie. 2000. Conservation and subsistence in small-scale societies. *Annual Review of Anthropology* 29: 493–524.

Smith, J. G. E. 1978. Economic uncertainty in an "original affluent society": caribou and caribou-eater Chipewyan adaptive strategies. *Arctic Anthropology* 15: 68–88.

Smith, L. Tuhiwai. 1999. *Decolonizing Methodologies: Research and Indigenous Peoples*. London: Zed Books.

Snodgrass, J. G. and K. Tiedje. 2008. Guest editors' introduction: indigenous nature reverence and conservation – seven ways of transcending an unnecessary dichotomy. *Journal for the Study of Religion, Nature and Culture* 2(1): 6–29.

Spak, S. 2005. The position of indigenous knowledge in Canadian co-management organizations. *Anthropologica* 47: 233–46.

Speck, F. G. 1915. The family hunting band as the basis of Algonkian social organization. *American Anthropologist* 17: 289–305.

Speck, F. G. 1935. *Naskapi: Savage Hunters of the Labrador Peninsula*. Norman, OK: University of Oklahoma Press.

Spencer, J. E. 1966. *Shifting Cultivation in Southeast Asia*. Berkeley and Los Angeles. CA: University of California Press.

SRISTI. 2011. Society for Research and Initiatives for Sustainable Technologies and Institution. Honey Bee Network. [online]: http://www.sristi.org/hbnew/index.php

Steadman, D. W. 1995. Prehistoric extinctions of Pacific island birds: biodiversity meets zooarcheology. *Science* 267: 1123–31.

Steinmetz, R., W. Chutipong, and N. Seuaturien. 2006. Collaborating to conserve large mammals in southeast Asia. *Conservation Biology* 20: 1391–401.

Stephenson, J. and H. Moller. 2009. Cross-cultural environmental research and management: challenges and progress. *Journal of the Royal Society of New Zealand* 39:139–49.

Stevenson, M. G. 1996. Indigenous knowledge in environmental assessment. *Arctic* 49: 278–91.

Stevenson, M. G. 2006. The possibility of difference: rethinking co-management. *Human Organization* 65: 167–80.

Steward, J. H. 1936. The economic and social basis of primitive bands. In *Essays in Anthropology Presented to A. L. Kroeber*. Berkeley, CA: University of California Press, 331–50.

Steward, J. H. 1955. *Theory of Culture Change*. Urbana, IL: University of Illinois Press.

Stoffle, R. W., D. B. Halmo, M. J. Evans, and J. E. Olmstead. 1990. Calculating the cultural significance of American Indian plants: Paiute and Shoshone ethnobotany at Yucca Mountain, Nevada. *American Anthropologist* 92: 416–32.

Strauss, S. 1992. Historical record be damned, they sell environmentalism by co-opting Chief Seattle. *Globe and Mail*, Toronto, February 8, 1992.

Sturtevant, W. C. 1964. Studies in ethnoscience. *American Anthropologist* 66: 99–131.

Subramanian, S. M. and B. Pisupati (eds). 2010. *Traditional Knowledge in Policy and Practice*. Tokyo: UN University Press.

Suchet-Pearson, S. and R. Howitt 2006. On teaching and learning resource and environmental management: reframing capacity-building in multicultural settings. *Australian Geographer* 37: 117–28.

Sullivan, B. L., C. L. Wood, M. J. Iliff *et al.* 2009. eBird: a citizen-based bird observation network in the biological sciences. *Biological Conservation* 142: 2282–92.

Sutton, I. 1975. *Indian Land Tenure*. New York: Clearwater.

Sutton, P. 1995. *Country: Aboriginal Boundaries and Land Ownership in Australia*. Canberra: Australian National University, Aboriginal History Monograph 3.

Suzuki, D. and A. McConnell. 1997. *The Sacred Balance: Rediscovering Our Place in Nature*. Vancouver: Greystone.

Swezey, S. L. and R. F. Heizer. 1993. Ritual management of salmonid fish resources in California. In *Before the Wilderness: Environmental Management by Native Californians* (T. C. Blackburn and K. Anderson, eds). Menlo Park, CA: Ballena Press, 299–327. (Originally published in *Journal of California Anthropology* 1977, 4: 6–29.)

Taiepa, T., P. Lyver, P. Horsley, J. Davis, M. Bragg, and H. Moller. 1997. Co-management of New Zealand's conservation estate by Maori and Pakeha: a review. *Environmental Conservation* 24: 236–50.

Tanner, A. 1979. *Bringing Home Animals: Religious Ideology and Mode of Production of the Mistassini Cree Hunter*. London: Hurst.

Taylor, B. R. (ed.). 2005. *Encyclopedia of Religion and Nature*. London and New York: Thoemmes Continuum.

Taylor, B. 2009. *Dark Green Religion. Nature Spirituality and the Planetary Future*. Berkeley: University of California Press.

Taylor, R. I. 1988. Deforestation and Indians in the Brazilian Amazonia. In *Biodiversity* (E. O. Wilson, ed.). Washington DC: National Academy Press, 138–44.

Thomas, W. H. 2003. One last chance: tapping indigenous knowledge to produce sustainable conservation policies. *Futures* 35: 989–98.

Thorpe, N., N. Hakongak, S. Eyegetok, and Kitikmeot Elders. 2001. *Thunder on the Tundra: Inuit Quajimajatuqangit of the Bathurst Caribou*. Vancouver: Generation Printing.

Tiki, W., G. Oba and T. Tvedt. 2011. Human stewardship or ruining cultural landscapes of the ancient Tula wells, southern Ethiopia. *The Geographical Journal* 177: 62–78.

Tobias, T. 2000. *Chief Kerry's Moose: A Guidebook to Land Use and Occupancy Mapping, Research Design and Data Collection*. Vancouver: Union of British Columbia Indian Chiefs. [online]: http://www.ubcic.bc.ca/files/PDF/Tobias_whole.pdf

Tobias, T. N. 2010. *Living Proof: The Essential Data Collection Guide for Indigenous Use and Occupancy Map Surveys*. Vancouver: Ecotrust Canada and Union of BC Indian Chiefs.

Toledo, V. M. 1992. What is ethnoecology? Origins, scope and implications of a rising discipline. *Ethnoecológica* 1(1): 5–21.

Toledo, V. M. 2001. Biodiversity and indigenous peoples. *Encyclopedia of Biodiversity,* Vol. 5. San Diego, CA: Academic Press, 330–40.

Toledo, V. M., B. Ortiz-Espejel, L. Cortés, P. Moguel, and M. D. J. Ordoñez. 2003. The multiple use of tropical forests by indigenous peoples in Mexico: a case of adaptive management. *Conservation Ecology* 7(3): 9. [online]: http://www.consecol.org/vol7/iss3/art9

Trosper, R. L. 1995. Traditional American Indian economic policy. *American Indian Culture and Research Journal* 19: 65–95.

Trosper, R. L. 1998. Land tenure and ecosystem management in Indian country. In *Who Owns America? Social Conflict Over Property Rights* (H. M. Jacobs, ed.). Madison, WI: University of Wisconsin Press, 208–26.

Trosper, R. L. 2002. Northwest coast indigenous institutions that supported resilience and sustainability. *Ecological Economics* 41: 329–44.

Trosper, R. L. 2007. Indigenous influence on forest management on the Menominee Indian Reservation. *Forest Ecology and Management* 249: 134–9.

Trosper, R. 2009. *Resilience, Reciprocity and Ecological Economics. Northwest Coast Sustainability.* London and New York: Routledge.

Trosper, R. and J. A. Parrotta. 2012. Introduction: the growing importance of traditional forest-related knowledge. In *Traditional Forest-Related Knowledge* (J. A. Parrotta and R. L. Trosper, eds). New York: Springer.

Tuan, Y. 1974. *Topophilia.* Englewood Cliffs, NJ: Prentice-Hall.

Turnbull, D. 1997. Reframing science and other local knowledge traditions. *Futures* 29: 551–62.

Turnbull, D. 2000. *Masons, Tricksters and Cartographers: Comparative Studies in the Sociology of Scientific and Indigenous Knowledge.* Reading: Harwood Academic Publishers.

Turnbull, D. (ed.). 2009. Futures of indigenous knowledges. *Futures* 41(1): 1–66.

Turner, B. L., W. C. Clark, R. W. Kates, J. F. Richards, J. T. Mathews, and W. B. Meyer (eds). 1990. *The Earth as Transformed by Human Action: Global and Regional Changes in the Biosphere Over the Past 300 Years.* Cambridge: Cambridge University Press.

Turner, N. J. 1988. The importance of a rose: evaluating the cultural significance of plants in Thompson and Lilooet Interior Salish. *American Anthropologist* 90: 272–90.

Turner, N. J. 1994. Burning mountain sides for better crops: Aboriginal landscape burning in British Columbia. *International Journal of Ecoforestry* 10: 116–22. (Originally published in *Archaeology in Montana* 1992, 32: 57–73.)

Turner, N. J. 1999. "Time to burn." Traditional use of fire to enhance resource production by aboriginal peoples in British Columbia. In *Indians, Fire and the Land in the Pacific Northwest* (R. Boyd, ed.). Corvallis, OR: Oregon State University Press, 185–218.

Turner, N. J. 2003. "Passing on the news": women's work, traditional knowledge and plant resource management in indigenous societies in NW N America. In *Women and Plants: Case Studies on Gender Relations in Local Plant Genetic Resource Management* (P. Howard, ed.). London: Zed Books, 133–49.

Turner, N. J. 2004. *Plants of Haida Gwaii.* Winlaw, British Columbia: Sono Nis.

Turner, N. J. 2005. *The Earth's Blanket: Traditional Teachings for Sustainable Living.* Vancouver: Douglas & McIntyre, and Seattle, WA: University of Washington Press.

Turner, N. J. and A. Davis. 1993. "When everything was scarce": the role of plants as famine foods in Northwestern North America. *Journal of Ethnobiology* 13: 171–201.

Turner, N. J. and F. Berkes. 2006. Coming to understanding: developing conservation through incremental learning in the Pacific Northwest. *Human Ecology* 34: 495–513.

Turner, N. J. and K. L. Turner. 2008. "Where our women used to get the food": cumulative effects and loss of ethnobotanical knowledge and practice; case study from coastal British Columbia. *Botany* 86: 103–115.

Turner, N. J. and H. Clifton 2009. "It's so different today": climate change and indigenous lifeways in British Colombia, Canada. *Global Environmental Change* 19: 180–190.

Turner, N. J., M. B. Ignace, and R. Ignace. 2000. Traditional ecological knowledge and wisdom of aboriginal peoples in British Columbia. *Ecological Applications* 10: 1275–87.

Turner, N. J., I. J. Davidson-Hunt, and M. O'Flaherty. 2003. Living on the edge: ecological and cultural edges as sources of diversity for social-ecological resilience. *Human Ecology* 31: 439–58.

Turner, N. J., Y. Ari, F. Berkes *et al.* 2009. Cultural management of living trees: an international perspective. *Journal of Ethnobiology* 29: 237–270.

Tyler, M. E. 1993. Spiritual stewardship in aboriginal resource management systems. *Environments* 22(1): 1–8.

Tyler, N. J. C., J. M. Turi, M. A. Sundset *et al.* 2007. Saami reindeer pastoralism under climate change: applying a generalized framework for vulnerability studies to a sub-arctic social-ecological system. *Global Environmental Change* 17: 191–206.

Usher, P. J. 2000. Traditional ecological knowledge in environmental assessment and management. *Arctic* 53: 183–93.

Valbo-Jorgensen, J. and A. F. Poulsen. 2001. Using local knowledge as a research tool in the study of river fish biology: experiences from the Mekong. *Environment, Development and Sustainability* 2: 253–76.

Valladolid, J. and F. Apffel-Marglin. 2001. Andean cosmovision and the nurturing of biodiversity. In *Indigenous Traditions and Ecology* (J. A. Grim, ed.). Cambridge, MA: Harvard University Press, 639–70.

Vandergeest, P. and N. L. Peluso. 1995. Territorialization and state power in Thailand. *Theory and Society* 35: 385–426.

Verschuuren, B., R. Wild, J.A .McNeely, and G. Oviedo (eds). 2010. *Sacred Natural Sites: Conserving Nature and Culture*. London: Earthscan.

Vestergaard, T. A. 1991. Living with pound nets: diffusion, invention and implications of a technology. *Folk* 33: 149–67.

Wallace, A. F. C. 1956. Revitalization movements: some theoretical considerations for their comparative study. *American Anthropologist* 58(2): 265.

Walsh, S. 2010. A Trojan horse of a word? "Development" in Bolivia's southern highlands: monocropping people, plants and knowledge. *Anthropologica* 52: 241–57.

Warner, G. 1997. Participatory management, popular knowledge and community empowerment: the case of sea urchin harvesting in the Vieux-Fort area of St. Lucia. *Human Ecology* 25: 29–46.

Warren, D. M. (ed.). 1991a. Indigenous agricultural knowledge systems and development. Special issue of *Agriculture and Human Values* 8(1/2).

Warren, D. M. 1991b. Using indigenous knowledge in agricultural development. *World Bank Discussion Papers* No. 127. Washington DC: World Bank.

Warren, D. M. 1995. Comments on article by Arun Agrawal. *Indigenous Knowledge and Development Monitor* 4(1): 13.

Warren, D. M. and J. Pinkston. 1998. Indigenous African resource management of a tropical rain forest ecosystem: a case study of the Yoruba of Ara, Nigeria. In *Linking Social and Ecological Systems* (F. Berkes and C. Folke, eds). Cambridge: Cambridge University Press, 158–89.

Warren, D. M., L. J. Slikkerveer, and D. Brokensha (eds). 1995. *The Cultural Dimension of Development: Indigenous Knowledge Systems*. London: Intermediate Technology Publications.

Watanabe, H. 1973. *The Ainu Ecosystem, Environment and Group Structure*. Seattle, WA: University of Washington Press.

Wavey, R. 1993. International Workshop on Indigenous Knowledge and Community-based Resource Management: keynote address. In *Traditional Ecological Knowledge: Concepts and Cases* (J. T. Inglis, ed.). Ottawa: Canadian Museum of Nature/International Development Research Centre, 11–16.

WCED (World Commission on Environment and Development). 1987. *Our Common Future*. Oxford and New York: Oxford University Press.

Wehi, P. M. 2009. Indigenous ancestral sayings contribute to modern conservation partnerships: examples using *Phormium texax. Ecological Applications* 19: 267–75.

Weinstein, M. S. 1993. Aboriginal land use and occupancy studies in Canada. Workshop on Spatial Aspects of Social Forestry Systems, Chiang Mai University, Thailand.

Weir, J.K. 2009. *Murray River Country: An Ecological Dialogue with Traditional Owners*. Canberra: Aboriginal Studies Press.

Wenzel, G. W. 2004. From TEK to IQ: Inuit Qaujimajatuqangit and Inuit cultural ecology. *Arctic Anthropology* 41: 238–50.

WFMC. 2011. Whitefeather forest initiative. Pikangikum, Ontario: Whitefeather Forest Management Corporation. [online]: http://www.whitefeatherforest.com

White, G. 2006. Cultures in collision: traditional knowledge and Euro-Canadian governance processes in northern land-claim boards. *Arctic* 59: 401–19.

White, L. 1967. The historical roots of our ecologic crisis. *Science* 155: 1203–7.

Whitehead, A. N. 1929. *Process and Reality: An Essay in Cosmology*. New York: Macmillan.

Wilkins, D. 1993. Linguistic evidence in support of a holistic approach to traditional ecological knowledge. In *Traditional Ecological Knowledge: Wisdom for Sustainable Development* (N. M.

Williams and G. Baines, eds). Canberra: Centre for Resource and Environmental Studies, Australian National University, 71–93.

Williams, N. M. and E. S. Hunn (eds). 1982. *Resource Managers: North American and Australian Hunter-Gatherers*. Washington, DC: American Association for the Advancement of Science.

Williams, N. M. and G. Baines (eds). 1993. *Traditional Ecological Knowledge: Wisdom for Sustainable Development*. Canberra: Centre for Resource and Environmental Studies, Australian National University.

Wilson, D. C. 2003. Examining the two cultures theory of fisheries knowledge: the case of bluefish management. *Society and Natural Resources* 16: 491–508.

Wilson, J. A., J. M. Acheson, M. Metcalfe, and P. Kleban. 1994. Chaos, complexity and communal management of fisheries. *Marine Policy* 18: 291–305.

Wilson, P. 1992. What Chief Seattle said. *Lewis and Clark Law School, Natural Resources Law Institute News* 3(2): 1, 12–15.

Winter, K. and W. McClatchley. 2009. The quantum co-evolution unit: an example of 'awa (kava—*Piper methysticum* G. Foster) in Hawaiian culture. *Economic Botany* 63: 353–62.

Winterhalder, B. 1983. The boreal forest, Cree-Ojibwa foraging and adaptive management. In *Resources and Dynamics of the Boreal Zone* (R. W. Wein, R. R. Riewe, and I. R. Methven, eds). Ottawa: Association of Canadian Universities for Northern Studies, 331–45.

Witt, N. and J. Hookimaw-Witt. 2003. Pinpinayhaytosowin [the way we do things]: a definition of traditional ecological knowledge (TEK) in the context of mining development on lands of the Attawapiskat First Nation and its effects on the design of research for a TEK study. *Canadian Journal of Native Studies* 23: 361–90.

Woo, M. K., P. Modeste, L. Martz *et al.* 2007. Science meets traditional knowledge: water and climate in the Sahtu (Great Bear Lake) region, Northwest Territories, Canada. *Arctic* 60: 37–46.

Worster, D. 1977. *Nature's Economy: A History of Ecological Ideas*. Cambridge: Cambridge University Press.

Worster, D. (ed.). 1988. *The Ends of the Earth: Perspectives on Modern Environmental History*. Cambridge: Cambridge University Press.

Wyndham, F. S. 2010. Environments of learning: Raramuri children's plant knowledge and experience of schooling, family, and landscapes in the Sierra Tarahumara, Mexico. *Human Ecology* 38: 87–99.

Xu, J., E. T. Ma, D. Tashi, Y. Fu, Z. Lu, and D. Melick. 2005. Integrating sacred knowledge for conservation: cultures and landscapes in southwest China. *Ecology and Society* 10(2): 7. [online]: http://www.ecologyandsociety.org/vol10/iss2/art7

Young, E. 1992. Aboriginal land rights in Australia: Expectations, achievements and implications. *Applied Geography* 12: 146–61.

Young, O. R., F. Berkhout, G. C. Gallopin, M. A. Janssen, E. Ostrom, and S. van der Leeuw. 2006. The globalization of socio-ecological systems: an agenda for scientific research. *Global Environmental Change* 16: 304–16.

Zachariah, M. 1984. The Berger Commission Inquiry Report and the revitalization of indigenous cultures. *Canadian Journal of Development Studies* 5: 65–77.

Zadeh, L. A. 1965. Fuzzy sets. *Information and Control* 8: 338–53.

Zadeh, L. A. 1973. Outline of a new approach to the analysis of complex systems and decision process. *Transactions on Systems, Man and Cybernetics* SMC-3: 28–44.

Zerbe, N. 2004. Biodiversity, ownership, and indigenous knowledge: exploring legal frameworks for community, farmers, and intellectual property rights in Africa. *Ecological Economics* 53: 493–506.

Web Links and Teaching Tips[1]

1 Context of Traditional Ecological Knowledge

The chapter provides a background to concepts, definitions, and origins of the different nomenclatures of knowledge systems, including what are widely known as traditional ecological knowledge (TEK) and indigenous knowledge (IK).

Wikipedia: Traditional Knowledge (TK)
http://en.wikipedia.org/wiki/Traditional_knowledge
Wiki site with background and reference links to TEK and Traditional Environmental Knowledge.

Wikipedia: Traditional Ecological Knowledge
http://en.wikipedia.org/wiki/Traditional_Ecological_Knowledge

What is Traditional Knowledge?
http://www.nativescience.org/html/traditional_knowledge.html
When an elder dies, a library burns. This site outlines basic aboriginal definitions and roots of TEK. It looks at structural differences between Western (non-traditional) and Traditional knowledge systems, as described by the Alaska Native

---

[1] Readers of the electronic version of this book can make use of hyperlinks embedded in the URLs in this section. Readers of the traditional, print-based version can access the same web pages by referring to the URLs and directions given.

Science Commission. "Related Links" include the Alaska Traditional Knowledge and Native Foods database.

What is Traditional Ecological Knowledge? E. Hunn
http://faculty.washington.edu/hunn/vitae/TEK_in_Baines.pdf

Convention on Biological Diversity, Article 8j
http://www.cbd.int/traditional
This is the CBD site outlining and giving information about the rights and responsibilities of Convention Parties with regards the protection and use of traditional knowledge, innovations and practices of indigenous communities.

Conservation Magazine. Old Science, New Science: Incorporating TEK into Contemporary Management
http://www.conservationmagazine.org/2008/07/old-science-new-science

Indigenous Knowledge and Science Revisited, G. S. Aikenhead, and M. Ogawa
http://www.springerlink.com/content/k04163q83u613v72
2007 paper in *Cultural Studies of Science Education.* (Subscription or payment required.)

Introduction to *Traditional Knowledge in Policy and Practice*
http://i.unu.edu/unu/u/publication/000/002/386/traditionalknowledgepolicyand-practice.pdf
Introductory chapter to the 2010 UN University Press book by S. M. Subramanian and B. Pisupati.

WWW Virtual Library. American Indians: Index of Indigenous Knowledge Resources on the Internet
http://www.hanksville.org/NAresources/indices/NAknowledge.html

UNESCO LINKS (Local Indigenous Knowledge Systems): What is Local Knowledge?
http://portal.unesco.org/science/en/ev.php-URL_ID=2034&URL_DO=DO_TOPIC&URL_SECTION=201.html
This site shows the many terms that encompass what we call local or place-based knowledge.

UNESCO MOST: Best Practices on Indigenous Knowledge
http://www.unesco.org/most/bpindi.htm
A database or clearinghouse of "best practices" for indigenous knowledge prepared by UNESCO's Management of Social Transformations (MOST) Programme. This page includes an analysis of IK definitions and gives the key aims of the database.

- **Management of Social Transformations (MOST) Programme**
  http://www.unesco.org/new/index.php?id=19159&L=0

UNEP: Indigenous Peoples

http://www.unep.org/indigenous
UNEP's Indigenous Peoples portal with news/events, activities, publications and archives. Includes contemporary issues such as climate change and indigenous resource mapping. Links include UNPFII and the International Day of Indigenous People.

UNPFII: UN Permanent Forum on Indigenous Issues

http://www.un.org/esa/socdev/unpfii
"The UN Permanent Forum on Indigenous Issues is an advisory body to the Economic and Social Council, with a mandate to discuss indigenous issues related to economic and social development, culture, the environment, education, health and human rights."

FAO: SARD (Sustainable Agriculture and Rural Development) and Indigenous Culture

http://www.fao.org/sard/en/init/964/2687/2453
"Indigenous Peoples worldwide are urgently calling for recognition of the vital and fundamental importance of culture for the viability of their traditional food and agro-ecological systems, as well as for sustainable development. Culture should be considered a fourth pillar of sustainable development, additional to the social, economic and environmental pillars."

Cultural Indicators of Indigenous Peoples' Food and Agro-ecological Systems

http://www.fao.org/sard/common/ecg/3045/en/Cultural_Indicators_paperApril2008.pdf
SARD (Sustainable Agriculture and Rural Development) Initiative report, by E. Woodley, E. Crowley, J. D. de Pryck, and A. Carmen.

Living Cybercartographic Atlas of Indigenous Perspectives and Knowledge

https://gcrc.carleton.ca/confluence/display/GCRCWEB/Living+Cybercartographic+Atlas+of+Indigenous+Perspectives+and+Knowledge
This is a project in Indigenous knowledge mapping undertaken by the Indigenous Knowledge group of the Geomatics and Cartographic Research Centre at Carleton University.

Traditional Knowledge Bulletin

http://tkbulletin.wordpress.com

TK Bulletin of the United Nations University Traditional Knowledge Institute, Australia.

SRISTI (Society for Research and Initiatives for Sustainable Technologies and Institutions)
http://www.sristi.org/cms/en

Honey Bee Network and Newsletter
http://www.sristi.org/hbnew

Aboriginal Canada Portal
http://www.aboriginalcanada.gc.ca/acp/site.nsf/eng
The Canadian Federal Government's portal for Aboriginal issues, policy and programs.

- **Elders: Traditional Knowledge**
  http://www.aboriginalcanada.gc.ca/acp/site.nsf/eng/ao26878.html
  A good collection of papers, presentations and other links on elders' issues.

Indigenous Peoples Literature
http://www.indigenouspeople.net
A beautiful site on and for indigenous peoples' literature, with additional links to stories, art, music, and other cultural sites.

- **Coyote Stories/poems**
  http://www.indigenouspeople.net/coyote.htm
  Many Coyote stories are listed here.

Exercise

Debate the proposition: "Since local/traditional/indigenous knowledge captures a range of kinds of knowledge, a diversity of terms and definitions is necessary. In fact, precise definitions of these concepts are neither possible nor desirable."

---

2 Emergence of the Field

This chapter reviews the literature and builds upon the concepts introduced in Chapter 1. It discusses the historical emergence of the field, and the development of a *critical mass* of knowledge around the values and potential roles of traditional ecological knowledge/indigenous knowledge in various areas of natural resource planning and management. The following links track the themes introduced in the chapter.

Time. Lost Tribes, Lost Knowledge
http://www.time.com/time/magazine/article/0,9171,973872-2,00.html
This *Time* magazine article by E. Linden, from 1991, marks the beginnings of popularization of TEK/IK. (Subscription required.)

Indigenous Knowledge and Development Monitor
http://www.iss.nl/ikdm/ikdm/ikdm
The *Indigenous Knowledge and Development Monitor* was a journal aimed at the international development community and scientists with an interest in indigenous knowledge. The *Monitor* was produced by Nuffic-CIRAN in cooperation with indigenous knowledge resource centres. Publication of the Monitor ceased in 2001.

Aboriginal Arts and Cultural Centre, Alice Springs
http://aboriginalart.com.au/culture/dreamtime2.html
"**The Dreamtime** According to Aboriginal belief, all life as it is today—Human, Animal, Bird and Fish is part of one vast unchanging network of relationships which can be traced to the Great Spirit ancestors of the Dreamtime. The Dreamtime continues as the "Dreaming" in the spiritual lives of aboriginal people today. The events of the ancient era of creation are enacted in ceremonies and danced in mime form. Song chant incessantly to the accompaniment of the didgeridoo or clap sticks relates the story of events of those early times and brings . . . the power of the dreaming to bear [on] life today."

Mystic Lands. Australia: Dreamtime
http://school.discoveryeducation.com/teachersguides/pdf/geography/ul/ml_australia_dreamtime_tg.pdf
http://school.discoveryeducation.com/teachersguides/pdf/geography/ds/ml_australia_dreamtime.pdf
Teaching materials related to the documentary "Australia: Dreamtime," from the series *Mystic Lands*.

Aboriginal Culture
http://www.aboriginalculture.com.au
This site contains a lot of very interesting historical, black-and-white photos from the New Territories, Australia archives.

- **Aboriginal Fishing Methods**
  http://www.aboriginalculture.com.au/fishingmethods.shtml
  Includes eel traps.

Indigenous and Community Conserved Areas
http://www.iccaforum.org

"Indigenous peoples and local communities, both sedentary and mobile, have for millennia played a critical role in conserving a variety of natural environments and species. They have done this for a variety of purposes, economic as well as cultural, spiritual and aesthetic. There are today many thousand Indigenous and Community Conserved Areas (ICCAs) across the world, including forests, wetlands, and landscapes, village lakes, water catchment, rivers and coastal stretches and marine areas."

Indigenous and Community Conserved Areas: A Bold New Frontier for Conservation
http://www.iucn.org/about/union/commissions/ceesp/topics/governance/icca

- **Theme on Indigenous Peoples, Local Communities, Equity and Protected Areas (TILCEPA)**
  http://www.iucn.org/about/union/commissions/ceesp/what_we_do/wg/tilcepa.cfm
- Biodiversity Governance by Indigenous Peoples and Local Communities
  http://www.iucn.org/about/union/commissions/ceesp/topics/governance
- **IUCN-CEESP ICCA Resources for Download**
  http://www.iucn.org/about/union/commissions/ceesp/ceesp_publications/index.cfm?uPage=7

Wikipedia: Environmental History
http://en.wikipedia.org/wiki/environmental_history

Environmental History online
http://www.environmentalhistory.net

Cultural Ecology: Indigenous Knowledge
http://culturalecology.info/version2/Indigenousknowledge.html#Topic247

COSMOS Project. People: Ecology: Place
http://www.culturalecology.info
"Sustainability Knowledge Organised to Manage the Environment Responsibly."

Terralingua
http://www.terralingua.org
A non-governmental organization concerned with the survival of world's languages, and biocultural diversity in general, Terralingua has a rich website. Of particular interest is the database on 45 biocultural diversity projects and initiatives included in the 2010 book *Biocultural Diversity Conservation*.

Global Diversity Foundation
http://www.globaldiversity.org.uk

"We are concerned about the future of the biodiversity that people tend, the languages they speak and the ways they interact with their cultural landscapes. We believe that globalisation can go hand-in-hand with diversity. But it requires education, research and sheer hard work in the form of long-term, community-based projects." Provides teaching guides.

Sahyadri e-News. People's Biodiversity Register
http://www.ces.iisc.ernet.in/biodiversity/sahyadri_enews/newsletter/issue15
Carried out in rural India, the People's Biodiversity Register is probably the most comprehensive people-and-biodiversity project. Note the link made between knowledge, livelihoods and biodiversity.

Managing People's Knowledge: An Indian Case Study of Building Bridges from Local to Global and from Oral to Scientific Knowledge
http://www.maweb.org/documents/bridging/bridging.13.pdf
Chapter by Y. Gokhale and colleagues in the 2006 book *Bridging Scales and Knowledge Systems*.

Biodiversity Institute, University of Oxford
http://www.biodiversity.ox.ac.uk
Contains resource material on conservation outside of formal protected areas: see the link to "Biodiversity beyond protected areas."

Indigenous Knowledge in Disaster Management
http://www.raipon.org/ikdm
A project in Russia aimed at studying and learning from indigenous peoples' traditional knowledge about disaster management.

Lived Knowledge
A number of sites provide examples of TEK/IK in practice.

Kupuna Kalo Hawaii
http://kupunakalo.com
Kupuna Kalo is an online resource about elders' (*kupuna*) knowledge of *kalo* (taro plant). An educational site that aims to reconnect native Hawaiians with *kalo*, the food that sustained their ancestors.

Wikipedia: Gary Paul Nabhan
http://en.wikipedia.org/wiki/Gary_Paul_Nabhan

Gary Nabhan's website
http://garynabhan.com/i

Gadii Mirrabooka: Australian Aboriginal Tales from the Dreaming
http://www.gadimirrabooka.com
A 2001 collection of Aboriginal stories.

The *Titi* Project

http://www.otago.ac.nz/titi

"Keep the *Titi* Forever" is a comprehensive project in New Zealand on Maori TEK/IK and science of the *titi*, which is a seabird (the sooty shearwater). It is a joint project of the Rakiura Maori and the University of Otago.

Limpopo River Awareness Kit: Indigenous/Traditional Knowledge

http://www.limpoporak.com/en/people/people+of+the+basin/cultural+diversity/
indigenous+traditional+knowledge.aspx

"The People and the River theme is an exploration of the diverse cultures, livelihoods and the dependency that . . . people in the Limpopo River basin have on the environment."

Atlantic First Nations Environmental Network

http://www.afnen.ca

Southern Gulf of St Lawrence Coalition on Sustainability

http://www.coalition-sgsl.ca

- **TEK Working Group**

http://www.coalition-sgsl.ca/groups_tek.php

Exercise

Following on from the "lived knowledge" sites listed above, carry out local research to check the feasibility of developing local cases (and websites) involving local, traditional, or indigenous knowledge in your area. Such "lived knowledge" may be gathered from farmers, ranchers, fishers, indigenous groups, naturalist organizations, urban service agencies, and others.

---

3 Intellectual Roots of Traditional Ecological Knowledge

This chapter expands on concepts and uses of TEK/IK and traces its roots from ethnoscience and human ecology. The following provides links to some key organizations and journals, and relevant resources for education and research.

Society of Ethnobiology

http://www.ethnobiology.org

"Ethnobiology is the scientific study of dynamic relationships among peoples, biota, and environments. The Society gathers and disseminates knowledge of ethnobiology and fosters ongoing appreciation for the richness of ethnobiology worldwide."

International Society of Ethnobiology

http://ethnobiology.net

Note the ISE Code of Ethics: it "aims to facilitate ethical conduct and equitable relationships by fostering a commitment to meaningful collaboration and reciprocal responsibility in research involving cultural knowledge."

People and Plants International (Ethnobotany)

http://www.peopleandplants.org

"We believe that cultural diversity is inherently linked to biological diversity and that effective stewardship of our Earth must involve local people. We also believe that traditional knowledge systems are critical to manage and conserve threatened landscapes and adapt to global change."

The Society for Human Ecology

http://www.societyforhumanecology.org

"SHE is an international interdisciplinary professional society that promotes the use of an ecological perspective in research, education, and application."

Some open-access journals in areas related to TEK/IK

- *Ecology and Society*
  http://www.ecologyandsociety.org
- *International Journal of the Commons*
  http://www.thecommonsjournal.org
- *Journal of Ethnobiology and Ethnomedicine*
  http://www.ethnobiomed.com

Native American and Indigenous Studies Association

http://naisa.org

"The Native American and Indigenous Studies Association is a professional organization dedicated to supporting scholars and others who work in the academic field of Native American and Indigenous studies."

Native American Science Curriculum

http://www.nativeamericanscience.org

Northwest Indian College

http://www.nwic.edu

Native American Ethnobotany, University of Michigan – Dearborn

http://herb.umd.umich.edu

Aboriginal Education Research Centre, University of Saskatchewan: Learning Indigenous Science from Place

http://aerc.usask.ca/projects/indigenous_science.html

AAAS Project on Traditional Ecological Knowledge

http://shr.aaas.org/tek

"In October 2002, the Science & Human Rights Program launched a new project exploring the intersection between traditional knowledge, intellectual property, and human rights. The goals of the project include: Exploring the role of the public domain as it applies to TK, examining issues affecting TK relating to the current intellectual property regime, and identifying and applying intellectual property options available to traditional knowledge holders." This site includes a link to a Handbook on TEK and Intellectual Property.

Smithsonian National Museum of Natural History: Arctic Studies Center

http://mnh.si.edu/ARCTIC

"The Arctic Studies Center, established in 1988, is the only U.S. government program with a special focus on northern cultural research and education. In keeping with this mandate, the Arctic Studies Center specifically studies northern peoples, exploring history, archaeology, social change and human lifeways across the circumpolar world."

World Agroforestry Centre

http://www.worldagroforestrycentre.org

The World Agroforestry Centre (ICRAF) is an independent not-for-profit research organization that works, among other things, on shifting cultivation systems.

Indigenous Peoples' Restoration Network: Traditional Ecological Knowledge

http://www.ser.org/iprn/tek.asp

Aboriginal Mapping Network

http://www.nativemaps.org

Working with Indigenous Knowledge: A Guide for Researchers

http://www.idrc.ca/EN/Resources/Publications/Pages/IDRCBookDetails.aspx?PublicationID=293

Sacred Ecology is not a book about TEK/IK research methodologies but this area can be pursued through the citations in Chapter 3. One open-access resource is the book by Louise Grenier, *Working with Indigenous Knowledge*: "Experience has shown us that development efforts that ignore local technologies, local systems of knowledge, and the local environment generally fail to achieve their desired objectives."

Exercise

The intellectual roots of TEK/IK in fact go beyond ethnoscience and human ecology. What are some of the other disciplines and subdisciplines, would you say, that have been important?

4 Traditional Knowledge Systems in Practice

Chapter 4 describes the workings of a sample of indigenous knowledge and resource management systems in a variety of ecosystem settings. Two themes run through the chapter: (1) TEK/IK represents the summation of millennia of ecological adaptations of human groups to their diverse environments; and (2) TEK/IK is compatible with some current ecological approaches, especially Adaptive Management.

Resilience Alliance

http://www.resalliance.org

"The RA is a multidisciplinary research group that explores the dynamics of complex adaptive systems, with special attention to resilience in the face of variation and change."

- Resiliance Alliance: Adaptive Management
  http://www.resalliance.org/index.php/adaptive_management
- Resiliance Alliance: Researcher Database
  http://www.resalliance.org/index.php/researcher_database?st=201

Stockholm Resilience Centre

http://www.stockholmresilience.org

Key site for understanding and application of resilience theory to social–ecological systems. In particular, see the "News and Videos" and "Research" areas, and, under "Research," the "Research Themes."

Traditional Water Harvesting

http://academic.evergreen.edu/g/grossmaz/palmbajp

TravelGood. Irrigation Secrets of the Ancients

http://www.travelgood.com/2005/05/irrigation-secrets-of-the-ancients

TreeHugger: Zuni Water Harvesting

http://www.treehugger.com/files/2005/06/zuni_water_harv.php

Wikipedia: Native American Use of Fire

http://en.wikipedia.org/wiki/Native_American_use_of_fire

Securing a Future: Cree Hunters' Resistance and Flexibility to Environmental Changes, Wemindji, James Bay

http://www.ecologyandsociety.org/articles/3828.html

2010 article by J. S. Sayles and M. E. Mulrennan in the journal *Ecology and Society*. Can indigenous people create cultural landscapes in sparsely populated areas?

Secretariat of the Pacific Community. Coastal Fisheries Programme: Traditional Marine Resource Management and Knowledge Information Bulletin

http://www.spc.int/coastfish/en/publications/bulletins/traditional-management.html

Locally Managed Marine Area Network

http://www.lmmanetwork.org

The following is a series of five sites about TEK/IK in practice, related to *ahupua'a* and ethnobotanical restoration efforts in Hawaii:

- **Wikipedia: Ahupua'a**
  http://en.wikipedia.org/wiki/Ahupua'a
- **HawaiiHistory.org: Ahupua'a**
  http://www.hawaiihistory.org/index.cfm?fuseaction=ig.page&CategoryID=299
- **Asia-Pacific Digital Library: Ethnobotany of the Ahupua'a**
  http://apdl.kcc.hawaii.edu/ahupuaa/botany
- **East Maui Watershed Partnership**
  http://eastmauiwatershed.org/Watersheds/Ahupuaa.htm
- **National Tropical Botanical Garden, Hawaii**
  http://ntbg.org

Wikipedia: Subak (Irrigation)

http://en.wikipedia.org/wiki/Subak_(irrigation)

National Science Foundation: Balinese Water Temples

http://artsci.wustl.edu/~anthro/research/Balinese Water Temples.htm

Forest Peoples' Programme

http://www.forestpeoples.org

Menominee Tribal Enterprises

http://www.mtewood.com

Exercise

Research the web and extend this list of TEK systems in practice.

---

5 Cree Worldview "From the Inside"

This chapter is an *emic* (insider) account of the eastern James Bay Cree worldview, as seen by the local people themselves. It relies heavily on a document conceived and prepared by Cree elders (Bearskin *et al.* 1989), follows their narratives and uses their quotations. The web links below aim to provide other cases of indigenous perspectives from a number of different groups.

Exercise

The following four open-access documents, three by the IUCN and its partners and one by Conservation International, provide a large number of case studies. Examine them and reflect on:

1   whether any of the cases may be considered *emic* accounts;
2   to what extent local worldviews dominate or shape the cases;
3   how some of these worldviews differ from Western worldview(s); and
4   which beliefs and worldviews seem consistent with Western conservation.

- **Amend, T., J. Brown, A. Kothari, A. Phillips, and S. Stolton (eds). 2008. *Protected Landscapes and Agrobiodiversity Values.* Volume 1 in the series *Protected Landscapes and Seascapes*, IUCN & GTZ. Heidelberg: Kasparek Verlag.**
  http://data.iucn.org/dbtw-wpd/edocs/2008-001.pdf
- **Mallarach, J.-M. (ed.). 2008. *Protected Landscapes and Cultural and Spiritual Values.* Volume 2 in the series *Values of Protected Landscapes and Seascapes*, IUCN, GTZ and Obra Social de Caixa Catalunya. Heidelberg: Kasparek Verlag.**
  http://data.iucn.org/dbtw-wpd/edocs/2008-055.pdf
- **Papayannis, T. and J.-M. Mallarach (eds). 2009. *The Sacred Dimension of Protected Areas: Proceedings of the Second Workshop of the Delos Initiative – Ouranoupolis 2007.* Gland, Switzerland: IUCN and Athens, Greece: Med-INA.**
  http://data.iucn.org/dbtw-wpd/edocs/2009-069.pdf
- **Painemilla, K. W., A. B. Rylands, A. Woofter, and C. Hughes (eds). 2010. *Indigenous Peoples and Conservation: From Rights to Resource Management.* Arlington, VA: Conservation International.**
  http://www.conservation.org/Documents/CI_ITPP_Indigenous_ Peoples_and_Conservation_Rights_Resource_Management.pdf

---

Northwest Center for Sustainable Resources, Oregon: Educator's Guide to American Indian Perspectives in Natural Resources
http://www.ncsr.org/Downloads/educatorguideindianperspectivesnaturalre- sources.pdf
With Frank Lake and Dennis Martinez.

Clayoquot Sound Scientific Panel: First Nations Perspectives Relating to Forest Practices Standards in Clayoquot Sound

http://www.cortex.ca/Rep3.pdf

An *emic* account. This is an older case but a classic. The controversy of forest management in Clayoquot Sound, British Colombia, was instrumental in initiating public discussion over indigenous knowledge and values in Canada, and the acceptance of the role of TEK/IK in natural resources decision-making.

See also the related book: Atleo, E. R. (Umeek). 2004. *Tsawalk: A Nuu-chah-nulth Worldview*. Vancouver: University of British Columbia Press.

Staying the Course, Staying Alive. Coastal First Nations Fundamental Truths: Biodiversity, Stewardship and Sustainability

http://www.biodiversitybc.org/assets/Default/BBC_Staying_the_Course_Web. pdf

An *emic* account. A small book, compiled by British Columbia First Nations authors, on the spiritual principles of BC coastal peoples.

Redstone Statement, 1 May 2010

http://indigenousenvirosummit10.unt.edu

Consensus statement of the International Summit on Indigenous Environmental Philosophy 2010. An international, indigenous, *emic* statement of environmental philosophy.

Canadian Museum of Civilization. Gateway to Aboriginal Heritage: Woodlands and Eastern Subarctic

http://www.civilization.ca/cmc/exhibitions/tresors/ethno/etb0160e.shtml

ArcticNet. IRIS 4 Research: Eastern Subarctic

http://www.arcticnet.ulaval.ca/research/iris_4.php

CreeCulture.ca: Aanischaaukamikw Cultural Institute

http://www.creeculture.ca/content/index.php?q=node/31

Whitefeather Forest Initiative

http://www.whitefeatherforest.com

A comprehensive project of resource development, indigenous conservation and cultural preservation, the WFI website provides much material on a group of NW Ontario (Canada) Anishinaabe (Ojibwa) people.

Gwich'in Social and Cultural Institute

http://www.gwichin.ca

Gwich'in Traditional Knowledge: Rat River Dolly Varden Char

http://www.grrb.nt.ca/pdf/fisheries/Rat River DV Char TK Report FINAL.pdf

Landscape Ecology and Community Knowledge for Conservation
http://www.lecol-ck.ca
A joint project of Parks Canada and the University of Manitoba, the site has much material on Inuit knowledge and several northern species of animals.

Wikipedia: Shamanism
http://en.wikipedia.org/wiki/Shamanism

Shamanism
http://www.angelfire.com/journal/cathbodua/Shamanism.html

We do not have Shamans: The Case Against "Shamans" in North American Indigenous Cultures
http://www.angelfire.com/electronic/awakening101/not_shamans.html

How to Practice Native American Shamanism
http://www.ehow.com/how_2145602_practice-native-american-shamanism.html

Shamana: The Raven Lodge
http://www.shamana.co.uk

Native Planet. The Mentawai: Shamans of the Siberut Jungle
http://www.nativeplanet.org/indigenous/cultures/indonesia/mentawai/mentawai.shtml

Dream-Catchers.org: Ojibwe Culture and History
http://www.dream-catchers.org/ojibwe-history.php

Dreaming Eagles' Eyrie
http://dreamingeagle.blogspot.com/2009/08/creation-story-of-ojibwe-people.html

Digital Partnerships with Indian Communities. Through Indigenous Eyes Stories: *Fair Wind's Drum*
http://www.sas.upenn.edu/dpic/indigeyes/ojibwe

National Film Board of Canada. *Ojigkwanong: Encounter with an Algonquin Sage* **(Video)**
http://www3.onf.ca/enclasse/doclens/visau/index.php?mode=view&filmId=5024 2&language=english&sort=title

Wikipedia: Pantheism
http://en.wikipedia.org/wiki/Pantheism

6 A Story of Caribou and Social Learning

Chapter 6 is the story of one major resource of Northern peoples, the caribou. Inuit, Dene, and Cree people are all hunters of the caribou. In Eurasia, many indigenous people, including the Saami, hunt or herd the reindeer, which is the same species as caribou but a different subspecies. The chapter also examines questions of conservation ethics and the development of conservation traditions.

Wikipedia: Conservation (Ethic)
http://en.wikipedia.org/wiki/Conservation_(ethic)

The Land Ethic
http://home.btconnect.com/tipiglen/landethic.html
An extract from Aldo Leopold's classic book, *A Sand County Almanac*.

The Philosophical Foundations of Aldo Leopold's Land Ethic
http://gadfly.igc.org/papers/leopold.htm
Discussion of the basis of Aldo Leopold's influential land ethic, by Ernest Partridge.

What Happened to Our Conservation Ethic?
http://www.landinstitute.org/vnews/display.v/ART/2003/11/10/3faffe2b56f9c
Essay by a "prairie writer" on what happened to the ethics of land/soil steward-ship prevalent among the early immigrants.

The Conservation Ethics Group
http://www.conservationethics.org/CEG/home.html

Traditional Knowledge Systems for Biodiversity Conservation
http://www.infinityfoundation.com/mandala/t_es/t_es_pande_conserve.htm
Article by Deep Narayan Pandey.

Conservation Ethos in Local Traditions: The West Bengal Heritage
http://www.scribd.com/doc/54084038/Nature-Conservation-Traditions-in-West
-Bengal
2001 article by D. Deb and K. C. Mahlotra in *Society and Natural Resources* journal.

Traditional Ecological Ethos and Norms as an Element of Social Capital and Its Role in Forest Management: A Case Study
http://www.shodh-research.org/links/ResearchProjects/minor/project12/
Winrock_case_study.pdf
2006 report by D. Mehra.

The Canadian Encyclopedia. Native People: Subarctic
http://www.thecanadianencyclopedia.com/index.cfm?PgNm=TCE&Params=A1
ARTA0009072

Wikipedia: Cree
http://en.wikipedia.org/wiki/Cree

The Grand Council of the Crees
http://www.gcc.ca

Dene Cultural Institute
http://www.deneculture.org

National Film Board of Canada. *Caribou Hunters* **(Video)**
http://www3.onf.ca/enclasse/doclens/visau/index.php?mode=view&language=e
nglish&filmId=13896

Ressources Naturelles et Faune, Québec: Caribou Migration Monitoring by Satellite Telemetry
http://www.mrnf.gouv.qc.ca/english/wildlife/maps-caribou

Nation. **Caribou Crisis**
http://nationnews.ca/index.php?option=com_zine&view=article&id=1076:car
ibou-crisis
2011 article in *Nation*, an independent Aboriginal publication.

The Reindeer Portal: EALAT
http://icr.arcticportal.org/index.php?option=com_content&view=frontpage&Ite
mid=78&lang=en

Saami Reindeer Pastoralism under Climate Change: Applying a Generalized Framework for Vulnerability Studies to a Sub-arctic Social–Ecological System
http://www.uio.no/studier/emner/annet/sum/SUM4015/h08/Tyler.pdf
2007 article by N. J. C. Tyler and colleages, in the journal *Global Environmental Change*.

Sami Culture: Reindeer Herding in Norway
http://www.utexas.edu/courses/sami/diehtu/siida/herding/herding-nr.htm

Sami Culture: Experiential Knowledge vs. Book/Classroom Knowledge
http://www.utexas.edu/courses/sami/dieda/socio/exper-book.htm
A comparision of book/classroom learning versus experiential processes of knowledge transfer.

Exercise
There are quite a few sites that belong to indigenous organizations or their cultural associations. Research and study some of them (perhaps those closer to your area), with conservation ethics in mind.

7 Cree Fishing Practices as Adaptive Management

How can we approach the dilemma of finding common ground between Western science and indigenous knowledge? Chapter 7 is a detailed human ecological analysis of one resource system, the Chisasibi Cree subsistence fishery in James Bay. It is an outsider's academic interpretation, an *etic* view.

"Ten Commandments" Could Improve Fisheries Management
http://www.science.oregonstate.edu/node/176
Article reporting on a conference presentation by Professor Mark Hixon and colleagues.

Traditional Knowledge and Harvesting of Salmon by *Huna* and *Hinyaa* Tlingit
http://alaska.fws.gov/asm/pdf/fisheries/reports/02-104final.pdf
2006 report by Steve J. Langdon.

US Fish and Wildlife Service Native American Liaison: Traditional Ecological Knowledge
http://www.fws.gov/nativeamerican/TEK.html

Anishinabek/Ontario Fisheries Resource Centre
http://www.aofrc.org/aofrc
Words of the Lagoon
http://books.google.cl/books?id=TloVDfV7QLoC&printsec=frontcover&dq=wo
rds+of+the+lagoon&source=bl&ots=WHMY2I2o71&sig=ek3iIsxBG0pVBIY9Jj
2P8nmGp7w&hl=es-419&ei=ZHk_TbLSOcSblgermYWPAw&sa=X&oi=book_
result&ct=result&resnum=3&ved=0CCsQ6AEwAg#v=onepage&q&f=false
R. E. (Bob) Johannes's classic 1981 book on a biologist's quest to discover, test, and record the knowledge of fishers of the Palau Islands of Micronesia. The book is out of print.

Introduction to *Fishers' Knowledge in Fisheries Science and Management*
http://publishing.unesco.org/chapters/978-92-3-104029-0.pdf
Introductory chapter to a 2007 UNESCO book edited by N. Haggan and colleagues.

Putting Fishermen's Knowledge to Work: The Promise and Pitfalls
http://www.penobscoteast.org/documents/PuttingFishermensKnowledge.pdf
Paper by Ted Ames, Gulf of Maine in the 2007 UNESCO book *Fishers' Knowledge in Fisheries Science and Management*.

Traditional Marine Resource Management in Vanuatu
http://www.vanuatu.usp.ac.fj/library/Online/Vanuatu/Hickey.pdf
Paper by F. R. Hickey in the 2007 UNESCO book *Fishers' Knowledge in Fisheries Science and Management*.

Back to the Future: Using Traditional Knowledge to Strengthen Biodiversity Conservation in Pohnpei, Federated States of Micronesia
http://lib-ojs3.lib.sfu.ca:8114/index.php/era/article/viewFile/29/18
2003 article by Bill Raynor and Mark Koska in the journal *Ethnobotany Research & Applications*.

Integrating Traditional and Evolutionary Knowledge in Biodiversity Conservation
http://www.ecologyandsociety.org/vol11/iss2/art4
2006 article by D. J. Fraser and colleagues in the journal *Ecology and Society*.

Mekong River Commission
http://www.mrcmekong.org

The Use of Local Knowledge in River Fisheries Research
http://www.fao.org/docrep/013/y5878e/y5878e03.pdf
Article by J. Valbo-Jorgensen in *FAO Aquaculture Newsletter* No. 32.

Using Local Knowledge as a Research Tool in the Study of River Fish Biology
http://www.unepscs.org/forum/attachment.php?attachmentid=30&d=1184767254
2000 article by J. Valbo-Jorgensen and A. F. Poulsen in the journal *Environment, Development and Sustainability*.

Instituto de Desenvolvimento Sustentável Mamirauá, Brazil
http://www.mamiraua.org.br
Mamirauá Sustainable Development Reserve, Brazil (in Portuguese).

Mamirauá Sustainable Development Reserve, Brazil: Lessons Learnt in Integrating Conservation with Poverty Reduction
http://pubs.iied.org/pdfs/9168IIED.pdf

Exercise
Are there alternative ways of resource management that rely mainly on contextual information, the reading of environmental signals, and qualitative mental models that provide information on trends in resource availability? Explore, using the references in Chapter 7 and the web links above.

---

8 Climate Change and Indigenous Ways of Knowing

This chapter is about indigenous knowledge of climate change, mainly in the Arctic. It is not TEK/IK in the sense of cognitive "knowledge" of climate change that is already fully formed and transmitted from one generation to the next. Rather, it is about knowledge as process, weather-related knowledge with sensitivity to critical signs in the environment and an understanding of what they mean.

UNEP/GRID-Arendal. *Arctic Times*: **The Uniqueness of the Arctic**
http://www.grida.no/publications/et/at/page.aspx

The Politics of Bridging Scales and Epistemologies: Science and Democracy in Global Environmental Governance
http://www.maweb.org/documents/bridging/bridging.16.pdf
Does international climate change science recognize IK/TEK? Chapter by C. Miller and P. Erickson, in the 2006 book *Bridging Scales and Knowledge Systems*.

Canada's Polar Life
http://www.arctic.uoguelph.ca/cpl

Listening to Our Past
http://www.tradition-orale.ca
Inuit oral traditions.

Inuit Qaujimajatuqangit Adventure Website
http://inuitq.ca
Inuit knowledge website.

Alaska Native Knowledge Network, University of Alaska Fairbanks
http://www.ankn.uaf.edu

Beaufort Sea Partnership
http://www.beaufortseapartnership.ca

- **Traditional and Local Knowledge Working Group**
  http://www.beaufortseapartnership.ca/knowledge.html

LibraryThing. *Decolonizing Methodologies: Research and Indigenous Peoples*
http://www.librarything.com/work/7464491
This page includes keywords and a list of books related to Linda Tuhiwai Smith's seminal book.

Review of *Decolonizing Methodologies*
http://www.msd.govt.nz/documents/about-msd-and-our-work/publications-resources/journals-and-magazines/social-policy-journal/spj17/17_pages214_217.pdf

Diversity and Technology for Engaging Communities (DTEC): Methodology
http://dtec.ed.uiuc.edu/methodology.html

DTEC, University of Illinois at Urbana Champaign methodology page. See in particular the section on "Decolonizing Approach."

Situating Knowledge Systems, from *Indigenous Research Methodologies*
http://www.sagepub.com/upm-data/41611_1.pdf
Chapter 1 from *Indigenous Research Methodologies* by Bagele Chilisa.

First Peoples: New Directions in Indigenous Studies. Blog: Research and Archiving with Respect
http://www.firstpeoplesnewdirections.org/blog/?p=2698

Sustainability Science: The Emerging Research Program
http://www.pnas.org/content/100/14/8059.full
A large project, based at Harvard University, that uses place-based cases, and local and indigenous knowledge, to explore sustainability. 2003 article by W. C. Clark and N. M. Dickson, in *Proceedings of the National Academy of Sciences*.

Indigenous Sustainability Science
http://www.infinityfoundation.com/indic_colloq/papers/paper_pandey2.pdf
Paper by Deep Narayan Pandey.

Understanding Local Weather and Climate Using Maori Environmental Knowledge
http://www.niwa.co.nz/news-and-publications/publications/all/wa/14-2/maori

IISD. Inuit Observations on Climate Change
http://www.iisd.org/casl/projects/inuitobs.htm
One of the first studies of indigenous views and observations of climate change.

- **Inuit Observations on Climate Change Videos**
  http://www.iisd.org/publications/pub.aspx?pno=429

Isuma *TV. Inuit Knowledge and Climate Change* (Video)
http://www.isuma.tv/hi/en/inuit-knowledge-and-climate-change
Film by Zacharias Kunuk and Ian Mauro (2010). An *emic* view of Inuit and climate change, co-directed by award-winning Inuk filmmaker Kunuk.

Arctic Science and Technology Information System (ASTIS) Database
http://www.aina.ucalgary.ca/astis

- ASTIS Database Subsets
  http://www.arctic.ucalgary.ca/index.php?page=astis_database

ACIA: Arctic Climate Impact Assessment
http://www.acia.uaf.edu

The major international scientific report of the project of the Arctic Council. The site contains full chapters of this authoritative volume, plus the short synthesis report and the policy report.

United Nations University Institute of Advanced Studies Traditional Knowledge Initiative: TK and Climate Change
http://www.unutki.org/default.php?doc_id=13

Greenpeace. Polar Meltdown: Background Report
http://archive.greenpeace.org/climate/polar/polrep
"It is my belief that the fate of the earth may very well depend on a new dialogue that must begin immediately between nation-states and the emerging Fourth World comprised of hundreds of millions of indigenous people."

Norma Kassi (Gwat-la-ey-ishi), Wolf Clan,
Vuntat Gwich'in Whitehorse, Yukon

National Film Board of Canada. *How to Build an Igloo* (Video)
http://www3.onf.ca/enclasse/doclens/visau/index.php?mode=view&filmId=11340&language=english&sort=title
This site has quite a few films about Arctic peoples and their environmental perception.

National Film Board of Canada. *If the Weather Permits* (Video)
http://www3.onf.ca/enclasse/doclens/visau/index.php?mode=view&filmId=51256&language=english&sort=title

Climate Change Adaptation

In recent years, the emphasis on climate change research has shifted to adaptation. There is a huge literature on this subject, including some freely available on the web.

IPCC. Climate Change 2007: Working Group II: Impacts, Adaption and Vulnerability
http://www.ipcc.ch/publications_and_data/ar4/wg2/en/ch17.html
Chapter 17 of IPCC Working Group II Report, by W. N. Adger and colleagues.

Theory and Practice in Assessing Vulnerability to Climate Change and Facilitating Adaptation
http://nome.colorado.edu/HARC/Readings/Kelly.pdf
2000 article by P. M. Kelly and W. N. Adger, in the journal *Climatic Change*.

Social Capital, Collective Action, and Adaptation to Climate Change
http://www.jstor.org/pss/30032945
2003 article by W. N. Adger, in the journal *Economic Geography*. (Subscription required.)

Knowledge Co-production in Climate Change Adaptation Projects: What are the Levers for Action?
http://cc2011.earthsystemgovernance.org/pdf/2011Colora_0153.pdf
2011 Colorado Conference on Earth System Governance paper by D. Hegger and colleagues.

Exercise
To what extent does climate change adaptation research use (or to what extend is it based upon) IK/TEK? How can the IK/TEK component of these studies be improved?

---

9 Complex Systems, Holism, and Fuzzy Logic

The chapter poses the question of how TEK/IK holders develop holistic approaches. It discusses rules-of-thumb, indigenous ways of monitoring, and reviews evidence for complex adaptive systems thinking in indigenous knowledge and practice. For example, how can fisher knowledge be construed as a fuzzy logic expert system? Finally, the chapter focuses on fuzzy logic for building collective mental models of the environment, as a way to explain how rules-of-thumb and other simple prescriptions can be used to deal with complexity.

Wikipedia: Complex System
http://en.wikipedia.org/wiki/Complex_system

Complexity Theory for a Sustainable Future
http://cup.columbia.edu/book/978-0-231-13460-6/complexity-theory-for-a-sustainable-future
2008 book, edited by J. Norberg and G. Cumming.

Local and Indigenous Knowledge as an Emergent Property of Complexity
http://westernsolomons.uib.no/docs/Woodley,Ellen/Woodley(2002)Local Knowledge in Vella Lavella (PhD Thesis).pdf
A 2002 University of Guelph Ph.D. thesis by E. Woodley, presenting a case study in the Solomon Islands.

Columbia River Inter-Tribal Fish Commission (CRITFC): First Salmon Feast
http://www.critfc.org/text/ceremony.html

ThinkQuest: The First Salmon Ceremony
http://library.thinkquest.org/2939/fsc.htm
For students.

Northwest Power and Conservation Council. Columbia River History: First-Salmon Ceremony

http://www.nwcouncil.org/history/firstsalmonceremony.asp

Upper Columbia Salmon Recovery Board: *First Salmon Ceremony* **(Video)**

http://vimeo.com/21653076

Wikibooks: Expert Systems/Fuzzy Logic

http://en.wikibooks.org/wiki/Expert_Systems/Fuzzy_Logic#About_Fuzzy_Logic

Fuzzy Logic. Fuzzy Logic Overview

http://www.austinlinks.com/Fuzzy/overview.html

Ecological Models Based on People's Knowledge: A Multi-step Fuzzy Cognitive Mapping Approach

http://levis.sggw.pl/~rew/scenes/pdf/Ozesmi.pdf

2003 article by U. Özesmi and S. L. Özesmi in the journal *Ecological Modelling*.

Managing Small-Scale Fisheries in the Caribbean: The Surface Longline Fishery in Gouyave, Grenada

http://umanitoba.ca/institutes/natural_resources/canadaresearchchair/thesis/S%20Grant%20thesis.pdf

A 2006 University of Manitoba Ph.D. thesis by Sandra Grant.

Monachus Guardian (Mediterranean Monk Seal)

http://www.monachus-guardian.org

A network of citizens' groups and scientists contribute to the conservation of the rarest mammal in Europe. See the "Monk Seal Library" on the website.

Civic Science for Sustainability

http://sciencepolicy.colorado.edu/students/envs_5100/backstrand.pdf

2003 article by Karin Bäckstrand in the journal *Global Environmental Politics*.

eBird

http://ebird.org

The eBird network relies on the observations of citizen scientists.

COASST (Coastal Observation and Seabird Survey Team), University of Washington

http://depts.washington.edu/coasst

The COASST vision is coastal communities contributing directly to the monitoring of marine birds and ecosystem health through a network of citizen scientists.

Unite Research with What Citizens Do for Fun: "Recreational Monitoring" of Marine Biodiversity

http://www.esajournals.org/doi/abs/10.1890/09-1546.1?prevSearch=[AllField%3A+goffredo]&searchHistoryKey=#aff1

Citizen science: recreational divers monitoring marine biodiversity. 2010 article by S. Goffredo and colleagues, in *Ecological Applications*. (Subscription required.)

Taiga Net

http://taiga.net

"A co-operative environmental and community web network dedicated to Northern Canada & Alaska." Nine featured sites including the Arctic Borderlands Ecological Knowledge Co-op.

Keep It Simple and Be Relevant: The First Ten Years of the Arctic Borderlands Ecological Knowledge Co-op

http://www.maweb.org/documents/bridging/bridging.10.pdf

J. Eamer's chapter in the 2006 book, *Bridging Scales and Knowledge Systems*.

Taiga Net. Yukon North Slope Traditional Knowledge

http://yukon.taiga.net/northslope

Taiga Net. A Yukon Historical Fishing Gallery

http://taiga.net/reports/traditional_fisheries/picturelist.htm

Integration of Local Ecological Knowledge and Conventional Science: A Study of Seven Community-Based Forestry Organizations in the USA

http://www.ecologyandsociety.org/vol13/iss2/art37

Involving local people and local knowledge in forestry. 2008 article by H. L. Ballard, M. E. Fernandez-Gimenez, and V. E. Sturtevant in *Ecology and Society*.

Wikipedia: Subak (Irrigation)

http://en.wikipedia.org/wiki/Subak_(irrigation)

A Case Study of Balinese Irrigation Management: Institutional Dynamics and Challenges

http://anu.academia.edu/RachelPLorenzen/Papers/506518/A_case_study_of_Balinese_irrigation_management_institutional_dynamics_and_challenges

Everyone and No One (Blog). Direct Water Democracy in Bali/J. S. Lansing: *A Thousand Years in Bali* (Video)

http://everybodyandnobody.wordpress.com/2009/12/05/direct-water-democracy-in-bali

J. S. Lansing's Website

http://www.u.arizona.edu/~jlansing/J._Stephen_Lansing/Welcome.html

> **Exercise**
>
> Go back to the web links for Chapter 4. Which of these cases show elements of complex systems thinking?

10 How Local Knowledge Develops: Cases from the West Indies

The chapter focuses on several aspects of the development of local and indigenous knowledge: how new knowledge arises and is elaborated upon, the processes involved, and the distinction between local and traditional knowledge. As well, the chapter discusses the relationship between knowledge/practice and the development of institutions, in particular, commons institutions that provide resource rights and the security of access on which local management systems can be based.

Environmental Understanding or Crisis Learning?

The chapter discusses two models, one emphasizing the gradual development of environmental knowledge, leading to increasingly more sophisticated understandings; and the second emphasizing the importance of resource crises and mistakes in shaping how environmental knowledge and practice develops. The two models are explored in the two lead papers of the special issue of *Human Ecology*, volume 34, number 4.

Developing Resource Management and Conservation
http://www.springerlink.com/content/0300-7839/34/4
Special issue of *Human Ecology*, volume 34, number 4. (Subscription or payment required.)

> **Exercise**
>
> Examine the other papers in the special issue of *Human Ecology* volume 34, number 4 (and additional cases from the citations): which case/example supports which model? How about the Caribbean examples in Chapter 10? Which case supports which model?

The Coexistence of Local Knowledge and GPS Technology
http://www.marecentre.nl/mast/documents/Mast82_Kalman_Correa.pdf
2009 article by J. Kalman and M. A. Liceaga Correa in the journal *MAST*.

Indicators as a Means of Communicating Knowledge
http://icesjms.oxfordjournals.org/content/62/3/606.full
2005 article in the *ICES Journal of Marine Science* by P. Degnbol.

Communicating Knowing Through Communities of Practice
http://ici-bostonready-pd-2009-2010.wikispaces.umb.edu/file/view/Communicat
ing+Knowing+Through+Communities+of+Practice.pdf
2008 article by Joel O. Iverson and Robert D. McPhee in the *Journal of Applied Communication Research.*

VITEK: Vitality Index of Traditional Environmental Knowledge
http://www.terralingua.org/projects/vitek/vitek.htm
"The development of TEK indicators represents the most recent chapter in the search for more effective policies. Such indicators are intended to identify and measure key components of TEK and thereby provide a clear and systematic basis for tracking changes over time."

Environmental Justice Foundation. Mangroves: Nature's Defence against Tsunamis: A Report on the Impact of Mangrove Loss and Shrimp Farm Development on Coastal Defences
http://www.ejfoundation.org/pdf/tsunami_report.pdf

Chonjo Magazine. **Mangrove Conservation: Traditional Wisdom Often Ignored**
http://www.lamuchonjo.com/articles/2011/03/29/mangrove-conservation
-traditional-wisdom-often-ignored

World Bank, ISME, center Aarhus: Draft Code of Conduct for the Sustainable Management of Mangrove Ecosystems
http://www.mangroverestoration.com/MBC_Code_AAA_WB070803_TN.pdf

CANARI (Caribbean Natural Resources Institute): A Guide to Teaching Participatory and Collaborative Approaches to Natural Resource Management
http://www.canari.org/267guide.pdf

CANARI: Free Downloadable PDF Documents
http://www.canari.org/pdf_files.html

Answers.com. *Seamoss Cultivation in the Caribbean* **(Video)**
http://video.answers.com/sea-moss-cultivation-in-the-caribbean-502319965

CANARI: Community Management of Seamoss at Blanchisseuse, Trinidad and Tobago
http://www.canari.org/Beat.htm

OceanVegetables.com. Harvesting Seaweed: Sea Vegetables for Food and Medicine
http://www.oceanvegetables.com/harvesting-seaweed.html

FAO Fisheries and Aquaculture Circular. Biology and Fishery Management of the White Sea Urchin, *Tripneustes ventricosus*, in the Eastern Caribbean
http://www.fao.org/docrep/013/i1751e/i1751e00.pdf

Grenada Case Study: The Lobster Fishery at Sauteurs
http://www.cavehill.uwi.edu/cermes/publications/Grenada lobstercasestudy.pdf
2003 research report by P. McConney.

Centre for Resource Management and Environmental Studies (CERMES), University of the West Indies
http://www.cavehill.uwi.edu/cermes/margov_profile.html#

Do We Need New Management Paradigms to Achieve Sustainability in Tropical Forests?
http://www.ecologyandsociety.org/issues/view.php?sf=27
Special issue of the journal *Ecology and Society*: 14(2), 2009.

Traditional Forest Knowledge (TFK), Commons and Forest Landscape Management: An Indian Perspective
http://iasc2008.glos.ac.uk/conference papers/papers/G/Gupta_210101.pdf
Conference paper by H. K. Gupta and A. Gupta.

Knowledge Management for Development
http://www.km4dev.org

11 Challenges for Indigenous Knowledge

This chapter deals with some of the popular myths of indigenous peoples, and builds a cultural evolutionary perspective to distinguish between invaders and natives. It then examines the differences between Western and indigenous notions of conservation, including the idea of wilderness. Next, the chapter discusses adapting traditional systems for contemporary livelihood needs.

Wikipedia: Chief Seattle
http://en.wikipedia.org/wiki/Chief_Seattle

Chief Seattle's Speech of 1854
http://www.halcyon.com/arborhts/chiefsea.html

Wikipedia: Noble Savage
http://en.wikipedia.org/wiki/Noble_savage

Wikipedia: Quaternary Extinction Event
http://en.wikipedia.org/wiki/Quaternary_extinction_event
The overkill hypothesis and other theories.

Terralingua: Biocultural Diversity Conservation
http://www.terralingua.org/bcdconservation
This portal on biocultural diversity projects responds to the question of the ability of indigenous people to conserve resources.

Biocultural Diversity for Endogenous Development
http://www.bioculturaldiversity.net/downloads/papers participants/maffi.pdf
Paper by L. Maffi.

Beauty and the Beast: Human Rights and Biocultural Diversity
http://www.garfieldfoundation.org/resources/Beauty & The Beast.pdf
2008 article in *Resurgence Magazine*, by J. Alcorn.

Rethinking Community-based Conservation
http://onlinelibrary.wiley.com/doi/10.1111/j.1523-1739.2004.00077.x/pdf   2004 article by F. Berkes, in the journal *Conservation Biology*. Republished as part of an open-access issue, titled *International Year of Biodiversity: Conservation Social Science*, in April 2010.

Wikipedia: Wise Use
http://en.wikipedia.org/wiki/Wise_use

Wilderness.net: Aldo Leopold
http://www.wilderness.net/index.cfm?fuse=feature0105

UNESCO World Heritage Convention: Cultural Landscapes
http://whc.unesco.org/en/activities/477

Cultural Landscapes
http://www.culturallandscapes.ca

Incentives for Indigenous Conservation

See the series of four open-access documents for which links are provided in the exercise at the beginning of the Chapter 5 web links (p. 333). TEK/IK often develops in tandem with commons institutions. In many cases, indigenous peoples' capacity to maintain and to adapt their systems can be enhanced through the defense of their land and resource rights. Protected rights provide incentives to conserve.

Parque de la Papa **(Video)**
The Potato Park outside of Cusco, Peru. Andean people repatriate traditional varieties of potato, and agrobiodiversity preservation is combined with community-based Andean ecotourism.
http://vimeo.com/17203020

ANDES
http://www.andes.org.pe/en
A Peruvian NGO dedicated to preserving traditional Andean biocultural and agro-biodiversity within a sustainable livelihoods framework.

ITeM (Instituto del Tercer Mundo): Rethinking Development and Progress
http://www.item.org.uy/node/49

Multiversity. Community-based Learning in the Peruvian Andes
http://vlal.bol.ucla.edu/multiversity/Right_menu_items/jorgeIshiwaza.htm
Article by J. Ishizawa about PRATEC, the Project on Andean Peasant Technologies.

Cosmovisions and Environmental Governance: The Case of In Situ Conservation of Native Cultivated Plants and Their Wild Relatives in Peru
http://www.maweb.org/documents/bridging/bridging.11.pdf
Chapter by J. Ishizawa in the 2006 book *Bridging Scales and Knowledge Systems*.

TV Multiversity: A Selection of videos from PRATEC (Project on Andean Peasant Technologies)
http://tvmultiversity.blogspot.com/2010/08/selection-of-films-from-pratec.html

Wikipedia: Pedanius Dioscorides
http://en.wikipedia.org/wiki/Pedanius_Dioscorides
Dioscorides, an Anatolian pharmacologist and botanist in the first century AD, was the author of an encyclopedia of herbal medicine which remained in use for over a thousand years.

Exercise

1 Most people believe in various myths about indigenous peoples (such as the "noble savage"). Reflect on yours.
2 Is "wilderness" a relative concept or merely a myth?
3 Find local/regional examples to discuss how conservation practice may (or may not) evolve.

---

12 Toward a Unity of Mind and Nature

TEK/IK is political because it threatens to change power relations between indigenous groups and the dominant society, and it poses challenges to the positivist–reductionist paradigm. Can TEK/IK be used alongside Western science? Many indigenous knowledge holders argue that the two kinds of knowledge may be best pursued in parallel (rather than combined). Contact points may be provided by certain kinds of holistic Western science, such as Adaptive Management, complexity, and fuzzy logic. TEK/IK inspires more participatory, community-based alternatives to top-down resource management; it injects a measure of ethics into the science of ecology.

Wikipedia: Political Ecology
http://en.wikipedia.org/wiki/Political_ecology

Journal of Political Ecology **(open access)**
http://jpe.library.arizona.edu

Intellectual Property Rights
http://www.psrast.org/vashipr.htm
Article by V. Shiva about Intellectual Property Rights and indigenous knowledge systems, including the example of neem.

Neem (*Azadirachta Indica*) in Context of Intellectual Property Rights (IPR)
http://recent-science.com/article/viewFile/7324/3770
2011 article by O. Singh and colleagues in *Recent Research in Science and Technology*.

Learning and Knowing Collectively
http://www.china-sds.org/kcxfzbg/addinfomanage/lwwk/data/kcx400.pdf
2004 article by R. B. Norgaard, in the journal *Ecological Economics*.

Sustainable Development: A Co-evolutionary View
http://neweconomicsinstitute.org/publications/essays/norgaard/richard/sustainable-development-a-co-evolutionary-view
Essay by R. B. Norgaard on the website of the New Economics Institute.

The Re-birth of Environmentalism as Pragmatic, Adaptive Management, Bryan Norton (Video)
http://www.youtube.com/watch?v=KwlQwILU1mg
2006 guest lecture at the Gund Institute for Ecological Economics, University of Vermont.

Wikipedia: Positivism
http://en.wikipedia.org/wiki/Positivism

Wikipedia: Social Constructivism
http://en.wikipedia.org/wiki/Social_constructivism

Why Political Ecology Has to Let Go of Nature, from *Politics of Nature*
http://www.studyplace.org/w/images/archive/3/34/20091008021135!Latour-Politics-of-Nature.pdf
Chapter 1 of Bruno Latour's 2004 book, *Politics of Nature*.

Exploring the Right to Diversity in Conservation Law, Policy, and Practice
http://www.iucn.org/about/union/commissions/ceesp/ceesp_publications/pm
October 2010 issue of the journal *Policy Matters*.

Indigenous Peoples' Knowledge and Rights Commission, International Geographical Union
http://www.indigenousgeography.net/ipkrc.shtm

Forests and Oceans for the Future
http://www.ecoknow.ca
Includes educational and other resource materials.

Global Diversity Fund: Biocultural Diversity Learning Network
http://www.bdln.net

TEK Initiative, Corvallis Oregon
http://tekinitiative.org
An organization founded in 2010 as an annual TEK conference by Valerie Goodness and Chris Dunn, with the direction and wisdom of Elder, Gail Woodside.

Interinstitutional Consortium for Indigenous Knowledge, Penn State College of Education
http://www.ed.psu.edu/ICIK
A network promoting communication among those interested in understanding diverse local knowledge systems as they meet a globalized world.

Agroecology in Action
http://agroeco.org
With M. Alteri; excellent "Related links."

AgriCultures Network
http://www.agriculturesnetwork.org
Mother Earth Journal. **Category Archive for "Traditional Knowledge"**
http://mother-earth-journal.com/category/traditional-knowledge

WordPress.com. Blogs About: Traditional Knowledge
http://en.wordpress.com/tag/traditional-knowledge

Cultural Perspectives on Biodiversity: Topic 4: How Do We Conserve and Empower Traditional Ecological Knowledge Before Its Disappearance? New Zealand Ecological Society
http://biodiversityvoice.wordpress.com/2010/09/27/topic4

Exercise

The note of pessimism of the last web link (how to "empower TEK before its disappearance") is at odds with the optimistic note at the beginning of Chapter 12. What is your own considered view of the future of TEK/IK?

Index

Note: page numbers in *italic* type refer to figures, tables, boxes, and photographs.